Precalculus
DeMYSTiFieD®

DeMYSTiFieD® Series

Accounting Demystified
Advanced Calculus Demystified
Advanced Physics Demystified
Advanced Statistics Demystified
Algebra Demystified
Alternative Energy Demystified
Anatomy Demystified
Astronomy Demystified
Audio Demystified
Biology Demystified
Biotechnology Demystified
Business Calculus Demystified
Business Math Demystified
Business Statistics Demystified
C++ Demystified
Calculus Demystified
Chemistry Demystified
Chinese Demystified
Circuit Analysis Demystified
College Algebra Demystified
Corporate Finance Demystified
Databases Demystified
Data Structures Demystified
Differential Equations Demystified
Digital Electronics Demystified
Earth Science Demystified
Electricity Demystified
Electronics Demystified
Engineering Statistics Demystified
Environmental Science Demystified
Ethics Demystified
Everyday Math Demystified
Fertility Demystified
Financial Planning Demystified
Forensics Demystified
French Demystified
Genetics Demystified
Geometry Demystified
German Demystified
Home Networking Demystified
Investing Demystified
Italian Demystified
Japanese Demystified
Java Demystified

JavaScript Demystified
Lean Six Sigma Demystified
Linear Algebra Demystified
Logic Demystified
Macroeconomics Demystified
Management Accounting Demystified
Math Proofs Demystified
Math Word Problems Demystified
MATLAB¤ Demystified
Medical Billing and Coding Demystified
Medical Terminology Demystified
Meteorology Demystified
Microbiology Demystified
Microeconomics Demystified
Nanotechnology Demystified
Nurse Management Demystified
OOP Demystified
Options Demystified
Organic Chemistry Demystified
Personal Computing Demystified
Pharmacology Demystified
Philosophy Demystified
Physics Demystified
Physiology Demystified
Pre-Algebra Demystified
Precalculus Demystified
Probability Demystified
Project Management Demystified
Psychology Demystified
Quality Management Demystified
Quantum Mechanics Demystified
Real Estate Math Demystified
Relativity Demystified
Robotics Demystified
Sales Management Demystified
Signals and Systems Demystified
Six Sigma Demystified
Spanish Demystified
sql Demystified
Statics and Dynamics Demystified
Statistics Demystified
Technical Analysis Demystified
Technical Math Demystified
Trigonometry Demystified

$$y^2 = -4x$$

$$A = x(50-x)$$

100 ft.
PICKET
FENCE

Precalculus
DeMYSTiFieD®

Rhonda Huettenmueller

Second Edition

McGraw Hill

New York   Chicago   San Francisco   Lisbon   London   Madrid   Mexico City
Milan   New Delhi   San Juan   Seoul   Singapore   Sydney   Toronto

The McGraw·Hill Companies

Cataloging-in-Publication Data is on file with the Library of Congress.

McGraw-Hill books are available at special quantity discounts to use as premiums and sales promotions, or for use in corporate training programs. To contact a representative please e-mail us at bulksales@mcgraw-hill.com.

Precalculus DeMYSTiFieD®, Second Edition

1 2 3 4 5 6 7 8 9 0   DOC/DOC   1 9 8 7 6 5 4 3 2

ISBN 978-0-07-177849-7
MHID 0-07-177849-7

Sponsoring Editor	**Proofreader**
Judy Bass	Cenveo Publisher Services
Acquisitions Coordinator	**Production Supervisor**
Bridget Thoreson	Pamela A. Pelton
Editing Supervisor	**Composition**
David E. Fogarty	Cenveo Publisher Services
Project Manager	**Art Director, Cover**
Sheena Uprety,	Jeff Weeks
Cenveo Publisher Services	**Cover Illustration**
Copy Editor	Lance Lekander
Cenveo Publisher Services	

Contents

Introduction

The purpose of this book is to prepare you for calculus. To succeed in calculus, you need strong algebra skills as well as an understanding of functions and their graphs. Most of the book is dedicated to covering the major families of functions (and their graphs): linear, quadratic, polynomial, rational, exponential, logarithmic, and trigonometric functions. Important calculus concepts are introduced in Chapters 2 and 3: the average rate of change of a function, the difference quotient, and increasing/decreasing intervals for a function. Chapter 6 introduces another important calculus concept: optimizing a function.

Before beginning your study of precalculus, you should have basic algebra skills: the ability to factor expressions, simplify fractions, solve equations and inequalities, and work with exponents and square roots. The Appendix contains a brief review of some of these topics. You should also have a basic knowledge of the xy plane, how to plot points and how to read graphs.

You will get the most from this book if you study the examples before working the Practice problems. If you get a problem wrong, make sure you understand where you went wrong (the solutions are worked out) before moving to the next topic. Study the Chapter Summary at the end of each chapter before taking the quiz and then take it as if you were in a classroom—without using notes or looking at the chapter.

Once you have worked through the chapters, you can take the Final Exam. Rather than try all 90 problems at once, treat the exam as three separate 30-problem tests. Try to improve your score with each attempt. If you do reasonably well on these exams, then you are ready for calculus.

I wish you the best of luck!

Rhonda Huettenmueller

About the Author

Rhonda Huettenmueller has taught mathematics at the college level for 20 years. She earned a PhD in mathematics from the University of North Texas and is the author of several books in the *Demystified* series, including the bestselling *Algebra Demystified*.

chapter **1**

Lines and Their Slopes

Most of an introductory course in calculus is concerned with the rate of change, that is, how fast a variable is changing. That rate of change is measured by the slope of a line, so we begin our preparation for calculus by studying lines and their slopes. We will learn an application from calculus for the slope of a line in Chapter 2. We will also use linear equations to help us solve applications (word problems) in this chapter.

CHAPTER OBJECTIVES

In this chapter, you will

- Find the slope of a line
- Work with horizontal and vertical lines
- Work with two lines that are parallel or perpendicular
- Find an equation of a line from two of its points
- Interpret the slope of a line
- Work with applications of lines

The Slope of a Line

The slope of a line measures its tilt. The sign of the slope tells us whether the line tilts up (if the slope is positive) or tilts down (if the slope is negative), see Figure 1-1. The larger the number, the steeper the slope (see Figure 1-2).

We can find the slope of a line by putting the coordinates of any two points on the line, (x_1, y_1) and (x_2, y_2), in the slope formula.

$$m = \frac{y_2 - y_1}{x_2 - x_1}$$

For example, $(0, 3)$, $(-2, 2)$, $(6, 6)$, and $(-1, \frac{5}{2})$ are all points on the same line. We can pick any pair of points to compute the slope.

$(0, 3)$ and $(-2, 2) : m = \dfrac{2 - 3}{-2 - 0}$ $(-2, 2)$ and $\left(-1, \dfrac{5}{2}\right) : m = \dfrac{\frac{5}{2} - 2}{-1 - (-2)}$

$\qquad\qquad\qquad = \dfrac{-1}{-2} = \dfrac{1}{2}$ $\qquad\qquad\qquad\quad = \dfrac{\frac{1}{2}}{1} = \dfrac{1}{2}$

$(6, 6)$ and $(0, 3) : m = \dfrac{3 - 6}{0 - 6}$ $(0, 3)$ and $\left(-1, \dfrac{5}{2}\right) : m = \dfrac{\frac{5}{2} - 3}{-1 - 0}$

$\qquad\qquad\qquad = \dfrac{-3}{-6} = \dfrac{1}{2}$ $\qquad\qquad\qquad\quad = \dfrac{-\frac{1}{2}}{-1} = \dfrac{1}{2}$

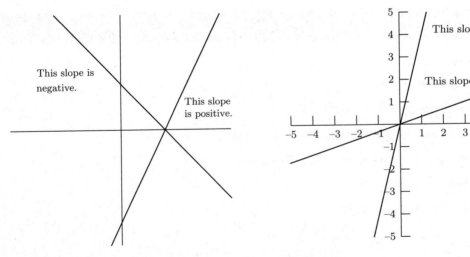

FIGURE 1-1   **FIGURE 1-2**

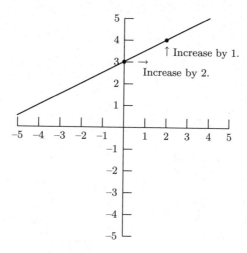

FIGURE 1-3

A slope of $\frac{1}{2}$ means that if we increase the x-value by 2, then we need to increase the y-value by 1 to get another point on the line. For example, knowing that $(0, 3)$ is on the line means that we know $(0 + 2, 3 + 1) = (2, 4)$ is also on the line (see Figure 1-3).

Because a horizontal line is not tilted at all, we expect the slope to be zero. As we can see from Figure 1-4 (on page 4), $(-4, -2)$ and $(1, -2)$ are two points on a horizontal line. When we put these points in the slope formula, we will see that the slope really is zero.

$$m = \frac{-2 - (-2)}{1 - (-4)} = \frac{0}{5} = 0$$

The y-values on a horizontal line do not change but the x-values do, so the numerator of the slope is always zero for a horizontal line. What happens to the slope formula for two points on a vertical line?

The points $(3, 2)$ and $(3, -1)$ are on the vertical line in Figure 1-5 (on page 4). Let's see what happens when we put them in the slope formula.

$$m = \frac{-1 - 2}{3 - 3} = \frac{-3}{0}$$

This is not a number, so the slope of a vertical line does not exist (we also say that it is undefined). The x-values on a vertical line do not change but the y-values do.

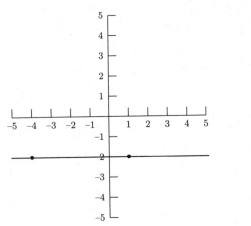

FIGURE 1-4

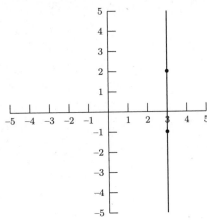

FIGURE 1-5

Linear Equations

Every line in the plane is the graph of a linear equation. The equation of a horizontal line is $y = a$ (where a is the y-value of every point on the line). Some examples of horizontal lines are $y = 4$, $y = 1$, and $y = -5$. These lines are sketched in Figure 1-6. The equation of a vertical line is $x = a$ (where a is the x-value of every point on the line). Some examples are $x = -3$, $x = 2$, and $x = 4$ (see Figure 1-7).

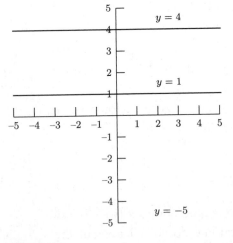

FIGURE 1-6

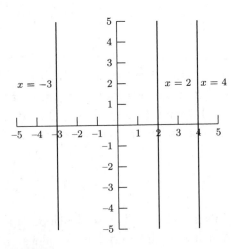

FIGURE 1-7

Other equations normally come in one of two forms: $Ax + By = C$ and $y = mx + b$. We will usually use the form $y = mx + b$ in this book. An equation in this form gives us two important pieces of information. The first is m, the slope. The second is b, the y-intercept (where the line crosses the y-axis). For this reason, this form is called the *slope-intercept* form. In the line $y = \frac{2}{3}x + 4$, the slope of the line is $\frac{2}{3}$ and the y-intercept is $(0, 4)$, or simply 4.

We can find an equation of a line from its slope and any point on the line. There are two common methods for finding this equation. One is to put m, x, and y (x and y are the coordinates of the point we know) in $y = mx + b$ and use algebra to find b. The other is to put these same numbers in the *point-slope* form of the line, $y - y_1 = m(x - x_1)$, and then use algebra to solve for y. We will use both methods in the next example.

EXAMPLE **1-1**

- Find an equation of the line with slope $-\frac{3}{4}$ containing the point $(8, -2)$.

   We let $m = -\frac{3}{4}$, $x = 8$, and $y = -2$ in $y = mx + b$ to find b.

   $$-2 = -\frac{3}{4}(8) + b \qquad \text{This gives us } -2 = -6 + b.$$

   $$4 = b \qquad\qquad\qquad \text{Add 6 to each side.}$$

   The line is $y = -\frac{3}{4}x + 4$.

   Now we let $m = -\frac{3}{4}$, $x_1 = 8$, and $y_1 = -2$ in $y - y_1 = m(x - x_1)$.

   $$y - (-2) = -\frac{3}{4}(x - 8)$$

   $$y + 2 = -\frac{3}{4}x + 6 \qquad \text{Simplify.}$$

   $$y = -\frac{3}{4}x + 4 \qquad \text{Subtract 2 from each side.}$$

- Find an equation of the line with slope 4, containing the point $(0, 3)$.

   We know the slope is 4 and the y-intercept is 3 [because $(0, 3)$ is on the line], so we can write the equation without having to do any work: $y = 4x + 3$.

- Find an equation of the horizontal line that contains the point $(5, -6)$.

Because the *y*-values are the same on a horizontal line, we know that this equation is $y = -6$. We can still find the equation algebraically using the fact that $m = 0$, $x = 5$, and $y = -6$. Then $y = mx + b$ becomes $-6 = 0(5) + b$. From here we can see that $b = -6$, so $y = 0x - 6$, or simply $y = -6$.

- Find an equation of the vertical line containing the point $(10, -1)$.

  Because the *x*-values are the same on a vertical line, we know that the equation is $x = 10$. We cannot find this equation algebraically because *m* does not exist.

  We can find an equation of a line if we know any two points on the line. First we need to use the slope formula to find *m*, and then we pick one of the points to put into $y = mx + b$.

EXAMPLE 1-2

Find an equation of the line containing the given points.

- $(-2, 3)$ and $(10, 15)$

  First, we find the slope. $m = \frac{15-3}{10-(-2)} = 1$

  We now use $x = -2$, $y = 3$, and $m = 1$ in $y = mx + b$ to find *b*.

  $$3 = 1(-2) + b$$

  $$5 = b \qquad\qquad \text{Add 2 to each side.}$$

  The equation is $y = 1x + 5$, or simply $y = x + 5$.

- $(\frac{1}{2}, -1)$ and $(4, 3)$

  Again, we begin by finding the slope.

  $$m = \frac{3 - (-1)}{4 - \frac{1}{2}} = \frac{4}{\frac{7}{2}} = 4 \div \frac{7}{2} = 4 \cdot \frac{2}{7} = \frac{8}{7}$$

  Using $x = 4$, $y = 3$, and $m = \frac{8}{7}$ in $y = mx + b$, we have

  $$3 = \frac{8}{7}(4) + b \qquad \frac{8}{7}(4) = \frac{32}{7}$$

  $$-\frac{11}{7} = b \qquad\qquad \text{Subtract: } 3 - \frac{32}{7} = \frac{21 - 32}{7} = -\frac{11}{7}.$$

  The equation is $y = \frac{8}{7}x - \frac{11}{7}$.

- $(0, 1)$ and $(12, 1)$

The *y*-values are the same, making this a horizontal line. The equation is $y = 1$.

If a graph is clear enough, we can find two points on the line or even its slope. In fact, if the slope and *y*-intercept are easy enough to see on the graph, we know right away what the equation is.

EXAMPLE **1-3**

The line in Figure 1-8 crosses the *y*-axis at 1, so $b = 1$. From this point, we can go right 2 and up 3 to reach the point $(2, 4)$ on the line. "Right 2" means that the denominator of the slope is 2. "Up 3" means that the numerator of the slope is 3. The slope is $\frac{3}{2}$, so the equation of the line is $y = \frac{3}{2}x + 1$.

The *y*-intercept for the line in Figure 1-9 is not easy to determine, but we do have two points. We can either find the slope by using the slope formula, or visually (as we did above). We can find the slope visually by asking how we can go from $(-4, 3)$ to $(2, -1)$: Down 4 (making the numerator of the slope -4) and right 6 (making the denominator 6). If we use the slope formula, we have

$$m = \frac{-1 - 3}{2 - (-4)} = \frac{-4}{6} = -\frac{2}{3}$$

Using $x = 2$ and $y = -1$ in $y = mx + b$, we have $-1 = -\frac{2}{3}(2) + b$. From this, we have $b = \frac{1}{3}$. The equation is $y = -\frac{2}{3}x + \frac{1}{3}$.

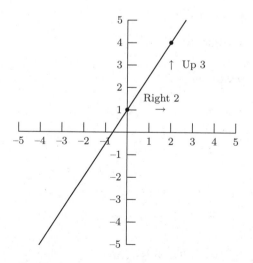

◆ FIGURE 1-8

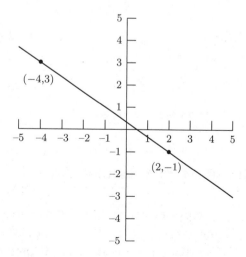

FIGURE 1-9

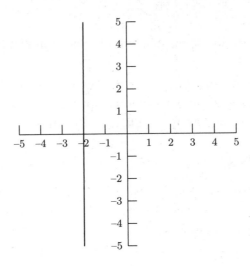

FIGURE 1-10

The line in Figure 1-10 is vertical, so it has the form $x = a$. All of the x-values are -2, so the equation is $x = -2$.

When an equation for a line is in the form $Ax + By = C$, we can find the slope by solving the equation for y. This puts the equation in the form $y = mx + b$.

EXAMPLE 1-4

- Find the slope of the line $6x - 2y = 3$.

$$6x - 2y = 3 \qquad \text{Solve this for } y.$$

$$-2y = -6x + 3 \qquad \text{Subtract } 6x.$$

$$y = 3x - \frac{3}{2} \qquad \text{Divide by } -2.$$

The slope is 3 (or $\frac{3}{1}$).

Parallel and Perpendicular Lines

Two lines are parallel if their slopes are equal (or if both lines are vertical), see Figure 1-11.

Two lines are perpendicular if their slopes are *negative reciprocals* of each other (or if one line is horizontal and the other is vertical), see Figure 1-12.

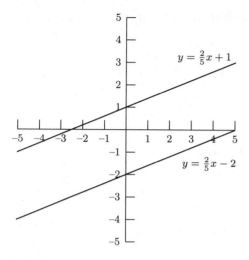

FIGURE 1-11

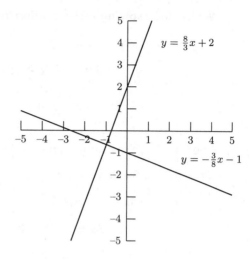

FIGURE 1-12

Two numbers are negative reciprocals of each other if one is positive and the other is negative and inverting one gets the other (if we ignore the sign).

EXAMPLE 1-5

- $\frac{5}{6}$ and $-\frac{6}{5}$ are negative reciprocals

- $-\frac{3}{4}$ and $\frac{4}{3}$ are negative reciprocals

- -2 and $\frac{1}{2}$ are negative reciprocals

- 1 and -1 are negative reciprocals

We can decide whether two lines are parallel or perpendicular or neither by writing them in the form $y = mx + b$ and then comparing their slopes.

EXAMPLE 1-6

Determine whether the lines are parallel or perpendicular or neither.

- $4x - 3y = -15$ and $4x - 3y = 6$

We begin by solving each equation for y, and then we compare their slopes.

$$4x - 3y = -15 \qquad\qquad 4x - 3y = 6$$
$$-3y = -4x - 15 \qquad\qquad -3y = -4x + 6$$
$$y = \frac{4}{3}x + 5 \qquad\qquad y = \frac{4}{3}x - 2$$

The lines have the same slope, so they are parallel.

- $3x - 5y = 20$ and $5x - 3y = -15$

$$3x - 5y = 20 \qquad\qquad 5x - 3y = -15$$
$$-5y = -3x + 20 \qquad\qquad -3y = -5x - 15$$
$$y = \frac{3}{5}x - 4 \qquad\qquad y = \frac{5}{3}x + 5$$

The slopes are reciprocals of each other but not *negative* reciprocals, so they are not perpendicular. They are not parallel, either.

- $x - y = 2$ and $x + y = -8$

$$x - y = 2 \qquad\qquad x + y = -8$$
$$y = x - 2 \qquad\qquad y = -x - 8$$

The slope of the first line is 1 and that of the second is -1. Because 1 and -1 are negative reciprocals, these lines are perpendicular.

- $y = 10$ and $x = 3$

The line $y = 10$ is horizontal, and the line $x = 3$ is vertical. They are perpendicular.

Sometimes we need to find an equation of a line when we know only a point on the line and an equation of another line that is either parallel or perpendicular to it. We need to find the slope of the line whose equation we have and use this to find the equation of the line we are looking for.

EXAMPLE 1-7

- Find an equation of the line containing the point $(-4, 5)$ that is parallel to the line $y = 2x + 1$.

The slope of $y = 2x + 1$ is 2. This is the same as the line we want, so we let $x = -4$, $y = 5$, and $m = 2$ in $y = mx + b$. We get

$5 = 2(-4) + b$, so $b = 13$. The equation of the line we want is $y = 2x + 13$.

- Find an equation of the line with x-intercept 4 that is perpendicular to $x - 3y = 12$.

The x-intercept is 4 means that the point $(4, 0)$ is on the line. The slope of the line we want is the negative reciprocal of the slope of the line $x - 3y = 12$. We find the slope of $x - 3y = 12$ by solving for y.

$$x - 3y = 12$$

$$y = \frac{1}{3}x - 4$$

The slope we want is -3, which is the negative reciprocal of $\frac{1}{3}$. When we let $x = 4$, $y = 0$, and $m = -3$ in $y = mx + b$, we have $0 = -3(4) + b$, which gives us $b = 12$. The line is $y = -3x + 12$.

- Find an equation of the line containing the point $(3, -8)$, perpendicular to the line $y = 9$.

The line $y = 9$ is horizontal, so the line we want is vertical. The vertical line passing through $(3, -8)$ is $x = 3$.

PRACTICE

When asked to find an equation for a line, put your answer in the form $y = mx + b$ unless the line is horizontal ($y = a$) or vertical ($x = a$).

1. Find the slope of the line containing the points $(4, 12)$ and $(-6, 1)$.

2. Find the slope of the line with x-intercept 5 and y-intercept -3.

3. Find an equation of the line containing the point $(-10, 4)$ with slope $-\frac{2}{5}$.

4. Find an equation of the line with y-intercept -5 and slope 2.

5. Find an equation of the line in Figure 1-13 (see page 12).

6. Find an equation of the line containing the points $(\frac{3}{4}, 1)$ and $(-2, -1)$.

7. Determine whether the lines $3x - 7y = 28$ and $7x + 3y = 3$ are parallel or perpendicular or neither.

8. Find an equation of the line containing the point $(2, 3)$ and perpendicular to the line $x - y = 5$.

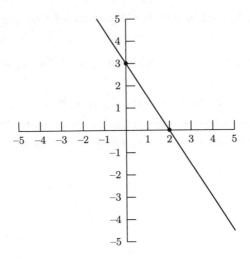

FIGURE 1-13

9. Find an equation of the line parallel to the line $x = 6$ containing the point $(-3, 2)$.

10. Determine whether the lines $2x - 3y = 1$ and $-4x + 6y = 5$ are parallel or perpendicular or neither.

 SOLUTIONS

1. $m = \dfrac{1 - 12}{-6 - 4} = \dfrac{-11}{-10} = \dfrac{11}{10}$

2. The x-intercept is 5 and the y-intercept is -3; this means that the points $(5, 0)$ and $(0, -3)$ are on the line.

$$m = \frac{-3 - 0}{0 - 5} = \frac{-3}{-5} = \frac{3}{5}$$

3. We put $x = -10$, $y = 4$, and $m = -\frac{2}{5}$ in $y = mx + b$ to find b.

$$4 = -\frac{2}{5}(-10) + b$$

$$0 = b$$

The equation is $y = -\frac{2}{5}x + 0$, or simply $y = -\frac{2}{5}x$.

4. $m = 2$, $b = -5$, so the line is $y = 2x - 5$.

5. From the graph, we can see that the *y*-intercept is 3. We can use the indicated points $(0, 3)$ and $(2, 0)$ to find the slope in two ways. One way is to put these numbers in the slope formula.

$$m = \frac{0-3}{2-0} = -\frac{3}{2}$$

The other way is to move from $(0, 3)$ to $(2, 0)$ by going down 3 (so the numerator of the slope is -3) and right 2 (so the denominator is 2). Either way, we have the slope $-\frac{3}{2}$. Because the *y*-intercept is 3, the equation is $y = -\frac{3}{2}x + 3$.

6. $m = \dfrac{-1-1}{-2-\frac{3}{4}} = \dfrac{-2}{-\frac{11}{4}} = -2 \div -\dfrac{11}{4} = -2 \cdot -\dfrac{4}{11} = \dfrac{8}{11}$

We use $x = -2$ and $y = -1$ in $y = mx + b$ to find *b*.

$$-1 = \frac{8}{11}(-2) + b \qquad\qquad \frac{8}{11}(-2) = -\frac{16}{11}$$

$$\frac{5}{11} = b \qquad\qquad -1 + \frac{16}{11} = \frac{-11+16}{11} = \frac{5}{11}$$

The equation is $y = \frac{8}{11}x + \frac{5}{11}$.

7. We solve for *y* in each equation so that we can compare their slopes.

$$3x - 7y = 28 \qquad\qquad 7x + 3y = 3$$

$$y = \frac{3}{7}x - 4 \qquad\qquad y = -\frac{7}{3}x + 1$$

The slopes are negative reciprocals of each other, so these lines are perpendicular.

8. Once we have found the slope for the line $x - y = 5$, we use its negative reciprocal as the slope of the line we want.

$$x - y = 5$$

$$y = x - 5$$

The slope of this line is 1. The negative reciprocal of 1 is -1. We use $x = 2$, $y = 3$, and $m = -1$ in $y = mx + b$.

$$3 = -1(2) + b$$

$$5 = b$$

The equation is $y = -1x + 5$, or simply $y = -x + 5$.

9. The line $x = 6$ is vertical, so the line we want is also vertical. The vertical line that goes through $(-3, 2)$, is $x = -3$.

10. We solve for y in each equation and compare their slopes.

$$2x - 3y = 1 \qquad\qquad -4x + 6y = 5$$

$$y = \frac{2}{3}x - \frac{1}{3} \qquad\qquad y = \frac{2}{3}x + \frac{5}{6}$$

The slopes are the same, so these lines are parallel.

Applications of Lines and Slopes

We can use the slope of a line to decide whether points in the plane form certain shapes. Here, we use the slope to decide whether or not three points form a right triangle and whether or not four points form a parallelogram. After we plot the points, we can decide which points to put into the slope formula.

EXAMPLE 1-8

• Show that $(-1, 2)$, $(4, -3)$, and $(5, 0)$ are the vertices of a right triangle.

From the graph in Figure 1-14, we see that the line segment between $(5, 0)$ and $(-1, 2)$ should be perpendicular to the line segment between $(5, 0)$ and $(4, -3)$. Once we have found the slopes of these line segments, we will see that they are negative reciprocals.

$$m = \frac{2 - 0}{-1 - 5} = -\frac{1}{3} \qquad m = \frac{-3 - 0}{4 - 5} = 3$$

• Show that $(-3, 1)$, $(3, -5)$, $(4, -1)$, and $(-2, 5)$ are the vertices of a parallelogram.

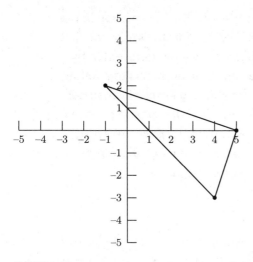

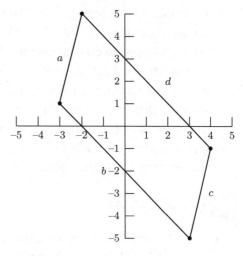

FIGURE 1-14   FIGURE 1-15

From the graph in Figure 1-15, we see that we need to show that sides *a* and *c* have the same slope as do *b* and *d*.

The slope for side *a* is $m = \dfrac{5 - 1}{-2 - (-3)} = 4,$

and the slope for side *c* is $m = \dfrac{-1 - (-5)}{4 - 3} = 4.$

The slope for side *b* is $m = \dfrac{-5 - 1}{3 - (-3)} = -1,$

and the slope for segment *d* is $m = \dfrac{-1 - 5}{4 - (-2)} = -1.$

There are many applications of linear equations to business and science. Suppose the property tax rate for a school district is \$1.50 per \$100 valuation. This is a linear relationship between the value of the property and the amount of tax on the property. The slope of the line in this relationship is $\frac{\text{tax change}}{\text{value change}} = \frac{\$1.50}{\$100}$. As the value of the property increases by \$100, the tax increases by \$1.50. Two variables are linearly related if a fixed increase in one variable causes a fixed increase or decrease in the other variable. These changes are proportional. For example, if a property increases in value by \$50, then its tax would increase by \$0.75 .

We can find an equation (also called a *model*) that describes the relationship between two variables if we are given two points or one point and the slope. As in most word problems, we must find the information in the statement of the problem; it is seldom spelled out for us. One of the first things we need to do is to decide which quantity will be represented by *x* and which by *y*. Sometimes it does not matter. In the problems that follow, it will matter. If we are instructed to "give variable 1 in terms of variable 2," then variable 1 will be *y* and variable 2 will be *x*. This is because in the equation $y = mx + b$, *y* is given in terms of *x*. For example, if we are asked to give the property tax in terms of property value, then *y* would represent the property tax and *x* would represent the property value.

 EXAMPLE 1-9

- A family paid $52.50 for water in January when they used 15,000 gallons (gal) and $77.50 in May when they used 25,000 gal. Find an equation that gives the amount of the water bill in terms of the number of gallons of water used.

Because we need to find the cost in terms of water used, we let *y* represent the cost and *x*, the amount of water used. Our ordered pairs are (water, cost): (15,000, 52.50) and (25,000, 77.50). Now we can compute the slope.

$$m = \frac{77.50 - 52.50}{25,000 - 15,000} = 0.0025$$

We use $x = 15,000$, $y = 52.50$, and $m = 0.0025$ in $y = mx + b$ to find *b*.

$$52.50 = 0.0025(15,000) + b$$

$$15 = b$$

The equation is $y = 0.0025x + 15$. With this equation, the family can predict its water bill by putting the amount of water used in the equation. For example, 32,000 gal would cost $0.0025(32,000) + 15 = \$95$.

- A bakery sells a special bread. It costs $6000 to produce 10,000 loaves of bread per day and $5900 to produce 9500 loaves. Find an equation that gives the daily costs in terms of the number of loaves of bread produced.

Because we want the cost in terms of the number of loaves produced, we let *y* represent the daily cost and *x*, the number of loaves produced in a day. Our points are of the form (number of loaves, daily cost): (10,000, 6000) and (9500, 5900).

$$m = \frac{5900 - 6000}{9500 - 10,000} = \frac{1}{5}$$

We use $x = 10{,}000$, $y = 6000$, and $m = \frac{1}{5}$ in $y = mx + b$.

$$6000 = \frac{1}{5}(10{,}000) + b$$

$$4000 = b$$

The equation is $y = \frac{1}{5}x + 4000$.

The slope and sometimes the y-intercept have important meanings in applied problems. In the first example, the household water bill was computed using $y = 0.0025x + 15$. The slope means that each gallon costs $0.0025 (or 0.25 cents). As the number of gallons increases by 1, the cost increases by $0.0025. The y-intercept is the cost when 0 gal is used. This additional monthly charge is $15. The slope in the bakery problem means that five loaves of bread costs $1 to produce (or each loaf costs $0.20). The y-intercept tells us the bakery's daily fixed costs are $4000. Fixed costs are costs that the bakery must pay regardless of the number of loaves produced. Fixed costs might include rent, equipment payments, insurance, taxes, etc.

In the following examples, information about the slope is given and a point is given or implied.

EXAMPLE 1-10

- The dosage of medication given to an adult cow is 500 milligrams (mg) plus 9 mg per pound. Find an equation that gives the amount of medication (in mg) per pound of weight.

  We use 500 mg as the y-intercept. The slope is $\frac{\text{increase in medication}}{\text{increase in weight}} = \frac{9}{1}$. The equation is $y = 9x + 500$, where x is in pounds and y is in milligrams.

- At the surface of the ocean, a certain object has 1500 pounds (lb) of pressure on it. For every foot below the surface, the pressure on the object increases about 43 lb. Find an equation that gives the pressure (in pounds) on the object in terms of its depth (in feet) in the ocean.

  At 0 feet (ft), the pressure on the object is 1500 lb, so the y-intercept is 1500. The slope is $\frac{\text{increase in pressure}}{\text{increase in depth}} = \frac{43}{1} = 43$. This makes the equation $y = 43x + 1500$, where x is the depth in feet and y is the pressure in pounds.

- A pancake mix requires $\frac{3}{4}$ cup of water for each cup of mix. Find an equation that gives the amount of water needed in terms of the amount of pancake mix.

  Although no point is directly given, we can assume that $(0, 0)$ is a point on the line because when there is no mix, no water is needed. The slope is $\frac{\text{increase in water}}{\text{increase in mix}} = \frac{3/4}{1} = \frac{3}{4}$. The equation is $y = \frac{3}{4}x + 0$, or simply $y = \frac{3}{4}x$.

 PRACTICE

1. Show that the points $(-5, 1)$, $(2, 0)$, and $(-2, -3)$ are the vertices of a right triangle (see Figure 1-16).

2. Show that the points $(-2, -3)$, $(3, 6)$, $(-5, 2)$, and $(6, 1)$ are the vertices of a parallelogram (see Figure 1-17).

3. A sales representative earns a monthly base salary plus a commission on sales. Her pay this month is $2000 on sales of $10,000. Last month, her pay was $2720 on sales of $16,000. Find an equation that gives her monthly pay in terms of her sales level.

4. The temperature scales Fahrenheit and Celsius are linearly related. Water freezes at 0°C and 32°F. Water boils at 212°F and 100°C. Find an equation that gives degrees Celsius in terms of degrees Fahrenheit.

5. A sales manager believes that each $100 spent on television advertising results in an increase of 45 units sold. If sales were 8250 units when $3600 was spent on television advertising, find an equation that gives the sales level in terms of the amount spent on advertising.

 **SOLUTIONS**

1. We show that the slope of the line segment between $(-5, 1)$ and $(-2, -3)$ is the negative reciprocal of the slope of the line segment between $(-2, -3)$ and $(2, 0)$. This will show that the angle at $(-2, -3)$ is a right angle.

$$m = \frac{-3 - 1}{-2 - (-5)} = -\frac{4}{3} \qquad m = \frac{0 - (-3)}{2 - (-2)} = \frac{3}{4}$$

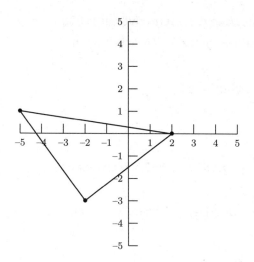

FIGURE 1-16   **FIGURE 1-17**

2. We show that the slope of the line segment between $(-5, 2)$ and $(-2, -3)$ is equal to the slope of the line segment between $(3, 6)$ and $(6, 1)$.

$$m = \frac{-3 - 2}{-2 - (-5)} = -\frac{5}{3} \qquad m = \frac{1 - 6}{6 - 3} = -\frac{5}{3}$$

Now we show that the slope of the line segment between $(-5, 2)$ and $(3, 6)$ is equal to the slope of the line segment between $(-2, -3)$ and $(6, 1)$.

$$m = \frac{6 - 2}{3 - (-5)} = \frac{1}{2} \qquad m = \frac{1 - (-3)}{6 - (-2)} = \frac{1}{2}$$

3. Because we want pay in terms of sales, y represents pay, and x represents monthly sales. The points are $(10{,}000, 2000)$ and $(16{,}000, 2720)$.

$$m = \frac{2720 - 2000}{16{,}000 - 10{,}000} = \frac{3}{25}$$

(This means that for every $25 in sales, the representative earns $3.) We use $x = 10,000$, $y = 2000$, and $m = \frac{3}{25}$ in $y = mx + b$.

$$2000 = \frac{3}{25}(10,000) + b$$

$$800 = b$$

The equation is $y = \frac{3}{25}x + 800$. (The y-intercept is 800, which means that her monthly base pay is $800.)

4. The points are (degrees Fahrenheit, degrees Celsius): $(32, 0)$ and $(212, 100)$.

$$m = \frac{100 - 0}{212 - 32} = \frac{5}{9}$$

(This means that a 9°F increase in temperature corresponds to an increase of 5°C.) We use $F = 32$, $C = 0$, and $m = \frac{5}{9}$ in $C = mF + b$.

$$0 = \frac{5}{9}(32) + b$$

$$-\frac{160}{9} = b$$

The equation is $C = \frac{5}{9}F - \frac{160}{9}$. (The y-intercept is $-\frac{160}{9}$, which means that the temperature 0°F corresponds to $-\frac{160}{9}°$C.)

5. The points are (amount spent on advertising, number of units sold). The slope is $\frac{\text{increase in sales}}{\text{increase in advertising spending}} = \frac{45}{100} = \frac{9}{20}$, and our point is $(3600, 8250)$.

$$8250 = \frac{9}{20}(3600) + b$$

$$6630 = b$$

The equation is $y = \frac{9}{20}x + 6630$. (The y-intercept is 6630, which means that if nothing were spent on television advertising, 6630 units would be sold.)

Summary

In this chapter, we learned how to

- *Use the slope formula to calculate the slope of a line.* When we have two points on a line, we put the x- and y-coordinates of these points in the slope formula, $m = \frac{y_2 - y_1}{x_2 - x_1}$. The slope of a horizontal line is zero, and the slope of a vertical line is not defined.

- *Determine the slope of a line from its graph.* If we can find two points, A and B, whose coordinates are easy to identify, we can measure the slope visually. The vertical distance from A to B is the numerator of the slope. The horizontal distance from A to B is the denominator of the slope.

- *Find an equation of a line from its slope and a point on its graph.* While there are several forms for an equation of a line, we usually worked with the slope-intercept form, $y = mx + b$. To find this equation from the slope of the line and one point, we find b by putting the slope and coordinates of the point, (x, y), in $y = mx + b$ and then solve the equation for b. A horizontal line has the form $y = a$, where a is the y-coordinate of every point on the line. A vertical line has the form $x = a$, where a is the x-coordinate of every point on the line.

- *Determine when two lines are parallel, perpendicular, or neither.* If neither line is vertical, then the lines are parallel if the slopes are equal. They are perpendicular if their slopes are negative reciprocals of each other. If the equations are in the form $y = mx + b$, we can simply compare their slopes. Otherwise, we can solve the equations for y and then compare the slopes. Two vertical lines are parallel, and a vertical line is perpendicular to a horizontal line.

- *Use the slope of a line to determine if points are vertices of some geometric figure.* Three points in the plane are the vertices of a right triangle if two of its sides are perpendicular. Four points in the plane are the vertices of a parallelogram if it has two pairs of parallel sides. It is usually helpful to plot the points before deciding which slopes to calculate and compare.

- *Use linear equations in applications.* If we have two quantities whose relationship can be approximated by a linear equation, we can find the equation after deciding which quantity to treat as x and which to treat as y. We then substitute the values given in the problem in the slope formula to find the slope, and then in $y = mx + b$ to find b. Once we have m and b, we have an equation that gives y in terms of x.

QUIZ

1. Find the slope of the line containing the points $(-4, 1)$ and $(2, 5)$.

   A. $\frac{3}{2}$ C. $-\frac{3}{5}$

   B. $-\frac{5}{3}$ D. $\frac{2}{3}$

2. Determine the slope of each line in Figure 1-18.

   A. The slope of L_1 is -3, and the slope of L_2 is $\frac{1}{3}$.

   B. The slope of L_1 is $-\frac{1}{3}$, and the slope of L_2 is 3.

   C. The slope of L_1 is $\frac{1}{3}$, and the slope of L_2 is -3.

   D. The slope of L_1 is 3, and the slope of L_2 is $-\frac{1}{3}$.

3. Find an equation of the line that contains the points $(11, 3)$ and $(1, 8)$.

   A. $-x + 2y = 30$ C. $x + 2y = 17$

   B. $-x + 2y = 19$ D. $2x + y = 10$

4. Are the lines $-3x + 4y = 20$ and $4x + 3y = 15$ parallel, perpendicular, or neither?

   A. Parallel   C. Neither

   B. Perpendicular   D. This cannot be determined

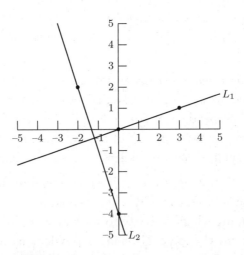

FIGURE 1-18

5. Find an equation of the line containing the point $(2, -7)$ and parallel to the line $-3x + 2y = 2.$

   A. $y = \frac{3}{2}x - 10$ C. $y = -\frac{2}{3}x - \frac{17}{3}$

   B. $y = \frac{2}{3}x - \frac{25}{3}$ D. $y = -\frac{3}{2}x - 4$

6. Describe the line $y = 15.$

   A. The line has slope 1 and y-intercept 15.

   B. The line has undefined slope and y-intercept 15.

   C. The line is vertical.

   D. The line is horizontal.

7. Find an equation of the vertical line that goes through the point $(10, -3)$.

   A. $x = 10$ C. $y = 10$

   B. $x = -3$ D. $y = -3$

8. Are the points $(-6, 23)$, $(-30, 5)$, $(-12, -19)$, and $(12, -1)$ the vertices of a rectangle? (See Figure 1-19.)

   A. Yes   C. This cannot be determined

   B. No

9. Are the lines $x = 9$ and $y = -9$ parallel, perpendicular, or neither?

   A. Parallel   C. Neither

   B. Perpendicular   D. This cannot be determined

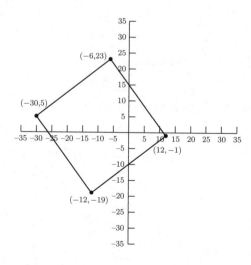

FIGURE 1-19

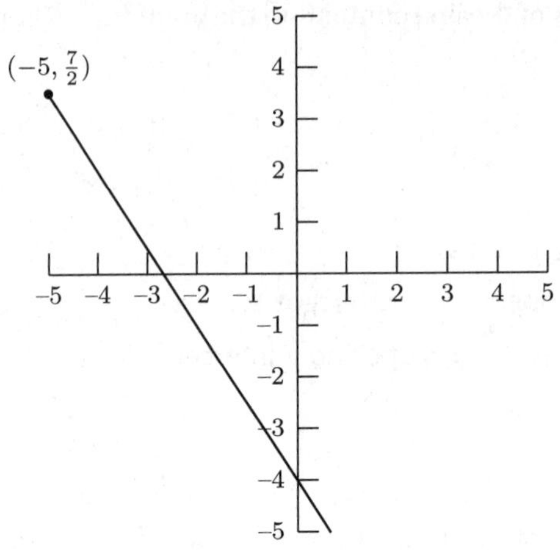

$\left(-5, \frac{7}{2}\right)$

FIGURE 1-20

10. A rental company charges $30 per day to rent a car plus $0.20 per mile. Find an equation that gives the daily rental in terms of the number of miles driven.

   A. $R = 30m + 0.20$

   B. $R = 0.20m + 30$

   C. $R = 0.30m + 20$

   D. $R = 20m + 0.30$

11. The Resendez family pays a monthly base charge for their electricity plus a charge for each kilowatt-hour (kWh) used. In April, their electric bill was $144.50 for 750 kWh and in May, it was $122.00 for 600 kWh. What is the charge per kilowatt-hour?

   A. $0.12

   B. $0.13

   C. $0.14

   D. $0.15

12. True or False: The slope of the line $x = 4$ is 0.

   A. True

   B. False

13. Find an equation of the line in Figure 1-20.

   A. $y = -\frac{2}{3}x - 4$

   B. $y = \frac{2}{3}x - 4$

   C. $y = -\frac{3}{2}x - 4$

   D. $y = \frac{3}{2}x - 4$

chapter 2

Introduction to Functions

While the concept of a function might seem simple at first, functions lie at the heart of calculus. The basic idea behind functions is *dependence*. If one variable *depends* on another, we say it is a function of the other variable. For example, because an hourly worker's weekly pay depends on how many hours he worked during the week, we say his pay is a function of hours worked.

CHAPTER OBJECTIVES

In this chapter, you will

- Learn the definition of a function
- Evaluate a function
- Compute the difference quotient
- Determine the domain of a function

The Definition of a Function

A *relation* between two sets A and B is a collection of ordered pairs, where the first coordinate comes from A and the second comes from B. For example, if $A = \{1, 2, 3, 4\}$ and $B = \{a, b, c\}$, one relation is the three pairs $\{(1, c), (1, a), (3, a)\}$. A *function* on sets A and B is a special kind of relation where *every* element of A is paired with *exactly one* element from B. The relation above fails to be a function in two ways. Not every element of A is paired with an element from B, 1 and 3 are used but not 2 and 4. Also, the element 1 is used *twice*, not *once*. There are no such restrictions on B; that is, elements from B can be paired with elements from A many times or not at all. For example, $\{(1, a), (2, a), (3, b), (4, b)\}$ is a function from A to B.

Functions exist all around us. The weekly pay of an hourly worker is a function of how many hours he worked. For any number of hours worked, there is exactly one pay amount that corresponds to that time. If A is the set of all triangles and B is the set of real numbers, then we have a function that pairs each triangle with exactly one real number that is its area. In this book, we will concern ourselves with functions from real numbers to real numbers. Set A is either all of the real numbers or some part of the real numbers, and B is the real numbers. For the most part, our functions will be in the form of an equation.

A linear function is one of the most basic kinds of functions. These functions have the form $f(x) = mx + b$. The only difference between $f(x) = mx + b$ and $y = mx + b$ is that y is replaced by $f(x)$. Very often $f(x)$ and y are the same. The letter f is the name of the function. Other common names of functions are g and h. The notation $f(x)$ is pronounced "f of x" or "f at x."

Evaluating a Function

Evaluating a function at a quantity means to substitute the quantity for x (or whatever the variable is). For example, evaluating the function $f(x) = 2x - 5$ at 6 means to substitute 6 for x.

$$f(6) = 2(6) - 5 = 7$$

We might also say $f(6) = 7$. The quantity inside the parentheses is x and the quantity on the right of the equal sign is y. One advantage to this notation is that we have both the x- and y-values without having to say anything about x and y. Functions that have no variables in them are called *constant functions*. All y-values for these functions are the same.

EXAMPLE 2-1

- Find $f(-2)$, $f(0)$, and $f(6)$ for $f(x) = \sqrt{x+3}$.

  We need to substitute -2, 0, and 6 for x in the function.

  $$f(-2) = \sqrt{-2+3} = \sqrt{1} = 1$$
  $$f(0) = \sqrt{0+3} = \sqrt{3}$$
  $$f(6) = \sqrt{6+3} = \sqrt{9} = 3$$

- Find $f(-8)$, $f(\pi)$, and $f(10)$ for $f(x) = 16$.

  $f(x) = 16$ is a constant function, so the y-value is 16 no matter what quantity is in the parentheses.

  $$f(-8) = 16 \qquad f(\pi) = 16 \qquad f(10) = 16$$

A *piecewise function* is a function with two or more formulas for computing y. Which formula we use depends on where x is. There is an interval for x written next to each formula for y (there is a review of intervals in the Appendix).

- $$f(x) = \begin{cases} x - 1 & \text{if } x \le -2 \\ 2x & \text{if } -2 < x < 2 \\ x^2 & \text{if } x \ge 2 \end{cases}$$

In this example, there are three formulas for y: $y = x - 1$, $y = 2x$, and $y = x^2$, and three intervals for x: $x \le -2$, $-2 < x < 2$, and $x \ge 2$ (Figure 2-1). When evaluating this function, we need to decide to which interval x belongs. Then we will use the corresponding formula for y.

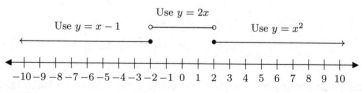

FIGURE 2-1

EXAMPLE 2-2

• Find $f(5)$, $f(-3)$, and $f(0)$ for the piecewise function above.

For $f(5)$, does $x = 5$ belong to $x \leq -2$, $-2 < x < 2$, or $x \geq 2$? Because $5 \geq 2$, we use $y = x^2$, the formula written next to $x \geq 2$.

$$f(5) = 5^2 = 25$$

For $f(-3)$, does $x = -3$ belong to $x \leq -2$, $-2 < x < 2$, or $x \geq 2$? Because $-3 \leq -2$, we use $y = x - 1$, the formula written next to $x \leq -2$.

$$f(-3) = -3 - 1 = -4$$

For $f(0)$, does $x = 0$ belong to $x \leq -2$, $-2 < x < 2$, or $x \geq 2$? Because $-2 < 0 < 2$, we use $y = 2x$, the formula written next to $-2 < x < 2$.

$$f(0) = 2(0) = 0$$

• Find $f(3)$, $f(1)$, and $f(-4)$ for

$$f(x) = \begin{cases} -x & \text{if } x \leq 1 \\ 5 & \text{if } x > 1 \end{cases}$$

$f(3) = 5$ because $3 > 1$

$f(1) = -1$ because $1 \leq 1$

$f(-4) = -(-4) = 4$ because $-4 \leq 1$

Piecewise functions come up in daily life. For example, suppose a company pays the regular hourly wage for someone who works up to 8 hours but time and a half for someone who works more than 8 hours but no more than 10 hours and double time for more than 10 hours. Then a worker whose regular hourly pay is $10 has the daily pay function below.

$$p(h) = \begin{cases} 10h & \text{if } 0 \leq h \leq 8 \\ 15(h-8) + 80 & \text{if } 8 < h \leq 10 \\ 20(h-10) + 110 & \text{if } 10 < h \leq 24 \end{cases}$$

Below is an example of a piecewise function based on data taken from Instructions for 1040-ES (2011) Schedule X from the Internal Revenue

Service (IRS). The *y*-value is the amount of estimated income tax for a single person. The *x*-value is the estimated taxable income.

$$f(x) = \begin{cases} 0.10x & \text{if } x \leq 8500 \\ 850 + 0.15(x - 8500) & \text{if } 8500 < x \leq 34{,}500 \\ 4750 + 0.25(x - 34{,}500) & \text{if } 34{,}500 < x \leq 83{,}600 \\ 17{,}025 + 0.28(x - 83{,}600) & \text{if } 83{,}600 < x \leq 174{,}400 \\ 42{,}449 + 0.33(x - 174{,}400) & \text{if } 174{,}400 < x \leq 379{,}150 \\ 110{,}016.50 + 0.35(x - 379{,}150) & \text{if } x > 379{,}150 \end{cases}$$

A single person who expects a taxable income of \$100,000 would pay \$17,025 + 0.28(100,000 − 83,600) = 21,617.

PRACTICE

1. Find $f(-1)$ and $f(0)$ for $f(x) = 3x^2 + 2x - 1$.

2. Evaluate $f(x) = \frac{1}{x+1}$ at $x = -3$, $x = 1$, and $x = \frac{1}{2}$.

3. Evaluate $g(x) = \sqrt{x - 6}$ at $x = 6$, $x = 8$, and $x = 10$.

4. Find $f(5)$, $f(3)$, $f(2)$, $f(0)$, and $f(-1)$.

$$f(x) = \begin{cases} x^2 + x & \text{if } x \leq -1 \\ 10 & \text{if } -1 < x \leq 2 \\ -6x & \text{if } x > 2 \end{cases}$$

5. The piecewise function below is based on data taken from Instructions for 1040-ES (2011) Schedule Y-1, from the Internal Revenue Service (IRS). The *y*-value is the amount of estimated income tax for a couple filing jointly. The *x*-value is the estimated taxable income. If a couple filing jointly expects a taxable income of \$150,000, what is their tax?

$$f(x) = \begin{cases} 0.10x & \text{if } x \leq 17{,}000 \\ 1700 + 0.15(x - 17{,}000) & \text{if } 17{,}000 < x \leq 69{,}000 \\ 9500 + 0.25(x - 69{,}000) & \text{if } 69{,}000 < x \leq 139{,}350 \\ 27{,}087.50 + 0.28(x - 139{,}350) & \text{if } 139{,}350 < x \leq 212{,}300 \\ 47{,}513.50 + 0.33(x - 212{,}300) & \text{if } 212{,}300 < x \leq 379{,}150 \\ 102{,}574 + 0.35(x - 379{,}150) & \text{if } x > 379{,}150 \end{cases}$$

✔ SOLUTIONS

1. $$f(-1) = 3(-1)^2 + 2(-1) - 1 = 3 - 2 - 1 = 0$$

$$f(0) = 3(0)^2 + 2(0) - 1 = -1$$

2. $$f(-3) = \frac{1}{-3+1} = \frac{1}{-2} \quad \text{or} \quad -\frac{1}{2}$$

$$f(1) = \frac{1}{1+1} = \frac{1}{2}$$

$$f\left(\frac{1}{2}\right) = \frac{1}{\frac{1}{2}+1} = \frac{1}{\frac{1}{2}+\frac{2}{2}} = \frac{1}{\frac{3}{2}} = 1 \div \frac{3}{2} = 1 \cdot \frac{2}{3} = \frac{2}{3}$$

3. $$g(6) = \sqrt{6-6} = \sqrt{0} = 0$$

$$g(8) = \sqrt{8-6} = \sqrt{2}$$

$$g(10) = \sqrt{10-6} = \sqrt{4} = 2$$

4. $$f(5) = -6(5) = -30 \qquad f(3) = -6(3) = -18$$

$$f(2) = 10 \qquad\qquad f(0) = 10$$

$$f(-1) = (-1)^2 + (-1) = 0$$

5. The tax is $27,087.50 + 0.28(150,000 - 139,350) = $30,069.50.

More on Evaluating Functions

Functions can be evaluated at quantities that are not numbers, but the idea is the same—we substitute the quantity in the parentheses for x and simplify.

▉ EXAMPLE 2-3

- Evaluate $f(a+3)$, $f(a^2)$, $f(u-v)$, and $f(a+h)$ for $f(x) = 8x + 5$.
  We let $x = a + 3$, $x = a^2$, $x = u - v$, and $x = a + h$ in the function.

$$f(a+3) = 8(a+3) + 5 = 8a + 24 + 5 = 8a + 29$$

$$f(a^2) = 8(a^2) + 5 = 8a^2 + 5$$

$$f(u-v) = 8(u-v) + 5 = 8u - 8v + 5$$

$$f(a+h) = 8(a+h) + 5 = 8a + 8h + 5$$

• Evaluate $f(10a)$, $f(-a)$, $f(a+h)$, and $f(x+1)$ for $f(x) = x^2 + 3x - 4$.

$$f(10a) = (10a)^2 + 3(10a) - 4 = 10^2a^2 + 30a - 4$$

$$= 100a^2 + 30a - 4$$

$$f(-a) = (-a)^2 + 3(-a) - 4 = a^2 - 3a - 4$$

Remember, $(-a)^2 = (-a)(-a) = a^2$, not $-a^2$.

$$f(a+h) = (a+h)^2 + 3(a+h) - 4$$

$$= (a+h)(a+h) + 3(a+h) - 4$$

$$= a^2 + 2ah + h^2 + 3a + 3h - 4$$

$$f(x+1) = (x+1)^2 + 3(x+1) - 4$$

$$= (x+1)(x+1) + 3(x+1) - 4$$

$$= x^2 + 2x + 1 + 3x + 3 - 4 = x^2 + 5x$$

• Find $f(a - 12)$, $f(a^2 + 1)$, $f(a+h)$, and $f(x+3)$ for $f(x) = -4$.
This is a constant function, so the y-value is -4 no matter what is in the parentheses.

$$f(a-12) = -4 \qquad f(a^2+1) = -4$$

$$f(a+h) = -4 \qquad f(x+3) = -4$$

• Find $f(2u+v)$, $f(\frac{1}{u})$, and $f(2x)$ for $f(x) = \frac{x+1}{x+2}$.

$$f(2u+v) = \frac{2u+v+1}{2u+v+2}$$

$$f\left(\frac{1}{u}\right) = \frac{\frac{1}{u}+1}{\frac{1}{u}+2} = \frac{\frac{1}{u}+\frac{u}{u}\cdot 1}{\frac{1}{u}+\frac{u}{u}\cdot 2}$$

$$= \frac{\frac{1}{u}+\frac{u}{u}}{\frac{1}{u}+\frac{2u}{u}} = \frac{\frac{1+u}{u}}{\frac{1+2u}{u}}$$

$$= \frac{1+u}{u} \div \frac{1+2u}{u} = \frac{1+u}{u}\cdot\frac{u}{1+2u} = \frac{1+u}{1+2u}$$

$$f(2x) = \frac{2x+1}{2x+2}$$

Very early in an introductory calculus course, students use function evaluation to evaluate an important formula called the *difference quotient*.

$$\frac{f(a+h) - f(a)}{h}$$

When evaluating the difference quotient, we are given a function such as $f(x) = x^2 + 3$. We need to find $f(a+h)$ and $f(a)$. Once we have these two quantities, we will put them into the quotient and simplify. Simplifying the quotient is usually the messiest part. For $f(x) = x^2 + 3$, we have $f(a+h) = (a+h)^2 + 3 = (a+h)(a+h) + 3 = a^2 + 2ah + h^2 + 3$, and $f(a) = a^2 + 3$. We will substitute $a^2 + 2ah + h^2 + 3$ for $f(a+h)$ and $a^2 + 3$ for $f(a)$.

$$\frac{f(a+h) - f(a)}{h} = \frac{\overbrace{a^2 + 2ah + h^2 + 3}^{f(a+h)} - \overbrace{(a^2 + 3)}^{f(a)}}{h}$$

Now we need to simplify this fraction.

$$\frac{a^2 + 2ah + h^2 + 3 - (a^2 + 3)}{h} = \frac{a^2 + 2ah + h^2 + 3 - a^2 - 3}{h}$$

$$= \frac{2ah + h^2}{h} \qquad \text{Factor } h.$$

$$= \frac{h(2a + h)}{h} = 2a + h$$

EXAMPLE 2-4

Evaluate the difference quotient for the given functions.

- $f(x) = 3x^2$

We begin by finding $f(a+h)$ and $f(a)$.

$$f(a+h) = 3(a+h)^2 = 3(a+h)(a+h) = 3(a^2 + 2ah + h^2)$$
$$= 3a^2 + 6ah + 3h^2$$
$$f(a) = 3a^2$$

We now substitute these quantities in the formula.

$$\frac{f(a+h) - f(a)}{h} = \frac{3a^2 + 6ah + 3h^2 - 3a^2}{h} = \frac{6ah + 3h^2}{h}$$
$$= \frac{h(6a + 3h)}{h} = 6a + 3h$$

- $f(x) = x^2 - 2x + 5$

$$f(a+h) = (a+h)^2 - 2(a+h) + 5$$
$$= (a+h)(a+h) - 2(a+h) + 5$$
$$= a^2 + 2ah + h^2 - 2a - 2h + 5$$
$$f(a) = a^2 - 2a + 5$$

$$\frac{f(a+h) - f(a)}{h} = \frac{a^2 + 2ah + h^2 - 2a - 2h + 5 - (a^2 - 2a + 5)}{h}$$
$$= \frac{a^2 + 2ah + h^2 - 2a - 2h + 5 - a^2 + 2a - 5}{h}$$
$$= \frac{2ah + h^2 - 2h}{h} = \frac{h(2a + h - 2)}{h}$$
$$= 2a + h - 2$$

- $f(x) = \dfrac{1}{x}$

$$f(a+h) = \frac{1}{a+h} \qquad \text{and} \qquad f(a) = \frac{1}{a}$$

$$\frac{f(a+h)-f(a)}{h}=\frac{\frac{1}{a+h}-\frac{1}{a}}{h}$$

$$=\frac{\frac{1}{a+h}\cdot\frac{a}{a}-\frac{1}{a}\cdot\frac{a+h}{a+h}}{h}$$

$$=\frac{\frac{a}{a(a+h)}-\frac{a+h}{a(a+h)}}{h}$$

$$=\frac{\frac{a-(a+h)}{a(a+h)}}{h}=\frac{\frac{a-a-h}{a(a+h)}}{h}$$

$$=\frac{\frac{-h}{a(a+h)}}{h}=\frac{-h}{a(a+h)}\div h$$

$$=\frac{-h}{a(a+h)}\cdot\frac{1}{h}=\frac{-1}{a(a+h)}$$

Do not worry—you will not spend a lot of time evaluating the difference quotient in calculus, there are formulas that do most of the work. What is the difference quotient, anyway? It is nothing more than the slope formula where $x_1 = a$, $y_1 = f(a)$, $x_2 = a + h$, and $y_2 = f(a+h)$.

$$m=\frac{y_2-y_1}{x_2-x_1}=\frac{f(a+h)-f(a)}{a+h-a}=\frac{f(a+h)-f(a)}{h}$$

Still Struggling

Be careful, factor h from each term in the numerator *before* canceling h from the denominator.

PRACTICE

1. Evaluate $f(u+1)$, $f(u^3)$, $f(a+h)$, and $f(2x-1)$ for $f(x)=7x-4$.

2. Find $f(-a)$, $f(2a)$, $f(a+h)$, and $f(x+5)$ for $f(x)=2x^2-x+3$.

3. Find $f(u+v)$, $f(u^2)$, $f(\frac{1}{u})$, and $f(x^2+3)$ for $f(x)=\frac{10x+1}{3x+2}$.

4. Evaluate the difference quotient for $f(x)=3x^2+2x-1$.

5. Evaluate the difference quotient for $f(x)=\frac{15}{2x-3}$.

✔ SOLUTIONS

1. $f(u+1) = 7(u+1) - 4 = 7u + 7 - 4 = 7u + 3$

$f(u^3) = 7(u^3) - 4 = 7u^3 - 4$

$f(a+h) = 7(a+h) - 4 = 7a + 7h - 4$

$f(2x-1) = 7(2x-1) - 4 = 14x - 7 - 4 = 14x - 11$

2. $f(-a) = 2(-a)^2 - (-a) + 3 = 2a^2 + a + 3$

$f(2a) = 2(2a)^2 - 2a + 3 = 2(4a^2) - 2a + 3 = 8a^2 - 2a + 3$

$f(a+h) = 2(a+h)^2 - (a+h) + 3 = 2(a+h)(a+h) - (a+h) + 3$

$\qquad = 2(a^2 + 2ah + h^2) - a - h + 3 = 2a^2 + 4ah + 2h^2 - a - h + 3$

$f(x+5) = 2(x+5)^2 - (x+5) + 3 = 2(x+5)(x+5) - (x+5) + 3$

$\qquad = 2(x^2 + 10x + 25) - x - 5 + 3 = 2x^2 + 19x + 48$

3. $$f(u+v) = \frac{10(u+v)+1}{3(u+v)+2} = \frac{10u + 10v + 1}{3u + 3v + 2}$$

$$f(u^2) = \frac{10u^2 + 1}{3u^2 + 2}$$

$$f\left(\frac{1}{u}\right) = \frac{10\left(\frac{1}{u}\right)+1}{3\left(\frac{1}{u}\right)+2}$$

$$= \frac{\frac{10}{u}+1}{\frac{3}{u}+2} = \frac{\frac{10}{u}+1 \cdot \frac{u}{u}}{\frac{3}{u}+2 \cdot \frac{u}{u}} = \frac{\frac{10}{u}+\frac{u}{u}}{\frac{3}{u}+\frac{2u}{u}}$$

$$= \frac{\frac{10+u}{u}}{\frac{3+2u}{u}} = \frac{10+u}{u} \div \frac{3+2u}{u}$$

$$= \frac{10+u}{u} \cdot \frac{u}{3+2u} = \frac{10+u}{3+2u}$$

$$f(x^2+3) = \frac{10(x^2+3)+1}{3(x^2+3)+2}$$

$$= \frac{10x^2 + 31}{3x^2 + 11}$$

4. $f(a+h) = 3(a+h)^2 + 2(a+h) - 1$

$\quad\quad = 3(a+h)(a+h) + 2(a+h) - 1$

$\quad\quad = 3(a^2 + 2ah + h^2) + 2a + 2h - 1$

$\quad\quad = 3a^2 + 6ah + 3h^2 + 2a + 2h - 1$

$f(a) = 3a^2 + 2a - 1$

$$\frac{f(a+h) - f(a)}{h} = \frac{3a^2 + 6ah + 3h^2 + 2a + 2h - 1 - (3a^2 + 2a - 1)}{h}$$

$$= \frac{3a^2 + 6ah + 3h^2 + 2a + 2h - 1 - 3a^2 - 2a + 1}{h}$$

$$= \frac{6ah + 3h^2 + 2h}{h}$$

$$= \frac{h(6a + 3h + 2)}{h} = 6a + 3h + 2$$

5. $f(a+h) = \dfrac{15}{2(a+h) - 3} = \dfrac{15}{2a + 2h - 3}$ and $f(a) = \dfrac{15}{2a - 3}$

$$\frac{f(a+h) - f(a)}{h} = \frac{\frac{15}{2a+2h-3} - \frac{15}{2a-3}}{h}$$

$$= \frac{\frac{15}{2a+2h-3} \cdot \frac{2a-3}{2a-3} - \frac{15}{2a-3} \cdot \frac{2a+2h-3}{2a+2h-3}}{h}$$

$$= \frac{\frac{15(2a-3) - 15(2a+2h-3)}{(2a+2h-3)(2a-3)}}{h} = \frac{\frac{30a-45-30a-30h+45}{(2a+2h-3)(2a-3)}}{h}$$

$$= \frac{\frac{-30h}{(2a+2h-3)(2a-3)}}{h} = \frac{-30h}{(2a+2h-3)(2a-3)} \div h$$

$$= \frac{-30h}{(2a+2h-3)(2a-3)} \cdot \frac{1}{h} = \frac{-30}{(2a+2h-3)(2a-3)}$$

Domain and Range

The *domain* of a function from set *A* to set *B* is all of set *A*. The *range* is set *B*. In our example at the beginning of the chapter, we had $A = \{1, 2, 3, 4\}$, $B = \{a, b, c\}$ and our function was $\{(1, a), (2, a), (3, b), (4, b)\}$. The domain of this function is $\{1, 2, 3, 4\}$, and the range is all of the elements from B that were paired with elements from A. These were $\{a, b\}$.

For the functions in this book, the domain consists of all the real numbers we are allowed to use for x. The range is all of the y-values. In this chapter, we will find the domain algebraically. In the next chapter, we will find both the domain and range from graphs of functions.

Very often, we find the domain of a function by thinking about what we cannot do. For now the things we cannot do are limited to division by zero and taking even roots of negative numbers. If a function has x in a denominator, set the denominator equal to zero and solve for x. The domain does *not* include the solution(s) to this equation (assuming the equation has a solution). If a function has x under an even root sign, set the quantity under the root greater than or equal to zero to find the domain. (Later when we learn about other functions, we will have other things we cannot do.) The domain and range are usually given in interval notation. There is a review of interval notation in the Appendix.

EXAMPLE 2-5

- $f(x) = \dfrac{x^2 - 4}{x + 3}$

We cannot let $x + 3$ to be zero, so we cannot let $x = -3$. The domain is $x \neq -3$, or $(-\infty, -3) \cup (-3, \infty)$.

- $f(x) = \dfrac{1}{x^3 + 2x^2 - x - 2}$

We use factoring by grouping to factor the denominator. (There is a review of factoring by grouping in the Appendix.)

$$x^3 + 2x^2 - x - 2 = 0$$

$$x^2(x + 2) - 1(x + 2) = 0$$

$$(x + 2)(x^2 - 1) = 0$$

$$(x + 2)(x - 1)(x + 1) = 0$$

$$x + 2 = 0 \qquad x - 1 = 0 \qquad x + 1 = 0$$

$$x = -2 \qquad x = 1 \qquad x = -1$$

The domain is all real numbers except 1, -1, and -2. The domain is shaded on the number line in Figure 2-2 (on the next page).

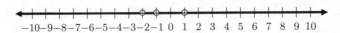

FIGURE 2-2

The domain is $(-\infty, -2) \cup (-2, -1) \cup (-1, 1) \cup (1, \infty)$.

- $g(x) = \dfrac{x + 5}{x^2 + 1}$

Because $x^2 + 1 = 0$ has no real number solution, we can let x equal any real number. The domain is all real numbers, or $(-\infty, \infty)$.

- $f(x) = \sqrt{x - 8}$

Because we can only take the square root of nonnegative numbers, $x - 8$ must be nonnegative. We represent "$x - 8$ must be nonnegative" as "$x - 8 \geq 0$." Solving $x - 8 \geq 0$, we get $x \geq 8$. The domain is $x \geq 8$, or $[8, \infty)$.

- $f(x) = \sqrt{x^2 - x - 2}$

(The Appendix has a review on solving nonlinear inequalities.) We need to solve $x^2 - x - 2 \geq 0$. Factoring $x^2 - x - 2$, we have $(x - 2)(x + 1)$, see Figure 2-3.

$$x - 2 = 0 \qquad x + 1 = 0$$

$$x = 2 \qquad x = -1$$

We use $x = -2$ as the test value to the left of -1, $x = 0$ for the test value between -1 and 2, and $x = 3$ for the test value to the right of 2 in $x^2 - x - 2 \geq 0$ to see which of these numbers makes it true.

Is $(-2)^2 - (-2) - 2 \geq 0$? Yes. Put "True" to the left of -1.

Is $0^2 - 0 - 2 \geq 0$? No. Put "False" between -1 and 2.

Is $3^2 - 3 - 2 \geq 0$? Yes. Put "True" to the right of 2, see Figure 2-4.

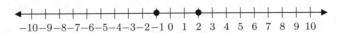

FIGURE 2-3

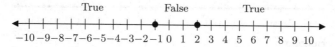

FIGURE 2-4

The inequality is true for $x \leq -1$ and $x \geq 2$, so the domain is $(-\infty, -1] \cup [2, \infty)$.

- $f(x) = \sqrt[4]{x^2 + 5}$

Because $x^2 + 5$ is always positive, we can let x be any real number. The domain is $(-\infty, \infty)$.

- $g(x) = \sqrt[3]{x + 7}$

We can take the cube root of any number, so the domain is all real numbers, or $(-\infty, \infty)$.

- $f(x) = x^4 - x^2 + 1$

There is no x in a denominator and no x under an even root sign, so the domain is all real numbers, or $(-\infty, \infty)$.

There are some functions that have x in a denominator and under an even root. At times, it is useful to shade a number line to keep track of the domain.

- $f(x) = \dfrac{x^2 + x - 3}{\sqrt{4 - x}}$

We cannot let $\sqrt{4 - x}$ be zero, and we cannot let $4 - x$ be negative. These restrictions mean that we must have $4 - x > 0$ (instead of $4 - x \geq 0$). The domain is $4 > x$ (or $x < 4$), which is the interval $(-\infty, 4)$.

- $h(x) = \dfrac{15 - x}{x^2 + 3x - 4} + \sqrt{x + 10}$

For $\sqrt{x + 10}$ we need $x + 10 \geq 0$, or $x \geq -10$, see Figure 2-5.

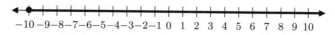

FIGURE 2-5

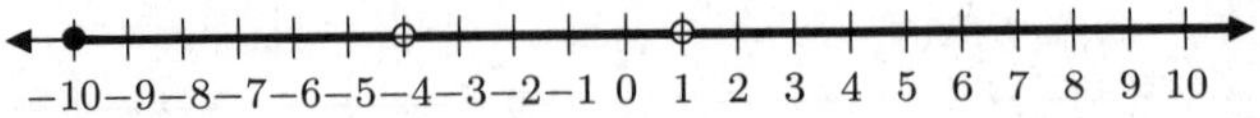

FIGURE 2-6

We also need for $x^2 + 3x - 4$ not to be zero.

$$x^2 + 3x - 4 = 0$$

$$(x + 4)(x - 1) = 0$$

$$x + 4 = 0 \qquad x - 1 = 0$$

$$x = -4 \qquad x = 1$$

We cannot let $x = -4$ and $x = 1$, so we exclude these numbers from $x \geq -10$. The domain is $[-10, -4) \cup (-4, 1) \cup (1, \infty)$, see Figure 2-6.

PRACTICE

For Problems 2 to 11, give the domain in interval notation.

1. A function consists of the ordered pairs $\{(h, 5), (z, 3), (i, 12)\}$. List the elements in the domain.

2. $f(x) = \dfrac{2x + 3}{x - 8}$

3. $f(x) = \dfrac{-1}{x^2 - 2x}$

4. $f(x) = \dfrac{x - 3}{x^2 + 10}$

5. $g(x) = \sqrt[3]{6 - x}$

6. $h(x) = \sqrt{x + 3}$

7. $f(x) = \sqrt{4 - x^2}$

8. $f(x) = \sqrt{3x^2 + 5}$

9. $f(x) = \dfrac{1}{\sqrt{x - 9}}$

10. $f(x) = 4x^3 - 2x + 5$

11. $f(x) = \dfrac{\sqrt{x + 5}}{x^2 + 2x - 8}$

 **SOLUTIONS**

1. The domain consists of the first coordinate of the ordered pairs: *h, z,* and *i*.

2. We cannot let $x - 8 = 0$, so we cannot let $x = 8$. The domain is $x \neq 8$, or $(-\infty, 8) \cup (8, \infty)$.

3. We cannot let $x^2 - 2x = x(x - 2) = 0$, so we cannot let $x = 0$ or $x = 2$. The domain is all real numbers except 0 and 2, or $(-\infty, 0) \cup (0, 2) \cup (2, \infty)$.

4. Because $x^2 + 10 = 0$ has no real number solution, the domain is all real numbers, or $(-\infty, \infty)$.

5. We can take the cube root of any number, so the domain is all real numbers, or $(-\infty, \infty)$.

6. We must have $x + 3 \geq 0$, or $x \geq -3$. The domain is $[-3, \infty)$.

7. We need to solve $4 - x^2 = (2 - x)(2 + x) \geq 0$, see Figure 2-7. The domain is $[-2, 2]$.

8. Because $3x^2 + 5 \geq 0$ is true for all real numbers, the domain is $(-\infty, \infty)$.

9. We need $x - 9 > 0$. The domain is $x > 9$, or $(9, \infty)$.

10. The domain is all real numbers, or $(-\infty, \infty)$.

11. From $x + 5 \geq 0$, we have $x \geq -5$, see Figure 2-8.
    Now we need to solve $x^2 + 2x - 8 = (x + 4)(x - 2) = 0$.

$$x + 4 = 0 \qquad\qquad x - 2 = 0$$

$$x = -4 \qquad\qquad x = 2$$

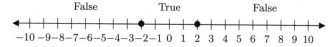

FIGURE 2-7

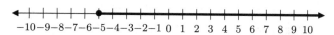

FIGURE 2-8

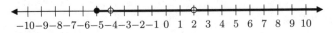

FIGURE 2-9

We must remove -4 and 2 from $x \geq -5$. The domain is $[-5, -4) \cup (-4, 2) \cup (2, \infty)$, see Figure 2-9.

At times the domain of a function matters when we are solving an applied problem. For example, suppose there is a 10×18 inch piece of cardboard that will be made into an open-topped box. After cutting a square $x \times x$ in from each corner, the sides will be folded up to form the box, see Figure 2-10.

The volume of the box is a function of x, $V(x) = x(18 - 2x)(10 - 2x)$. What is the domain of this function? We obviously cannot cut a negative number of inches from each corner. If we cut 0 in from each corner, we do not have a box, so x must be positive. Finally, the box is only 10 in wide, so if we cut out 5 in from each corner, then we will not have any cardboard left. These facts make the domain $0 < x < 5$. Maximizing the volume of this box is a typical problem in a first semester of calculus. The solutions to the mathematical problem are $\frac{14 \pm \sqrt{61}}{3}$ (approximately 2.0635 and 7.27008). Only one of these numbers is in the domain of the applied function, so only one of these numbers is the solution.

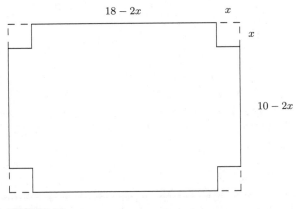

FIGURE 2-10

Summary

In this chapter, we learned how to

- *Evaluate a function.* We work with functions in the form of equations in x and y. To evaluate such a function means to substitute a number for x and to simplify to find y [for the most part, y and $f(x)$ are the same]. For example, to evaluate $f(5)$ for some function f, we replace x with 5 and then simplify.

- *Evaluate a piecewise function.* A piecewise function has more than one formula to compute y-values. The function is written with the formula for computing y-values next to an interval for x. The formula we use to compute y depends on the interval containing the x-value we have.

- *Evaluate the difference quotient.* The difference quotient is $\frac{f(a+h)-f(a)}{h}$. When given a function f, we evaluate the difference quotient by simplifying $f(a+h)$ and then putting this and $f(a)$ into the fraction. Once this is done, we simplify the fraction.

- *Find the domain of a function.* If we have an equation in which y is a function of x, then the domain is the set of x-values that make sense for the equation. If any x-values cause the denominator to be 0, then such x-values are not in the domain. If any x-values cause the expression under an even root to be negative, then such x-values are not in the domain.

QUIZ

1. Find $f(-2)$ for $f(x) = x^2$.

   A. -2

   B. 2

   C. -4

   D. 4

2. Find $g(2a)$ for $g(x) = x^3 + 1$.

   A. $2a^3 + 1$

   B. $8a^3 + 1$

   C. $2a^3 + 2$

   D. $8a^3 + 8$

3. Find the domain for the function $g(x) = \frac{8x-4}{x+1}$.

   A. $(-\infty, -1) \cup (-1, \infty)$

   B. $(-1, \infty)$

   C. $(-\infty, -1) \cup (-1, 2) \cup (2, \infty)$

   D. $(-\infty, -1] \cup [-1, \infty)$

4. Evaluate the difference quotient for the function $f(x) = 3x + 4$.

   A. $3 + h$

   B. 3

   C. $3a + h$

   D. 1

5. Find $f(\frac{1}{2})$ for $f(x) = \frac{5}{x}$.

   A. 10

   B. $\frac{5}{2}$

   C. 2

   D. $\frac{2}{5}$

6. Find the domain for the function $f(x) = \sqrt{6 - 3x}$.

   A. $[-2, \infty)$

   B. $[2, \infty)$

   C. $(-\infty, 2]$

   D. $(-\infty, 2) \cup (2, \infty)$

7. Evaluate the difference quotient for the function $f(x) = 4x^2 - 7$.

   A. $8ah + 4h$

   B. $8a + 4h^2$

   C. $8a + 4$

   D. $8a + 4h$

8. Find the domain for the function $f(x) = \frac{1}{x^2+9}$.

   A. $(-\infty, -3) \cup (3, \infty)$

   B. All real numbers

   C. $(-\infty, -3) \cup (-3, 3) \cup (3, \infty)$

   D. $(-\infty, -3) \cup (-3, \infty)$

9. Find the domain for the function $g(x) = \frac{\sqrt{x-2}}{x-6}$.

   A. $(-\infty, 6) \cup (6, \infty)$

   B. $(-\infty, 2) \cup (2, 6) \cup (6, \infty)$

   C. $[2, \infty)$

   D. $[2, 6) \cup (6, \infty)$

chapter 3

Functions and Their Graphs

In Chapter 2, we learned how to evaluate a function and how to find its domain. In this chapter, we will learn how to do these things by studying the graph of a function. The graph of a function can tell us almost anything we want to know about the function, where the function is increasing or decreasing, where it has a maximum or minimum, where its intercepts are, and more. Being able to draw conclusions about a function from its graph will help you with certain concepts in calculus.

CHAPTER OBJECTIVES

In this chapter, you will

- Evaluate a function from its graph
- Use the Vertical Line Test to determine whether *y* is a function of *x*
- Determine the domain and range of a function from its graph
- Determine where a function is increasing and where it is decreasing
- Compute the average rate of change of a function
- Recognize symmetry in a graph
- Determine whether a function is even, odd, or neither

Evaluating a Function

To say that $f(-3) = 1$ means that when $x = -3$, $y = 1$, so the point $(-3, 1)$ is on the graph of $f(x)$. Similarly, if $(5, 4)$ is a point on the graph of $f(x)$, then $f(5) = 4$.

 EXAMPLE 3-1

- The graph in Figure 3-1 is the graph of $f(x) = x^3 - x^2 - 4x + 4$. Find $f(-1)$, $f(0)$, $f(3)$, and $f(-2)$.

The point $(-1, 6)$ is on the graph means that $f(-1) = 6$.
The point $(0, 4)$ is on the graph means that $f(0) = 4$.
The point $(3, 10)$ is on the graph means that $f(3) = 10$.
The point $(-2, 0)$ is on the graph means that $f(-2) = 0$.

The graph also shows the *intercepts* of the graph. Rememeber that an *x*-intercept is a point where the graph intersects (touches or crosses) the *x*-axis, and the *y*-intercept is a point where the graph intersects the *y*-axis. We can tell that the *y*-intercept for the graph in Figure 3-1 is 4 [or $(0, 4)$] and the *x*-intercepts are -2, 1, and 2 [or $(-2, 0)$, $(1, 0)$, and $(2, 0)$].

The Vertical Line Test

An equation "gives y as a function of x" means that for every x-value, there is a unique y-value. From this fact we can look at a graph of an equation to decide if the equation gives y as a function of x. If an equation is not a function, then at least one x-value has more than one y-value in the equation, and there is more than one point on the graph that has the same x-coordinate. A line through points having the same x-coordinate is vertical. This is the idea behind the *Vertical Line Test*. The graph of an equation passes the Vertical Line Test if every vertical line intersects the graph at one point or not at all. If so, then the equation is a function.

The graph of $y^2 = x$ is shown in Figure 3-2. The vertical line $x = 4$ intersects the graph in two places, $(4, 2)$ and $(4, -2)$, so y is not a function of x in the equation $y^2 = x$.

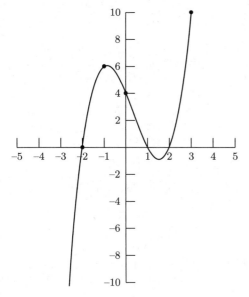

FIGURE 3-1

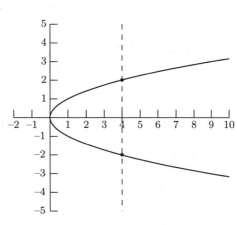

FIGURE 3-2

The Domain and Range

You might remember from Chapter 2 that if y is a function of x, then the domain consists of all possible values for x. We can find the domain of a function by looking at its graph. The graph's extension horizontally shows the function's domain. The range of a function consists of all possible y-values, so the graph's vertical extension shows the function's range.

 EXAMPLE 3-2

The graph of a function is given. Find the domain and range of the function, and give your answer in interval notation.

- **The graph in Figure 3-3 extends horizontally from $x = -5$ to $x = 4$. Because there are closed dots on these endpoints (instead of open dots), $x = -5$ and $x = 4$ are part of the domain, too. The domain is $[-5, 4]$. The graph extends vertically from $y = -4$ to $y = 3$, so the range is $[-4, 3]$.**

- **The graph in Figure 3-4 extends horizontally from $x = -3$ to $x = 2$. Because open dots are used on $(-3, 5)$ and $(2, 0)$, these points are not on**

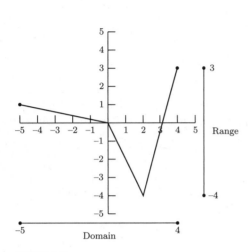

FIGURE 3-3

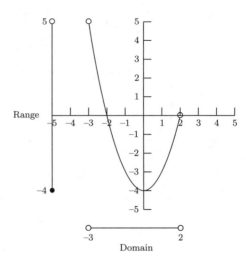

FIGURE 3-4

the graph, so $x = -3$ and $x = 2$ are not part of the domain. The domain is $(-3, 2)$.

- The graph in Figure 3-5 extends vertically from $y = -4$ and $y = 5$. The range is $[-4, 5)$. We need to use a bracket around -4 because $(0, -4)$ is a point on the graph, and a parenthesis around 5 because the point $(-3, 5)$ is not a point on the graph.

   The graph extends horizontally from $x = -2$ on the left and vertically from below $y = 0$. The domain is $[-2, \infty)$, and the range is $(-\infty, 0]$.

Increasing/Decreasing Intervals

A function is increasing on an interval if moving toward the right in the interval means the graph is going up. A function is decreasing on an interval if moving toward the right in the interval means the graph is going down. The function whose graph is in Figure 3-6 is increasing from $x = -3$ to $x = 0$ as well as to the right of $x = 2$. It is decreasing to the left of $x = -3$ and between $x = 0$ and $x = 2$. Using interval notation, we say the function is increasing on the intervals $(-3, 0)$ and $(2, \infty)$ and decreasing on the intervals $(-\infty, -3)$ and $(0, 2)$. For reasons covered in calculus, parentheses are used for the interval notation.

A function is constant on an interval if the y-values do not change. This part of the graph is part of a horiztonal line.

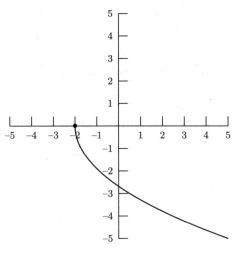

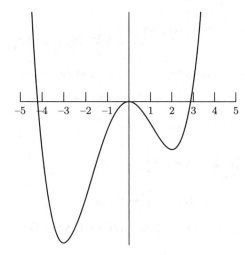

FIGURE 3-5   **FIGURE 3-6**

◼ EXAMPLE 3-3

Determine the intervals on which the functions are increasing, decreasing, or constant.

- This function in Figure 3-7 is increasing on $(-5, -2)$ and $(4, 5)$. It is decreasing on $(-2, 2)$ and constant on $(2, 4)$.

- The function in Figure 3-8 is increasing on all of its domain, $(0, \infty)$.

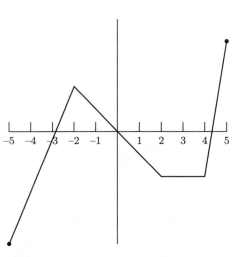

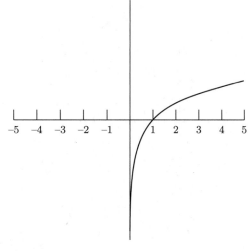

FIGURE 3-7   **FIGURE 3-8**

Still Struggling

Be careful, a function is increasing or decreasing on intervals of x, not y.

 PRACTICE

1. Is the graph in Figure 3-9 the graph of a function?

2. Refer to the graph of $f(x)$ in Figure 3-10.

   a. What is $f(-3)$?

   b. What is $f(5)$?

   c. What is the domain?

   d. What is the range?

   e. What are the x-intercepts?

   f. What is the y-intercept?

   g. What is/are the increasing interval(s)?

   h. What is/are the decreasing interval(s)?

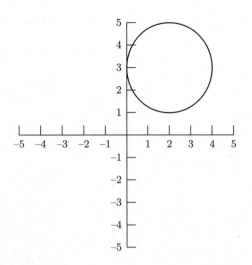

FIGURE 3-9

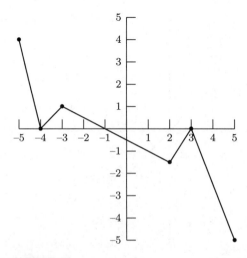

FIGURE 3-10

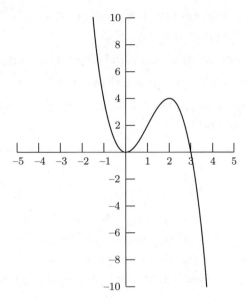

FIGURE 3-11

3. Refer to the graph of $f(x)$ in Figure 3-11.

   a. What is $f(2)$? $f(1)$?

   b. What are the *x*-intercepts? What is the *y*-intercept?

   c. What is the domain? Range?

   d. What is the increasing interval? What are the decreasing intervals?

SOLUTIONS _____

1. No. The graph fails the Vertical Line Test.
2. a. $f(-3) = 1$ because $(-3, 1)$ is a point on the graph.
   b. $f(5) = -5$ because $(5, -5)$ is a point on the graph.
   c. The domain is $[-5, 5]$.
   d. The range is $[-5, 4]$.
   e. The *x*-intercepts are -4, -1, and 3.
   f. The *y*-intercept is $-\frac{1}{2}$.
   g. The increasing intervals are $(-4, -3)$ and $(2, 3)$.
   h. The decreasing intervals are $(-5, -4)$, $(-3, 2)$, and $(3, 5)$.

3. a. $f(2) = 4$ because $(2, 4)$ is a point on the graph. $f(1) = 2$ because $(1, 2)$ is a point on the graph.

   b. The *x*-intercepts are 0 and 3. The *y*-intercept is 0.

   c. The domain and range are all real numbers, $(-\infty, \infty)$.

   d. The increasing interval is $(0, 2)$, and the decreasing intervals are $(-\infty, 0)$ and $(2, \infty)$.

Graphs of Data

Graphs are useful tools for presenting a lot of information in a small space. Being able to read a graph and draw conclusions from it are important in many subjects in addition to mathematics. In the example below, we will practice drawing conclusions based on information given in the graph in Figure 3-12.

 EXAMPLE 3-4

This graph shows the daily balance of a checking account for about 2 weeks. No more than one transaction (a deposit or a check written) is made in 1 day. For example, the balance at the end of the second day is $350 and $300 at the end of the third day, so a $50 check was written during the third day.

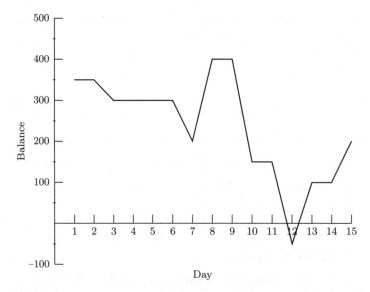

FIGURE 3-12

1. **On what day was a check for $200 written?**

   On the 12th day when the balance dropped from $150 to −$50.

2. **What is the largest deposit?**

   The largest increase was $200, on the eighth day when the balance increased from $200 to $400.

3. **What is the largest check written?**

   The largest check was written on the 10th day when the balance dropped from $400 to $150.

4. **When was the account overdrawn?**

   The balance was negative on the 12th day.

5. **What was the longest period of inactivity?**

   From the third day until the sixth day, the balance did not change, so the longest period of inactivity was 3 days.

Average Rate of Change

Calculus deals with the rate of change. A familiar example of a rate of change is speed (or more accurately, velocity). Velocity is the rate of change of distance per unit of time. A car traveling in city traffic generally has a lower rate of change of distance per hour than a car traveling on an interstate freeway. A glass of water placed in a refrigerator has a lower rate of temperature change than a glass of water placed in a freezer. In calculus, you will study instantaneous rates of change of functions at different values of x. We will study the *average rate of change* in this book. As you will see in the following examples, the average rate of change can hide a lot of variation.

 EXAMPLE 3-5

- Suppose $1000 was invested in company stock for some manufacturing company. The value of the investment at the beginning of each year is given in Table 3-1.

1. How much did the stock increase per year on average from the beginning of Year 3 to the beginning of Year 6?

   For this 3-year period the investment increased in value from $1162 to $1252. The average rate of change is

   $$\frac{1252 - 1162}{6 - 3} = \frac{90}{3} = 30 \text{ per year}$$

TABLE 3-1	The Value of an Investment over 10 Years	
Year	Value (in Dollars)	Change from the Previous Year
1	1000	New investment of $1000
2	1205	Gain of $205
3	1162	Loss of $43
4	1025	Loss of $137
5	1190	Gain of $165
6	1252	Gain of $62
7	1434	Gain of $182
8	1621	Gain of $187
9	2015	Gain of $394
10	2845	Gain of $830

2. What was the average annual loss from the beginning of Year 2 to the beginning of Year 5?

The average rate of change during this 3-year period is

$$\frac{1190 - 1205}{5 - 2} = \frac{-15}{3} = -5 \text{ per year}$$

The negative symbol means that this change is a loss, not a gain.

3. What was the average annual increase over the full period?

The average increase in the investment over the full 9 years is

$$\frac{2845 - 1000}{10 - 1} = \frac{1845}{9} = 205 \text{ per year}$$

• Find the average rate of change between the points $(-3, 9)$ and $(-1, 3)$ and between the points $(1, 1.5)$ and $(3, 1.125)$ for the function whose graph is given in Figure 3-13.

The average rate of change of a function between two points on the graph is the slope of the line containing the two points. For the points $(-3, 9)$ and $(-1, 3)$, $x_1 = -3$, $y_1 = 9$ and $x_2 = -1$, $y_2 = 3$.

$$\text{Average rate of change} = \frac{y_2 - y_1}{x_2 - x_1} = \frac{3 - 9}{-1 - (-3)} = \frac{-6}{2} = \frac{-3}{1} = -3$$

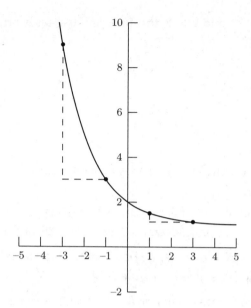

FIGURE 3-13

Between $x = -3$ and $x = -1$, the *y*-values of this function *decrease* by 3 as *x* increases by 1, on average.

For the points $(1, 1.5)$ and $(3, 1.125)$, $x_1 = 1$, $y_1 = 1.5$ and $x_2 = 3$, $y_2 = 1.125$.

$$\text{Average rate of change} = \frac{y_2 - y_1}{x_2 - x_1} = \frac{1.125 - 1.5}{3 - 1} = \frac{-0.375}{2} = -0.1875$$

Between $x = 1$ and $x = 3$, the *y*-values of this function decrease on average by 0.1875 as *x* increases by 1.

- Find the average rate of change of $f(x) = -3x^2 + 10$ between $x = -1$ and $x = 2$.

Once we find the *y*-values by putting them into the function, we will find the slope of the line containing these two points.

$$y_1 = f(x_1) = f(-1) = -3(-1)^2 + 10 = 7$$

$$y_2 = f(x_2) = f(2) = -3(2)^2 + 10 = -2$$

$$\text{Average rate of change} = \frac{y_2 - y_1}{x_2 - x_1} = \frac{-2 - 7}{2 - (-1)} = \frac{-9}{3} = \frac{-3}{1} = -3$$

Between $x = -1$ and $x = 2$, this function decreases on average by 3 as x increases by 1.

 **PRACTICE**

1. A sales representative's pay is based on his sales. Table 3-2 shows his salary during 1 year.

   How much did his monthly pay change on average between January and July? Between July and December? Between October and December?

2. Find the average rate of change between the indicated points of the function whose graph is given in Figure 3-14.

3. Find the average rate of change for $f(x) = 2 - x^3$ between $x = -2$ and $x = 1$.

4. Find the average rate of change for $f(x) = 6x - 3$ between $x = -5$ and $x = 3$ and between $x = 0$ and $x = 8$.

TABLE 3-2 A Sales Representative's Pay over 12 Months	
Month	**Pay**
January (1)	2100
February (2)	2000
March (3)	2400
April (4)	2700
May (5)	2500
June (6)	3000
July (7)	3500
August (8)	3600
September (9)	2500
October (10)	2000
November (11)	2000
December (12)	2100

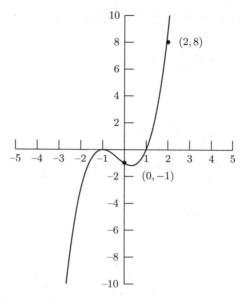

FIGURE 3-14

 **SOLUTIONS**

1. The average monthly increase between January and July is the slope of the line containing the points (1,2100) and (7,3500).

$$\frac{3500 - 2100}{7 - 1} \approx 233$$

The average monthly decrease between July and December is the slope of the line containing the points (7,3500) and (12,2100).

$$\frac{2100 - 3500}{12 - 7} = -280$$

The average monthly increase from October to December is the slope of the line containing the points (10,2000) and (12,2100).

$$\frac{2100 - 2000}{12 - 10} = 50$$

2. $x_1 = 0$, $y_1 = -1$ and $x_2 = 2$, $y_2 = 8$

$$\text{Average rate of change} = \frac{8-(-1)}{2-0} = \frac{9}{2}$$

3.
$$y_1 = f(x_1) = f(-2) = 2-(-2)^3 = 10$$
$$y_2 = f(x_2) = f(1) = 2-(1)^3 = 1$$
$$\text{Average rate of change} = \frac{1-10}{1-(-2)} = -3$$

4. For $x_1 = -5$ and $x_2 = 3$,

$$y_1 = f(x_1) = f(-5) = 6(-5) - 3 = -33$$
$$y_2 = f(x_2) = f(3) = 6(3) - 3 = 15$$
$$\text{Average rate of change} = \frac{15-(-33)}{3-(-5)} = 6$$

For $x_1 = 0$ and $x_2 = 8$,

$$y_1 = f(x_1) = f(0) = 6(0) - 3 = -3$$
$$y_2 = f(x_2) = f(8) = 6(8) - 3 = 45$$
$$\text{Average rate of change} = \frac{45-(-3)}{8-0} = 6$$

The average rate of change between *any* two points on a linear function is the slope.

It is worth noting that the difference quotient gives the average rate of change of $f(x)$ between $x_1 = a$ and $x_2 = a+h$.

$$y_1 = f(x_1) = f(a) \qquad y_2 = f(x_2) = f(a+h)$$
$$\text{Average rate of change} = \frac{y_2-y_1}{x_2-x_1} = \frac{f(a+h)-f(a)}{a+h-a}$$
$$= \frac{f(a+h)-f(a)}{h}$$

Even and Odd Functions

A graph is *symmetric* if one half looks like the other half. We might also say that one half of the graph is a reflection of the other.

When a graph has symmetry, we usually say that it is symmetric with respect to a line or a point. The graph in Figure 3-15 is symmetric with respect to the x-axis because the half of the graph above the x-axis is a reflection of the half below the x-axis. The graph in Figure 3-16 is symmetric with respect to the y-axis.

The graph in Figure 3-17 is symmetric with respect to the vertical line $x = 2$.

One type of symmetry that is a little harder to see is *origin symmetry*. A graph has origin symmetry if folding the graph along the x-axis then again along the y-axis would have one part of the graph coincide with the other part. The graphs in Figures 3-18 and 3-19 have origin symmetry.

Knowing in advance whether or not the graph of a function is symmetric can make sketching the graph less work. We can use algebra to decide if the graph of a function has y-axis symmetry or origin symmetry. Except for the function $f(x) = 0$, the graph of a function does not have x-axis symmetry because x-axis symmetry would cause a graph to fail the Vertical Line Test.

For the graph of a function to be symmetric with respect to the y-axis, a point on the left side of the y-axis must have a mirror image on the right side of the graph (see Figure 3-20).

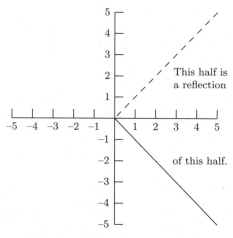

FIGURE 3-15

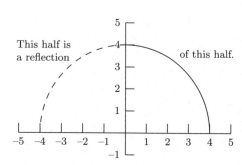

FIGURE 3-16

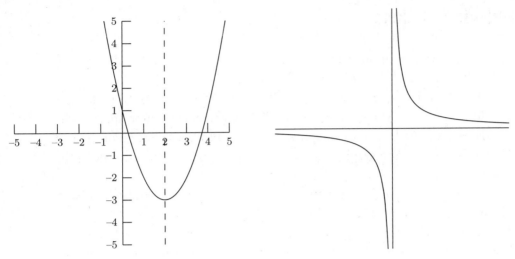

FIGURE 3-17   FIGURE 3-18

The graph of a function with y-axis symmetry has the property that (x, y) is on the graph means that $(-x, y)$ is also on the graph. The functional notation for this idea is $f(x) = f(-x)$. "$f(x) = f(-x)$" says that the y-value for x ($f(x)$) is the same as the y-value for $-x$ ($f(-x)$). If evaluating a function at $-x$ does not change the equation, then its graph has y-axis symmetry. Such functions are called *even functions*.

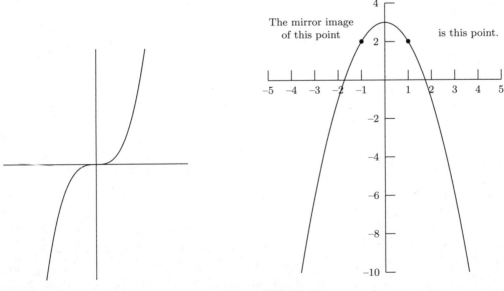

FIGURE 3-19   FIGURE 3-20

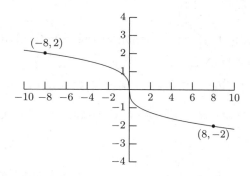

FIGURE 3-21

For a function whose graph is symmetric with respect to the origin, the mirror image of (x, y) is $(-x, -y)$ (see Figure 3-21).

The functional notation for this idea is $f(-x) = -f(x)$. "$f(-x) = -f(x)$" says that the y-value for $-x$ ($f(-x)$) is the opposite of the y-value for x ($-f(x)$). If evaluating a function at $-x$ changes the equation to its negative, then the graph of the function is symmetric with respect to the origin. These functions are called *odd functions*.

In order to work the following problems, we will use the following facts.

$$a(-x)^{\text{even power}} = ax^{\text{even power}} \text{ and } a(-x)^{\text{odd power}} = -ax^{\text{odd power}}$$

EXAMPLE 3-6

Determine if the given function is even (its graph is symmetric with respect to the y-axis), odd (its graph is symmetric with respect to the origin), or neither.

- $f(x) = x^2 - 2$

  Does evaluating $f(x)$ at $-x$ change the function? If so, is $f(-x) = -(x^2 - 2) = -f(x)$?

$$f(-x) = (-x)^2 - 2 = x^2 - 2$$

  Evaluating $f(x)$ at $-x$ does not change the function, so the function is even.

- $f(x) = x^3 + 5x$

  Does evaluating $f(x)$ at $-x$ change the function? If so, is $f(-x) = -(x^3 + 5x) = -f(x)$?

  $$f(-x) = (-x)^3 + 5(-x) = -x^3 - 5x = -(x^3 + 5x) = -f(x)$$

  Evaluating $f(x)$ at $-x$ gives us $-f(x)$, so the function is odd.

- $f(x) = \dfrac{x}{x+1}$

  Does evaluating $f(x)$ at $-x$ change the function? If so, is $f(-x) = -\frac{x}{x+1} = -f(x)$?

  $$f(-x) = \frac{-x}{-x+1}$$

  Because $f(-x)$ is not the same as $f(x)$ nor the same as $-f(x)$, the function is neither even nor odd.

 PRACTICE

For Problems 1 to 4, determine whether or not the graph has symmetry. If it does, determine the kind of symmetry it has. For Problems 5 to 8, determine if the function is even, odd, or neither.

1. See Figure 3-22

2. See Figure 3-23

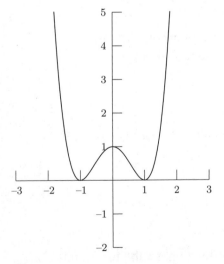

FIGURE 3-22

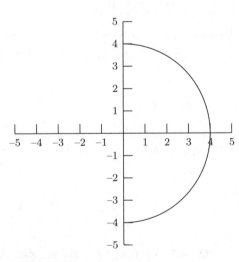

FIGURE 3-23

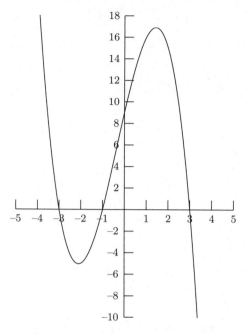

FIGURE 3-24

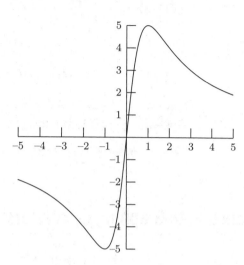

FIGURE 3-25

3. See Figure 3-24

4. See Figure 3-25

5. $f(x) = x^3 + 6$

6. $f(x) = 3x^2 - 2$

7. $f(x) = \dfrac{x^2 - 3}{x^3 + 2x}$

8. $g(x) = \sqrt[3]{x}$

 **SOLUTIONS**

1. This graph has **y**-axis symmetry.

2. This graph has **x**-axis symmetry.

3. This graph does not have symmetry.

4. This graph has origin symmetry.

5. $f(-x) = (-x)^3 + 6 = -x^3 + 6$

   $f(-x) \neq f(x)$ and $f(-x) \neq -f(x)$, making $f(x)$ neither even nor odd.

6. $f(-x) = 3(-x)^2 - 2 = 3x^2 - 2$

   $f(-x) = f(x)$, making $f(x)$ even.

7. $f(-x) = \dfrac{(-x)^2 - 3}{(-x)^3 + 2(-x)} = \dfrac{x^2 - 3}{-x^3 - 2x} = \dfrac{x^2 - 3}{-(x^3 + 2x)}$

   $= -\dfrac{x^2 - 3}{x^3 + 2x} = -f(x)$

   $f(-x) = -f(x)$, making $f(x)$ odd.

8. $g(-x) = \sqrt[3]{-x} = -\sqrt[3]{x} = -g(x)$

   $g(-x) = -g(x)$, making $g(x)$ odd.

Introduction to Graphing Calculators

A graphing calculator is a powerful tool in algebra. For now, we will learn how to use it to plot the graph of a function and to evaluate a function. The screens and keystrokes are for a TI-84® calculator (the screens and keystrokes are the same for a TI-83®). We begin by entering the function in the Y = Editor. Press the Y = key and then enter the function. Once a function is entered, you might need to adjust the viewing window, that is, the part of the graph that will be displayed. In the *standard window*, the x- and y-values range from −10 to 10, and the scale (the distance between tickmarks) is 1. You can change the viewing window by pressing the WINDOW key and making the changes. Once the function is entered and the window set, display the graph by pressing the GRAPH key.

EXAMPLE 3-7

• Use a graphing calculator to plot the graph of $f(x) = 4x - 8$.

We begin by pressing Y = and entering $4x - 8$. (See Figure 3-26.) From what we know about the graph of the line $y = 4x - 8$, we know that the standard viewing window is a good window for displaying the graph of this function. (See Figure 3-27.) Finally, press the GRAPH key to display the graph. (See Figure 3-28.)

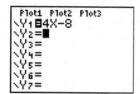

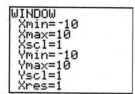

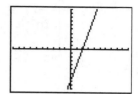

FIGURE 3-26   FIGURE 3-27   FIGURE 3-28

A calculator can help us to evaluate a function. One method locates a point on the graph. In order for this method to work, the point (or at least its *x*-coordinate) must be in the viewing window. The other method involves the TABLE feature. We will see how to use these methods in the following example.

 EXAMPLE 3-8

Evaluate $f(3)$ for $f(x) = 4x - 8$.

   We already have this function entered in the Y = Editor, and $x = 3$ is in the viewing window. To use the VALUE feature, press the 2nd key followed by the TRACE key to get on the CALCULATE menu. Because the VALUE feature is the first choice, you only need to press the ENTER key. (See Figure 3-29.) At the "$x =$" prompt, enter 3 and press ENTER . The cursor goes to the point on the graph for $x = 3$ and shows us that $y = 4$. From this, we know that $f(3) = 4$. (See Figure 3-30.)

   In order to use the TABLE feature to evaluate a function, you should adjust the calculator to allow you to input values for *x*. Go to the TABLE SETUP menu by pressing 2nd key followed by the WINDOW key. Cursor to "Ask" on the line, "Indpnt: Auto Ask " and press ENTER . (See Figure 3-31.) Now, go to the TABLE menu (2nd followed by GRAPH) and enter 3. (See Figure 3-32.)

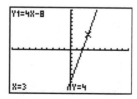

FIGURE 3-29   FIGURE 3-30

FIGURE 3-31   FIGURE 3-32

 PRACTICE

Use the standard viewing window to plot the graphs.

1. Let $f(x) = x^2 - 4$.

   a. Plot the graph.

   b. Evaluate $f(3)$ using the VALUE feature.

2. Let $f(x) = 4\sqrt{x}$.

   a. Plot the graph.

   b. Evaluate $f(100)$ using the TABLE feature.

SOLUTIONS

1. See Figures 3-33 and 3-34.

2. See Figures 3-35 and 3-36.

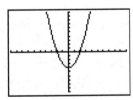

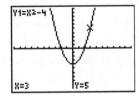

FIGURE 3-33   FIGURE 3-34

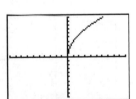

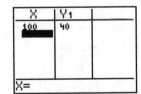

FIGURE 3-35   FIGURE 3-36

Summary

In this chapter, we learned how to

- *Evaluate a function from its graph.* We find $f(a)$ from the graph of f by locating the point on the graph for $x = a$. The y-coordinate of this point is $f(a)$.

- *Determine whether or not a graph is the graph of a function.* If every vertical line intersects the graph of an equation in at most one point, then the equation is a function. In other words, if any vertical line intersects the graph of an equation in more than one point, then the equation is not a function (i.e., y is not a function of x).

- *Use the graph of a function to find its domain and range.* We find the domain and range of a function from its graph by seeing how far it extends horizontally (the domain) and how far it extends vertically (the range). If the function has an endpoint, we must decide whether to use a parenthesis or bracket around the endpoint. We use a parenthesis if the endpoint is shown by an open dot, and we use a bracket if the endpoint is shown by a closed dot.

- *Determine where a function is increasing and where it is decreasing.* A function is increasing on an interval (of x-values) if its graph goes up as we move from left to right in the interval. A function is decreasing on an interval if its graph goes down as we move from left to right in the interval. If the graph is horizontal on an interval, then the function is constant on that interval. Because you will likely use open intervals in calculus when describing increasing/decreasing/constant intervals, we use parentheses here.

- *Find the average rate of change of a function.* The average rate of change of a function between two values of x is the slope of the line containing the two points on the graph at these x-values. If we are only given the x-values, we use the function to compute the y-values before finding the slope.

- *Recognize symmetry in a graph.* A graph is symmetric with respect to the y-axis if the part of the graph that is to the left of the y-axis is a reflection of the part of the graph to the right of the y-axis. If a graph has y-axis symmetry, then the point (a, b) on the graph implies the point $(-a, b)$ is also on the graph. Similarly, if a graph has x-axis symmetry, then the part of the graph below the x-axis is a reflection of the part of the graph above the x-axis, and the point (a, b) on the graph implies the point $(a, -b)$ is also on the graph. A graph has origin symmetry if (a, b) is on the graph implies $(-a, -b)$ is also on the graph. Visually, we can tell if a graph has origin symmetry if we (mentally) make two folds in the graph, once along the y-axis and again along the x-axis. If the parts of the graph would coincide, then the graph has origin symmetry.

• *Determine whether a function is even, odd, or neither.* A function is even if its graph has y-axis symmetry. A function is odd if its graph has origin symmetry. We can algebraically determine if a function is even, odd, or neither by evaluating the function at $-x$. If $f(-x) = f(x)$ (the equation does not change with this substitution), then the function is even. If $f(-x) = -f(x)$ (the expression is the opposite of the original expression), then the function is odd.

QUIZ

Problems 1 to 4 refer to the function whose graph is in Figure 3.37.

1. **What is the domain of the function?**

   A. $(2, \infty)$

   B. $[0, \infty)$

   C. $[-4, \infty)$

   D. All real numbers

2. **What is the range of the function?**

   A. $(2, \infty)$

   B. $[0, \infty)$

   C. $[-4, \infty)$

   D. All real numbers

3. **What is the y-intercept?**

   A. 0

   B. 2

   C. -4

   D. The graph does not have a y-intercept.

4. **Find the average rate of change of the function between $x = 0$ and $x = 5$.**

   A. $\frac{1}{5}$

   B. $-\frac{1}{5}$

   C. 5

   D. -5

Problems 5 to 8 refer to the function whose graph is in Figure 3-38.

5. **Where is the function increasing?**

   A. $(-5, 5)$

   B. $(-4, 4)$

   C. $(0, 4)$

   D. $(-4, 0)$

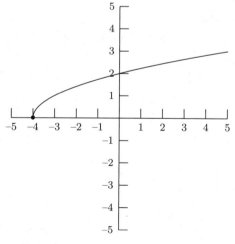

FIGURE 3-37

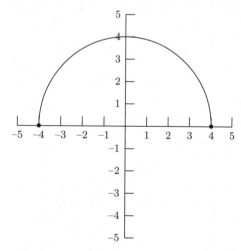

FIGURE 3-38

6. **What is the range of the function?**

   A. $[-5, 5]$ C. $[0, 4]$

   B. $[-4, 4]$ D. $[-4, 0]$

7. **What symmetry does the graph have?**

   A. x-axis symmetry   C. Origin symmetry

   B. y-axis symmetry   D. The graph does not have symmetry.

8. **Is the function even, odd, or neither?**

   A. Even   C. Neither

   B. Odd

9. **Find the average rate of change for the function $f(x) = 10 - x$ between $x = -1$ and $x = 1$.**

   A. -1 C. 1

   B. -2 D. 2

10. **Is the function $f(x) = \frac{6x^3}{x^2+5}$ even, odd, or neither?**

    A. Even   C. Neither

    B. Odd   D. It is impossible to tell without the graph.

11. **Find the average rate of change for the function $g(x) = 2x^3 - 5$ between $x = 1$ and $x = 2$.**

    A. 14   C. -14

    B. 15   D. 8

12. **Is the function $f(x) = 4x^3 - 6$ even, odd, or neither?**

    A. Even   C. Neither

    B. Odd   D. It is impossible to tell without the graph.

chapter 4

Combinations of Functions

Most ... e some combination of simple ... ortant ways of combining fu ... position. Being able to see ho ... elp you to use formulas in calc ... an arithmetic combination a ... e chapter, we will work with ... use in later chapters.

CH...

In this ...

- Fin...
- Fin...
- Fin... ctions
- Fir...
- Fir... ition of simpler functions
- De...
- Find the inverse of a function

Arithmetic Combinations

We can add two functions, $(f + g)(x)$, subtract them, $(f - g)(x)$, multiply them, $(fg)(x)$, and divide them $(\frac{f}{g})(x)$. The domain of $(f + g)(x)$, $(f - g)(x)$, and $(fg)(x)$ is the intersection of the domain of $f(x)$ and $g(x)$. In other words, their domain is where the domain of $f(x)$ overlaps the domain of $g(x)$. The domain of $(\frac{f}{g})(x)$ is the same, except we need to exclude any x that makes $g(x) = 0$.

 EXAMPLE 4-1

Find $(f + g)(x)$, $(f - g)(x)$, $(fg)(x)$, $(\frac{f}{g})(x)$, and their domain.

- $f(x) = x^2 - 2x + 5$ and $g(x) = 6x - 10$

$$(f + g)(x) = f(x) + g(x) = \overbrace{(x^2 - 2x + 5)}^{f(x)} + \overbrace{(6x - 10)}^{g(x)} = x^2 + 4x - 5$$

$$(f - g)(x) = f(x) - g(x) = (x^2 - 2x + 5) - (6x - 10) = x^2 - 8x + 15$$

$$(fg)(x) = f(x)g(x) = (x^2 - 2x + 5)(6x - 10)$$

$$= 6x^3 - 10x^2 - 12x^2 + 20x + 30x - 50$$

$$= 6x^3 - 22x^2 + 50x - 50$$

$$\left(\frac{f}{g}\right)(x) = \frac{f(x)}{g(x)} = \frac{x^2 - 2x + 5}{6x - 10}$$

The domain of $(f + g)(x)$, $(f - g)(x)$, and $(fg)(x)$ is $(-\infty, \infty)$. The domain of $(\frac{f}{g})(x)$ is $x \neq \frac{5}{3}$ (from $6x - 10 = 0$), or $(-\infty, \frac{5}{3}) \cup (\frac{5}{3}, \infty)$.

- $f(x) = x - 3$ and $g(x) = \sqrt{x + 2}$

$$(f + g)(x) = x - 3 + \sqrt{x + 2} \qquad (f - g)(x) = x - 3 - \sqrt{x + 2}$$

$$(fg)(x) = (x - 3)\sqrt{x + 2} \qquad \left(\frac{f}{g}\right)(x) = \frac{x - 3}{\sqrt{x + 2}}$$

The domain for $(f + g)(x)$, $(f - g)(x)$, and $(fg)(x)$ is $[-2, \infty)$ (from $x + 2 \geq 0$). The domain for $(\frac{f}{g})(x)$ is $(-2, \infty)$ because we need $\sqrt{x + 2} \neq 0$.

Function Composition

An important combination of two functions is *function composition*. This involves evaluating one function at another function. The notation for composing f with g is $(f \circ g)(x)$. By definition, $(f \circ g)(x) = f(g(x))$, which means that we substitute $g(x)$ for x in $f(x)$. For now, we find the composition of two functions. Later, we will find the domain of the composition.

 EXAMPLE 4-2

Find $(f \circ g)(x)$ and $(g \circ f)(x)$ for the given functions.

- $f(x) = x^2 + 1$ and $g(x) = 3x + 2$

$$(f \circ g)(x) = f(g(x)) \qquad \text{This is the definition of composition.}$$

$$= f(3x + 2) \qquad \text{Replace } g(x) \text{ with } 3x + 2.$$

$$= (3x + 2)^2 + 1 \qquad \text{Substitute } 3x + 2 \text{ for } x \text{ in } f(x).$$

$$= (3x + 2)(3x + 2) + 1 = 9x^2 + 12x + 5$$

$$(g \circ f)(x) = g(f(x)) \qquad \text{This is the definition of composition.}$$

$$= g(x^2 + 1) \qquad \text{Replace } f(x) \text{ with } x^2 + 1.$$

$$= 3(x^2 + 1) + 2 \qquad \text{Substitute } x^2 + 1 \text{ for } x \text{ in } g(x).$$

$$= 3x^2 + 3 + 2 = 3x^2 + 5$$

- $f(x) = \sqrt{5x - 2}$ and $g(x) = x^2$

$$(f \circ g)(x) = f(g(x)) \qquad \text{This is the definition of composition.}$$

$$= f(x^2) \qquad \text{Replace } g(x) \text{ with } x^2.$$

$$= \sqrt{5x^2 - 2} \qquad \text{Substitute } x^2 \text{ for } x \text{ in } f(x).$$

$$(g \circ f)(x) = g(f(x)) \qquad \text{This is the definition of composition.}$$

$$= g(\sqrt{5x - 2}) \qquad \text{Replace } f(x) \text{ with } \sqrt{5x - 2}.$$

$$= (\sqrt{5x - 2})^2 \qquad \text{Substitute } \sqrt{5x - 2} \text{ for } x \text{ in } g(x).$$

$$= 5x - 2$$

- $f(x) = \frac{1}{x+1}$ and $g(x) = \frac{2x-1}{x+3}$

$$(f \circ g)(x) = f(g(x)) = f\left(\frac{2x-1}{x+3}\right)$$

$$= \frac{1}{\frac{2x-1}{x+3}+1} = \frac{1}{\frac{2x-1}{x+3}+1 \cdot \frac{x+3}{x+3}}$$

$$= \frac{1}{\frac{2x-1+x+3}{x+3}} = \frac{1}{\frac{3x+2}{x+3}} \qquad \text{Simplify the denominator.}$$

$$= 1 \div \frac{3x+2}{x+3} = 1 \cdot \frac{x+3}{3x+2}$$

$$= \frac{x+3}{3x+2}$$

$$(g \circ f)(x) = g(f(x)) = g\left(\frac{1}{x+1}\right)$$

$$= \frac{2\left(\frac{1}{x+1}\right)-1}{\frac{1}{x+1}+3} = \frac{\frac{2}{x+1}-1 \cdot \frac{x+1}{x+1}}{\frac{1}{x+1}+3 \cdot \frac{x+1}{x+1}} \qquad \text{Simplify.}$$

$$= \frac{\frac{2-(x+1)}{x+1}}{\frac{1+3(x+1)}{x+1}} = \frac{\frac{-x+1}{x+1}}{\frac{3x+4}{x+1}}$$

$$= \frac{-x+1}{x+1} \div \frac{3x+4}{x+1} = \frac{-x+1}{x+1} \cdot \frac{x+1}{3x+4}$$

$$= \frac{-x+1}{3x+4}$$

At times, we only need to find $(f \circ g)(a)$ for a particular value of $x = a$. The y-value for $g(x)$ becomes the x-value for $f(x)$. The steps are almost the same as before except that we work with numbers instead of variables. We begin by computing the y-value, which is $g(a)$.

EXAMPLE 4-3

- Find $(f \circ g)(-1)$, $(f \circ g)(0)$, and $(g \circ f)(1)$ for $f(x) = 4x + 3$ and $g(x) = 2 - x^2$.

$$(f \circ g)(-1) = f(g(-1)) \qquad g(-1) = 2 - (-1)^2 = 1$$

$$= f(1) \qquad \text{Replace } g(-1) \text{ with 1.}$$

$$= 4(1) + 3 = 7 \qquad \text{Evaluate } f(x) \text{ at } x = 1.$$

$$(f \circ g)(0) = f(g(0)) \qquad g(0) = 2 - 0^2 = 2$$

$$= f(2) \qquad \text{Replace } g(0) \text{ with 2.}$$

$$= 4(2) + 3 = 11 \qquad \text{Evaluate } f(x) \text{ at } x = 2.$$

$$(g \circ f)(1) = g(f(1)) \qquad f(1) = 4(1) + 3 = 7$$

$$= g(7) \qquad \text{Replace } f(1) \text{ with 7.}$$

$$= 2 - 7^2 = -47 \qquad \text{Evaluate } g(x) \text{ at } x = 7.$$

We can compose two functions for a single x-value by looking at the graphs of the individual functions. To find $(f \circ g)(a)$, we look at the graph of $g(x)$ to find the point whose x-coordinate is a. The y-coordinate of this point is $g(a)$. Then we look at the graph of $f(x)$ to find the point whose x-coordinate is $g(a)$. The y-coordinate of this point is $f(g(a)) = (f \circ g)(a)$.

EXAMPLE 4-4

Refer to Figure 4-1. The solid graph is the graph of $f(x)$, and the dashed graph is the graph of $g(x)$.

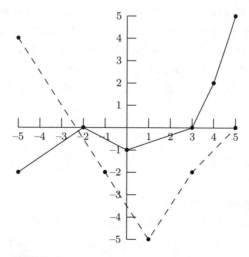

FIGURE 4-1

• Find $(f \circ g)(-1)$, $(f \circ g)(3)$, $(f \circ g)(5)$, and $(g \circ f)(0)$.

$(f \circ g)(-1) = f(g(-1))$ Look for $x = -1$ on the graph of $g(x)$.

$\qquad\qquad = f(-2)$ $(-1, -2)$ is on the graph of $g(x)$, so $g(-1) = -2$.

$\qquad\qquad = 0$ $(-2, 0)$ is on the graph of $f(x)$, so $f(-2) = 0$.

$(f \circ g)(3) = f(g(3))$ Look for $x = 3$ on the graph of $g(x)$.

$\qquad\qquad = f(-2)$ $(3, -2)$ is on the graph of $g(x)$, so $g(3) = -2$.

$\qquad\qquad = 0$ $(-2, 0)$ is on the graph of $f(x)$, so $f(-2) = 0$.

$(f \circ g)(5) = f(g(5))$ Look for $x = 5$ on the graph of $g(x)$.

$\qquad\qquad = f(0)$ $(5, 0)$ is on the graph of $g(x)$, so $g(5) = 0$.

$\qquad\qquad = -1$ $(0, -1)$ is on the graph of $f(x)$, so $f(0) = -1$.

$(g \circ f)(0) = g(f(0))$ Look for $x = 0$ on the graph of $f(x)$.

$\qquad\qquad = g(-1)$ $(0, -1)$ is on the graph of $f(x)$, so $f(0) = -1$.

$\qquad\qquad = -2$ $(-1, -2)$ is on the graph of $g(x)$, so $g(-1) = -2$.

Before we get to the official definition for the domain of $f \circ g$, remember that the y-value for g [which is $g(x)$] becomes the x-value for $f(x)$. This means that the y-values for g *must* be allowed into f. For example, if $f(x) = \frac{1}{x}$ and $g(x) = x - 3$, then $x - 3$ cannot be zero. When finding the domain for $f \circ g$, we begin with the domain for g and then remove any x-value whose y-value is not allowed into f. With this in mind, here is the official definition for the domain of $f \circ g$: The domain of $(f \circ g)(x)$ is the set of all real numbers x such that $g(x)$ is in the domain of $f(x)$.

EXAMPLE 4-5

Find the domain for $(f \circ g)(x)$.

• $f(x) = \frac{1}{x^2}$ and $g(x) = \sqrt{2x - 6}$

The domain for $g(x)$ is $x \geq 3$ (from $2x - 6 \geq 0$). Are there any x-values in $[3, \infty)$ which we cannot put into $\frac{1}{(\sqrt{2x-6})^2}$? We cannot allow $(\sqrt{2x - 6})^2$ to be zero, so we cannot allow $x = 3$. The domain for $(f \circ g)(x)$ is $(3, \infty)$.

- $f(x) = \frac{1}{x}$ and $g(x) = \frac{x-1}{x+1}$

The domain for $g(x)$ is $x \neq -1$. Are there any x-values we need to remove from $x \neq -1$? We need to find any real numbers that are not in the domain for

$$(f \circ g)(x) = f(g(x)) = f\left(\frac{x-1}{x+1}\right) = \frac{1}{\frac{x-1}{x+1}}$$

The denominator of this fraction is $\frac{x-1}{x+1}$, so we cannot allow $\frac{x-1}{x+1}$ to be zero. A fraction equals zero only when the numerator is zero, so we cannot allow $x - 1$ to be zero. We must remove $x = 1$ from the domain of $g(x)$. The domain of $(f \circ g)(x)$ is $x \neq -1, 1$, or $(-\infty, -1) \cup (-1, 1) \cup (1, \infty)$. This function simplifies to $(f \circ g)(x) = \frac{x+1}{x-1}$, which hides the fact that we cannot let $x = -1$.

Still Struggling

When finding the domain of $(f \circ g)(x)$, a value might *not* be in the domain of $f(x)$ but *is* in the domain of the composition.

Any number of functions can be composed together. Functions can even be composed with themselves. When composing functions, we work from the right to the left, performing one composition at a time.

 EXAMPLE 4-6

Find $(f \circ f)(x)$ and $(f \circ g \circ h)(x)$.

Notice that these examples involve two separate problems, finding $(f \circ f)$ (x) and finding $(f \circ g \circ h)(x)$. After computing $(f \circ f)(x)$, we will begin our work for $(f \circ g \circ h)(x)$ by computing $g(h(x))$ and then we will evaluate f at this quantity.

- $f(x) = x^3$, $g(x) = 2x - 5$, and $h(x) = x^2 + 1$.

$$(f \circ f)(x) = f(f(x)) = f(x^3) = (x^3)^3 = x^9$$

For $(f \circ g \circ h)(x)$, we begin with $(g \circ h)(x) = g(h(x)) = g(x^2 + 1) = 2(x^2 + 1) - 5 = 2x^2 - 3$. Now we need to evaluate $f(x)$ at $2x^2 - 3$.

$$(f \circ g \circ h)(x) = f(g(h(x))) = f(g(x^2 + 1))$$
$$= f(2x^2 - 3) = (2x^2 - 3)^3$$

- $f(x) = 3x + 7$, $g(x) = |x - 2|$, and $h(x) = x^4 - 5$

$$(f \circ f)(x) = f(f(x)) = f(3x + 7) = 3(3x + 7) + 7 = 9x + 28$$
$$(f \circ g \circ h)(x) = (f \circ g)(h(x)) = f(g(h(x)))$$
$$g(h(x)) = g(x^4 - 5) = |(x^4 - 5) - 2| = |x^4 - 7|$$
$$(f \circ g)(h(x)) = f(g(h(x))) = f(|x^4 - 7|)$$
$$= 3|x^4 - 7| + 7$$

In order for calculus students to use certain formulas, they need to recognize complicated functions as a combination of simpler functions. Sums, differences, products, and quotients are easy to see, but some compositions of functions are less obvious.

EXAMPLE 4-7

Find functions $f(x)$ and $g(x)$ so that $h(x) = (f \circ g)(x)$.

- $h(x) = \sqrt{x + 16}$

  Although there are many possibilities for $f(x)$ and $g(x)$, there is one pair of functions that is obvious. Usually we want $g(x)$ to be the computation that is done first and $f(x)$, the computation to be done last. Here, when computing the y-value for $h(x)$, we would calculate $x + 16$. This is $g(x)$. The last calculation is to take the square root. This is $f(x)$. If we let $f(x) = \sqrt{x}$ and $g(x) = x + 16$, we have $(f \circ g)(x) = f(g(x)) = f(x + 16) = \sqrt{x + 16} = h(x)$.

- $h(x) = \dfrac{2}{x^2 + 1}$

  When computing a y-value for $h(x)$, we would first find $x^2 + 1$. This will be $g(x)$. This number is the denominator of a fraction whose numerator is 2. This is $f(x)$, a fraction whose numerator is 2 and whose denominator is x. If $f(x) = \frac{2}{x}$ and $g(x) = x^2 + 1$, $(f \circ g)(x) = f(g(x)) = f(x^2 + 1) = \frac{2}{x^2+1} = h(x)$.

PRACTICE

1. $f(x) = 3x^2 + x$ and $g(x) = x - 4$

   a. Find $(f + g)(x)$, $(f - g)(x)$, $(fg)(x)$, and $(\frac{f}{g})(x)$.

   b. What is the domain for $(\frac{f}{g})(x)$?

   c. Find $(f \circ g)(x)$ and $(g \circ f)(x)$.

   d. What is the domain for $(f \circ g)(x)$?

   e. Find $(f \circ g)(1)$ and $(g \circ f)(0)$.

   f. Find $(f \circ f)(x)$.

2. Find $(f \circ g)(x)$, $(g \circ f)(x)$, and the domain for $(f \circ g)(x)$.

$$f(x) = \frac{2x - 3}{x + 4} \text{ and } g(x) = \frac{x}{x - 1}$$

3. Refer to the graphs in Figure 4-2. The solid graph is the graph of $f(x)$, and the dashed graph is the graph of $g(x)$. Find $(f \circ g)(1)$, $(f \circ g)(4)$, and $(g \circ f)(-2)$.

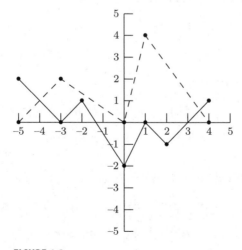

FIGURE 4-2

4. Find $(f \circ g \circ h)(x)$ for $f(x) = \frac{1}{x+3}$, $g(x) = 4x + 9$, and $h(x) = 5x^2 - 1$.

5. Find functions $f(x)$ and $g(x)$ so that $h(x) = (f \circ g)(x)$, where $h(x) = (x - 5)^3 + 2$.

 SOLUTIONS

1. a. $(f + g)(x) = (3x^2 + x) + (x - 4) = 3x^2 + 2x - 4$

$(f - g)(x) = (3x^2 + x) - (x - 4) = 3x^2 + 4$

$(fg)(x) = (3x^2 + x)(x - 4) = 3x^3 - 11x^2 - 4x$

$\left(\dfrac{f}{g}\right)(x) = \dfrac{3x^2 + x}{x - 4}$

b. The domain is $x \neq 4$, (from $x - 4 = 0$), or $(-\infty, 4) \cup (4, \infty)$.

c. $(f \circ g)(x) = f(g(x)) = f(x - 4) = 3(x - 4)^2 + (x - 4)$

$= 3(x - 4)(x - 4) + x - 4 = 3x^2 - 23x + 44$

$(g \circ f)(x) = g(f(x)) = g(3x^2 + x) = 3x^2 + x - 4$

d. The domain for $g(x)$ is all real numbers. We can let x be any real number for $f(x)$, so we do not need to remove anything from the domain of $g(x)$. The domain of $(f \circ g)(x)$ is all real numbers, or $(-\infty, \infty)$.

e. $(f \circ g)(1) = f(g(1))$

$\qquad = f(-3) \qquad\qquad g(1) = 1 - 4 = -3$

$\qquad = 24 \qquad\qquad f(-3) = 3(-3)^2 + (-3) = 24$

$(g \circ f)(0) = g(f(0))$

$\qquad = g(0) \qquad\qquad f(0) = 3(0)^2 + 0 = 0$

$\qquad = -4 \qquad\qquad g(0) = 0 - 4 = -4$

f. $(f \circ f)(x) = f(f(x)) = f(3x^2 + x) = 3(3x^2 + x)^2 + (3x^2 + x)$

$\qquad = 3(3x^2 + x)(3x^2 + x) + 3x^2 + x$

$\qquad = 27x^4 + 18x^3 + 6x^2 + x$

2.
$$(f \circ g)(x) = f(g(x)) = f\left(\frac{x}{x-1}\right)$$

$$= \frac{2\left(\frac{x}{x-1}\right) - 3}{\frac{x}{x-1} + 4} = \frac{\frac{2x}{x-1} - 3 \cdot \frac{x-1}{x-1}}{\frac{x}{x-1} + 4 \cdot \frac{x-1}{x-1}}$$

$$= \frac{\frac{2x-3(x-1)}{x-1}}{\frac{x+4(x-1)}{x-1}} = \frac{\frac{-x+3}{x-1}}{\frac{5x-4}{x-1}}$$

$$= \frac{-x+3}{x-1} \div \frac{5x-4}{x-1} = \frac{-x+3}{x-1} \cdot \frac{x-1}{5x-4}$$

$$= \frac{-x+3}{5x-4}$$

$$(g \circ f)(x) = g(f(x)) = g\left(\frac{2x-3}{x+4}\right)$$

$$= \frac{\frac{2x-3}{x+4}}{\frac{2x-3}{x+4} - 1} = \frac{\frac{2x-3}{x+4}}{\frac{2x-3}{x+4} - 1 \cdot \frac{x+4}{x+4}}$$

$$= \frac{\frac{2x-3}{x+4}}{\frac{2x-3-(x+4)}{x+4}} = \frac{\frac{2x-3}{x+4}}{\frac{x-7}{x+4}}$$

$$= \frac{2x-3}{x+4} \div \frac{x-7}{x+4} = \frac{2x-3}{x+4} \cdot \frac{x+4}{x-7}$$

$$= \frac{2x-3}{x-7}$$

The domain of $g(x)$ is $x \neq 1$. Now we need to see if there is anything we need to remove from $x \neq 1$. Before simplifying $(f \circ g)(x)$, we have

$$f(g(x)) = \frac{2\left(\frac{x}{x-1}\right) - 3}{\frac{x}{x-1} + 4}$$

The denominator of this fraction cannot be zero, so we must have $\frac{x}{x-1} + 4 \neq 0$.

$$\frac{x}{x-1} + 4 = 0$$

$$(x-1)\left(\frac{x}{x-1}+4\right)=(x-1)0 \qquad \text{Clear the fraction.}$$

$$x+4(x-1)=0$$

$$5x-4=0$$

$$x=\frac{4}{5}$$

The domain is $x \neq 1, \frac{4}{5}$, or $(-\infty, \frac{4}{5}) \cup (\frac{4}{5}, 1) \cup (1, \infty)$.

While it seems that $x = -4$ might not be allowed in the domain of $(f \circ g)(x)$, $x = -4$ is in the domain.

$$(f \circ g)(-4) = f(g(-4))$$

$$= f\left(\frac{4}{5}\right) \qquad g(-4) = \frac{-4}{-4-1} = \frac{4}{5}$$

$$= -\frac{7}{24} \qquad f\left(\frac{4}{5}\right) = \frac{2\left(\frac{4}{5}\right)-3}{\frac{4}{5}+4} = -\frac{7}{24}$$

3. $(f \circ g)(1) = f(g(1))$ Look for $x = 1$ on the graph of $g(x)$.

$\qquad\qquad = f(4)$ $(1, 4)$ is on the graph of $g(x)$, so $g(1) = 4$.

$\qquad\qquad = 1$ $(4, 1)$ is on the graph of $f(x)$, so $f(4) = 1$.

$(f \circ g)(4) = f(g(4))$ Look for $x = 4$ on the graph of $g(x)$.

$\qquad\qquad = f(0)$ $(4, 0)$ is on the graph of $g(x)$, so $g(4) = 0$.

$\qquad\qquad = -2$ $(0, -2)$ is on the graph of $f(x)$, so $f(0) = -2$.

$(g \circ f)(-2) = g(f(-2))$ Look for $x = -2$ on the graph of $f(x)$.

$\qquad\qquad = g(1)$ $(-2, 1)$ is on the graph of $f(x)$, so $f(-2) = 1$.

$\qquad\qquad = 4$ $(1, 4)$ is on the graph of $g(x)$, so $g(1) = 4$.

4. $(f \circ g \circ h)(x) = (f \circ g)(h(x)) = f(g(h(x)))$

$$g(h(x)) = g(5x^2 - 1) = 4(5x^2 - 1) + 9 = 20x^2 + 5$$

$$f(g(h(x))) = f(20x^2 + 5) = \frac{1}{(20x^2 + 5) + 3} = \frac{1}{20x^2 + 8}$$

5. One possibility is $g(x) = x - 5$ and $f(x) = x^3 + 2$.

$$(f \circ g)(x) = f(g(x)) = f(x - 5) = (x - 5)^3 + 2 = h(x)$$

Inverse Functions

In the same way operations on real numbers (like addition and multiplication) have identities and inverses, operations on functions can have identities and inverses. We can apply many operations on functions that we can apply to real numbers—adding, multiplying, raising to powers, etc. These operations can have identities and functions in the same way that real numbers have. The additive identity for function addition is $i(x) = 0$. Each function has an additive inverse; $-f(x)$ is the additive inverse for $f(x)$. The multiplicative identity for function multiplication is $i(x) = 1$, and the multiplicative inverse for $f(x)$ is $\frac{1}{f(x)}$.

If we look at function composition as an operation on functions, then we can ask whether or not there is an identity for this operation and whether or not functions have inverses for this operation. There is an identity for this operation, $i(x) = x$. For any function $f(x)$, $(f \circ i)(x) = f(i(x)) = f(x)$. *Some* functions have inverses. Later we will see which functions have inverses and how to find the inverses. The notation for the inverse function of $f(x)$ is $f^{-1}(x)$. This is different from $(f(x))^{-1}$, which is the reciprocal for $f(x)$. For now, we will be given two functions that are said to be inverses of each other. We can determine whether or not two functions are inverses of each other by composing one function with the other. If $(f \circ g)(x) = x$ and $(g \circ f)(x) = x$ (both compositions simplify to x), then the functions are inverses.

EXAMPLE 4-8

Verify that $f(x)$ and $g(x)$ are inverses.

- $f(x) = 2x + 5$ and $g(x) = \frac{1}{2}x - \frac{5}{2}$
  We show that $(f \circ g)(x) = x$ and $(g \circ f)(x) = x$.

$$(f \circ g)(x) = f(g(x)) = f\left(\frac{1}{2}x - \frac{5}{2}\right)$$

$$= 2\left(\frac{1}{2}x - \frac{5}{2}\right) + 5 = x - 5 + 5 = x$$

$$(g \circ f)(x) = g(f(x)) = g(2x + 5) = \frac{1}{2}(2x + 5) - \frac{5}{2}$$

$$= x + \frac{5}{2} - \frac{5}{2} = x$$

We have just verified the fact that $f(x)$ and $g(x)$ are inverses of each other.

- $f(x) = 5x^3 - 6$ and $g(x) = \sqrt[3]{\frac{x+6}{5}}$

$$(f \circ g)(x) = f(g(x)) = f\left(\sqrt[3]{\frac{x+6}{5}}\right) = 5\left(\sqrt[3]{\frac{x+6}{5}}\right)^3 - 6$$

$$= 5\left(\frac{x+6}{5}\right) - 6 = x + 6 - 6 = x$$

$$(g \circ f)(x) = g(f(x)) = g(5x^3 - 6) = \sqrt[3]{\frac{5x^3 - 6 + 6}{5}}$$

$$= \sqrt[3]{\frac{5x^3}{5}} = \sqrt[3]{x^3} = x$$

- $f(x) = \frac{2x-1}{x+4}$ and $g(x) = \frac{4x+1}{2-x}$

$$(f \circ g)(x) = f(g(x)) = f\left(\frac{4x+1}{2-x}\right) = \frac{2\left(\frac{4x+1}{2-x}\right) - 1}{\frac{4x+1}{2-x} + 4}$$

$$= \frac{\frac{2(4x+1)}{2-x} - 1 \cdot \frac{2-x}{2-x}}{\frac{4x+1}{2-x} + 4 \cdot \frac{2-x}{2-x}}$$

$$= \frac{\frac{8x+2-(2-x)}{2-x}}{\frac{4x+1+4(2-x)}{2-x}} = \frac{\frac{9x}{2-x}}{\frac{9}{2-x}}$$

$$= \frac{9x}{2-x} \div \frac{9}{2-x} = \frac{9x}{2-x} \cdot \frac{2-x}{9} = x$$

$$(g \circ f)(x) = g(f(x)) = g\left(\frac{2x-1}{x+4}\right) = \frac{4\left(\frac{2x-1}{x+4}\right)+1}{2-\frac{2x-1}{x+4}}$$

$$= \frac{\frac{4(2x-1)}{x+4}+1 \cdot \frac{x+4}{x+4}}{2 \cdot \frac{x+4}{x+4}-\frac{2x-1}{x+4}} = \frac{\frac{8x-4+x+4}{x+4}}{\frac{2(x+4)-(2x-1)}{x+4}}$$

$$= \frac{\frac{9x}{x+4}}{\frac{9}{x+4}} = \frac{9x}{x+4} \div \frac{9}{x+4}$$

$$= \frac{9x}{x+4} \cdot \frac{x+4}{9} = x$$

If we think of a function as a collection of points on a graph, or ordered pairs, then the only thing that makes $f(x)$ different from $f^{-1}(x)$ is that their x-coordinates and y-coordinates are reversed. For example, if $(3, -1)$ is point on the graph of $f(x)$, then $(-1, 3)$ is a point on the graph of $f^{-1}(x)$.

EXAMPLE **4-9**

The graph of a function $f(x)$ is given in Figure 4-3. Use the graph of $f(x)$ to sketch the graph of $f^{-1}(x)$.

We make a table of values for $f(x)$ and switch the x and y columns for $f^{-1}(x)$.

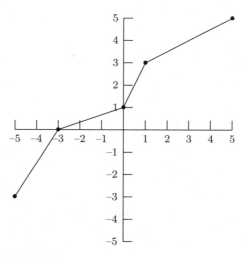

FIGURE 4-3

TABLE 4-1			
x	$y = f(x)$	x	$y = f^{-1}(x)$
-5	-3	-3	-5
-3	0	0	-3
0	1	1	0
1	3	3	1
5	5	5	5

The solid graph in Figure 4-4 is the graph of $f(x)$, and the dashed graph is the graph of $f^{-1}(x)$.

You might have noticed the symmetry between the graphs in Figure 4-4. This kind of symmetry occurs between any function and its inverse: If $f(x)$ is a function that has an inverse, then the graph of $f^{-1}(x)$ is a reflection of the graph of $f(x)$ across the line $y = x$. The solid and dashed graphs in Figures 4-5 and 4-6 are inverses of each other. As you can see, they reflect each other across the line $y = x$.

A function has an inverse if its graph passes the Horizontal Line Test—if any horizontal line touches the graph in more than one place, then the function does not have an inverse. Functions whose graphs pass the Horizontal Line Test are called *one-to-one* functions. For a one-to-one function, every x is paired with

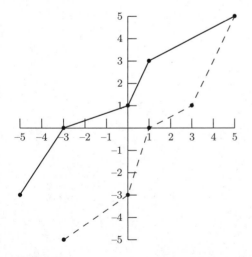

FIGURE 4-4

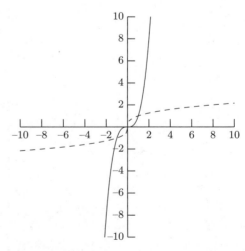

FIGURE 4-5

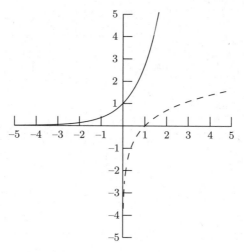

FIGURE 4-6

exactly one *y and* every *y* is paired with exactly one *x*. For example, while (1, 3) and (5, 3) could be points on the graph of a function, they cannot be points on the graph of a one-to-one function because 3 is paired with *two x*-values.

EXAMPLE 4-10

- **The graph of *f(x)* is given in Figure 4-7. Is *f(x)* one-to-one?**
  As you can see, this graph fails the Horizontal Line Test (the horizontal line in Figure 4-8 intersects the graph more than once), so *f(x)* is not one-to-one.

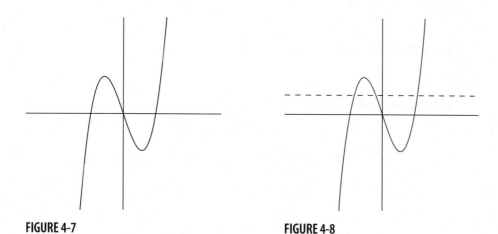

FIGURE 4-7   **FIGURE 4-8**

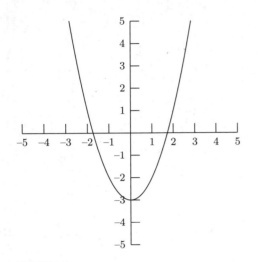

FIGURE 4-9   **FIGURE 4-10**

For functions that are not one-to-one, we can restrict the domain to force the function to be one-to-one. The function whose graph is in Figure 4-9, $f(x) = x^2 - 3$, is not one-to-one. If we restrict the domain to $x \geq 0$, then the new function is one-to-one. As you can see, the graph in Figure 4-10 does pass the Horizontal Line Test.

Finding the inverse function is not hard, but it can be a little tedious. The steps below show the process of algebraically switching x and y.

1. Replace $f(x)$ with x, and replace x with y.
2. Solve this equation for y.
3. Replace y with $f^{-1}(x)$.

 EXAMPLE 4-11

Find $f^{-1}(x)$.

- $f(x) = 6x + 14$

$$x = 6y + 14 \qquad \text{Step 1}$$

$$x - 14 = 6y \qquad \text{Step 2}$$

$$\frac{x - 14}{6} = y$$

$$f^{-1}(x) = \frac{x - 14}{6} \qquad \text{Step 3}$$

- $f(x) = 9(x - 4)^5$

$$x = 9(y - 4)^5 \qquad \text{Step 1}$$

$$\frac{x}{9} = (y - 4)^5 \qquad \text{Step 2}$$

$$\sqrt[5]{\frac{x}{9}} = y - 4$$

$$\sqrt[5]{\frac{x}{9}} + 4 = y$$

$$f^{-1}(x) = \sqrt[5]{\frac{x}{9}} + 4 \qquad \text{Step 3}$$

- $f(x) = \dfrac{1 - x}{2 - x}$

$$x = \frac{1 - y}{2 - y} \qquad \text{Step 1}$$

$$x(2 - y) = 1 - y \qquad \text{Step 2}$$

$$2x - xy = 1 - y$$

$$2x - 1 = xy - y \qquad \text{y terms on one side, non-y terms on other side}$$

$$2x - 1 = y(x - 1) \qquad \text{Factor } y$$

$$\frac{2x - 1}{x - 1} = y$$

$$f^{-1}(x) = \frac{2x - 1}{x - 1} \qquad \text{Step 3}$$

PRACTICE

1. Show that $f(x) = \frac{1}{2}x + 7$ and $g(x) = 2x - 14$ are inverses.

2. Show that $f(x) = \sqrt[3]{x - 8}$ and $g(x) = x^3 + 8$ are inverses.

3. Show that $f(x) = \frac{x+2}{x-3}$ and $g(x) = \frac{3x+2}{x-1}$ are inverses.

4. Use the graph of $f(x)$ in Figure 4-11 to sketch the graph of $f^{-1}(x)$.

5. Find $f^{-1}(x)$ for $f(x) = 5x + 12$.

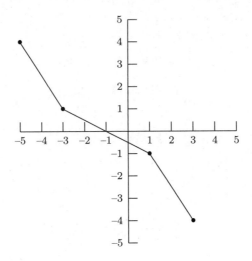

FIGURE 4-11

6. Find $g^{-1}(x)$ for $g(x) = \sqrt[3]{2x} - 1$.

7. Find $f^{-1}(x)$ for $f(x) = \frac{2x-3}{6x+1}$.

✓ SOLUTIONS

1. $(f \circ g)(x) = f(g(x)) = f(2x - 14) = \dfrac{1}{2}(2x - 14) + 7$

$$= x - 7 + 7 = x$$

$(g \circ f)(x) = g(f(x)) = g\left(\dfrac{1}{2}x + 7\right) = 2\left(\dfrac{1}{2}x + 7\right) - 14$

$$= x + 14 - 14 = x$$

2. $(f \circ g)(x) = f(g(x)) = f(x^3 + 8) = \sqrt[3]{(x^3 + 8) - 8}$

$$= \sqrt[3]{x^3} = x$$

$(g \circ f)(x) = g(f(x)) = g(\sqrt[3]{x - 8}) = (\sqrt[3]{x - 8})^3 + 8$

$$= x - 8 + 8 = x$$

3. $$(f \circ g)(x) = f(g(x)) = f\left(\frac{3x+2}{x-1}\right) = \frac{\frac{3x+2}{x-1}+2}{\frac{3x+2}{x-1}-3}$$

$$= \frac{\frac{3x+2}{x-1}+2\cdot\frac{x-1}{x-1}}{\frac{3x+2}{x-1}-3\cdot\frac{x-1}{x-1}} = \frac{\frac{3x+2+2(x-1)}{x-1}}{\frac{3x+2-3(x-1)}{x-1}}$$

$$= \frac{\frac{5x}{x-1}}{\frac{5}{x-1}} = \frac{5x}{x-1} \div \frac{5}{x-1}$$

$$= \frac{5x}{x-1} \cdot \frac{x-1}{5} = x$$

$$(g \circ f)(x) = g(f(x)) = g\left(\frac{x+2}{x-3}\right) = \frac{3\left(\frac{x+2}{x-3}\right)+2}{\frac{x+2}{x-3}-1}$$

$$= \frac{\frac{3(x+2)}{x-3}+2\cdot\frac{x-3}{x-3}}{\frac{x+2}{x-3}-1\cdot\frac{x-3}{x-3}} = \frac{\frac{3x+6+2(x-3)}{x-3}}{\frac{x+2-(x-3)}{x-3}}$$

$$= \frac{\frac{5x}{x-3}}{\frac{5}{x-3}} = \frac{5x}{x-3} \div \frac{5}{x-3}$$

$$= \frac{5x}{x-3} \cdot \frac{x-3}{5} = x$$

4. The solid graph in Figure 4-12 (on page 92) is the graph of $f(x)$, and the dashed graph is the graph of $f^{-1}(x)$.

5. $$x = 5y + 12$$

$$x - 12 = 5y$$

$$\frac{x-12}{5} = y \text{ so, } f^{-1}(x) = \frac{x-12}{5}$$

6. $$x = \sqrt[3]{2y} - 1$$

$$x + 1 = \sqrt[3]{2y}$$

$$(x+1)^3 = 2y$$

$$\frac{(x+1)^3}{2} = y \text{ so } g^{-1}(x) = \frac{(x+1)^3}{2}$$

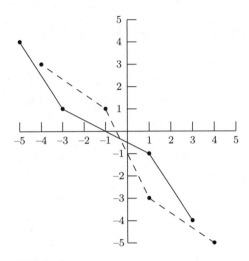

FIGURE 4-12

7.

$$x = \frac{2y - 3}{6y + 1}$$

$$x(6y + 1) = 2y - 3$$

$$6xy + x = 2y - 3$$

$$x + 3 = 2y - 6xy$$

$$x + 3 = y(2 - 6x)$$

$$\frac{x + 3}{2 - 6x} = y \text{ so } f^{-1}(x) = \frac{x + 3}{2 - 6x}$$

Summary

In this chapter, we learned how to

- *Arithmetically combine two functions.* We find the combination $(f + g)(x)$ by adding $f(x)$ to $g(x)$. Similarly, we find $(f - g)(x)$ by subtractring $g(x)$ from $f(x)$; $(fg)(x)$ by multiplying $f(x)$ by $g(x)$; and $(\frac{f}{g})(x)$ by dividing $f(x)$ by $g(x)$. The domain of $(f \pm g)(x)$ and $(fg)(x)$ consists of any x-value that is in each of the domains of $f(x)$ and $g(x)$. For $(\frac{f}{g})(x)$, not only must x be in each of the domains of $f(x)$ and $g(x)$, but $g(x) \neq 0$.

- *Compose one function with another.* To compose $f(x)$ with $g(x)$ means to evaluate $f(x)$ at $g(x)$. The notation is $(f \circ g)(x) = f(g(x))$. Basically, we replace x in f with $g(x)$.

- *Evaluate* $(f \circ g)(x)$ *one x-value at a time.* To find $(f \circ g)(a)$, we first compute $g(a)$ and then evaluate $f(x)$ at this number. If we need to use graphs to find $(f \circ g)(a)$, we use the graph of $g(x)$ to find the y-value for $x = a$, that is, $g(a)$. We then locate the point on the graph of $f(x)$ whose x-coordinate is $g(a)$. The y-value of this point is $(f \circ g)(a)$.

- *Find the domain of* $(f \circ g)(x)$. We begin with the domain of g and exclude any x-value whose y-value is not allowed as an x-value in f.

- *Recognize a function as the composition of two simpler functions.* If we have a function $h(x)$, we can sometimes find two simpler functions $f(x)$ and $g(x)$ whose composition is $h(x)$. That is, we want to find $f(x)$ and $g(x)$ so that $(f \circ g)(x) = h(x)$. Often, the g function is the first operation(s) performed, and f is the last operation(s) performed.

- *Determine whether or not two functions are inverses of each other.* We can determine whether or not $f(x)$ and $g(x)$ are inverses of each other by computing $(f \circ g)(x)$ and $(g \circ f)(x)$. If these compositions simplify to x, then $f(x)$ and $g(x)$ are inverses of each other.

- *Determine whether or not a function has an inverse.* Only one-to-one functions have an inverse. A function is one-to-one if every x has a unique y, *and* every y has a unique x. The graph of a one-to-one function passes the Horizontal Line Test: Every horizontal line in the plane intersects the graph of the function at most once. If a function is not one-to-one, we can restrict its domain and force it to be one-to-one.

- *Find the inverse of a function.* The relationship between a function and its inverse is that their x- and y-coordinates are reversed. In other words, if (a, b) is a point on the graph of $f(x)$, then (b, a) is a point on the graph of $f^{-1}(x)$. We find $f^{-1}(x)$ using this fact: Reverse x and y in the equation and then solve for y.

QUIZ

Problems 1 to 4 refer to the functions $f(x) = x^2 + 1$ and $g(x) = \frac{1}{x-4}$.

1. **Find the domain for $(fg)(x)$.**

   A. $(4, \infty)$

   B. $(-\infty, 4) \cup (4, \infty)$

   C. $(-\infty, 4] \cup [4, \infty)$

2. **Find $(f \circ g)(x)$.**

   A. $\frac{1}{x^2-3}$

   B. $\frac{1}{(x-4)^2} + 1$

   C. $\frac{x-4}{x^2+1}$

   D. $\frac{x^2+1}{x-4}$

3. **Find $(g \circ f)(x)$.**

   A. $\frac{1}{x^2-3}$

   B. $\frac{1}{(x-4)^2} + 1$

   C. $\frac{x-4}{x^2+1}$

   D. $\frac{x^2+1}{x-4}$

4. **Find $g^{-1}(x)$.**

   A. $x - 4$

   B. $\frac{-1}{x-4}$

   C. $\frac{4x+1}{x}$

   D. $g^{-1}(x)$ does not exist because $g(x)$ is not a one-to-one function.

5. **Let $f(x) = \sqrt{x+2}$ and $g(x) = 4x + 2$. Find $f(g(3))$.**

   A. 4

   B. $4\sqrt{11} + 2$

   C. $4\sqrt{13}$

   D. $f(g(3))$ does not exist.

6. **If $f(3) = -8$, then find $f^{-1}(-8)$.**

   A. 3

   B. -3

   C. 8

   D. -8

7. **The graph of $f(x)$ is in Figure 4-13. Does $f^{-1}(x)$ exist?**

   A. Yes

   B. No

   C. It is impossible to tell without the equation.

8. **Are the functions $f(x) = 5x - 6$ and $g(x) = \frac{x+6}{5}$ inverses of each other?**

   A. Yes

   B. No

   C. It is impossible to tell.

9. **Find $f^{-1}(x)$ if $f(x) = x^3 + 1$.**

   A. $\sqrt[3]{x} - 1$

   B. $\sqrt[3]{x} + 1$

   C. $\frac{1}{x^3+1}$

   D. $\sqrt[3]{x - 1}$

10. **What is the domain for $(f \circ g)(x)$ if $f(x) = \frac{x}{x-1}$ and $g(x) = x^2 - 3$?**

    A. $x \neq -2, 2$

    B. $x \neq -2, 1, 2$

    C. $x \neq -2, 0, 2$

    D. $x \neq -2, 0, 1, 2$

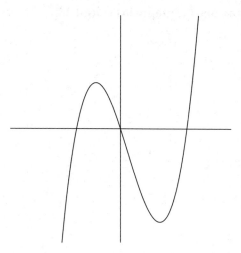

FIGURE 4-13   FIGURE 4-14

11. The solid graph in Figure 4-14 is the graph of $f(x)$ and the dashed graph is the graph of $g(x)$. Use the graphs to evaluate $(f \circ g)(0)$.

    A. -1 C. 1

    B. 2 D. $(f \circ g)(0)$ is not defined.

12. If $h(x) = \sqrt{2x + 3}$ and $g(x) = 2x + 3$, what is $f(x)$ if $h(x) = (f \circ g)(x)$?

    A. $f(x) = x$ C. $f(x) = \sqrt{x}$

    B. $f(x) = x^2$ D. It is impossible to determine.

13. The graph of $f(x)$ is in Figure 4-15. Identify the graph of $f^{-1}(x)$ in Figure 4-16.

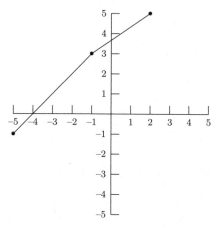

FIGURE 4-15

Choose the graph of the inverse function from among the graphs in Figure 4-16.

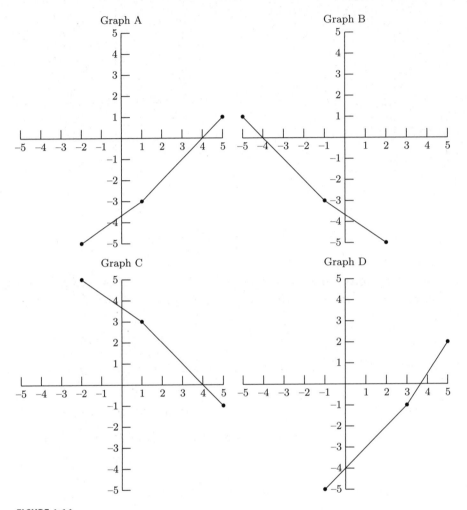

FIGURE 4-16

chapter 5

Transformations of Functions

When working with functions in calculus, you need to know how a function behaves when all you have is the function's equation. For example, just by looking at a linear function, such as $f(x) = 3x - 4$, you could sketch a rough graph without having to plot points. In this chapter, we will develop the skills you need to be able to do the same with a larger family of functions. (These skills will also help you to use a graphing calculator.) We will work with several basic families of functions, whose graphs are shown in Table 5-1. We will learn how algebraic changes to these functions affect their graphs. As we learn new functions throughout the book, we will use what we learn here to sketch their graphs without having to spend too much time plotting points.

CHAPTER OBJECTIVES

In this chapter, you will

- Work with graphs of several basic functions
- Shift graphs vertically and horizontally
- Reflect graphs across the *x*-axis and *y*-axis
- Stretch graphs vertically and horizontally

TABLE 5-1

Linear Function $f(x) = mx + b$	Absolute Value Function $f(x) = |x|$
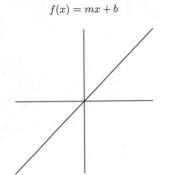	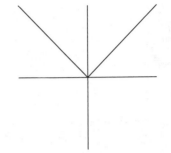
Quadratic Function $f(x) = x^2$	Square Root Function $f(x) = \sqrt{x}$
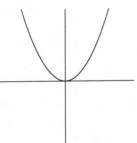	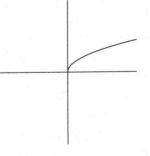
Cubic Function $f(x) = x^3$	Reciprocal Function $f(x) = \frac{1}{x}$
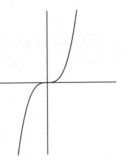	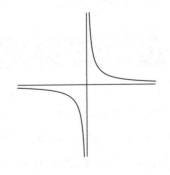

Shifting Graphs

What effect does adding 1 to a function have on its graph? It depends on where we put "+1." Adding 1 to x shifts the graph to the *left* 1 unit. Adding 1 to y shifts the graph *up* 1 unit. Let us see how adding 1 to some part of the function $f(x) = |x|$ affects its graph.

- $y = |x + 1|$, 1 is added to x, shifting the graph to the left 1 unit. See Figure 5-1.

- $y = |x| + 1$, 1 is added to y (which is $|x|$), shifting the graph up 1 unit. See Figure 5-2.

(For the graphs in this chapter, the solid graph will be the graph of the original function, and the dashed graph will be the graph of the transformed function.)

Adding 2 to some part of the function $f(x) = \sqrt{x}$ has the same kind of effect.

- $y = \sqrt{x + 2}$, 2 is added to x, shifting the graph to the left 2 units. See Figure 5-3.

- $y = \sqrt{x} + 2$, 2 is added to y (which is $\sqrt{x}$), shifting the graph up 2 units. See Figure 5-4.

From these examples, we see that adding a positive number to x shifts the graph to the left, and adding a positive number to y shifts the graph up. The opposite is true when subtracting a positive number from x and from y:

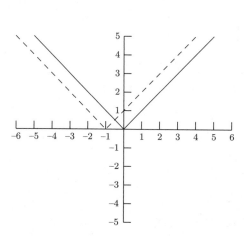

FIGURE 5-1

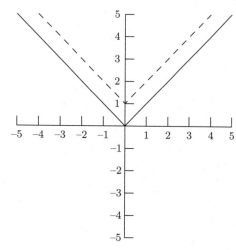

FIGURE 5-2

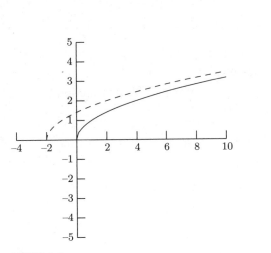

FIGURE 5-3   **FIGURE 5-4**

Subtracting a positive number from x shifts the graph to the right, whereas subtracting a positive number from y shifts the graph down.

- $y = (x - 1)^3$, 1 is subtracted from x, shifting the graph to the right 1 unit. See Figure 5-5.

- $y = x^3 - 1$, 1 is subtracted from y (which is x^3), shifting the graph down 1 unit. See Figure 5-6.

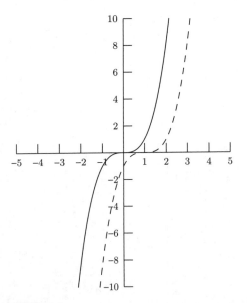

FIGURE 5-5

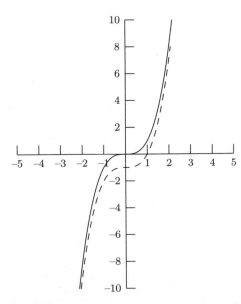

FIGURE 5-6

Still Struggling

For $f(x + h) + k$, if k is positive, the graph moves in the *positive* direction for y. However, if h is positive, the graph moves in the *negative* direction for x.

Stretching and Compressing Graphs

Multiplying the x-values or y-values by a number changes the graph, usually by stretching or compressing it. Multiplying the x-values or y-values by -1 reverses the graph. If a is a number larger than 1 ($a > 1$), then multiplying x by a horizontally compresses the graph, but multiplying y by a vertically stretches the graph. If a is positive but less than 1 ($0 < a < 1$), then multiplying x by a horizontally stretches the graph, but multiplying y by a vertically compresses the graph.

- $y = \sqrt{2x}$, the graph is horizontally compressed. See Figure 5-7.
- $y = 2\sqrt{x}$, the graph is vertically stretched. See Figure 5-8.
- $y = \left(\frac{1}{2}x\right)^3$, the graph is horizontally stretched. See Figure 5-9.
- $y = \frac{1}{2}x^3$, the graph is vertically compressed. See Figure 5-10.

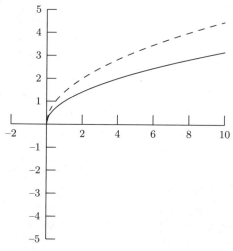

FIGURE 5-7

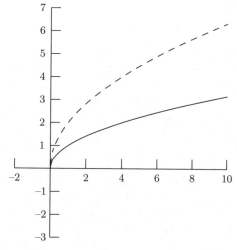

FIGURE 5-8

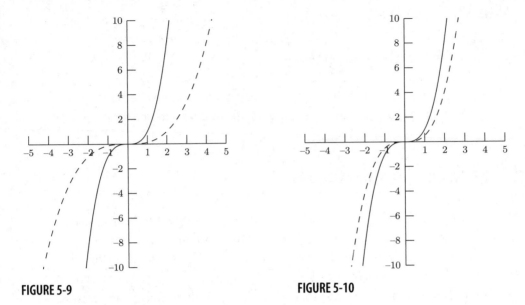

FIGURE 5-9   FIGURE 5-10

For many functions, but not all, vertical compression is the same as horizontal stretching, and vertical stretching is the same as horizontal compression.

Reflecting Graphs

Multiplying the x-values by −1 reverses the graph horizontally. This is called *reflecting the graph across the y-axis* (see Figure 5-11). Multiplying the y-values by −1 reverses the graph vertically. This is called *reflecting the graph across the x-axis* (see Figure 5-12).

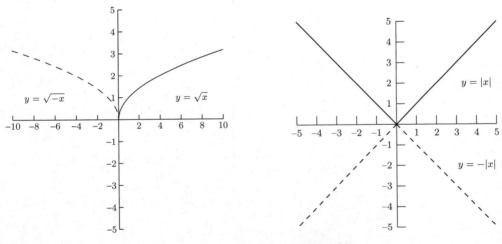

FIGURE 5-11   FIGURE 5-12

When a function is even, reflecting the graph across the y-axis does not change the graph. When a function is odd, reflecting the graph across the y-axis is the same as reflecting it across the x-axis.

We can use function notation to summarize these transformations.

$$y = af(x - h) + k$$

- If h is positive, the graph is shifted to the right h units.
- If h is negative, the graph is shifted to the left h units.
- If k is positive, the graph is shifted up k units.
- If k is negative, the graph is shifted down k units.
- If $a > 1$, the graph is vertically stretched. The larger a is, the greater is the stretch.
- If $0 < a < 1$, the graph is vertically compressed. The closer to zero a is, the greater is the compression.
- The graph of $-f(x)$ is reflected across the x-axis.
- The graph of $f(-x)$ is reflected across the y-axis.

The graphs below are various transformations of the graph of $y = |x|$. The graph in Figure 5-13 is the graph of the original function shifted to the right 1 unit and up 2 units. The graph in Figure 5-14 is reflected across the x-axis and vertically compressed. The graph in Figure 5-15 is the graph shifted to the left

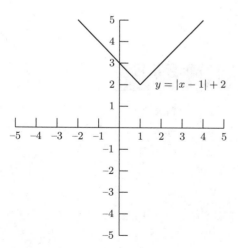

FIGURE 5-13

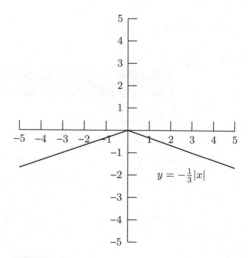

FIGURE 5-14

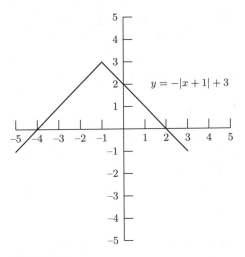

FIGURE 5-15

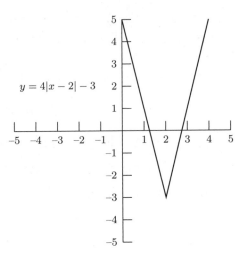

FIGURE 5-16

1 unit, reflected across the x-axis, and shifted up 3 units. Finally, the graph in Figure 5-16 is the graph shifted to the right 2 units, down 3 units, and vertically stretched.

 EXAMPLE 5-1

The graph of $y = f(x)$ is given in Figure 5-17. Sketch the transformations.

We sketch the graph by moving the points $(-4, 5)$, $(-1, -1)$, $(1, 3)$, and $(4, 0)$.

- $y = f(x + 1) - 3$

TABLE 5-2			
Original Point	Left 1 $x - 1$	Down 3 $y - 3$	Plot This Point
$(-4, 5)$	$-4 - 1 = -5$	$5 - 3 = 2$	$(-5, 2)$
$(-1, -1)$	$-1 - 1 = -2$	$-1 - 3 = -4$	$(-2, -4)$
$(1, 3)$	$1 - 1 = 0$	$3 - 3 = 0$	$(0, 0)$
$(4, 0)$	$4 - 1 = 3$	$0 - 3 = -3$	$(3, -3)$

The graph of this transformation is the dashed graph in Figure 5-18.

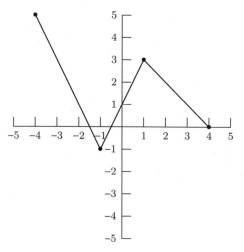

FIGURE 5-17

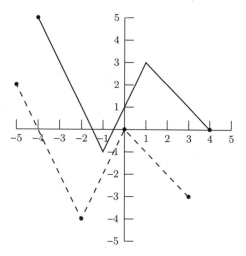

FIGURE 5-18

- $y = -f(x)$

TABLE 5-3			
Original Point	x Does Not Change x	Oppposite of y −y	Plot This Point
$(-4, 5)$	-4	-5	$(-4, -5)$
$(-1, -1)$	-1	$-(-1) = 1$	$(-1, 1)$
$(1, 3)$	1	-3	$(1, -3)$
$(4, 0)$	4	$-0 = 0$	$(4, 0)$

The graph of this transformation is the dashed graph in Figure 5-19.

- $y = 2f(x - 3)$

TABLE 5-4			
Original Point	Right 3 x + 3	Stretched 2y	Plot This Point
$(-4, 5)$	$-4 + 3 = -1$	$2(5) = 10$	$(-1, 10)$
$(-1, -1)$	$-1 + 3 = 2$	$2(-1) = -2$	$(2, -2)$
$(1, 3)$	$1 + 3 = 4$	$2(3) = 6$	$(4, 6)$
$(4, 0)$	$4 + 3 = 7$	$2(0) = 0$	$(7, 0)$

The dashed graph in Figure 5-20 is the graph of this transformation.

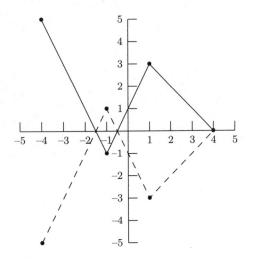

FIGURE 5-19

FIGURE 5-20

- $y = \dfrac{1}{2} f(-x) + 2$

TABLE 5-5			
Original Point	**Opposite of x** $-x$	**Compressed and up 2** $\frac{1}{2}y + 2$	**Plot This Point**
$(-4, 5)$	$-(-4) = 4$	$\frac{1}{2}(5) + 2 = \frac{9}{2}$	$(4, \frac{9}{2})$
$(-1, -1)$	$-(-1) = 1$	$\frac{1}{2}(-1) + 2 = \frac{3}{2}$	$(1, \frac{3}{2})$
$(1, 3)$	-1	$\frac{1}{2}(3) + 2 = \frac{7}{2}$	$(-1, \frac{7}{2})$
$(4, 0)$	-4	$\frac{1}{2}(0) + 2 = 2$	$(-4, 2)$

The dashed graph in Figure 5-21 is the graph of this transformation.

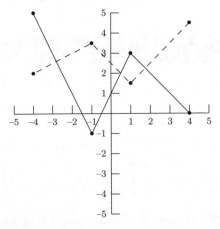

FIGURE 5-21

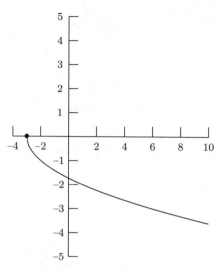

FIGURE 5-22

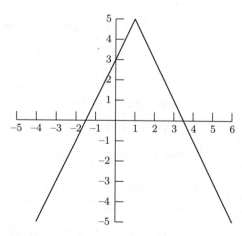

FIGURE 5-23

 PRACTICE

For Problems 1 to 4, match the graph with its function on page 108. Some functions will be left over.

1. See Figure 5-22

2. See Figure 5-23

3. See Figure 5-24

4. See Figure 5-25

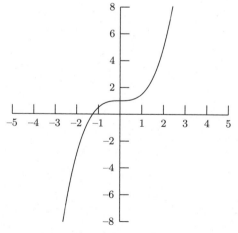

FIGURE 5-24

FIGURE 5-25

$$f(x) = -2|x - 1| + 5 \qquad f(x) = -\sqrt{x + 3} \qquad f(x) = \sqrt{3 - x}$$

$$f(x) = -\frac{1}{2}x^3 + 1 \qquad f(x) = |x + 2| - 3 \qquad f(x) = \frac{1}{2}x^3 + 1$$

For Problems 5 to 8, use the statements below to describe the transformations on $f(x)$.

Some of the statements are used more than once, and others will not be
used.

(A) Shifts the graph to the left.

(B) Shifts the graph to the right.

(C) Shifts the graph up.

(D) Shifts the graph down.

(E) Reflects the graph across the y-axis.

(F) Reflects the graph across the x-axis.

(G) Vertically compresses the graph.

(H) Vertically stretches the graph.

(I) Reflects the graph across the x-axis and vertically compresses the
graph.

(J) Reflects the graph across the y-axis and vertically stretches the
graph.

5. For the function $f(-x) + 3$

    a. What does "+3" do?

    b. What does the negative sign on x do?

6. For the function $3 f(x - 1) - 4$

    a. What does 3 do?

    b. What does "−1" do?

    c. What does "−4" do?

7. For the function $-\frac{1}{2} f(x + 3) + 1$

    a. What does $-\frac{1}{2}$ do?

    b. What does "+3" do?

    c. What does "+1" do?

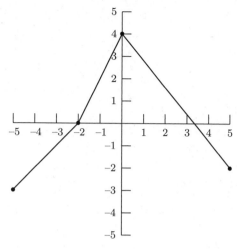

FIGURE 5-26

8. For the function $\frac{1}{3} f(-x) - 1$

   a. What does $\frac{1}{3}$ do?

   b. What does the negative sign on *x* do?

   c. What does "−1" do?

Refer to the graph of $f(x)$ in Figure 5-26 for Problems 9 to 10.

9. Sketch the graph of $f(-x) - 1$.

10. Sketch the graph of $-\frac{1}{2} f(x + 3) + 1$.

✔ **SOLUTIONS**

   1. $f(x) = -\sqrt{x + 3}$

   2. $f(x) = |x + 2| - 3$

   3. $f(x) = \frac{1}{2}x^3 + 1$

   4. $f(x) = -2|x - 1| + 5$

   5. C, E

   6. H, B, D

   7. I, A, C

   8. G, E, D

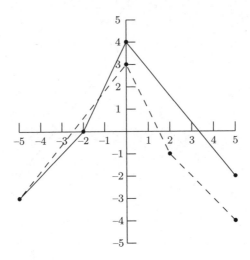

FIGURE 5-27

9. See Figure 5-27

Refer to Table 5-6 for the graph in Figure 5-27.

TABLE 5-6			
Original Point	**Opposite of x** $-x$	**Down 1** $y - 1$	**Plot This Point**
$(-5, -3)$	$-(-5) = 5$	$-3 - 1 = -4$	$(5, -4)$
$(-2, 0)$	$-(-2) = 2$	$0 - 1 = -1$	$(2, -1)$
$(0, 4)$	$-0 = 0$	$4 - 1 = 3$	$(0, 3)$
$(5, -2)$	-5	$-2 - 1 = -3$	$(-5, -3)$

10. See Figure 5-28

Refer to Table 5-7 for the graph in Figure 5-28.

TABLE 5-7			
Original Point	**Left 3** $x - 3$	**Opposite of y, Compressed, Up 1** $-\frac{1}{2}y + 1$	**Plot This Point**
$(-5, -3)$	$-5 - 3 = -8$	$-\frac{1}{2}(-3) + 1 = \frac{5}{2}$	$(-8, \frac{5}{2})$
$(-2, 0)$	$-2 - 3 = -5$	$-\frac{1}{2}(0) + 1 = 1$	$(-5, 1)$
$(0, 4)$	$0 - 3 = -3$	$-\frac{1}{2}(4) + 1 = -1$	$(-3, -1)$
$(5, -2)$	$5 - 3 = 2$	$-\frac{1}{2}(-2) + 1 = 2$	$(2, 2)$

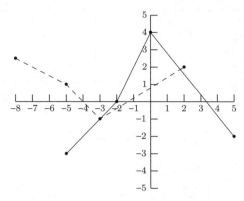

FIGURE 5-28

Function Transformations and Graphing Calculators

Now that we are familiar with a larger family of functions, we can use what we have learned to display their graphs on a graphing calculator. For example, we know that the standard viewing window will not show any part of the graph of $y = x^2 + 20$. Because the graph does not even *start* until $y = 20$, we do not really need any part of the window below $y = 20$. The graph of this function (see Figure 5-30) is displayed in the following window: $-10 \leq x \leq 10$ and $20 \leq y \leq 30$. (See Figure 5-29 for this window.)

If you do want the x-axis to be displayed, you can change the y-scale (the distance between vertical tickmarks) and allow the window to include negative y-values. (See Figures 5-31 and 5-32.)

If the graph of a function is stretched or compressed, we can adjust the x-values or the y-values or both. For example, the graph of $y = 10\sqrt{x}$ is shown in Figure 5-33. We do not see much of the graph in the standard window.

We can get a better picture of the graph by shifting the axes and by changing the y-scale. (See Figures 5-34 and 5-35.)

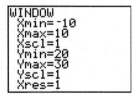

FIGURE 5-29

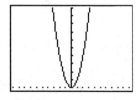

FIGURE 5-30

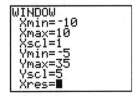

FIGURE 5-31

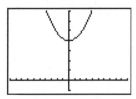

FIGURE 5-32

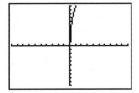

FIGURE 5-33

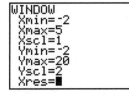

FIGURE 5-34

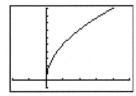

FIGURE 5-35

 PRACTICE

Two windows are given for each function. Before plotting the graph in a graphing calculator, decide which window would give a more complete picture of the graph. Experiment with different windows to see which windows display the graphs well.

1. $y = x^3 - 10$; Window A: $-20 \leq x \leq 20$, $-5 \leq y \leq 25$ and Window B: $-5 \leq x \leq 5$, $-30 \leq y \leq 10$

2. $y = (x - 25)^2$; Window A: $20 \leq x \leq 30$, $-5 \leq y \leq 10$ and Window B: $-10 \leq x \leq 10$, $-25 \leq y \leq 25$

3. $y = 10|x|$ (The absolute value function is on the Math Menu: press the MATH key, cursor to the right to "NUM" and press ENTER.) Window A: $-5 \leq x \leq 5$, $-5 \leq y \leq 15$ and Window B: $-10 \leq x \leq 10$, $-15 \leq y \leq 5$

4. $y = -\sqrt{x}$; Window A: $-10 \leq x \leq 10$, $0 \leq y \leq 10$ and Window B: $-5 \leq x \leq 10$, $-10 \leq y \leq 5$

5. $y = 0.10(\frac{1}{x})$; Window A: $-2 \leq x \leq 10$, $-2 \leq y \leq 10$ and Window B: $-2 \leq x \leq 2$, $-2 \leq y \leq 2$

✔ SOLUTIONS

1. Window B, see Figure 5-36

2. Window A, see Figure 5-37

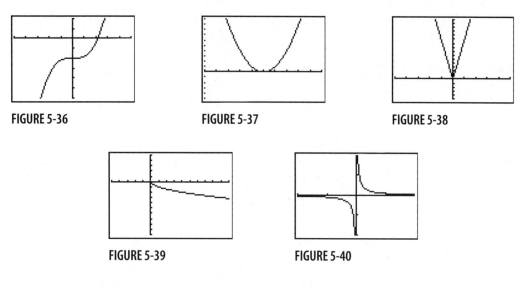

FIGURE 5-36   **FIGURE 5-37**   **FIGURE 5-38**

FIGURE 5-39   **FIGURE 5-40**

3. Window A, see Figure 5-38

4. Window B, see Figure 5-39

5. Window B, see Figure 5-40

Summary

In this chapter, we learned how certain algebraic changes to a function caused changes in its graph. Table 5-8 summarizes the changes we studied. In this table, a, h, and k are positive numbers.

TABLE 5-8	
Algebraic Change	**Effect on the Graph**
$y = f(x - h)$	The graph of $f(x)$ is shifted to the right h units.
$y = f(x + h)$	The graph of $f(x)$ is shifted to the left h units.
$y = f(x) + k$	The graph of $f(x)$ is shifted up k units.
$y = f(x) - k$	The graph of $f(x)$ is shifted down k units.
$y = a\,f(x)$	If $a > 1$, the graph of $f(x)$ is vertically stretched.
	If $0 < a < 1$, the graph of $f(x)$ is vertically compressed.
$y = -f(x)$	The graph of $f(x)$ is reflected across the x-axis.
$y = f(-x)$	The graph of $f(x)$ is reflected across the y-axis.

QUIZ

Match the graphs in Figures 5-41 to 5-44 with the functions in Problems 1 to 4.

1. $f(x) = \sqrt{-x}$.

2. $f(x) = 2\sqrt{x}$.

3. $f(x) = \sqrt{x-1}$.

4. $f(x) = \sqrt{x+1}$.

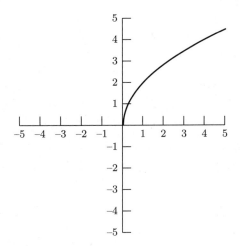

FIGURE 5-41

FIGURE 5-42

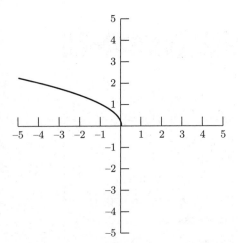

FIGURE 5-43

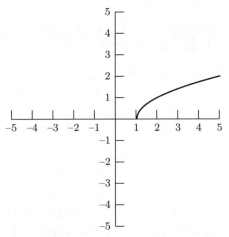

FIGURE 5-44

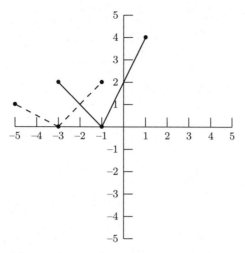

FIGURE 5-45

5. **The graph of $y = f(x - 1) + 3$ is the graph of $y = f(x)$.**

   A. Shifted to the left 1 unit and down 3 units.

   B. Shifted to the right 1 unit and up 3 units.

   C. Shifted to the left 3 units and down 1 unit.

   D. Shifted to the right 3 units and up 1 unit.

6. **The graph of $y = -f(x)$ is the graph of $y = f(x)$.**

   A. Reflected across the x-axis.

   B. Reflected across the y-axis.

   C. Reflected across the line $y = x$.

7. **The solid graph in Figure 5-45 is the graph of $f(x)$, and the dashed graph is the graph of a transformation of $f(x)$. What is the transformation?**

   A. $\frac{1}{2} f(x - 2)$

   B. $\frac{1}{2} f(x + 2)$

   C. $f(x - 2) + \frac{1}{2}$

   D. $f(x + 2) - \frac{1}{2}$

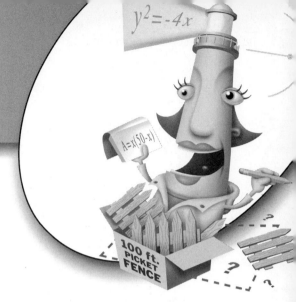

chapter 6

Quadratic Functions

In Chapter 5, we were introduced to the quadratic function $f(x) = x^2$ (see Figure 6-1) and how changes to this function affected its graph. In this chapter, we will learn how to select a few points to sketch an accurate graph of a quadratic function. We will also use the fact that these functions have either a highest point or a lowest point to optimize certain applied problems. This will be a preview to some of the optimization problems you will solve in calculus.

CHAPTER OBJECTIVES

In this chapter, you will

- Identify the vertex for the graph of a quadratic function
- Find the intercepts for the graph of a quadratic function
- Sketch the graph of a quadratic function
- Rewrite a quadratic function in standard form
- Solve applications involving quadratic functions

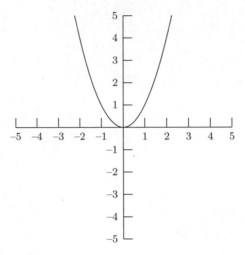

FIGURE 6-1

The Graph of a Quadratic Function

When a quadratic function is written in standard form, $f(x) = a(x - h)^2 + k$, we have a pretty good idea of what its graph (called a *parabola*) looks like: h causes the graph to shift horizontally, and k causes it to shift vertically. The point $(0, 0)$ on $y = x^2$ has shifted to (h, k). This point is the *vertex*. On a parabola that opens up (when a is positive), the vertex is the lowest point on the graph. On a graph that opens down (when a is negative), the vertex is the highest point on the graph.

To sketch the graph of a quadratic function, we begin with the vertex. Once we have the vertex, we find two points to its left and two points to its right. We should choose points that show the curvature around the vertex and how fast the ends are going up or down. It does not matter which points we choose, but a good rule of thumb is to find $h - 2a$, $h - a$, $h + a$, and $h + 2a$. Because a parabola is symmetric about the line $x = h$ (the vertical line that goes through the vertex), the y-values for $h - a$ and $h + a$ are the same and the y-values for $h - 2a$ and $h + 2a$ are the same, too. We also find the intercepts. Of course, not every quadratic function has x-intercepts. If you know that the vertex is above the x-axis, and the graph opens up, then the graph cannot have x-intercepts.

 **EXAMPLE 6-1**

Sketch the graph for the following quadratic functions. Find the *y*-intercept and the *x*-intercepts, if any.

TABLE 6-1

	x	y	Plot This Point
$h - 2a$	$1 - 2(1) = -1$	$(-1 - 1)^2 - 4 = 0$	$(-1, 0)$
$h - a$	$1 - 1 = 0$	$(0 - 1)^2 - 4 = -3$	$(0, -3)$
h	1	-4	$(1, -4)$
$h + a$	$1 + 1 = 2$	$(2 - 1)^2 - 4 = -3$	$(2, -3)$
$h + 2a$	$1 + 2(1) = 3$	$(3 - 1)^2 - 4 = 0$	$(3, 0)$

- $f(x) = (x - 1)^2 - 4$

Because $a = 1$ is positive, $h = 1, k = -4$, we know that the parabola opens up and the vertex is $(1, -4)$.

To find the y-intercept, we let $x = 0$ in the function. The y-intercept is $(0 - 1)^2 - 4 = -3$. To find the x-intercepts, we let $y = 0$ and solve for x.

$$(x - 1)^2 - 4 = 0 \quad \text{Substitute 0 for } f(x).$$

$$(x - 1)^2 = 4 \quad \text{Add 4 to each side.}$$

$$x - 1 = \pm 2 \quad \text{Take the square root of each side.}$$

$$x = 1 \pm 2 = 1 + 2, 1 - 2 = 3, -1$$

The x-intercepts are 3 and -1. Using the points in Table 6-1, we can sketch the graph of the function (see Figure 6-2).

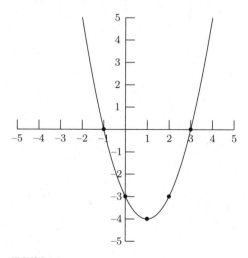

FIGURE 6-2

TABLE 6-2

	x	y	Plot This Point
$h - 2a$	$-1 - 2(-2) = 3$	$-2(3 + 1)^2 + 18 = -14$	$(3, -14)$
$h - a$	$-1 - (-2) = 1$	$-2(1 + 1)^2 + 18 = 10$	$(1, 10)$
h	-1	18	$(-1, 18)$
$h + a$	$-1 + (-2) = -3$	$-2(-3 + 1)^2 + 18 = 10$	$(-3, 10)$
$h + 2a$	$-1 + 2(-2) = -5$	$-2(-5 + 1)^2 + 18 = -14$	$(-5, -14)$

- $g(x) = -2(x + 1)^2 + 18$

  Because $a = -2$, $h = -1$, $k = 18$, we know that the parabola opens down, and the vertex is $(-1, 18)$. We now find the intercepts.

  $$y = -2(0 + 1)^2 + 18 \qquad -2(x + 1)^2 + 18 = 0$$
  $$y = 16 \qquad\qquad\qquad -2(x + 1)^2 = -18$$
  $$(x + 1)^2 = 9$$
  $$x + 1 = \pm 3$$
  $$x = -1 \pm 3 = -1 - 3,$$
  $$-1 + 3 = -4, 2$$

  The y-intercept is 16 and the x-intercepts are -4 and 2. We sketch the graph of the function by plotting the points from Table 6-2. The graph is sketched in Figure 6-3.

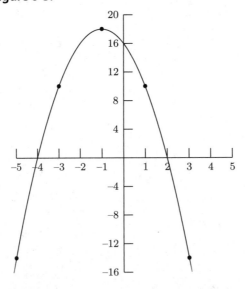

FIGURE 6-3

TABLE 6-3

	x	y	Plot This Point
$h - 2a$	$-1 - 2\left(\frac{1}{2}\right) = -2$	$\frac{1}{2}(-2+1)^2 + 2 = 2\frac{1}{2}$	$\left(-2, 2\frac{1}{2}\right)$
$h - a$	$-1 - \frac{1}{2} = -1\frac{1}{2}$	$\frac{1}{2}\left(-1\frac{1}{2}+1\right)^2 + 2 = 2\frac{1}{8}$	$\left(-1\frac{1}{2}, 2\frac{1}{8}\right)$
h	-1	2	$(-1, 2)$
$h + a$	$-1 + \frac{1}{2} = -\frac{1}{2}$	$\frac{1}{2}\left(-\frac{1}{2}+1\right)^2 + 2 = 2\frac{1}{8}$	$\left(-\frac{1}{2}, 2\frac{1}{8}\right)$
$h + 2a$	$-1 + 2\left(\frac{1}{2}\right) = 0$	$\frac{1}{2}(0+1)^2 + 2 = 2\frac{1}{2}$	$\left(0, 2\frac{1}{2}\right)$

- $f(x) = \dfrac{1}{2}(x+1)^2 + 2$

Because $a = \frac{1}{2}$, $h = -1$, $k = 2$, we know that the parabola opens up, and the vertex is $(-1, 2)$. There are no x-intercepts because the parabola opens up ($a = \frac{1}{2}$ is positive) and the vertex is above the x-axis ($k = 2$ is positive). If we were to solve the equation $\frac{1}{2}(x+1)^2 + 2 = 0$, we would not get a real number solution. The y-intercept is $y = \frac{1}{2}(0+1)^2 + 2 = 2\frac{1}{2}$. See Table 6-3 for points to plot and Figure 6-4 for the graph.

Finding a Quadratic Function

Having the vertex and one other point on a parabola, we can find an equation for the quadratic function. Once we know the vertex, we have h and k in $y = a(x - h)^2 + k$. We can find a if we know one other point on its graph. After

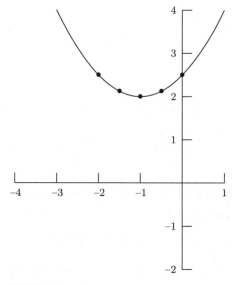

FIGURE 6-4

substituting the x- and y-values for the second point in the equation, we can algebraically solve for a.

 EXAMPLE 6-2

- **The vertex for a quadratic function is $(-3, 4)$, and the y-intercept is -10. Find an equation for this function.**
  Let $h = -3$, $k = 4$ in $y = a(x - h)^2 + k$ to get $y = a(x + 3)^2 + 4$. Saying that the y-intercept is -10 is another way of saying $(0, -10)$ is a point on the graph. We can let $x = 0$ and $y = -10$ in $y = a(x + 3)^2 + 4$ to find a.

  $$-10 = a(0 + 3)^2 + 4$$

  $$-14 = 9a$$

  $$-\frac{14}{9} = a$$

  An equation for this function is $y = -\frac{14}{9}(x + 3)^2 + 4$.

Finding the Vertex

Quadratic equations are not normally written in the convenient form $f(x) = a(x - h)^2 + k$. We can complete the square on a quadratic function in the form $f(x) = ax^2 + bx + c$ to find (h, k). Begin by completing the square on the terms containing x^2 and x. (There is a review of completing the square in the Appendix.)

 EXAMPLE 6-3

Find the vertex.

- $y = x^2 - 6x - 2$

  $$y = x^2 - 6x - 2$$

  $$y = \left[x^2 - 6x + \left(\frac{6}{2}\right)^2\right] - 2 + ?$$

  We need to balance putting $+(\frac{6}{2})^2 = 9$ inside the parentheses by adding -9 outside the parentheses.

  $$y = (x^2 - 6x + 9) - 2 - 9$$

  $$y = (x - 3)^2 - 11 \qquad \text{The vertex is } (3, -11).$$

- $f(x) = 4x^2 + 8x + 1$

We begin by factoring $a = 4$ from $4x^2 + 8x$, and then we complete the square on the terms containing x^2 and x.

$$f(x) = 4x^2 + 8x + 1$$

$$f(x) = 4(x^2 + 2x) + 1$$

$$f(x) = 4(x^2 + 2x + 1) + 1 + ?$$

By putting $+1$ inside the parentheses, we are adding $4(1) = 4$. We need to balance this by adding -4 outside the parentheses.

$$f(x) = 4(x^2 + 2x + 1) + 1 + (-4)$$

$$f(x) = 4(x + 1)^2 - 3 \qquad \text{The vertex is } (-1, -3).$$

When factoring an unusual quantity from two or more terms, it is not obvious what terms go in the parentheses. We can find the terms that go in the parentheses by writing the terms to be factored as numerators of fractions and the number to be factored as the denominator. The terms that go inside the parentheses are the simplified fractions.

- $f(x) = -3x^2 + 9x + \dfrac{1}{4}$

We need to factor $a = -3$ from $-3x^2 + 9x$.

$$\frac{-3x^2}{-3} + \frac{9x}{-3} = x^2 - 3x$$

$$f(x) = -3x^2 + 9x + \frac{1}{4}$$

$$f(x) = -3(x^2 - 3x) + \frac{1}{4}$$

$$f(x) = -3\left(x^2 - 3x + \frac{9}{4}\right) + \frac{1}{4} + ? \qquad \left(\frac{3}{2}\right)^2 = \frac{9}{4}$$

By putting $+\frac{9}{4}$ inside the parentheses, we are adding $-3(\frac{9}{4})$.

We need to balance this by adding $\frac{27}{4}$ outside the parentheses.

$$f(x) = -3\left(x^2 - 3x + \frac{9}{4}\right) + \frac{1}{4} + \frac{27}{4} = -3\left(x^2 - 3x + \frac{9}{4}\right) + \frac{28}{4}$$

$$f(x) = -3\left(x - \frac{3}{2}\right)^2 + 7 \qquad \text{The vertex is } \left(\frac{3}{2}, 7\right).$$

- $g(x) = \dfrac{2}{3}x^2 + x - 2$

Factoring $a = \frac{2}{3}$ from $\frac{2}{3}x^2 + x$, we have

$$\frac{\left(\frac{2}{3}\right)x^2}{\frac{2}{3}} + \frac{x}{\frac{2}{3}} = x^2 + x \div \frac{2}{3} = x^2 + x \cdot \frac{3}{2} = x^2 + \frac{3}{2}x.$$

$$g(x) = \frac{2}{3}\left(x^2 + \frac{3}{2}x\right) - 2$$

$$= \frac{2}{3}\left(x^2 + \frac{3}{2}x + \frac{9}{16}\right) - 2 + ? \qquad \left(\frac{1}{2} \cdot \frac{3}{2}\right)^2 = \frac{9}{16}$$

By adding $\frac{9}{16}$ inside the parentheses, we are adding $\frac{2}{3} \cdot \frac{9}{16} = \frac{3}{8}$.

We need to balance this by adding $-\frac{3}{8}$ outside the parentheses.

$$g(x) = \frac{2}{3}\left(x^2 + \frac{3}{2}x + \frac{9}{16}\right) - 2 - \frac{3}{8}$$

$$g(x) = \frac{2}{3}\left(x + \frac{3}{4}\right)^2 - \frac{19}{8} \qquad \text{The vertex is } \left(-\frac{3}{4}, -\frac{19}{8}\right).$$

One advantage in the form $f(x) = ax^2 + bx + c$ is that it is usually easier to use to find the intercepts. We can use factoring and the quadratic formula when it is in this form. Also, c is the y-intercept. Because a is the same number in both forms, we can tell whether the parabola opens up or down. It can be tedious to complete the square on $f(x) = ax^2 + bx + c$ to find the vertex. Fortunately, there is a shortcut, called the vertex formula.

$$h = \frac{-b}{2a} \quad \text{and} \quad k = f(h) = f\left(\frac{-b}{2a}\right)$$

This shortcut comes from completing the square to rewrite $f(x) = ax^2 + bx + c$ as $f(x) = a(x - h)^2 + k$.

$$f(x) = ax^2 + bx + c$$

$$= a\left(x^2 + \frac{b}{a}x\right) + c$$

$$= a\left[x^2 + \frac{b}{a}x + \left(\frac{b}{2a}\right)^2\right] + c - a \cdot \left(\frac{b}{2a}\right)^2$$

$$= a\left(x + \frac{b}{2a}\right)^2 + c - \frac{b^2}{4a} \qquad \text{The vertex is } \left(\frac{-b}{2a}, c - \frac{b^2}{4a}\right).$$

It is easier to find k by evaluating the function at $x = \frac{-b}{2a}$ than by using this formula.

EXAMPLE 6-4

Use the vertex formula to find the vertex.

- $f(x) = -3x^2 + 9x + 4$

$$h = \frac{-b}{2a} = \frac{-9}{2(-3)} = \frac{3}{2} \text{ and } k = f\left(\frac{3}{2}\right) = -3\left(\frac{3}{2}\right)^2 + 9\left(\frac{3}{2}\right) + 4 = \frac{43}{4}$$

The vertex is $\left(\frac{3}{2}, \frac{43}{4}\right)$.

A graphing calculator can help us to locate the vertex for the graph of a quadratic function. Using the TRACE button, we can travel along the graph, with the calculator displaying the coordinates of each point we cross. We can get a better approximation for the vertex with the *minimum* or *maximum* features. The steps for using these features are summarized after Example 6-5.

EXAMPLE 6-5

- Use a calculator to locate the vertex for the graph of $y = x^2 - x - 3$.
  We begin by displaying the graph in the standard window (see Figure 6-5).

  Because the parabola opens up, we want to use the *minimum* feature. Go to the CALCULATE menu (2nd key followed by the TRACE key) and cursor to "3:minimum" and press ENTER. Because a graph can have multiple

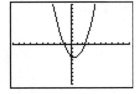

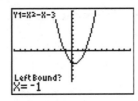

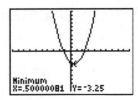

FIGURE 6-5   **FIGURE 6-6**   **FIGURE 6-7**

minimum or maximum values (we will see some of these functions later), the calculator needs an interval containing the vertex. Because there is only one minimum in the window, we could use $-10 \leq x \leq 10$ as the interval containing the minimum. Because smaller intervals work better, we will use $x = -1$ and $x = 4$. These will be the values we enter at the "Left Bound?" and "Right Bound?" prompts. Enter -1 at the "Left Bound?" prompt (see Figure 6-6) and 4 at the "Right Bound?" prompt. We can ignore the "Guess?" prompt by pressing ENTER (or we could enter a guess). The calculator gives us an approximation for the coordinates of the vertex. See Figure 6-7.

These steps are summarized in Table 6-4.

An important topic in calculus is optimizing functions; that is, finding a maximum and/or minimum value for the function. Precalculus students can use algebra to optimize quadratic functions. A quadratic function has a minimum value (if its graph opens up) or a maximum value (if its graph opens down). If a is positive, then k is the minimum functional value. If a is negative, then k is the maximum functional value. These values occur at $x = h$.

TABLE 6-4

Using a Calculator to Locate the Vertex
1. Enter the function on the Y = Editor, and set an appropriate window.
2. Go to the CALCULATE menu (2nd key followed by the TRACE key), cursor to "3:minimum" or "4:maximum" and press ENTER.
3. Enter a left bound and a right bound at the prompts. The x-coordinate of the vertex must be between these values.
4. Either enter a guess at the "Guess?" prompt or ignore it by pressing ENTER.
5. The cursor goes to the vertex and its approximate coordinates are displayed.

EXAMPLE 6-6

Find the minimum or maximum functional value and where it occurs.

- $f(x) = -(x-3)^2 + 25$

  The parabola opens down because $a = -1$ is negative. This means that $k = 25$ is the maximum functional value. It occurs at $x = 3$.

- $y = 0.01x^2 - 6x + 2000$

  We find the vertex with the vertex formula.

  $$h = \frac{-b}{2a} = \frac{-(-6)}{2(0.01)} = 300 \text{ and } k = 0.01(300)^2 - 6(300) + 2000 = 1100$$

  Because $a = 0.01$ is positive, $k = 1100$ is the minimum functional value. The minimum occurs at $x = 300$.

Still Struggling

For a function in the form $f(x) = -(x-h)^2 + k$, the negative symbol does not affect the sign of h. For example, the vertex for $f(x) = -(x-4)^2 + 3$ and $g(x) = (x-4)^2 + 3$ is (4, 3) for each function.

PRACTICE

For Problems 1 to 3, sketch the graph and identify the vertex and intercepts.

1. $y = -(x-1)^2 + 4$

2. $f(x) = \frac{2}{3}(x+1)^2 + 2$

3. $y = -\frac{1}{2}x^2 - x + 12$

4. Rewrite $f(x) = -\frac{3}{5}x^2 - 6x - 11$ in the form $f(x) = a(x-h)^2 + k$, using completing the square.

5. Find the maximum or minimum functional value for $g(x) = -0.002x^2 + 5x + 150$. (Hint: Use the vertex formula.)

6. Find an equation for the quadratic function whose vertex is $(2, 5)$ and whose graph contains the point $(-8, 15)$.

7. Use a graphing calculator to find the vertex for the graph of $f(x) = -x^2 + 2x + 4$.

 SOLUTIONS

1. The vertex is $(1, 4)$. The y-intercept is $-(0-1)^2 + 4 = 3$.

$$-(x-1)^2 + 4 = 0$$
$$-(x-1)^2 = -4$$
$$(x-1)^2 = 4$$
$$x - 1 = \pm 2$$
$$x = 1 \pm 2 = 1 + 2, 1 - 2 = 3, -1$$

The x-intercepts are 3 and -1. The graph is sketched in Figure 6-8.

2. The vertex is $(-1, 2)$. The y-intercept is $\frac{2}{3}(0+1) + 2 = \frac{8}{3}$. There are two ways we can tell that there are no x-intercepts. The parabola opens up and the vertex is above the x-axis, so the parabola is always above the x-axis. Also, the equation $\frac{2}{3}(x+1)^2 + 2 = 0$ has no real number solution. The graph is sketched in Figure 6-9.

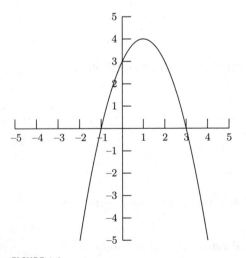

FIGURE 6-8

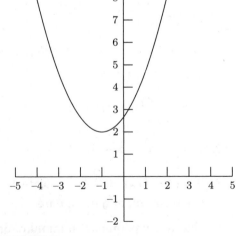

FIGURE 6-9

3. The vertex is $\left(-1, \frac{25}{2}\right)$.

$$h = \frac{-b}{2a} = \frac{-(-1)}{2 \cdot \frac{-1}{2}} = -1 \text{ and } k = -\frac{1}{2}(-1)^2 - (-1) + 12 = \frac{25}{2}$$

The y-intercept is $-\frac{1}{2}(0)^2 - 0 + 12 = 12$.

$$0 = -\frac{1}{2}x^2 - x + 12 \qquad \text{Multiply each side by } -2.$$

$$-2(0) = -2\left(-\frac{1}{2}x^2 - x + 12\right)$$

$$0 = x^2 + 2x - 24 \qquad \text{Factor.}$$

$$0 = (x + 6)(x - 4)$$

$$x + 6 = 0 \qquad\qquad x - 4 = 0$$

$$x = -6 \qquad\qquad x = 4$$

The x-intercepts are -6 and 4, see Figure 6-10.

4. $f(x) = -\frac{3}{5}x^2 - 6x - 11 \qquad$ Factor $-\frac{3}{5}$ from the x^2 and x terms.

$$f(x) = -\frac{3}{5}(x^2 + 10x) - 11 \qquad \frac{-6x}{-\frac{3}{5}} = -6x \div -\frac{3}{5}$$

$$= -6x \cdot -\frac{5}{3} = 10x$$

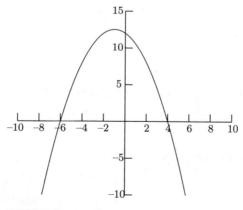

FIGURE 6-10

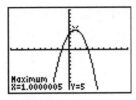

FIGURE 6-11

$$f(x) = -\frac{3}{5}(x^2 + 10x + 25) - 11 + 15$$

$$f(x) = -\frac{3}{5}(x + 5)^2 + 4$$

5. This function has a maximum value because $a = -0.002$ is negative. The answer is *k*.

$$h = \frac{-b}{2a} = \frac{-5}{2(-0.002)} = 1250 \quad \text{and} \quad k = g(1250)$$

$$= -0.002(1250)^2 + 5(1250) + 150 = 3275$$

The maximum functional value is 3275.

6. $h = 2$, $k = 5$ which makes $y = a(x - h)^2 + k$ become $y = a(x - 2)^2 + 5$. We can find *a* by letting $x = -8$ and $y = 15$.

$$y = a(x - 2)^2 + 5$$

$$15 = a(-8 - 2)^2 + 5$$

$$10 = a(-10)^2$$

$$10 = 100a$$

$$0.1 = a$$

The equation is $y = 0.1(x - 2)^2 + 5$.

7. The graph is plotted in the standard window in Figure 6-11.

Optimizing Quadratic Functions

These techniques to maximize/minimize quadratic functions can be applied to problems outside of mathematics. We can maximize an enclosed area, minimize the surface area of a box, maximize revenue, and optimize many other problems. In the first problems, the functions to be optimized are given. Later, we will have to find the functions based on the information given in the problem. The answers to these problems are one or both coordinates of the vertex.

 EXAMPLE 6-7

- **The weekly profit function for a product is given by $P(x) = -0.0001x^2 + 3x - 12,500$, where x is the number of units produced per week, and $P(x)$ is the profit (in dollars). What is the maximum weekly profit? How many units should be produced for this profit?**

  The profit function is a quadratic function which has a maximum value. What information does the vertex give us? h is the number of units needed to maximize the weekly profit, and k is the maximum weekly profit.

  Number of units that maximizes weekly profit.
  $$h = \frac{-b}{2a} = \frac{-3}{2(-0.0001)} = 15{,}000 \quad \text{and}$$

  Maximum weekly profit
  $$k = -0.0001(15{,}000)^2 + 3(15{,}000) - 12{,}500 = 10{,}000$$

  Maximize the weekly profit by producing 15,000 units. The maximum weekly profit is $10,000.

- **The number of units of a product sold depends on the amount of money spent on advertising. If $y = -26x^2 + 2600x + 10{,}000$ gives the number of units sold after x thousands of dollars is spent on advertising, find the amount spent on advertising that results in the most sales.**

  h gives us the amount to spend on advertising in order to maximize sales, and k tells us the maximum sales level. We only need to find h.

  $$h = \frac{-b}{2a} = \frac{-2600}{2(-26)} = 50$$

  Spend $50,000 on advertising to maximize sales. (Because x is in thousands of dollars, $h = 50$ represents $50,000.)

The height of an object propelled upward (neglecting air resistance) is given by the quadratic function $s(t) = -16t^2 + v_0t + s_0$, where s is the height in feet, and t is the number of seconds after the initial thrust. The initial velocity (in feet per second) of the object is v_0, and s_0 is the initial height (in feet) of the object. For example, if an object is tossed up at the rate of 10 feet per second, then $v_0 = 10$. If an object is propelled upward from a height of 50 feet, then $s_0 = 50$. If an object is dropped, its initial velocity is zero, so $v_0 = 0$.

EXAMPLE 6-8

- An object is tossed upward with an initial velocity of 15 feet per second from a height of 4 feet. What is the object's maximum height? How long does it take the object to reach its maximum height?

Because the initial velocity is 15 feet per second, $v_0 = 15$, and the initial height is 4 feet, so $s_0 = 4$. The function that gives the height of the object (in feet) after t seconds is $s(t) = -16t^2 + 15t + 4$.

$$h = \frac{-b}{2a} = \frac{-15}{2(-16)} = 0.46875 \quad \text{and}$$

$$k = -16(0.46875)^2 + 15(0.46875) + 4 = 7.515625$$

The object reaches its maximum height of 7.515625 feet after 0.46875 seconds.

- A projectile is fired from the ground with an initial velocity of 120 miles per hour. What is the projectile's maximum height? How long does it take to reach its maximum height?

Because the projectile is being fired from the ground, its initial height is zero, so $s_0 = 0$. The initial velocity is given as 120 miles per hour—we need to convert this to feet per second. There are 5280 feet per mile, so 120 miles is 120(5280) = 633,600 feet. There are 60(60) = 3600 seconds per hour.

$$\frac{120 \text{ miles}}{1 \text{ hour}} = \frac{633,600 \text{ feet}}{3600 \text{ seconds}} = 176 \text{ feet per second}$$

Now we have the function: $s(t) = -16t^2 + 176t + 0 = -16t^2 + 176t$

$$h = \frac{-b}{2a} = \frac{-176}{2(-16)} = 5.5 \quad \text{and} \quad k = -16(5.5)^2 + 176(5.5) = 484$$

The projectile reaches its maximum height of 484 feet after 5.5 seconds.

Another problem involving the maximum vertical height is one where we know the horizontal distance traveled instead of the time it has traveled. The x-coordinates describe the object's horizontal distance, and the y-coordinates describe its height. Here we find the maximum height and how far it traveled horizontally to reach the maximum height.

EXAMPLE 6-9

- A ball is thrown across a field. Its path can be described by the equation $y = -0.002x^2 + 0.2x + 5$, where x is the horizontal distance (in feet) and y is the height (in feet). See Figure 6-12. What is the ball's maximum height? How far had it traveled horizontally to reach its maximum height?

k answers the first question, and h answers the second.

$$h = \frac{-b}{2a} = \frac{-0.2}{2(-0.002)} = 50 \text{ and } k = -0.002(50)^2 + 0.2(50) + 5 = 10$$

The ball reached a maximum height of 10 feet when it traveled 50 feet horizontally.

The revenue of a product or service can depend on its price in two ways. An increase in the price means that more revenue per unit is earned but fewer units are sold. A decrease in the price means that less revenue is earned per unit but more units are sold. If one of these revenue functions is modeled by a quadratic function, we can easily find the price that maximizes revenue. In the next problems, a current price and sales level are given. We are told how a price increase or decrease affects the sales level. We let x represent the number of price increases/decreases. Suppose every $10 decrease in the price results in an increase of five customers. Then the revenue function is (old price $- 10x$)(old sales level $+ 5x$). If every $50 increase in the price results in a loss of one customer, then the revenue function is (old price $+ 50x$)(old sales level $- 1x$). These functions are quadratic functions which have a maximum value.

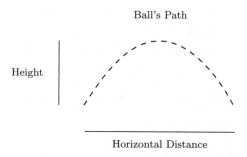

Ball's Path

Height

Horizontal Distance

FIGURE 6-12

The vertex tells us the maximum revenue and how many increases/decreases in the price yields the maximum revenue.

EXAMPLE 6-10

- A management firm has determined that 60 apartments in a complex can be rented if the monthly rent is $900, and that for each $50 increase in the rent, three tenants are lost with little chance of being replaced. What rent should be charged to maximize revenue? What is the maximum revenue?

Let x represent the number of $50 increases in the rent. This means if the rent is raised $50, $x = 1$, if the rent is increased $100, $x = 2$, and if the rent is increased $150, $x = 3$; so the rent function is $900 + 50x$. The number of tenants depends on the number of $50 increases in the rent. So, if the rent is raised $50, there are $60 - 3(1)$ tentants; if the rent is raised $100, then there are $60 - 3(2)$ tenants; and if the rent is raised $150, there are $60 - 3(3)$ tenants. If the rent is raised $50x$, there are $60 - 3x$ tenants. The revenue function is $R = (900 + 50x)(60 - 3x) = -150x^2 + 300x + 54,000$.

$$h = \frac{-b}{2a} = \frac{-300}{2(-150)} = 1 \quad \text{and} \quad k = -150(1)^2 + 300(1) + 54,000$$
$$= 54,150$$

The maximum revenue is $54,150. Maximize revenue by charging $900 + 50(1) = 950$ per month for rent.

- A cinema multiplex averages 2500 tickets sold on a Saturday when ticket prices are $8. Concession revenue averages $1.50 per ticket sold. A research firm has determined that for each $0.50 increase in the ticket price, 100 fewer tickets are sold. What is the maximum revenue (including concession revenue) and what ticket price maximizes the revenue?

Let x represent the number of $0.50 increases in the price. The ticket price is $8 + 0.50x$. The average number of tickets sold is $2500 - 100x$. The average ticket revenue is $(8.00 + 0.50x)(2500 - 100x)$. The average concession revenue is $1.50(2500 - 100x)$. The total revenue is:

$$R = (8.00 + 0.50x)(2500 - 100x) + 1.50(2500 - 100x)$$
$$= -50x^2 + 300x + 23,750$$
$$h = \frac{-b}{2a} = \frac{-300}{2(-50)} = 3 \text{ and } k = -50(3)^2 + 300(3) + 23,750 = 24,200$$

To maximize revenue, the ticket price should be $8.00 + 0.50(3) = \$9.50$, and the maximum revenue is $24,200.

- The manager of a performing arts company offers a group discount price of $45 per person for groups of 20 or more and will drop the price by $1.50 per person for each additional person. What is the maximum revenue? What size group maximizes the revenue?

  Because the price does not change until more than 20 people are in the group, we let x represent the additional people in the group. What is the price per person if the group size is more than 20? If one extra person is in the group, the price is $45 - 1(1.50)$. If there are two extra people, the price is $45 - 2(1.50)$; and if there are three extra people, the price is $45 - 3(1.50)$. So, if there are x additional people, the price is $45 - 1.50x$. The revenue is:

  $$R = (20 + x)(45 - 1.50x) = -1.50x^2 + 15x + 900$$

  $$h = \frac{-b}{2a} = \frac{-15}{2(-1.50)} = 5 \text{ and } k = -1.50(5)^2 + 15(5) + 900 = 937.50$$

  The group size that maximizes revenue is $20 + 5 = 25$. The maximum revenue is $937.50.

Optimizing geometric figures are common calculus and precalculus problems. In many of these problems, there are more than two variables. We are given enough information in the problem to eliminate one of the variables. For example, if we want the area of a rectangle, the formula is $A = LW$. If we know the perimeter is 20, then we can use the equation $2L + 2W = 20$ to solve for either L or W and then substitute this quantity in the area function, reducing the equation from three to two variables. The new area function is quadratic.

EXAMPLE 6-11

- A parks department has 1200 meters of fencing available to enclose two adjacent playing fields (see Figure 6-13). What dimensions maximize the enclosed area? What is the maximum enclosed area?

  The total enclosed area is $A = LW$. Because there is 1200 meters of fencing available, we must have $L + W + W + W + L = 1200$ (see Figure 6-14).

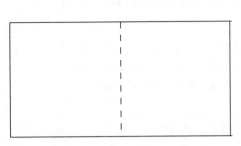

FIGURE 6-13

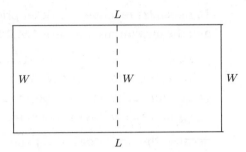

FIGURE 6-14

We can solve for L or W in this equation and substitute it in $A = LW$, reducing the equation to two variables. We solve for L in $2L + 3W = 1200$.

$$2L + 3W = 1200$$

$$L = \frac{1200 - 3W}{2}$$

Now $A = LW$ becomes $A = \frac{1200 - 3W}{2} \cdot W = -\frac{3}{2}W^2 + 600W$. This function has a maximum value.

$$h = \frac{-b}{2a} = \frac{-600}{2\left(-\frac{3}{2}\right)} = 200 \text{ and } k = -\frac{3}{2}(200)^2 + 600(200) = 60{,}000$$

The width that maximizes the enclosed area is 200 meters; the length is $\frac{1200 - 3(200)}{2} = 300$ meters. The maximum enclosed area is 60,000 square meters.

Another common fencing problem is one where only three sides of a rectangular area need to be fenced. The fourth side is some other boundary like a stream or the side of a building. We call two sides W and the third side L. Then "$2W + L$ = amount of fencing" allows us to solve for L and substitute "L = amount of fencing $-2W$" in $A = LW$ to reduce the area formula to two variables.

EXAMPLE 6-12

- A farmer has 1000 feet of fencing materials available to fence a rectangular pasture next to a river (see Figure 6-15). If the side along the river does not need to be fenced, what dimensions maximize the enclosed area? What is the maximum enclosed area?

Using the fact that $2W + L = 1000$, we can solve for L and substitute this quantity in the area formula $A = LW$.

$$2W + L = 1000$$
$$L = 1000 - 2W$$
$$A = LW$$
$$A = (1000 - 2W)W = -2W^2 + 1000W$$

This quadratic function has a maximum value.

$$h = \frac{-b}{2a} = \frac{-1000}{2(-2)} = 250 \text{ and } k = -2(250)^2 + 1000(250) = 125{,}000$$

Maximize the enclosed area by letting $W = 250$ feet and $L = 1000 - 2(250) = 500$ feet. The maximum enclosed area is 125,000 square feet.

In the last problems, we maximize the area of a figure but we have to work a little harder to find the area function to maximize.

EXAMPLE 6-13

- A window is to be constructed in the shape of a rectangle surmounted by a semicircle (see Figure 6-16). The perimeter of the window needs to be 18 feet. What dimensions admit the greatest amount of light?

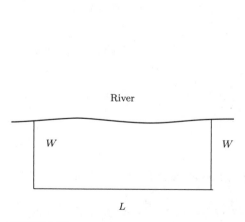

FIGURE 6-15

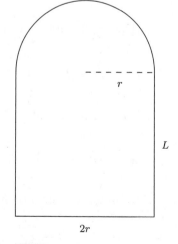

FIGURE 6-16

The dimensions that will admit the greatest amount of light are the same that will maximize the area of the window. The area of the window is the rectangular area plus the area of the semicircle. The area of the rectangular region is $L\,W$. Because the width of the window is the diameter (or twice the radius) of the semicircle, we can rewrite the area as $L(2r) = 2rL$. The area of the semicircle is half of the area of a circle with radius r, or $\frac{1}{2}\pi r^2$. The total area of the window is:

$$A = 2rL + \frac{1}{2}\pi r^2$$

Now we use the fact that the perimeter is 18 feet to help us replace L with an expression using r. The perimeter is made up of the two sides $(2L)$ and the bottom of the rectangle $(2r)$ and the length around the semicircle. The length around the outside of the semicircle is half of the circumference of a circle with radius r, $\frac{1}{2}(2\pi r) = \pi r$. The total perimeter is $P = 2L + 2r + \pi r$. This is equal to 18. We solve the equation $2L + 2r + \pi r = 18$ for L.

$$2L + 2r + \pi r = 18$$

$$2L = 18 - 2r - \pi r$$

$$L = \frac{18 - 2r - \pi r}{2} = 9 - r - \frac{1}{2}\pi r$$

Now we substitute $9 - r - \frac{1}{2}\pi r$ for L in the area formula.

$$A = 2rL + \frac{1}{2}\pi r^2 \qquad\qquad \text{Substitute for } L.$$

$$A = 2r\left(9 - r - \frac{1}{2}\pi r\right) + \frac{1}{2}\pi r^2 \qquad\qquad \text{Distribute } 2r.$$

$$A = 18r - 2r^2 - \pi r^2 + \frac{1}{2}\pi r^2 \qquad\qquad \text{Combine like terms.}$$

$$= 18r - 2r^2 - \frac{1}{2}\pi r^2 = 18r - \left(2 + \frac{1}{2}\pi\right)r^2 \qquad \text{Factor } r^2.$$

$$A = -\left(2 + \frac{1}{2}\pi\right)r^2 + 18r$$

This quadratic function has a maximum value.

$$h = \frac{-b}{2a} = \frac{-18}{2\left[-\left(2 + \frac{1}{2}\pi\right)\right]} = \frac{18}{4 + \pi} \approx 2.52$$

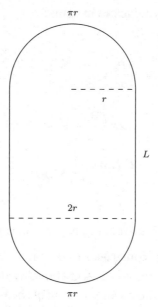

πr

r

L

$2r$

πr

FIGURE 6-17

Maximize the amount of light admitted in the window by letting the radius of the semicircle be about 2.52 feet, and the length about $9 - 2.52 - \frac{\pi}{2}(2.52) \approx 2.52$ feet.

- A track is to be constructed so that it is shaped like Figure 6-17, a rectangle with a semicircle at each end. If the inside perimeter of the track is to be $\frac{1}{4}$ mile, what is the maximum area of the rectangle?

The length of the rectangle is L. Its width is the diameter of the semicircles (or twice their radius). The area formula for the rectangle is $A = LW = L(2r) = 2rL$. The perimeter of the figure is the two sides of the rectangle ($2L$) plus the length around each semicircle (πr). The total perimeter is $2L + 2\pi r$. Although we could work with the dimensions in miles, it is easier to convert $\frac{1}{4}$ mile to feet. There are $\frac{5280}{4} = 1320$ feet in $\frac{1}{4}$ mile. We solve $2L + 2\pi r = 1320$ for L. Solving for r works, too.

$$2L + 2\pi r = 1320$$

$$2L = 1320 - 2\pi r$$

$$L = \frac{1320 - 2\pi r}{2} = 660 - \pi r$$

$$A = 2rL$$

$$A = 2r(660 - \pi r) = -2\pi r^2 + 1320r$$

The area function has a maximum value.

$$h = \frac{-b}{2a} = \frac{-1320}{2(-2\pi)} = \frac{330}{\pi}$$

$$k = -2\pi \left(\frac{330}{\pi}\right)^2 + 1320 \left(\frac{330}{\pi}\right)$$

$$= \frac{217{,}800}{\pi} \approx 69{,}328$$

The maximum area of the rectangular region is about 69,328 square feet.

• A rectangle is to be constructed so that it is bounded below by the x-axis, on the left by the y-axis, and above by the line $y = -2x + 12$ (see Figure 6-18). What is the maximum area of the rectangle?

The coordinates of the corners can help us to see how we can find the length and width of the rectangle. The coordinates of the corners are marked in Figure 6-19.

The height of the rectangle is y and the width is x. This makes the area $A = xy$. We need to eliminate x or y. Because $y = -2x + 12$, we can substitute

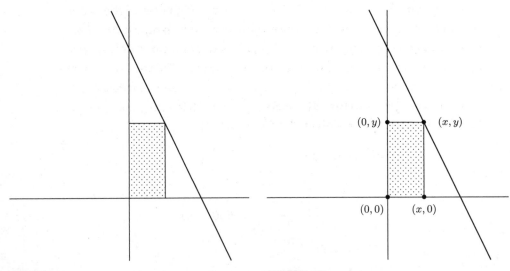

FIGURE 6-18   **FIGURE 6-19**

$-2x + 12$ for y in $A = xy$ to make it the quadratic function $A = xy = x(-2x + 12) = -2x^2 + 12x$.

$$h = \frac{-b}{2a} = \frac{-12}{2(-2)} = 3 \quad \text{and} \quad k = -2(3)^2 + 12(3) = 18$$

The maximum area is 18 square units.

 PRACTICE

1. The average cost of a product can be approximated by the function $C(x) = 0.00025x^2 - 0.25x + 70.5$, where x is the number of units produced and $C(x)$ is the average cost in dollars. What level of production minimizes the average cost?

2. A frog jumps from a rock to the shore of a pond. Its path is given by the equation $y = -\frac{5}{72}x^2 + \frac{5}{3}x$, where x is the horizontal distance in inches, and y is the height in inches. What is the frog's maximum height? How far had it traveled horizontally when it reached its maximum height?

3. A projectile is fired upward from a 10-feet platform. The projectile's initial velocity is 108 miles per hour. What is the projectile's maximum height? When will it reach its maximum height?

4. Attendance at home games for a college basketball team averages 1000 and the ticket price is $12. Concession sales average $2 per person. A student survey reveals that for every $0.25 decrease in the ticket price, 25 more students would attend the home games. What ticket price maximizes revenue? What is the maximum revenue?

5. A school has 1600 feet of fencing available to enclose three playing fields (see Figure 6-20). What dimensions maximize the enclosed area?

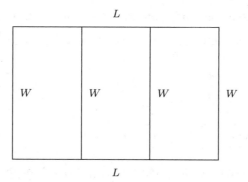

FIGURE 6-20

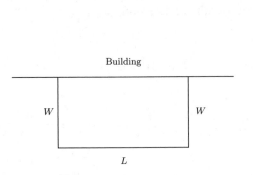

Building

W W

L

FIGURE 6-21

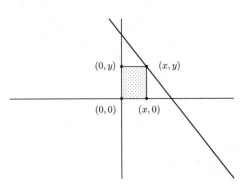

$(0, y)$ (x, y)

$(0, 0)$ $(x, 0)$

FIGURE 6-22

6. The manager of a large warehouse wants to enclose an area behind the building. He has 900 feet of fencing available (see Figure 6-21). What dimensions maximize the enclosed area? What is the maximum area?

7. A swimming pool is to be constructed in the shape of a rectangle with a semicircle at one end (refer again to Figure 6-16). If the perimeter is to be 120 feet, what dimensions maximize the area? What is the maximum area?

8. A rectangle is to be constructed so that it is bounded by the *x*-axis, the *y*-axis, and the line *y* = −3*x* + 4 (see Figure 6-22). What is the maximum area of the rectangle?

 SOLUTIONS

1. We only need to find *h*.

$$h = \frac{-b}{2a} = \frac{-(-0.25)}{2(0.00025)} = 500$$

Minimize the average cost by producing 500 units.

2. *k* answers the first question, and *h* answers the second.

$$h = \frac{-b}{2a} = \frac{-\frac{5}{3}}{2\left(-\frac{5}{72}\right)} = \frac{\frac{5}{3}}{\frac{5}{36}} = \frac{5}{3} \div \frac{5}{36} = \frac{5}{3} \cdot \frac{36}{5} = 12$$

$$k = -\frac{5}{72}(12)^2 + \frac{5}{3}(12) = 10$$

The frog reached a maximum height of 10 inches and had traveled 12 inches horizontally when it reached its maximum height.

3. The formula $s(t) = -16t^2 + v_0 t + s_0$ is in feet and seconds, so we need to convert 108 miles per hour to feet per second. There are 5280 feet in a mile and 60(60) = 3600 seconds in an hour.

$$\frac{108 \text{ miles}}{1 \text{ hour}} = \frac{108(5280) \text{ feet}}{3600 \text{ seconds}} = 158.4 \text{ feet per second}$$

Replacing v_0 with 158.4 and s_0 with 10, we have the function giving the height of the projectile after t seconds, $s(t) = -16t^2 + 158.4t + 10$.

$$h = \frac{-b}{2a} = \frac{-158.4}{2(-16)} = 4.95 \quad \text{and}$$

$$k = -16(4.95)^2 + 158.4(4.95) + 10 = 402.04$$

The projectile reaches a maximum height of 402.04 feet after 4.95 seconds.

4. We let x represent the number of $0.25 decreases in the ticket price. The ticket price is $12 - 0.25x$ and the average number attending the games is $1000 + 25x$. Ticket revenue is $(12 - 0.25x)(1000 + 25x)$. Revenue from concession sales is $2(1000 + 25x)$. Total revenue is:

$$R = (12 - 0.25x)(1000 + 25x) + 2(1000 + 25x)$$

$$= -6.25x^2 + 100x + 14{,}000$$

$$h = \frac{-b}{2a} = \frac{-100}{2(-6.25)} = 8 \quad \text{and}$$

$$k = -6.25(8)^2 + 100(8) + 14{,}000 = 14{,}400$$

The ticket price that maximizes revenue is $12 - 0.25(8) = \$10$ and the maximum revenue is $14,400.

5. The total area is $A = LW$. Because there is 1600 feet of fencing available, $2L + 4W = 1600$. Solving this equation for L, we have $L = 800 - 2W$. Substitute $800 - 2W$ for L in $A = LW$.

$$A = LW$$

$$= (800 - 2W)W = -2W^2 + 800W$$

$$h = \frac{-b}{2a} = \frac{-800}{2(-2)} = 200$$

Maximize the enclosed area by letting the width be 200 feet and the length be $800 - 2(200) = 400$ feet.

6. The enclosed area is $A = LW$. Because 900 feet of fencing is available, $2W + L = 900$. Solving this for L, we have $L = 900 - 2W$. We substitute $900 - 2W$ for L in $A = LW$.

$$A = LW$$
$$= (900 - 2W)W = -2W^2 + 900W$$
$$h = \frac{-b}{2a} = \frac{-900}{2(-2)} = 225 \quad \text{and} \quad k = -2(225)^2 + 900(225)$$
$$= 101{,}250$$

Maximize the enclosed area by letting the width be 225 feet and the length be $900 - 2(225) = 450$ feet. The maximum enclosed area is 101,250 square feet.

7. The area of the rectangle is $2rL$ (the width is twice the radius of the semicircle). The area of the semicircle is half the area of a circle with radius r, $\frac{1}{2}\pi r^2$. The total area of the pool is $A = 2rL + \frac{1}{2}\pi r^2$. After finding an equation for the perimeter, we solve the equation for L and substitute this for L in $A = 2rL + \frac{1}{2}\pi r^2$. The perimeter of the rectangular part is $L + 2r + L = 2r + 2L$. The length around the semicircle is half the circumference of a circle with radius r, $\frac{1}{2}(2\pi r) = \pi r$. The total length around the pool is $2L + 2r + \pi r$ which equals 120 feet.

$$2L + 2r + \pi r = 120$$
$$2L = 120 - 2r - \pi r$$
$$L = \frac{120 - 2r - \pi r}{2} = 60 - r - \frac{1}{2}\pi r$$
$$A = 2rL + \frac{1}{2}\pi r^2$$
$$= 2r\left(60 - r - \frac{1}{2}\pi r\right) + \frac{1}{2}\pi r^2$$

Substitute $60 - r - \frac{1}{2}\pi r$ for L.

$$= 120r - 2r^2 - \pi r^2 + \frac{1}{2}\pi r^2$$

$$= -2r^2 - \frac{1}{2}\pi r^2 + 120r$$

$$= \left(-2 - \frac{1}{2}\pi\right) r^2 + 120r$$

$$h = \frac{-b}{2a} = \frac{-120}{2\left(-2 - \frac{1}{2}\pi\right)} = \frac{-120}{-4 - \pi} = \frac{-120}{-(4 + \pi)}$$

$$= \frac{120}{4 + \pi} \approx 16.8$$

$$k = \left(-2 - \frac{1}{2}\pi\right)\left(\frac{120}{4 + \pi}\right)^2 + 120\left(\frac{120}{4 + \pi}\right)$$

$$= \frac{7200}{4 + \pi} \approx 1008.2$$

Maximize the area by letting the radius of the semicircle be about 16.8 feet and the length of the rectangle be about $60 - 16.8 - \frac{1}{2}\pi(16.8) \approx 16.8$ feet. The maximum area is about 1008.2 square feet.

8. The area is $A = LW$. The length of the rectangle is y [the distance from $(0, 0)$ and $(0, y)$]. The width is x [the distance between $(0, 0)$ and $(x, 0)$]. The area is now $A = xy$. Because $y = -3x + 4$, we can substitute $-3x + 4$ for y in $A = xy$.

$$A = xy$$

$$A = x(-3x + 4) = -3x^2 + 4x$$

$$h = \frac{-4}{2(-3)} = \frac{2}{3} \quad \text{and} \quad k = -3\left(\frac{2}{3}\right)^2 + 4\left(\frac{2}{3}\right) = \frac{4}{3}$$

The maximum area is $\frac{4}{3}$ square units.

Summary

In this chapter, we learned how to

- *Identify the vertex for the graph of a quadratic function.* If the equation is in standard form, $f(x) = a(x - h)^2 + k$, then the vertex is (h, k). If the equation is in the form $f(x) = ax^2 + bx + c$, we can either complete the square to rewrite it in standard form, or we can use the formula for h: $h = \frac{-b}{2a}$. Once we have h, we find k by computing $k = f(h) = f(\frac{-b}{2a})$.

- *Sketch the graph of a quadratic function.* We sketch the graph of a quadratic function by finding the vertex and by plotting a couple of points on either side of the vertex, usually $x = h \pm a$ and $x = h \pm 2a$. We find the x-intercepts (if there are any) by setting the function equal to zero. We find the y-intercept by evaluating the function at $x = 0$.

- *Use a graphing calculator to locate the vertex for a quadratic function.* A graphing calculator can find the highest point in a window or the lowest point.

- *Find a quadratic function when given its vertex and another point on its graph.* If we know (h, k), then the only number we need is a for $f(x) = a(x - h)^2 + k$. We find a by putting h and k in the formula as well as the coordinates of the other point. We then solve this equation for a.

- *Use quadratic functions to solve optimization problems.* Because a quadratic function has either a maximum value (when the graph opens down) or a minimum value (when the graph opens up), we can optimize many problems involving quadratic functions. The answer to these problems is h, k, or both.

QUIZ

1. What is the vertex for the graph of $f(x) = -3(x - 2)^2 + 1$?

   A. $(2, 1)$ C. $(6, 1)$

   B. $(-2, 1)$ D. $(-6, 1)$

2. Complete the square on $y = x^2 - 10x + 3$ to write the function in standard form, $y = a(x - h)^2 + k$.

   A. $y = (x - 10)^2 - 97$ C. $y = (x - 10)^2 + 103$

   B. $y = (x - 5)^2 - 22$ D. $y = (x - 5)^2 + 28$

3. Complete the square on $y = -2x^2 - 8x + 5$ to write the function in standard form.

   A. $y = -2(x + 2)^2 + 13$ C. $y = -2(x - 2)^2 + 13$

   B. $y = -2(x + 2)^2 + 9$ D. $y = -2(x - 2)^2 - 3$

4. What are the x- and y-intercepts for the graph of $f(x) = 2x^2 + 5x - 3$?

   A. The x-intercepts are $-\frac{1}{2}$ and 3, and the y-intercept is -3.

   B. The x-intercepts are $-\frac{1}{2}$ and 3, and the y-intercept is 3.

   C. The x-intercepts are $\frac{1}{2}$ and -3, and the y-intercept is -3.

   D. The x-intercepts are $\frac{1}{2}$ and -3, and the y-intercept is 3.

5. What is the vertex for the graph of $y = -0.004x^2 + 0.4x + 15$?

   A. $(50, 25)$ C. $(100, 54.6)$

   B. $(-50, 25)$ D. $(-100, 15)$

6. Find the maximum or minimum value for the function $f(x) = 2(x - 5)^2 + 8$.

   A. The minimum functional value is 5.   C. The maximum functional value is 8.

   B. The maximum functional value is 10.   D. The minimum functional value is 8.

7. Find the maximum or minimum value for the function $y = x^2 - 12x + 9$.

   A. The minimum functional value is 45.   C. The maximum functional value is 45.

   B. The minimum functional value is -27.   D. The maximum functional value is -27.

8. Find the quadratic function whose vertex is $(-3, 10)$ and whose graph contains the point $(\frac{1}{2}, 59)$.

   A. $f(x) = -4(x - 3)^2 + 10$ C. $f(x) = 4(x + 3)^2 + 10$

   B. $f(x) = 8(x + 3)^2 + 10$ D. $f(x) = 17(x - 3)^2 + 10$

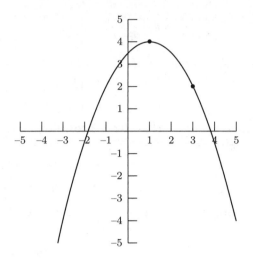

FIGURE 6-23

9. What is the function whose graph is in Figure 6-23?

   A. $y = -x^2 + 2x + 3$

   B. $y = -\frac{1}{2}x^2 + x + \frac{7}{2}$

   C. $y = -\frac{1}{8}x^2 - \frac{1}{4}x + \frac{31}{8}$

   D. $y = \frac{1}{8}x^2 - \frac{1}{4}x + \frac{33}{8}$

10. Noel, a hot dog vendor at an arts festival, averages 28 hot dogs sold per hour when the price is $4. He believes that for every $0.50 increase in the price, 2 fewer hot dogs are sold in an hour. What is the most revenue he can average in an hour?

   A. $100

   B. $107

   C. $114

   D. $121

11. The owner of an office complex wants to fence part of the parking lot adjacent to the building. He has 240 feet of fencing material in storage. If he only uses the fencing material in storage, and does not need to fence the side along the building, what is the maximum area he can enclose?

   A. 6800 square feet

   B. 7000 square feet

   C. 7200 square feet

   D. 7500 square feet

12. Find the maximum area of a rectangle bounded below by the x-axis, on one side by the y-axis, and above by the line $y = -\frac{4}{3}x + 6$. (Refer again to Figure 6-22.)

   A. $\frac{25}{2}$

   B. $\frac{25}{4}$

   C. $\frac{27}{2}$

   D. $\frac{27}{4}$

chapter 7

Polynomial Functions

We now add to our knowledge of functions by studying a major family of functions—polynomial functions. As we did with linear and quadratic functions, we will learn how to look at a polynomial function and have a good idea of what its graph looks like. Many of the functions that you will see in calculus are polynomial functions or are some combination of functions involving polynomials. Not only are polynomial functions worth studying for their own sake, but also polynomials are used to model all sorts of problems in the real world. In fact, graphing calculators have a feature (called *regression*) that helps find a polynomial that models a set of data.

CHAPTER OBJECTIVES

In this chapter, you will

- Recognize the general shape of the graph of a polynomial function from its equation
- Find the *x*-intercepts from the factors of a polynomial function
- Sketch the graph of a polynomial function
- Use polynomial division to find the zeros of a polynomial
- Perform arithmetic with complex numbers
- Find complex zeros for a polynomial function

Introduction to Polynomial Functions and Their Graphs

A polynomial function is a function in the form $f(x) = a_n x^n + a_{n-1} x^{n-1} + \cdots + a_1 x + a_0$, where each a_i is a real number and the powers on x are whole numbers. There is no x under a root sign and no x in a denominator. The number a_i is called a *coefficient*. For example, in the polynomial function $f(x) = -2x^3 + 5x^2 - 4x + 8$, the coefficients are -2, 5, -4, and 8. The *constant* term (the term with no variable) is 8. The powers on x are 3, 2, and 1. The *degree* of the polynomial is the highest power on x. In this example, the degree is 3. Quadratic functions are degree 2. Linear functions of the form $f(x) = mx + b$ (if $m \neq 0$) are degree 1. Constant functions of the form $f(x) = b$ are degree zero (this is because $x^0 = 1$, making $f(x) = bx^0$).

The *leading term* of a polynomial is the term having x to the highest power. Usually, but not always, the leading term is written first. The *leading coefficient* is the coefficient on the leading term. In our example, the leading term is $-2x^3$, and the leading coefficient is -2. The leading term tells us about the *end behavior* of the graph. The "end behavior of the graph" means what the graph is doing for large values of x (large in the positive and the negative directions). For example, we know that both ends of the graph of $y = x^2 + x + 1$ go up because the parabola opens up. Understanding the end behavior of the graph of a function will help to prepare you for a fundamental concept in calculus called a *limit*.

The end behavior of the graph of $f(x) = a_n x^n + a_{n-1} x^{n-1} + \cdots + a_1 x + a_0$ is the same as the end behavior of $y = a_n x^n$; so we begin our study of polynomial functions with the graph of $y = x^n$. The graph of $y = x^n$ (with n at least 2) has one of two basic shapes, the graph of a quadratic function is typical of the graph of $y = x^n$ when n is even, and the graph of the cubic function is typical of the graph of $y = x^n$ when n is odd, see Table 7-1.

To see how the end behavior of the graph of $f(x) = a_n x^n + a_{n-1} x^{n-1} + \cdots + a_1 x + a_0$ is the same as the graph of $y = ax^n$, the graphs of two polynomial functions are shown in Figures 7-1 and 7-2 as well as the graphs of $y = a_n x^n$.

From what we see in the examples above and from what we learned in Chapter 5, we know what the graph of $y = a_n x^n$ looks like. Now, we can determine the end behavior for the graph of *any* polynomial function, (see Table 7-2).

Determining the end behavior for the graph of a polynomial function from its leading term is called the *Leading Coefficient Test*. How can one term in a polynomial function give us this information? For x-values large enough (both large positive numbers and large negative numbers), the other terms do not contribute as much to the size of the y-values.

TABLE 7-1

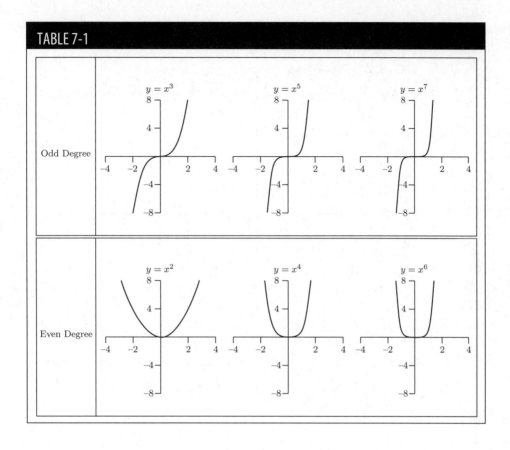

FIGURE 7-1

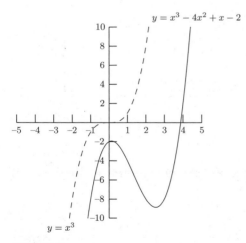

FIGURE 7-2

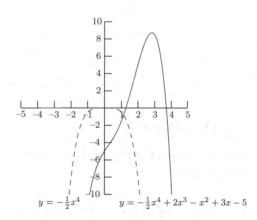

TABLE 7-2

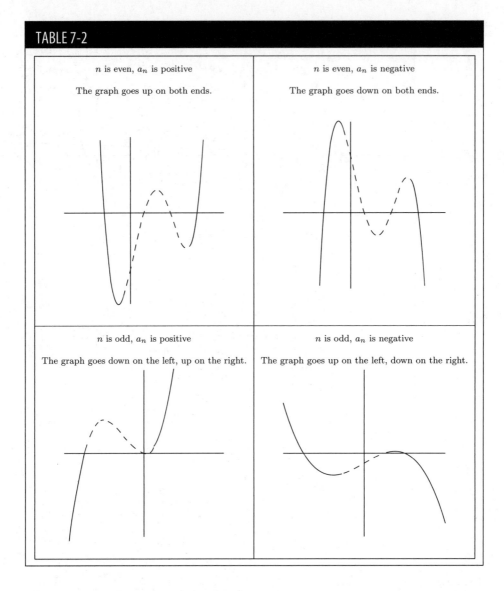

n is even, a_n is positive

The graph goes up on both ends.

n is even, a_n is negative

The graph goes down on both ends.

n is odd, a_n is positive

The graph goes down on the left, up on the right.

n is odd, a_n is negative

The graph goes up on the left, down on the right.

EXAMPLE 7-1

Use the Leading Coefficient Test to determine the end behavior for the graph of the function.

- $f(x) = 4x^5 + 6x^3 - 2x^2 + 8x + 11$

  We only need to look at the leading term, $4x^5$. The degree, 5, is odd, and the leading coefficient, 4, is positive, so the graph goes down on the left and up on the right.

- $P(x) = 5 + 2x - 6x^2$

  The leading term is $-6x^2$. The degree, 2, is even, and the leading coefficient, -6, is negative, so the graph goes down on the left and down on the right.

- $h(x) = -2x^3 + 4x^2 - 7x + 9$

  The leading term is $-2x^3$. The degree, 3, is odd, and the leading coefficient, -2, is negative, so the graph goes up on the left and down on the right.

- $g(x) = x^4 + 4x^3 - 8x^2 + 3x - 5$

  The leading term is x^4. The degree, 4, is even, and the leading coefficient, 1, is positive, so the graph goes up on the left and up on the right.

The Real Zeros of a Polynomial Function

Finding the x-intercepts (if any) for the graph of a polynomial function is very important. The x-intercept of any graph is where the graph intersects (touches or crosses) the x-axis. We found the x-intercepts for some quadratic functions by factoring and setting each factor equal to zero. This is how we will find the x-intercepts for polynomial functions. It is not always easy to do. In fact, some polynomials are so hard to factor that the best we can do is approximate the x-intercepts (using graphing calculators or calculus). This is not the case for the polynomials in this book, however. Every polynomial here can be factored using techniques covered here.

Because an x-intercept for $f(x) = a_n x^n + a_{n-1} x^{n-1} + \cdots + a_1 x + a_0$ is a solution to the equation $0 = a_n x^n + a_{n-1} x^{n-1} + \cdots + a_1 x + a_0$, x-intercepts are also called *zeros* of the polynomial. All of the following statements have the same meaning for a polynomial. Let c be a real number, and let $P(x)$ be a polynomial function.

1. c is an x-intercept for the graph of $P(x)$.

2. c is a zero for $P(x)$. [This is so because $P(c) = 0$.]

3. $x - c$ is a factor of $P(x)$.

EXAMPLE 7-2

- $x - 1$ is a factor means that 1 is an x-intercept and a zero.

- $x + 5$ is a factor means that -5 is an x-intercept and a zero.

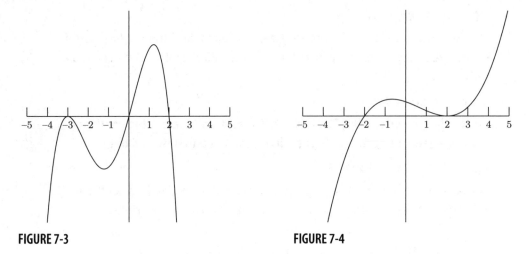

FIGURE 7-3   FIGURE 7-4

- x is a factor means that 0 is an x-intercept and a zero.

- 3 is a zero means that $x - 3$ is a factor and 3 is an x-intercept.

We can find the zeros of a function (or at least the approximate zeros) by looking at its graph.

The x-intercepts for the graph in Figure 7-3 are -3, 0, and 2, which tell us that $x + 3$, x, and $x - 2$ are factors of the polynomial.

The x-intercepts for the graph in Figure 7-4 are 2 and -2, so we know that $x - 2$ and $x + 2$ [which is $x - (-2)$] are factors of the polynomial.

The graph of the polynomial function in Figure 7-5 has x-intercepts of -1, 1, and 2. This means that $x - 1$, $x - 2$, and $x + 1$ [as $x - (-1)$] are factors of the polynomial.

The x-intercepts for the graph in Figure 7-6 are -3, 0, and 2, making $x + 3$, x (as $x - 0$), and $x - 2$ factors of the polynomial.

Now that we know about the end behavior for the graph of a polynomial function and the relationship between x-intercepts and factors, we can look at a polynomial and have a pretty good idea of what its graph looks like. In Example 7-3, we will match polynomial functions to their graphs.

▮ EXAMPLE 7-3

Match the functions with the graphs in Figures 7-3 to 7-6.

- $f(x) = \dfrac{1}{10}x^2(x + 3)(x - 2) = \dfrac{1}{10}x^4 + \dfrac{1}{10}x^3 - \dfrac{3}{5}x^2$

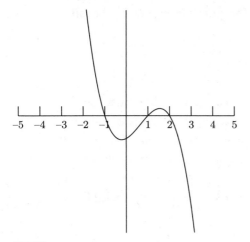

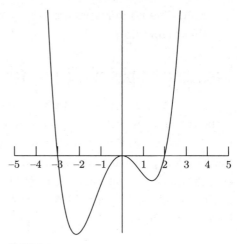

FIGURE 7-5   FIGURE 7-6

Because $f(x)$ is a polynomial whose degree is even and whose leading coefficient is positive, we look for a graph that goes up on the left and up on the right. Because the factors are x^2, $x + 3$, and $x - 2$, we also look for a graph with x-intercepts 0, -3, and 2. The graph in Figure 7-6 satisfies these conditions.

- $g(x) = -\dfrac{1}{2}(x - 1)(x - 2)(x + 1) = -\dfrac{1}{2}x^3 + x^2 + \dfrac{1}{2}x - 1$

Because $g(x)$ is a polynomial whose degree is odd and whose leading coefficient is negative, we look for a graph that goes up on the left and down on the right. The factors are $x - 1$, $x - 2$, and $x + 1$, so we also look for a graph with 1, 2, and -1 as x-intercepts. The graph in Figure 7-5 satisifies these conditions.

- $P(x) = \dfrac{1}{10}(x - 2)^2(x + 2) = \dfrac{1}{10}x^3 - \dfrac{1}{5}x^2 - \dfrac{2}{5}x + \dfrac{4}{5}$

Because $P(x)$ is a polynomial whose degree is odd and whose leading term is positive, we look for a graph that goes down on the left and up on the right. The x-intercepts are 2 and -2. The graph in Figure 7-4 satisfies these conditions.

- $h(x) = -\dfrac{1}{5}x(x + 3)^2(x - 2) = -\dfrac{1}{5}x^4 - \dfrac{4}{5}x^3 + \dfrac{3}{5}x^2 + \dfrac{18}{5}x$

Because $h(x)$ is a polynomial whose degree is even and whose leading term is negative, we look for a graph that goes down on the left and down on the right. The *x*-intercepts are −3, 0, and 2. The graph in Figure 7-3 satisfies these conditions.

Sketching Graphs of Polynomials

To sketch the graph of most polynomial functions accurately, we must use calculus (do not let that scare you—the calculus part is easier than the algebra part!). We can still get a pretty good graph using algebra alone. The general method is to plot *x*-intercepts (if there are any), a point to the left of the smallest *x*-intercept, a point between any two *x*-intercepts, and a point to the right of the largest *x*-intercept. Because the *y*-intercept is easy to find, it would not hurt to plot this, too.

 EXAMPLE 7-4

- $f(x) = -(2x - 1)(x + 2)(x - 3)$

  The *x*-intercepts are −2, 3, and $\frac{1}{2}$ (from $2x - 1 = 0$). In addition to the *x*-intercepts, we plot the points for $x = -2.5$ (to the left of $x = -2$), $x = -1$ (between $x = -2$ and $x = \frac{1}{2}$), $x = 2$ (between $x = \frac{1}{2}$ and $x = 3$), and $x = 3.5$ (to the right of $x = 3$). The points are computed in Table 7-3.

  The reason we used $x = -2.5$ instead of $x = -3$ and $x = 3.5$ instead of $x = 4$ is that their *y*-values were too large for our graph. The graph is given in Figure 7-7.

TABLE 7-3	
x	$f(x)$
−2.5	16.5
−2	0
−1	−12
0	−6
$\frac{1}{2}$	0
2	12
3	0
3.5	−16.5

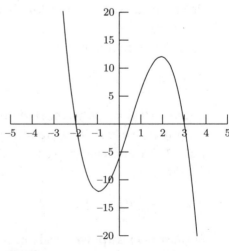

FIGURE 7-7

 **PRACTICE**

Use the Leading Coefficient Test to determine the end behavior for the graph of the function in Problems 1 to 4.

    1. $f(x) = -8x^3 + 4x^2 - 9x + 3$

    2. $f(x) = 4x^5 + 10x^4 - 3x^3 + x^2$

    3. $P(x) = -x^2 + x - 6$

    4. $g(x) = 1 + x + x^2 + x^3$

Identify the *x*-intercepts and factors for the polynomial function whose graphs are given.

    5. See Figure 7-8

    6. See Figure 7-9

    7. See Figure 7-10

Match the polynomial function in Problems 8 to 10 with one of the graphs in Figures 7-8 through 7-10.

    8. $f(x) = -\dfrac{1}{8}(x+4)(x+2)(x-2)(x-4) = -\dfrac{1}{8}x^4 + \dfrac{5}{2}x^2 - 8$

    9. $P(x) = -\dfrac{1}{2}x^2(x+2)(x-1) = -\dfrac{1}{2}x^4 - \dfrac{1}{2}x^3 + x^2$

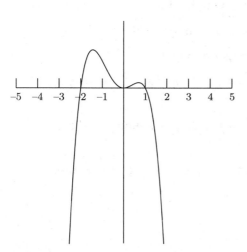

FIGURE 7-8

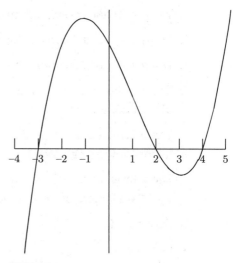

FIGURE 7-9

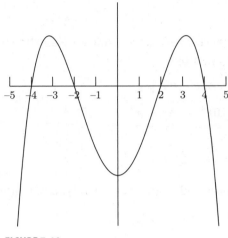

FIGURE 7-10

10. $R(x) = \frac{1}{2}(x+3)(x-2)(x-4) = \frac{1}{2}x^3 - \frac{3}{2}x^2 - 5x + 12$

11. Sketch the graph of $f(x) = \frac{1}{2}x(x-2)(x+2)$

12. Sketch the graph of $h(x) = -\frac{1}{10}(x+4)(x+1)(x-2)(x-3)$

✔ SOLUTIONS _____

1. The graph goes up on the left and down on the right.

2. The graph goes down on the left and up on the right.

3. The graph goes down on the left and down on the right.

4. The graph goes down on the left and up on the right.

5. The x-intercepts are -2, 0, and 1, so $x+2$, x, and $x-1$ are factors of the polynomial.

6. The x-intercepts are -3, 2, and 4, so $x+3$, $x-2$, and $x-4$ are factors of the polynomial.

7. The x-intercepts are -4, -2, 2, and 4, so $x+4$, $x+2$, $x-2$, and $x-4$ are factors of the polynomial.

8. Figure 7-10

9. Figure 7-8

10. Figure 7-9

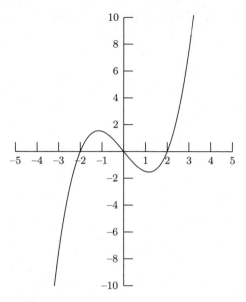

FIGURE 7-11   **FIGURE 7-12**

11. **See Figure 7-11**

12. **See Figure 7-12**

Polynomial Division

Polynomials can be divided in much the same way as whole numbers. When we take the quotient of two whole numbers (where the divisor is not zero), we get a quotient and a remainder. The same happens when we take the quotient of two polynomials. Polynomial division is useful when factoring polynomials.

Polynomial division problems usually come in one of the two forms.

$$\frac{\text{dividend polynomial}}{\text{divisor polynomial}} \quad \text{or} \quad \text{dividend polynomial} \div \text{divisor polynomial}$$

According to the division algorithm for polynomials, for any polynomials $f(x)$ and $g(x)$ [with $g(x)$ not the zero function]

$$\frac{f(x)}{g(x)} = q(x) + \frac{r(x)}{g(x)}$$

where $q(x)$ is the quotient (which might be zero) and $r(x)$ is the remainder, which has degree *strictly* less than the degree of $g(x)$. Multiplying by $g(x)$ to clear the fraction, we also get $f(x) = g(x)q(x) + r(x)$. First we perform polynomial division using long division.

$$
g(x) \overline{\smash{\big)}\, f(x)} \quad \genfrac{}{}{0pt}{}{q(x)}{} \atop r(x)
$$

 EXAMPLE 7-5

Find the quotient and remainder using long division.

• $$\dfrac{4x^2 + 3x - 5}{x + 2}$$

$$
x + 2 \,\overline{\smash{\big)}\, 4x^2 + 3x - 5}
$$

We begin by dividing the leading term of the dividend by the leading term of the divisor. For the first step in this example, we will divide $4x^2$ by x. You might see right away that $4x^2 \div x$ is $4x$. If not, write $4x^2 \div x$ as a fraction then reduce: $\dfrac{4x^2}{x} = 4x$. This is the first term of the quotient.

$$
\begin{array}{r}
4x \phantom{{}+3x-5} \\
x + 2 \,\overline{\smash{\big)}\, 4x^2 + 3x - 5}
\end{array}
$$

Multiply $4x$ by the divisor: $4x(x + 2) = 4x^2 + 8x$. Subtract this from the first two terms of the dividend. Be careful to subtract all of $4x^2 + 8x$, not just $4x^2$.

$$
\begin{array}{r}
4x \phantom{{}+3x-5} \\
x + 2 \,\overline{\smash{\big)}\, 4x^2 + 3x - 5} \\
-(4x^2 + 8x) \phantom{{}-5} \\
\hline
-5x \phantom{{}-5}
\end{array}
$$

Bring down the next term.

$$
\begin{array}{r}
4x \phantom{{}+3x-5} \\
x + 2 \,\overline{\smash{\big)}\, 4x^2 + 3x - 5} \\
-(4x^2 + 8x) \phantom{{}-5} \\
\hline
-5x - 5
\end{array}
$$

Start the process again with $-5x \div x = -5$. The next term in the quotient is -5. Multiply $x + 2$ by -5: $-5(x + 2) = -5x - 10$. Subtract this from $-5x - 5$.

$$
\begin{array}{r}
4x - 5 \\
x + 2 \overline{\smash{\big)}\ 4x^2 + 3x - 5} \\
\underline{-(4x^2 + 8x)} \\
-5x - 5 \\
\underline{-(-5x - 10)} \\
5
\end{array}
$$

We are finished because $5 \div x = \frac{5}{x}$ cannot be a term in a polynomial. The remainder is 5 and the quotient is $4x - 5$.

- $x^2 + 2x - 3 \overline{\smash{\big)}\ 3x^4 + 5x^3 - 4x^2 + 7x - 1}$

Divide $3x^4$ by x^2 to get the first term of the quotient: $\frac{3x^4}{x^2} = 3x^2$. Multiply $x^2 + 2x - 3$ by $3x^2$: $3x^2(x^2 + 2x - 3) = 3x^4 + 6x^3 - 9x^2$. Subtract this from the first three terms in the dividend.

$$
\begin{array}{r}
3x^2 \\
x^2 + 2x - 3 \overline{\smash{\big)}\ 3x^4 + 5x^3 - 4x^2 + 7x - 1} \\
\underline{-(3x^4 + 6x^3 - 9x^2)} \\
-x^3 + 5x^2
\end{array}
$$

Divide $-x^3$ by x^2 to get the second term in the quotient: $\frac{-x^3}{x^2} = -x$. Multiply $x^2 + 2x - 3$ by $-x$: $-x(x^2 + 2x - 3) = -x^3 - 2x^2 + 3x$. Subtract this from $-x^3 + 5x^2 + 7x$.

$$
\begin{array}{r}
3x^2 - x \\
x^2 + 2x - 3 \overline{\smash{\big)}\ 3x^4 + 5x^3 - 4x^2 + 7x - 1} \\
\underline{-(3x^4 + 6x^3 - 9x^2)} \\
-x^3 + 5x^2 + 7x \\
\underline{-(-x^3 - 2x^2 + 3x)} \\
7x^2 + 4x
\end{array}
$$

Divide $7x^2$ by x^2 to get the third term in the quotient: $\frac{7x^2}{x^2} = 7$. Multiply $x^2 + 2x - 3$ by 7: $7(x^2 + 2x - 3) = 7x^2 + 14x - 21$. Subtract this from $7x^2 + 4x - 1$.

$$
\begin{array}{r}
3x^2 - \quad x + 7 \\
x^2 + 2x - 3 \overline{\smash{\big)}\ 3x^4 + 5x^3 - 4x^2 + 7x - 1} \\
\underline{-(3x^4 + 6x^3 - 9x^2)} \\
-x^3 + 5x^2 + 7x \\
\underline{-(-x^3 - 2x^2 + 3x)} \\
7x^2 + 4x - 1 \\
\underline{-(7x^2 + 14x - 21)} \\
-10x + 20
\end{array}
$$

Because $\frac{-10x}{x^2}$ cannot be a term in a polynomial, we are done. The quotient is $3x^2 - x + 7$, and the remainder is $-10x + 20$.

It is important that every power of x, from the highest power to the constant term, be represented in the polynomial. Although it is possible to perform long division without all powers represented, it is very easy to make an error. Also, it is not possible to perform synthetic division (later in this chapter) without a coefficient for *every* term. If a power of x is not written, we need to rewrite the polynomial (either the dividend, divisor, or both) using a coefficient of zero on the missing powers. For example, we would write $x^3 - 1$ as $x^3 + 0x^2 + 0x - 1$.

■ EXAMPLE 7-6

• $(x^3 - 8) \div (x + 1)$

Rewrite as $(x^3 + 0x^2 + 0x - 8) \div (x + 1)$

$$
\begin{array}{r}
x^2 - \ x + 1 \\
x + 1 \overline{\smash{\big)}\ x^3 + 0x^2 + 0x - 8} \\
\underline{-(x^3 + x^2)} \\
-x^2 + 0x \\
\underline{-(-x^2 - x)} \\
x - 8 \\
\underline{-(x + 1)} \\
-9
\end{array}
$$

The quotient is $x^2 - x - 1$, and the remainder is -9.

Polynomial division is a little trickier when the leading coefficient of the divisor is not 1. The terms of the quotient are harder to find and are likely to be fractions.

EXAMPLE 7-7

Find the quotient and remainder using long division.

- $$\frac{x^2 - x + 2}{2x - 1}$$

Find the first term in the quotient by dividing the first term of the dividend by the first term in the divisor: $\frac{x^2}{2x} = \frac{x}{2} = \frac{1}{2}x$.

$$
\begin{array}{r}
\frac{1}{2}x \\
2x - 1 \overline{\big)\ x^2 - x + 2} \\
\underline{-(x^2 - \frac{1}{2}x)} \\
-\frac{1}{2}x + 2
\end{array}
$$

The second term in the quotient is

$$\frac{-\frac{1}{2}x}{2x} = \frac{-\frac{1}{2}}{2} = -\frac{1}{2} \div 2 = -\frac{1}{2} \cdot \frac{1}{2} = -\frac{1}{4}.$$

Multiply $2x - 1$ by $-\frac{1}{4}$: $-\frac{1}{4}(2x - 1) = -\frac{1}{2}x + \frac{1}{4}$.

$$
\begin{array}{r}
\frac{1}{2}x - \frac{1}{4} \\
2x - 1 \overline{\big)\ x^2 - x + 2} \\
\underline{-(x^2 - \frac{1}{2}x)} \\
-\frac{1}{2}x + 2 \\
\underline{-(-\frac{1}{2}x + \frac{1}{4})} \\
\frac{7}{4}
\end{array}
$$

The quotient is $\frac{1}{2}x - \frac{1}{4}$, and the remainder is $\frac{7}{4}$.

- $(4x^2 + 5x - 6) \div \left(\frac{2}{3}x - 1\right)$

Find the first term in the quotient by dividing the leading term in the quotient by the first term in the divisor.

$$\frac{4x^2}{\frac{2}{3}x} = \frac{4x}{\frac{2}{3}} = 4x \div \frac{2}{3} = 4x \cdot \frac{3}{2} = 6x$$

$$6x\left(\frac{2}{3}x - 1\right) = 4x^2 - 6x$$

$$
\begin{array}{r}
6x \\
\frac{2}{3}x - 1 \overline{\smash{\big)}\ 4x^2 + 5x - 6} \\
\underline{-(4x^2 - 6x)} \\
11x - 6
\end{array}
$$

$$
\frac{11x}{\frac{2}{3}x} = \frac{11}{\frac{2}{3}} = 11 \div \frac{2}{3} = 11 \cdot \frac{3}{2} = \frac{33}{2}
$$

$$
\frac{33}{2}\left(\frac{2}{3}x - 1\right) = 11x - \frac{33}{2}
$$

$$
\begin{array}{r}
6x + \frac{33}{2} \\
\frac{2}{3}x - 1 \overline{\smash{\big)}\ 4x^2 + 5x - 6} \\
\underline{-(4x^2 - 6x)} \\
11x - 6 \\
\underline{-(11x - \frac{33}{2})} \\
\frac{21}{2}
\end{array}
$$

The quotient is $6x + \frac{33}{2}$, and the remainder is $\frac{21}{2}$.

Synthetic division of polynomials is much easier than long division. It only works when the divisor is of a certain form. Here, we use synthetic division when the divisor is of the form "$x -$ number" or "$x +$ number."

For a problem of the form

$$
\frac{a_n x^n + a_{n-1} x^{n-1} + \cdots + a_1 x + a_0}{x - c}
$$

or $(a_n x^n + a_{n-1} x^{n-1} + \cdots + a_1 x + a_0) \div (x - c),$

write

$$
c \,\big|\ a_n \quad a_{n-1} \quad \cdots \quad a_1 \quad a_0
$$

Every power of x must be represented.

In synthetic division, the tedious work in long division is reduced to a few steps.

 **EXAMPLE 7-8**

Find the quotient and remainder using synthetic division.

- $$\frac{4x^3 - 5x^2 + x - 8}{x - 2}$$

$$2 \,\rvert\, 4 \quad -5 \quad 1 \quad -8$$

Bring down the first coefficient.

$$2 \,\rvert\, 4 \quad -5 \quad 1 \quad -8$$
$$\overline{ 4}$$

Multiply this coefficient by 2 (which is c) and put the product under -5, the next coefficient.

$$2 \,\rvert\, 4 \quad -5 \quad 1 \quad -8$$
$$ 8$$
$$\overline{ 4}$$

Add -5 and 8. Put the sum under 8.

$$2 \,\rvert\, 4 \quad -5 \quad 1 \quad -8$$
$$ 8$$
$$\overline{ 4 \quad 3}$$

Multiply 3 by 2 and put the product under 1, the next coefficient.

$$2 \,\rvert\, 4 \quad -5 \quad 1 \quad -8$$
$$ 8 \quad 6$$
$$\overline{ 4 \quad 3}$$

Add 1 and 6. Put the sum under 6.

$$2 \,\rvert\, 4 \quad -5 \quad 1 \quad -8$$
$$ 8 \quad 6$$
$$\overline{ 4 \quad 3 \quad 7}$$

Multiply 7 by 2. Put the product under -8, the last coefficient.

$$2 \,\rvert\, 4 \quad -5 \quad 1 \quad -8$$
$$ 8 \quad 6 \quad 14$$
$$\overline{ 4 \quad 3 \quad 7}$$

Add -8 and 14. Put the sum under 14. This is the last step.

$$
\begin{array}{r|rrrr}
2 & 4 & -5 & 1 & -8 \\
  &   & 8 & 6 & 14 \\
\hline
  & 4 & 3 & 7 & 6 \\
\end{array}
$$

The numbers on the last row are the coefficients of the quotient and the remainder. The remainder is a constant (which is a term of degree zero), and the degree of the quotient is exactly one less degree than the degree of the dividend. In this example, the degree of the dividend is 3, so the degree of the quotient is 2. The last number on the bottom row is the remainder. The numbers before it are the coefficients of the quotient, in order from the highest degree to the lowest. The remainder in this example is 6. The coefficients of the quotient are 4, 3, and 7. The quotient is $4x^2 + 3x + 7$.

- $(3x^4 - x^2 + 2x + 9) \div (x + 5)$

  Because $x + 5 = x - (-5)$, $c = -5$.

$$
\begin{array}{r|rrrrr}
-5 & 3 & 0 & -1 & 2 & 9
\end{array}
$$

Bring down 3, the first coefficient. Multiply it by -5. Put $3(-5) = -15$ under 0.

$$
\begin{array}{r|rrrrr}
-5 & 3 & 0 & -1 & 2 & 9 \\
   &   & -15 & & & \\
\hline
   & 3 & & & & \\
\end{array}
$$

Add $0 + (-15) = -15$. Multiply -15 by -5 and put $(-15)(-5) = 75$ under -1.

$$
\begin{array}{r|rrrrr}
-5 & 3 & 0 & -1 & 2 & 9 \\
   &   & -15 & 75 & & \\
\hline
   & 3 & -15 & & & \\
\end{array}
$$

Add -1 and 75. Multiply $-1 + 75 = 74$ by -5 and put $(74)(-5) = -370$ under 2.

$$
\begin{array}{r|rrrrr}
-5 & 3 & 0 & -1 & 2 & 9 \\
   &   & -15 & 75 & -370 & \\
\hline
   & 3 & -15 & 74 & & \\
\end{array}
$$

Add 2 to -370. Multiply $2 + (-370) = -368$ by -5 and put $(-368)(-5) = 1840$ under 9.

$$
\begin{array}{r|rrrrr}
-5 & 3 & 0 & -1 & 2 & 9 \\
   &   & -15 & 75 & -370 & 1840 \\
\hline
   & 3 & -15 & 74 & -368 \\
\end{array}
$$

Add 9 to 1840. Put $9 + 1840 = 1849$ under 1840.

$$
\begin{array}{r|rrrrr}
-5 & 3 & 0 & -1 & 2 & 9 \\
   &   & -15 & 75 & -370 & 1840 \\
\hline
   & 3 & -15 & 74 & -368 & 1849 \\
\end{array}
$$

The dividend has degree 4, so the quotient has degree 3. The quotient is $3x^3 - 15x^2 + 74x - 368$, and the remainder is 1849.

When dividing a polynomial $f(x)$ by $x - c$, the remainder tells us two things. If we get a remainder of zero, then both the divisor, $(x - c)$, and quotient are factors of $f(x)$. Another fact we get from the remainder is that $f(c) = $ remainder.

$$f(x) = (x - c)q(x) + \text{remainder}$$

$$f(c) = (c - c)q(c) + \text{remainder} \qquad \text{Evaluate } f(x) \text{ at } x = c.$$

$$f(c) = 0q(c) + \text{remainder}$$

$$f(c) = \text{remainder}$$

The fact that $f(c)$ is the remainder, is called the *Remainder Theorem*. It is useful when trying to evaluate complicated polynomials. We can also use this fact to check our work with synthetic division and long division (providing the divisor is $x - c$).

- $(x^3 - 6x^2 + 4x - 5) \div (x - 3)$

  By the Remainder Theorem, we should get the remainder to be $3^3 - 6(3^2) + 4(3) - 5 = -20$.

$$
\begin{array}{r|rrrr}
3 & 1 & -6 & 4 & -5 \\
  &   & 3 & -9 & -15 \\
\hline
  & 1 & -3 & -5 & -20 \\
\end{array}
$$

EXAMPLE 7-9

Use synthetic division and the Remainder Theorem to evaluate $f(c)$.

- $f(x) = 14x^3 - 16x^2 + 10x + 8; c = 1$.

  We first perform synthetic division with $x - c = x - 1$.

$$
\begin{array}{r|rrrr}
1 & 14 & -16 & 10 & 8 \\
  &   & 14 & -2 & 8 \\
\hline
  & 14 & -2 & 8 & 16 \\
\end{array}
$$

The remainder is 16, so $f(1) = 16$.

Now we use synthetic division and the Remainder Theorem to factor polynomials. Suppose $x = c$ is a zero for a polynomial $f(x)$. Let us see what happens when we divide $f(x)$ by $x - c$.

$$f(x) = (x - c)q(x) + r(x)$$

Because $x = c$ is a zero, the remainder is zero, so $f(x) = (x - c)q(x) + 0$, which means $f(x) = (x - c)q(x)$. The next step in completely factoring $f(x)$ is factoring $q(x)$.

EXAMPLE 7-10

Completely factor the polynomials.

- $f(x) = x^3 - 4x^2 - 7x + 10, c = 1$ is a zero.

  We use the fact that $c = 1$ is a zero to get started. We use synthetic division to divide $f(x)$ by $x - 1$.

$$
\begin{array}{r|rrrr}
1 & 1 & -4 & -7 & 10 \\
  &   & 1 & -3 & -10 \\
\hline
  & 1 & -3 & -10 & 0 \\
\end{array}
$$

The quotient is $x^2 - 3x - 10$. We now have $f(x)$ partially factored.

$$f(x) = x^3 - 4x^2 - 7x + 10$$

$$= (x - 1)(x^2 - 3x - 10)$$

Because the quotient is quadratic, we can factor it directly or by using the quadratic formula.

$$x^2 - 3x - 10 = (x - 5)(x + 2)$$

Now we have the complete factorization of $f(x)$:

$$f(x) = x^3 - 4x^2 - 7x + 10$$
$$= (x - 1)(x - 5)(x + 2)$$

- $R(x) = x^3 - 2x + 1, c = 1$ is a zero.

$$
\begin{array}{r|rrrr}
1 & 1 & 0 & -2 & 1 \\
  &   & 1 & 1 & -1 \\
\hline
  & 1 & 1 & -1 & 0 \\
\end{array}
$$

$$R(x) = x^3 - 2x + 1 = (x - 1)(x^2 + x - 1)$$

We must use the quadratic formula to find the two zeros of $x^2 + x - 1$.

$$x = \frac{-1 \pm \sqrt{1^2 - 4(1)(-1)}}{2(1)}$$

$$\frac{-1 \pm \sqrt{5}}{2} = \frac{-1 + \sqrt{5}}{2}, \frac{-1 - \sqrt{5}}{2}$$

The factors for these zeros are $x - \frac{-1+\sqrt{5}}{2}$ and $x - \frac{-1-\sqrt{5}}{2}$.

$$R(x) = (x - 1)\left(x - \frac{-1 + \sqrt{5}}{2}\right)\left(x - \frac{-1 - \sqrt{5}}{2}\right)$$

PRACTICE

For Problems 1 to 4, use long division to find the quotient and remainder. For Problems 5 and 6, use synthetic division.

1. $(6x^3 - 2x^2 + 5x - 1) \div (x^2 + 3x + 2)$

2. $(x^3 - x^2 + 2x + 5) \div (3x - 4)$

3. $\dfrac{3x^3 - x^2 + 4x + 2}{-\frac{1}{2}x^2 + 1}$

4. $\dfrac{x^3 - 1}{x - 1}$

5. $\dfrac{x^3 + 2x^2 + x - 8}{x + 3}$

6. $(x^3 + 8) \div (x + 2)$

7. Use synthetic division and the Remainder Theorem to evaluate $f(c)$.

$$f(x) = 6x^4 - 8x^3 + x^2 + 2x - 5; c = -2$$

8. Completely factor the polynomial. $f(x) = x^3 + 2x^2 - x - 2; c = 1$ is a zero.

9. Completely factor the polynomial. $P(x) = x^3 - 5x^2 + 5x + 3; c = 3$ is a zero.

SOLUTIONS

1.
$$
\begin{array}{r}
6x - 20 \\
x^2 + 3x + 2 \overline{\smash{\big)}\ 6x^3 - 2x^2 + 5x - 1} \\
-(6x^3 + 18x^2 + 12x) \\
\hline
-20x^2 - 7x - 1 \\
-(-20x^2 - 60x - 40) \\
\hline
53x + 39
\end{array}
$$

The quotient is $6x - 20$, and the remainder is $5x + 39$.

2.
$$
\begin{array}{r}
\frac{1}{3}x^2 + \frac{1}{9}x \\
3x - 4 \overline{\smash{\big)}\ x^3 - x^2 + 2x + 5} \\
-(x^3 - \frac{4}{3}x^2) \\
\hline
\frac{1}{3}x^2 + 2x \\
-(\frac{1}{3}x^2 - \frac{4}{9}x) \\
\hline
\frac{22}{9}x + 5
\end{array}
$$

$$\frac{\frac{22}{9}x}{3x} = \frac{\frac{22}{9}}{3} = \frac{22}{9} \cdot \frac{1}{3} = \frac{22}{27}$$

$$\frac{22}{27}(3x - 4) = \frac{22}{9}x - \frac{88}{27}$$

$$\frac{1}{3}x^2 + \frac{1}{9}x + \frac{22}{27}$$

$$3x - 4 \overline{) \quad x^3 - x^2 + 2x + 5 }$$

$$\underline{-(x^3 - \tfrac{4}{3}x^2)}$$

$$\tfrac{1}{3}x^2 + 2x$$

$$\underline{-(\tfrac{1}{3}x^2 - \tfrac{4}{9}x)}$$

$$\tfrac{22}{9}x + 5$$

$$\underline{-(\tfrac{22}{9}x - \tfrac{88}{27})}$$

$$\tfrac{223}{27}$$

The quotient is $\frac{1}{3}x^2 + \frac{1}{9}x + \frac{22}{27}$, and the remainder is $\frac{223}{27}$.

3.

$$\frac{3x^3}{-\frac{1}{2}x^2} = \frac{3x}{-\frac{1}{2}} = 3x \div -\frac{1}{2} = 3x \cdot (-2) = -6x$$

$$-6x\left(-\frac{1}{2}x^2 + 0x + 1\right) = 3x^3 + 0x^2 - 6x$$

$$-6x$$

$$-\tfrac{1}{2}x^2 + 0x + 1 \overline{) \quad 3x^3 - x^2 + 4x + 2 }$$

$$\underline{-(3x^3 - 0x^2 - 6x)}$$

$$-x^2 + 10x + 2$$

$$\frac{-x^2}{-\frac{1}{2}x^2} = \frac{1}{\frac{1}{2}} = 1 \div \frac{1}{2} = 1 \cdot 2 = 2$$

$$2\left(-\frac{1}{2}x^2 + 0x + 1\right) = -x^2 + 0x + 2$$

$$-6x + 2$$

$$-\tfrac{1}{2}x^2 + 0x + 1 \overline{) \quad 3x^3 - x^2 + 4x + 2 }$$

$$\underline{-(3x^3 - 0x^2 - 6x)}$$

$$-x^2 + 10x + 2$$

$$\underline{-(-x^2 + 0x + 2)}$$

$$10x + 0$$

The quotient is $-6x + 2$, and the remainder is $10x$.

$$
\begin{array}{r}
x^2 + x + 1 \\
x - 1 \overline{\big)\ x^3 + 0x^2 + 0x - 1} \\
-(x^3 - x^2) \\
\hline
x^2 + 0x \\
-(x^2 - x) \\
\hline
x - 1 \\
-(x - 1) \\
\hline
0
\end{array}
$$

4.

The quotient is $x^2 + x + 1$, and the remainder is 0.

5.
$$
-3 \,\overline{\big|}
\begin{array}{rrrr}
1 & 2 & 1 & -8 \\
 & -3 & 3 & -12 \\
\hline
1 & -1 & 4 & -20
\end{array}
$$

The quotient is $x^2 - x + 4$, and the remainder is -20.

6.
$$
-2 \,\overline{\big|}
\begin{array}{rrrr}
1 & 0 & 0 & 8 \\
 & -2 & 4 & -8 \\
\hline
1 & -2 & 4 & 0
\end{array}
$$

The quotient is $x^2 - 2x + 4$, and the remainder is 0.

7.
$$
-2 \,\overline{\big|}
\begin{array}{rrrrr}
6 & -8 & 1 & 2 & -5 \\
 & -12 & 40 & -82 & 160 \\
\hline
6 & -20 & 41 & -80 & 155
\end{array}
$$

The remainder is 155, so $f(-2) = 155$.

8.
$$
1 \,\overline{\big|}
\begin{array}{rrrr}
1 & 2 & -1 & -2 \\
 & 1 & 3 & 2 \\
\hline
1 & 3 & 2 & 0
\end{array}
$$

$$f(x) = (x - 1)(x^2 + 3x + 2)$$
$$= (x - 1)(x + 1)(x + 2)$$

9.
$$
3 \,\overline{\big|}
\begin{array}{rrrr}
1 & -5 & 5 & 3 \\
 & 3 & -6 & -3 \\
\hline
1 & -2 & -1 & 0
\end{array}
$$

$$P(x) = (x - 3)(x^2 - 2x - 1)$$

In order to factor $x^2 - 2x - 1$, we must first find its zeros.

$$x = \frac{-(-2) \pm \sqrt{(-2)^2 - 4(1)(-1)}}{2(1)}$$

$$= \frac{2 \pm \sqrt{8}}{2} = \frac{2 \pm 2\sqrt{2}}{2}$$

$$= \frac{2(1 \pm \sqrt{2})}{2} = 1 \pm \sqrt{2}$$

$$= 1 + \sqrt{2}, 1 - \sqrt{2}$$

Because $x = 1 + \sqrt{2}$ is a zero, $x - (1 + \sqrt{2}) = x - 1 - \sqrt{2}$ is a factor. Because $x = 1 - \sqrt{2}$ is a zero, $x - (1 - \sqrt{2}) = x - 1 + \sqrt{2}$ is a factor.

$$P(x) = (x - 3)(x - 1 - \sqrt{2})(x - 1 + \sqrt{2})$$

The Rational Zero Theorem

In the above examples and Practice Problems, a zero was given to help us get started with factoring. Usually, we have to find a starting point ourselves. The *Rational Zero Theorem* gives us a place to start. The Rational Zero Theorem says that if a polynomial function $f(x)$, with integer coefficients, has a rational number p/q as a zero, then p is a divisor of the constant term and q is a divisor of the leading coefficient. Not all polynomials have rational zeros, but most of those in precalculus courses do.

We use the Rational Zero Theorem to create a list of candidates for zeros. These candidates are rational numbers whose numerators divide the polynomial's constant term and whose numerators divide its leading coefficient. Once we have this list, we will try each number in the list to see which, if any, are zeros. Once we have found a zero, we can begin to factor the polynomial.

EXAMPLE 7-11

List the possible rational zeros.

- $f(x) = 4x^3 + 6x^2 - 2x + 9$

The numerators in our list are the divisors of 9: 1, 3, and 9 as well as their negatives, -1, -3, and -9. The denominators are the divisors of 4: 1, 2, and 4. The list of possible rational zeros is—

$$\frac{1}{1}, \frac{3}{1}, \frac{9}{1}, -\frac{1}{1}, -\frac{3}{1}, -\frac{9}{1}, \frac{1}{2}, \frac{3}{2}, \frac{9}{2}, -\frac{1}{2}, -\frac{3}{2}, -\frac{9}{2}, \frac{1}{4}, \frac{3}{4}, \frac{9}{4},$$

$$-\frac{1}{4}, -\frac{3}{4}, \text{ and } -\frac{9}{4}$$

This list could be written with a little less effort as $\pm 1, \pm 3, \pm 9,$ $\pm\frac{1}{2}, \pm\frac{3}{2}, \pm\frac{9}{2}, \pm\frac{1}{4}, \pm\frac{3}{4}, \pm\frac{9}{4}$.

We only need to list the numerators with negative numbers and not the denominators. The reason is that no new numbers are added to the list; only duplicates of numbers are there. For example, $\frac{-1}{2}$ and $\frac{1}{-2}$ are the same number.

- $g(x) = 6x^4 - 5x^3 + 2x - 8$

The possible numerators are the divisors of 8: ± 1, ± 2, ± 4, and ± 8. The possible denominators are the divisors of 6: 1, 2, 3, and 6. The list of possible rational zeros is—

$$\pm 1, \pm 2, \pm 4, \pm 8, \pm\frac{1}{2}, \pm\frac{2}{2}, \pm\frac{4}{2}, \pm\frac{8}{2}, \pm\frac{1}{3}, \pm\frac{2}{3}, \pm\frac{4}{3}, \pm\frac{8}{3}, \pm\frac{1}{6},$$

$$\pm\frac{2}{6}, \pm\frac{4}{6}, \pm\frac{8}{6}$$

There are several duplicates on this list. There are duplicates when the constant term and leading coefficient have common factors. The duplicates do not really hurt anything, but they could waste time when checking the list for zeros.

Now that we have a starting place, we can factor many polynomials. Here is the strategy. First we will see if the polynomial can be factored directly. If not, we need to list the possible rational zeros. Then we will try the numbers in this list, one at a time, until we find a zero. Once we have found a zero, we will use polynomial division (long division or synthetic division) to find the quotient. Next, we will factor the quotient. If the quotient is a quadratic factor, we will either factor it directly or use the quadratic formula to find its zeros. If the quotient is a polynomial of degree 3 or higher, we will need to start over to factor the quotient. Eventually, we will have a quotient that is quadratic.

EXAMPLE 7-12

Completely factor each polynomial.

- $f(x) = 3x^4 - 2x^3 - 7x^2 - 2x$

  First we factor x from each term: $f(x) = x(3x^3 - 2x^2 - 7x - 2)$. The possible rational zeros for $3x^3 - 2x^2 - 7x - 2$ are $\pm 1, \ \pm 2, \ \pm\frac{1}{3}, \ \pm\frac{2}{3}$.

  $$3(1)^3 - 2(1)^2 - 7(1) - 2 \neq 0$$

  $$3(-1)^3 - 2(-1)^2 - 7(-1) - 2 = 0$$

  We now use synthetic division to find the quotient for $(3x^3 - 2x^2 - 7x - 2) \div (x + 1)$.

  $$
  \begin{array}{r|rrrr}
  -1 & 3 & -2 & -7 & -2 \\
     &   & -3 & 5 & 2 \\
  \hline
     & 3 & -5 & -2 & 0
  \end{array}
  $$

  The quotient is $3x^2 - 5x - 2$ which factors as $(3x + 1)(x - 2)$.

  $$
  \begin{aligned}
  f(x) &= 3x^4 - 2x^3 - 7x^2 - 2x \\
       &= x(3x^3 - 2x^2 - 7x - 2) \\
       &= x(x + 1)(3x^2 - 5x - 2) \\
       &= x(x + 1)(3x + 1)(x - 2)
  \end{aligned}
  $$

- $h(x) = 3x^3 + 4x^2 - 18x + 5$

  The possible rational zeros are $\pm 1, \ \pm 5, \ \pm\frac{1}{3},$ and $\pm\frac{5}{3}$.

  $$h(1) = 3(1^3) + 4(1^2) - 18(1) + 5 \neq 0$$

  $$h(-1) = 3(-1)^3 + 4(-1)^2 - 18(-1) + 5 \neq 0$$

  $$h(5) = 3(5^3) + 4(5^2) - 18(5) + 5 \neq 0$$

Continuing in this way, we see that $h(-5) \neq 0$, $h(\frac{1}{3}) \neq 0$, $h(-\frac{1}{3}) \neq 0$, and $h(\frac{5}{3}) = 0$.

$$
\begin{array}{r|rrrr}
\frac{5}{3} & 3 & 4 & -18 & 5 \\
 & & 5 & 15 & -5 \\
\hline
 & 3 & 9 & -3 & 0
\end{array}
$$

$h(x) = \left(x - \dfrac{5}{3}\right)(3x^2 + 9x - 3)$ Factor 3 from the second factor.

$\quad = \left(x - \dfrac{5}{3}\right)(3)(x^2 + 3x - 1)$ Move the 3 to the first factor.

$\quad = \left[3\left(x - \dfrac{5}{3}\right)\right](x^2 + 3x - 1)$ Distribute 3.

$\quad = (3x - 5)(x^2 + 3x - 1)$

We find the zeros of $x^2 + 3x - 1$ using the quadratic formula.

$$x = \frac{-3 \pm \sqrt{3^2 - 4(1)(-1)}}{2(1)}$$

$$= \frac{-3 \pm \sqrt{13}}{2} = \frac{-3 + \sqrt{13}}{2}, \; \frac{-3 - \sqrt{13}}{2}$$

$$h(x) = (3x - 5)\left(x - \frac{-3 + \sqrt{13}}{2}\right)\left(x - \frac{-3 - \sqrt{13}}{2}\right)$$

Still Struggling

The Rational Zero Thereom only lists rational numbers that might be zeros for a polynomial having integer coefficients. Irrational zeros are not in this list, so you cannot find all the zeros simply by checking all of the numbers in this list.

Two Helpful Theorems

There are a couple of algebra facts that can help us to eliminate some of the possible rational zeros. The first we will learn is *Descartes' Rule of Signs*. The second is the *Upper and Lower Bounds Theorem*. Descartes' Rule of Signs counts the number of positive zeros and negative zeros. For instance, according to the rule, $f(x) = x^3 + x^2 + 4x + 6$ has no positive zeros at all. This shrinks the list of possible rational zeros from $\pm1,\ \pm2,\ \pm3,$ and ±6 to $-1, -2, -3,$ and -6. Another advantage of the sign test is that if we know that there are two positive zeros and we have found one of them, then we *know* that there is exactly one more.

The Upper and Lower Bounds Theorem gives us an idea of how large (in both the positive and negative directions) the zeros can be. For example, we can use the Upper and Lower Bounds Theorem to show that all of the zeros for $f(x) = 5x^3 + 20x^2 - 9x - 36$ are between -5 and 5. This shrinks the list of possible rational zeros from $\pm1,\ \pm2,\ \pm3,\ \pm4,\ \pm6,\ \pm9,\ \pm12,\ \pm18,\ \pm36,$ $\pm\frac{1}{5},\ \pm\frac{2}{5},\ \pm\frac{3}{5},\ \pm\frac{4}{5},\ \pm\frac{6}{5},\ \pm\frac{9}{5},\ \pm\frac{12}{5},\ \pm\frac{18}{5},$ and $\pm\frac{36}{5}$ to $\pm1,\ \pm2,\ \pm3,\ \pm4,\ \pm\frac{1}{5},$ $\pm\frac{2}{5},\ \pm\frac{3}{5},\ \pm\frac{4}{5},\ \pm\frac{6}{5},\ \pm\frac{9}{5},\ \pm\frac{12}{5},$ and $\pm\frac{18}{5}$.

Descartes' Rule of Signs

Let P be a polynomial function with real coefficients.

- Let m be the number of sign changes in the coefficients of $P(x)$. The number of positive zeros is either m or m less an even whole number.

- Let n be the number of sign changes in the coefficients of $P(-x)$. The number of negative zeros is either n or n less an even whole number.

Ignore any zero coefficient when counting sign changes.

Descartes' Rule of Signs counts the number of positive zeros and the number of negative zeros by counting sign changes. The maximum number of positive zeros for a polynomial function is the number of sign changes in $f(x) = a_n x^n + a_{n-1}x^{n-1} + \cdots + a_1 x + a_0$. The possible number of positive zeros is the number of sign changes minus an even whole number. For example, if there are 5 sign changes, there are 5 or 3 or 1 positive zeros. If there are 6 sign changes, there are 6 or 4 or 2 or 0 positive zeros. The polynomial function $f(x) = 3x^4 - 2x^3 + 7x^2 + 5x - 8$ has 3 sign changes: from 3 to -2, from -2 to 7, and from 5 to -8. There are either 3 or 1 positive zeros. The maximim number of negative zeros is the number of sign changes in the polynomial $f(-x)$. The possible number of negative zeros is the number of sign changes in $f(-x)$ minus an even whole number.

 EXAMPLE 7-13

Use Descartes' Rule of Signs to count the possible number of positive zeros and negative zeros for the polynomial functions.

- $f(x) = 5x^3 - 6x^2 - 10x + 4$

  There are 2 sign changes: from 5 to -6 and from -10 to 4. This means that there are either 2 or 0 positive zeros. Before we count the possible number of negative zeros, remember from earlier in the book that for a number a, $a(-x)^{\text{even power}} = ax^{\text{even power}}$ and $a(-x)^{\text{odd power}} = -ax^{\text{odd power}}$

$$f(-x) = 5(-x)^3 - 6(-x)^2 - 10(-x) + 4$$
$$= -5x^3 - 6x^2 + 10x + 4$$

  There is 1 sign change, from -6 to 10, so there is exactly 1 negative zero.

- $P(x) = x^5 + x^3 + x + 4$

  There are no sign changes, so there are no positive zeros.

$$P(-x) = (-x)^5 + (-x)^3 + (-x) + 4$$
$$= -x^5 - x^3 - x + 4$$

  There is 1 sign change, so there is exactly 1 negative zero.

The Upper and Lower Bounds Theorem

Let P be a polynomial function with a positive leading coefficient. Let a be a negative number and b, a positive number.

- If synthetic division is performed on $\frac{P(x)}{x-a}$ and the bottom row alternates between nonnegative and nonpositive entries, then $x = a$ is a lower bound for the real zeros of P.

- If synthetic division is performed on $\frac{P(x)}{x-b}$ and the bottom row consists only of nonnegative entries, then $x = b$ is an upper bound for the real zeros of P.

The Upper and Lower Bounds Theorem helps us to find a range of *x*-values that contains all real zeros. For a negative number $x = a$, the statement "*a* is a lower bound for the real zeros" means that there is no number to the left of $x = a$ on the *x*-axis that is a zero. For a positive number $x = b$, the statement "*b* is an upper bound for the real zeros" means that there is no number to the right of $x = b$ on the *x*-axis that is a zero. In other words, all of the *x*-intercepts are between *a* and *b*.

To determine whether a negative number $x = a$ is a lower bound for a polynomial, we use synthetic division. If the numbers in the bottom row alternate between nonpositive and nonnegative numbers, then $x = a$ is a lower bound for the real zeros. A "nonpositive" number is zero or negative, and a "nonnegative" number is zero or positive.

To determine whether a positive number $x = b$ is an upper bound for the positive zeros, again we use synthetic division. If the numbers on the bottom row are all nonnegative, then $x = b$ is an upper bound on the real zeros.

 EXAMPLE 7-14

Show that the given values for *a* and *b* are lower and upper bounds, respectively, for the following polynomials.

- $f(x) = x^4 + x^3 - 16x^2 - 4x + 48; a = -5$ and $b = 5$

$$
\begin{array}{r|rrrrr}
-5 & 1 & 1 & -16 & -4 & 48 \\
   &   & -5 & 20 & -20 & 120 \\
\hline
   & 1 & -4 & 4 & -24 & 168 \\
\end{array}
$$

The bottom row alternates between positive and negative numbers, so $a = -5$ is a lower bound for the real zeros of $f(x)$.

$$
\begin{array}{r|rrrrr}
5 & 1 & 1 & -16 & -4 & 48 \\
  &   & 5 & 30 & 70 & 330 \\
\hline
  & 1 & 6 & 14 & 66 & 378 \\
\end{array}
$$

The entries on the bottom row are all positive, so $b = 5$ is an upper bound for the real zeros of $f(x)$. All of the real zeros for $f(x)$ are between $x = -5$ and $x = 5$.

If zero appears on the bottom row when testing for an upper bound, we can consider zero to be positive. If zero appears in the bottom row when testing for a lower bound, we can consider zero to be negative if the previous entry is positive and positive if the previous entry is negative. In other words, consider zero to be the opposite sign as the previous entry.

- $P(x) = 4x^4 + 20x^3 + 7x^2 + 3x - 6$ with $a = -5$

$$
\begin{array}{r|rrrrr}
-5 & 4 & 20 & 7 & 3 & -6 \\
   &   & -20 & 0 & -35 & 160 \\
\hline
   & 4 & 0 & 7 & -32 & 154
\end{array}
$$

Because zero follows a positive number, we consider zero to be negative. This makes the bottom row alternate between positive and negative entries, so $a = -5$ is a lower bound for the real zeros of $P(x)$.

The Upper and Lower Bounds Theorem has some limitations. For instance, it does not tell us *how* to find upper and lower bounds for the zeros of a polynomial. For any polynomial, there are infinitely many upper and lower bounds. For instance, if $x = 5$ is an upper bound, then any number larger than 5 is also an upper bound. For many polynomials, a starting place is the quotient of the constant term and the leading coefficient and its negative: $\pm \frac{\text{constant term}}{\text{leading coefficient}}$. First show that these are bounds for the zeros, then work your way inward. For example, if $f(x) = 2x^3 - 7x^2 + x + 50$, let $a = -\frac{50}{2} = -25$ and $b = \frac{50}{2} = 25$. Then, let a and b get closer together, say $a = -10$ and $b = 10$.

Graphing Calculators and the Zeros of a Polynomial

For a polynomial such as $f(x) = 5x^3 + 20x^2 - 9x - 36$, the list of possible rational zeros is quite long—36! Fortunately, a graphing calculator can help us to find the zeros of this function. We can plot the graph of the function and see if any of these rational numbers is a zero. Once we have identitified a rational zero, we can use synthetic division to partially factor the polynomial.

The graph (shown in Figure 7-13) is plotted in the window $-5 \le x \le 5$ and $-50 \le y \le 50$. It appears that $x = -4$ is a zero, so we divide the polynomial by $x + 4$.

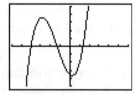

FIGURE 7-13

$$\begin{array}{r|rrrr}
-4 & 5 & 20 & -9 & -36 \\
  &   & -20 & 0 & 36 \\
\hline
  & 5 & 0 & -9 & 0
\end{array}$$

Because the remainder is zero, we see that $x + 4$ and the quotient, $5x^2 - 9$, are factors, so $f(x) = (x + 4)(5x^2 - 9)$. We solve $5x^2 - 9 = 0$ to find the other zeros.

$$5x^2 - 9 = 0$$

$$5x^2 = 9$$

$$x^2 = \frac{9}{5}$$

$$x = \pm\sqrt{\frac{9}{5}} = \pm\frac{3}{\sqrt{5}}$$

$$= \pm\frac{3}{\sqrt{5}} \cdot \frac{\sqrt{5}}{\sqrt{5}}$$

$$= \pm\frac{3\sqrt{5}}{5} = \frac{3\sqrt{5}}{5}, \; -\frac{3\sqrt{5}}{5}$$

$$f(x) = (x + 4)\left(x - \frac{3\sqrt{5}}{5}\right)\left(x + \frac{3\sqrt{5}}{5}\right)$$

The Upper and Lower Bounds Theorem can help us to find a window that will display *all* the x-intercepts for the graph of a polynomial function. In Example 7-14, we found that $x = -5$ and $x = 5$ are bounds for the zeros of $f(x) = x^4 + x^3 - 16x^2 - 4x + 48$. This tells us that we can set the window to using these values (and $-50 \le y \le 50$), knowing that all of the x-intercepts will be displayed. The graph (in Figure 7-14) displays all four x-intercepts for this graph.

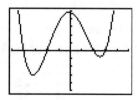

FIGURE 7-14

PRACTICE

1. List the candidates for rational zeros. Do not try to find the zeros.

$$f(x) = 3x^4 + 8x^3 - 11x^2 + 3x + 4$$

2. List the candidates for rational zeros. Do not try to find the zeros. $P(x) = 6x^4 - 24$

3. Completely factor $h(x) = 2x^3 + 5x^2 - 23x + 10$.

4. Completely factor $P(x) = 7x^3 + 26x^2 - 15x + 2$.

5. Use Descartes' Rule of Signs to count the possible number of positive zeros and the possible number of negative zeros of $f(x) = 2x^4 - 6x^3 - x^2 + 4x - 8$.

6. Use Descartes' Rule of Signs to count the possible number of positive zeros and the possible number of negative zeros of $f(x) = -x^3 - x^2 + x + 1$.

7. Show that the given values for a and b are lower and upper, respectively, bounds for the zeros of $f(x) = x^3 - 6x^2 + x + 5; a = -3, b = 7$.

8. Show that the given values for a and b are lower and upper, respectively, bounds for the zeros of $f(x) = x^4 - x^2 - 2; a = -2, b = 2$.

9. Sketch the graph for $g(x) = x^3 - x^2 - 17x - 15$.

✓ SOLUTIONS

1. Possible numerators: $\pm 1, \pm 2, \pm 4$

   Possible denominators: 1 and 3

   Possible rational zeros: $\pm 1, \pm 2, \pm 4, \pm \frac{1}{3}, \pm \frac{2}{3}, \pm \frac{4}{3}$

2. Possible numerators: $\pm 1, \pm 2, \pm 3, \pm 4, \pm 6, \pm 8, \pm 12, \pm 24$

   Possible denominators: 1, 2, 3, 6

   Possible rational zeros (with duplicates omitted): $\pm 1, \pm 2, \pm 3, \pm 4, \pm 6, \pm 8, \pm 12, \pm 24, \pm \frac{1}{2}, \pm \frac{3}{2}, \pm \frac{1}{3}, \pm \frac{2}{3}, \pm \frac{4}{3}, \pm \frac{8}{3}, \pm \frac{1}{6}$

3. The possible rational zeros are $\pm 1, \pm 2, \pm 5, \pm 10, \pm \frac{1}{2}$, and $\pm \frac{5}{2}$. Because $h(2) = 0, x = 2$ is a zero of $h(x)$.

$$
\begin{array}{r|rrrr}
2 & 2 & 5 & -23 & 10 \\
  &   & 4 & 18 & -10 \\
\hline
  & 2 & 9 & -5 & 0
\end{array}
$$

$$h(x) = (x - 2)(2x^2 + 9x - 5)$$

$$h(x) = (x - 2)(2x - 1)(x + 5)$$

4. The possible rational zeros are ± 1, ± 2, $\pm\frac{1}{7}$, and $\pm\frac{2}{7}$. Because $P(\frac{2}{7}) = 0$, $x = \frac{2}{7}$ is a zero for $P(x)$.

$$
\begin{array}{r|rrrr}
\frac{2}{7} & 7 & 26 & -15 & 2 \\
  &   & 2 & 8 & -2 \\
\hline
  & 7 & 28 & -7 & 0 \\
\end{array}
$$

$$P(x) = \left(x - \frac{2}{7}\right)(7x^2 + 28x - 7)$$

$$= \left(x - \frac{2}{7}\right)(7)(x^2 + 4x - 1) = \left[7\left(x - \frac{2}{7}\right)\right](x^2 + 4x - 1)$$

$$= (7x - 2)(x^2 + 4x - 1)$$

We use the quadratic formula to find the zeros for $x^2 + 4x - 1$.

$$x = \frac{-4 \pm \sqrt{4^2 - 4(1)(-1)}}{2(1)} = \frac{-4 \pm \sqrt{20}}{2}$$

$$= \frac{-4 \pm 2\sqrt{5}}{2} = \frac{2(-2 \pm \sqrt{5})}{2}$$

$$= -2 \pm \sqrt{5} = -2 + \sqrt{5},\ -2 - \sqrt{5}$$

$$x^2 + 4x - 1 = [x - (-2 + \sqrt{5})][x - (-2 - \sqrt{5})]$$

$$= (x + 2 - \sqrt{5})(x + 2 + \sqrt{5})$$

$$P(x) = (7x - 2)(x + 2 - \sqrt{5})(x + 2 + \sqrt{5})$$

5. There are 3 sign changes in $f(x)$, so there are 3 or 1 positive zeros.

$$f(-x) = 2(-x)^4 - 6(-x)^3 - (-x)^2 + 4(-x) - 8$$

$$= 2x^4 + 6x^3 - x^2 - 4x - 8$$

There is 1 sign change in $f(-x)$, so there is exactly 1 negative zero.

6. There is 1 sign change in $f(x)$, so there is exactly 1 positive zero.

$$f(-x) = -(-x)^3 - (-x)^2 + (-x) + 1$$

$$= x^3 - x^2 - x + 1$$

There are 2 sign changes in $f(-x)$, so there are 2 or 0 negative zeros.

7.
$$
\begin{array}{r|rrrr}
-3 & 1 & -6 & 1 & 5 \\
   &   & -3 & 27 & -84 \\
\hline
   & 1 & -9 & 28 & -79
\end{array}
$$

The entries in the bottom row alternate between positive and negative (or nonnegative and nonpositive), so $a = -3$ is a lower bound for the real zeros of $f(x)$.

$$
\begin{array}{r|rrrr}
7 & 1 & -6 & 1 & 5 \\
  &   & 7 & 7 & 56 \\
\hline
  & 1 & 1 & 8 & 61
\end{array}
$$

The entries in the bottom are positive (nonnegative), so $b = 7$ is an upper bound for the real zeros of $f(x)$.

8.
$$
\begin{array}{r|rrrrr}
-2 & 1 & 0 & -1 & 0 & -2 \\
   &   & -2 & 4 & -6 & 12 \\
\hline
   & 1 & -2 & 3 & -6 & 10
\end{array}
$$

The entries in the bottom row alternate between positive and negative, so $a = -2$ is a lower bound for the real zeros of $f(x)$.

$$
\begin{array}{r|rrrrr}
2 & 1 & 0 & -1 & 0 & -2 \\
  &   & 2 & 4 & 6 & 12 \\
\hline
  & 1 & 2 & 3 & 6 & 10
\end{array}
$$

The entries in the bottom row are all positive, so $b = 2$ is an upper bound for the real zeros of $f(x)$.

9. The possible rational zeros are $\pm 1, \pm 3, \pm 5,$ and ± 15; $g(-1) = 0$.

$$
\begin{array}{r|rrrr}
-1 & 1 & -1 & -17 & -15 \\
   &   & -1 & 2 & 15 \\
\hline
   & 1 & -2 & -15 & 0
\end{array}
$$

$$g(x) = (x+1)(x^2 - 2x - 15)$$

$$= (x+1)(x+3)(x-5)$$

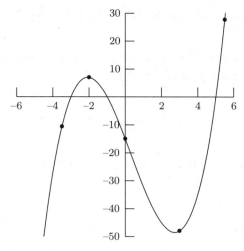

FIGURE 7-15

The **x-intercepts** are **−3, −1,** and **5.** We plot points for **x =
−3.5, x = −2, x = 0, x = 3,** and **x = 5.5,** see Figure 7-15.

Complex Numbers

Arithmetic with Complex Numbers

Until now, zeros of polynomials have been real numbers. The next topic
involves *complex* zeros. These zeros come from even roots of negative numbers
like $\sqrt{-1}$. Before working with complex zeros of polynomials, we will first learn
some complex number arithmetic. Complex numbers are normally written in
the form $a + bi$, where a and b are real numbers and $i = \sqrt{-1}$. A number such
as $4 + \sqrt{-9}$ would be written as $4 + 3i$ because $\sqrt{-9} = \sqrt{9}\sqrt{-1} = 3i$. Real
numbers are complex numbers where $b = 0$. Generally, though, when we refer
to complex numbers in this book, we mean complex numbers that are not real.

 EXAMPLE 7-15

Write the complex numbers in the form $a + bi$, where a and b are real numbers.

- $\sqrt{-64} = \sqrt{64}\sqrt{-1} = 8i$
- $\sqrt{-27} = \sqrt{27}\sqrt{-1} = \sqrt{27}\,i = \sqrt{9 \cdot 3}\,i = \sqrt{9}\sqrt{3}\,i = 3\sqrt{3}\,i$

  Be careful, $\sqrt{3i} \neq \sqrt{3}\,i$.

$$\bullet\ 6 + \sqrt{-8} = 6 + \sqrt{8}i = 6 + \sqrt{4 \cdot 2}i = 6 + \sqrt{4}\sqrt{2}i = 6 + 2\sqrt{2}i$$

Adding complex numbers is a matter of adding like terms. Add the real parts, *a* and *c*, and the imaginary parts, *b* and *d*.

$$(a + bi) + (c + di) = (a + c) + (b + d)i$$

Subtract two complex numbers by distributing the minus sign in the parentheses, then adding the like terms.

$$a + bi - (c + di) = a + bi - c - di = (a - c) + (b - d)i$$

 EXAMPLE 7-16

Perform the arithmetic. Write the sum or difference in the form *a + bi*, where *a* and *b* are real numbers.

- $(3 - 5i) + (4 + 8i) = (3 + 4) + (-5 + 8)i = 7 + 3i$

- $2i - 6 + 9i = -6 + 11i$

- $7 - \sqrt{-18} + 3 + 5\sqrt{-2} = 7 - \sqrt{18}i + 3 + 5\sqrt{2}i$

$$= 7 - \sqrt{9 \cdot 2}i + 3 + 5\sqrt{2}i$$
$$= 7 - 3\sqrt{2}i + 3 + 5\sqrt{2}i$$
$$= 10 + 2\sqrt{2}i$$

- $11 - 3i - (7 + 6i) = 11 - 3i - 7 - 6i = 4 - 9i$

- $7 + \sqrt{-8} - (1 - \sqrt{-18}) = 7 + \sqrt{8}i - 1 + \sqrt{18}i$

$$= 7 + 2\sqrt{2}i - 1 + 3\sqrt{2}i = 6 + 5\sqrt{2}i$$

Multiplying complex numbers is not as straightforward as adding and subtracting them. First we will take the product of two purely imaginary numbers (numbers whose real parts are zero). Remember that $i = \sqrt{-1}$, which makes $i^2 = -1$. In most complex number multiplication problems, we have a term with i^2. Replace i^2 with -1. Multiply two complex numbers in the form $a + bi$ using the FOIL method (see a review of the FOIL method in the Appendix), substituting -1 for i^2 and combining like terms.

EXAMPLE 7-17

Write the product in the form $a + bi$, where a and b are real numbers.

- $(5i)(6i) = 30i^2 = 30(-1) = -30$
- $(2i)(-9i) = -18i^2 = -18(-1) = 18$
- $(\sqrt{-6})(\sqrt{-9}) = (\sqrt{6}\,i)(\sqrt{9}\,i) = (\sqrt{6})(3)i^2 = 3\sqrt{6}(-1) = -3\sqrt{6}$
- $(4 + 2i)(5 + 3i) = 20 + 12i + 10i + 6i^2 = 20 + 22i + 6(-1)$

$$= 14 + 22i$$

- $(8 - 2i)(8 + 2i) = 64 + 16i - 16i - 4i^2 = 64 - 4(-1) = 68$

The complex numbers $a + bi$ and $a - bi$ are called *complex conjugates*. The only difference between a complex number and its conjugate is the sign between the real part and the imaginary part. The product of any complex number and its conjugate is a real number.

$$(a + bi)(a - bi) = a^2 - abi + abi - b^2 i^2$$

$$= a^2 - b^2(-1)$$

$$= a^2 + b^2$$

EXAMPLE 7-18

- **The complex conjugate of $3 + 2i$ is $3 - 2i$.**
- **The complex conjugate of $-7 - i$ is $-7 + i$.**
- **The complex conjugate of $10i$ is $-10i$.**
- **$(7 - 2i)(7 + 2i)$**

  Here, $a = 7$ and $b = 2$, so $a^2 = 49$ and $b^2 = 4$, making $(7 - 2i)(7 + 2i) = 49 + 4 = 53$

- **$(1 - i)(1 + i)$**

  Here $a = 1$ and $b = 1$, so $a^2 = 1$ and $b^2 = 1$, making $(1 - i)(1 + i) = 1 + 1 = 2$

Dividing two complex numbers can be a little complicated. These problems are normally written as fractions. If the denominator is purely imaginary, we can simply multiply the fraction by $\frac{i}{i}$ and simplify.

EXAMPLE 7-19

Perform the division. Write the quotient in the form $a + bi$, where a and b are real numbers.

- $$\frac{2 + 3i}{i} = \frac{2 + 3i}{i} \cdot \frac{i}{i} = \frac{(2 + 3i)i}{i^2}$$

$$= \frac{2i + 3i^2}{i^2} = \frac{2i + 3(-1)}{-1}$$

$$= \frac{-3 + 2i}{-1} = -(-3 + 2i)$$

$$= 3 - 2i$$

- $$\frac{4 + 5i}{2i} = \frac{4 + 5i}{2i} \cdot \frac{i}{i} = \frac{4i + 5i^2}{2i^2}$$

$$= \frac{4i + 5(-1)}{2(-1)} = \frac{4i - 5}{-2} = \frac{-(4i - 5)}{2} = \frac{-(-5 + 4i)}{2}$$

$$= \frac{5 - 4i}{2} = \frac{5}{2} - 2i$$

When the divisor (denominator) is in the form $a + bi$, multiplying the fraction by $\frac{i}{i}$ does not work, as you can see in this problem.

$$\frac{2 - 5i}{3 + 6i} \cdot \frac{i}{i} = \frac{2i - 5i^2}{3i + 6i^2} = \frac{5 + 2i}{-6 + 3i}$$

What *does* work is to multiply the fraction by the denominator's conjugate over itself. This works because the product of any complex number and its conjugate is a real number. We use the FOIL method in the numerator (if necessary) and the fact that $(a + bi)(a - bi) = a^2 + b^2$ in the denominator.

EXAMPLE 7-20

Write the quotient in the form $a + bi$, where a and b are real numbers.

- $$\frac{2 + 7i}{6 + i} = \frac{2 + 7i}{6 + i} \cdot \frac{6 - i}{6 - i} = \frac{12 - 2i + 42i - 7i^2}{6^2 + 1^2}$$

$$= \frac{12 + 40i - 7(-1)}{37} = \frac{12 + 40i + 7}{37}$$

$$= \frac{19 + 40i}{37} = \frac{19}{37} + \frac{40}{37}i$$

$$\frac{4 - 9i}{5 - 2i} = \frac{4 - 9i}{5 - 2i} \cdot \frac{5 + 2i}{5 + 2i} = \frac{20 + 8i - 45i - 18i^2}{5^2 + 2^2}$$

$$= \frac{20 - 37i - 18(-1)}{25 + 4} = \frac{20 - 37i + 18}{29}$$

$$= \frac{38 - 37i}{29} = \frac{38}{29} - \frac{37}{29}i$$

Still Struggling

Make sure you multiply the numerator and denominator of a complex division problem by the denominator's *conjugate*, not the denominator itself. This is a very common mistake.

There are reasons to write complex numbers in the form $a + bi$. One is that complex numbers are plotted in the plane (real numbers are plotted on the number line), where the horizontal axis is the *real* axis, and the vertical axis is the *imaginary* axis. The number $3 - 4i$ is plotted in Figure 7-16.

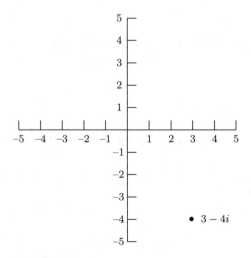

FIGURE 7-16

PRACTICE

For Problems 1 to 3, write the complex number in the form $a + bi$, where a and b are real numbers.

1. $\sqrt{-25}$

2. $\sqrt{-24}$

3. $14 - \sqrt{-36}$

For Problems 4 to 15, perform the arithmetic. Write answers in the form $a + bi$, where a and b are real numbers.

4. $18 - 4i + (-15) + 2i$

5. $5 + i + 5 - i$

6. $7 + i + 12 + i$

7. $-5 + \sqrt{-12} + 7 + 4\sqrt{-12}$

8. $\sqrt{-48} - (-1 - \sqrt{-75})$

9. $(2i)(10i)$

10. $(4\sqrt{-25})(2\sqrt{-25})$

11. $\sqrt{-6} \cdot \sqrt{-15}$

12. $(15 + 3i)(-2 + i)$

13. $(3 + 2i)(3 - 2i)$

14. $(8 - 10i)(8 + 10i)$

15. $(1 - 9i)(1 + 9i)$

For Problems 16 to 18, identify the complex conjugate.

16. $15 + 7i$

17. $-3 + i$

18. $-9i$

For Problems 19 to 21, write the quotient in the form $a + bi$, where a and b are real numbers.

19. $\dfrac{4 - 9i}{-3i}$

20. $\dfrac{4 + 2i}{1 - 3i}$

21. $\dfrac{6 + 4i}{6 - 4i}$

✓ SOLUTIONS

1. $\sqrt{-25} = \sqrt{25}\,i = 5i$

2. $\sqrt{-24} = \sqrt{24}\,i = \sqrt{4 \cdot 6}\,i = 2\sqrt{6}\,i$

3. $14 - \sqrt{-36} = 14 - \sqrt{36}\,i = 14 - 6i$

4. $18 - 4i + (-15) + 2i = 3 - 2i$

5. $5 + i + 5 - i = 10 + 0i = 10$

6. $7 + i + 12 + i = 19 + 2i$

7. $-5 + \sqrt{-12} + 7 + 4\sqrt{-12} = -5 + \sqrt{12}\,i + 7 + 4\sqrt{12}\,i$

$$= -5 + \sqrt{4 \cdot 3}\,i + 7 + 4\sqrt{4 \cdot 3}\,i$$

$$= -5 + 2\sqrt{3}\,i + 7 + 4 \cdot 2\sqrt{3}\,i$$

$$= -5 + 2\sqrt{3}\,i + 7 + 8\sqrt{3}\,i$$

$$= 2 + 10\sqrt{3}\,i$$

8. $\sqrt{-48} - (-1 - \sqrt{-75}) = \sqrt{48}\,i + 1 + \sqrt{75}\,i$

$$= \sqrt{16 \cdot 3}\,i + 1 + \sqrt{25 \cdot 3}\,i$$

$$= 4\sqrt{3}\,i + 1 + 5\sqrt{3}\,i = 1 + 9\sqrt{3}\,i$$

9. $(2i)(10i) = 20i^2 = 20(-1) = -20$

10. $(4\sqrt{-25})(2\sqrt{-25}) = 4(5i)[2(5i)] = 200i^2 = 200(-1) = -200$

11. $\sqrt{-6} \cdot \sqrt{-15} = \sqrt{6}\,i \cdot \sqrt{15}\,i = \sqrt{6 \cdot 15}\,i^2 = \sqrt{90}\,i^2$
    $= 3\sqrt{10}(-1) = -3\sqrt{10}$

12. $(15 + 3i)(-2 + i) = -30 + 15i - 6i + 3i^2$
    $= -30 + 9i + 3(-1) = -33 + 9i$

13. $(3 + 2i)(3 - 2i) = 9 - 6i + 6i - 4i^2 = 9 - 4(-1) = 13$
    (or $3^2 + 2^2 = 13$)

14. $(8 - 10i)(8 + 10i) = 64 + 80i - 80i - 100i^2 = 64 - 100(-1)$
    $= 164$ (or $8^2 + 10^2 = 164$)

15. $(1 - 9i)(1 + 9i) = 1 + 9i - 9i - 81i^2 = 1 - 81(-1) = 82$
    (or $1^2 + 9^2 = 82$)

16. The complex conjugate of $15 + 7i$ is $15 - 7i$.

17. The complex conjugate of $-3 + i$ is $-3 - i$.

18. The complex conjugate of $-9i$ is $9i$.

19.
$$\frac{4 - 9i}{-3i} = \frac{4 - 9i}{-3i} \cdot \frac{i}{i} = \frac{4i - 9i^2}{-3i^2}$$

$$= \frac{4i - 9(-1)}{-3(-1)} = \frac{9 + 4i}{3} = 3 + \frac{4}{3}i$$

20.
$$\frac{4 + 2i}{1 - 3i} = \frac{4 + 2i}{1 - 3i} \cdot \frac{1 + 3i}{1 + 3i} = \frac{4 + 12i + 2i + 6i^2}{1^2 + 3^2}$$

$$= \frac{4 + 14i + 6(-1)}{10} = \frac{-2 + 14i}{10} = -\frac{1}{5} + \frac{7}{5}i$$

21.
$$\frac{6 + 4i}{6 - 4i} = \frac{6 + 4i}{6 - 4i} \cdot \frac{6 + 4i}{6 + 4i} = \frac{36 + 24i + 24i + 16i^2}{6^2 + 4^2}$$

$$= \frac{36 + 48i + 16(-1)}{36 + 16} = \frac{20 + 48i}{52} = \frac{5}{13} + \frac{12}{13}i$$

Complex Solutions to Quadratic Equations

As we know, some quadratic functions do not have x-intercepts. For example, the graph of $f(x) = x^2 + 1$ does not have an x-intercept. (See Figure 7-17.) Every quadratic equation has a solution, however. These solutions might be real

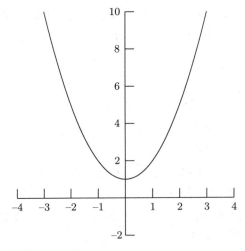

FIGURE 7-17

or complex. The real solutions for a quadratic equation are the x-intercepts for the graph of its related quadratic function.

The function $f(x) = x^2 + 1$ does have two complex zeros because the equation $x^2 + 1 = 0$ has two complex solutions.

$$x^2 + 1 = 0$$

$$x^2 = -1$$

$$x = \pm\sqrt{-1}$$

$$= \pm i$$

The quadratic equations in Example 7-21 have complex solutions.

■ EXAMPLE **7-21**

Solve the equation and write the solutions in the form $a + bi$, where a and b are real numbers.

- $x^2 - 3x + 6 = 0$

$$x = \frac{-(-3) \pm \sqrt{(-3)^2 - 4(1)(6)}}{2(1)} = \frac{3 \pm \sqrt{9 - 24}}{2}$$

$$= \frac{3 \pm \sqrt{-15}}{2} = \frac{3 \pm \sqrt{15}\,i}{2}$$

$$= \frac{3}{2} \pm \frac{\sqrt{15}}{2}i = \frac{3}{2} - \frac{\sqrt{15}}{2}i, \ \frac{3}{2} + \frac{\sqrt{15}}{2}i$$

- $3x^2 + 8x + 14 = 0$

$$x = \frac{-8 \pm \sqrt{8^2 - 4(3)(14)}}{2(3)} = \frac{-8 \pm \sqrt{-104}}{6}$$

$$= \frac{-8 \pm 2\sqrt{26}\,i}{6} = \frac{2(-4 \pm \sqrt{26}\,i)}{6}$$

$$= \frac{-4 \pm \sqrt{26}\,i}{3} = -\frac{4}{3} \pm \frac{\sqrt{26}}{3}i$$

$$= -\frac{4}{3} + \frac{\sqrt{26}}{3}i, \ -\frac{4}{3} - \frac{\sqrt{26}}{3}i$$

In these problems, the complex solutions to the quadratic equation came in conjugate pairs. This always happens when the solutions are complex numbers. A quadratic expression that has complex zeros is called *irreducible* (over the reals) because it cannot be factored using real numbers.

We can tell which quadratic factors are irreducible without having to use the quadratic formula. We only need part of the quadratic formula, $b^2 - 4ac$. When this number is negative, the quadratic factor has two complex zeros, $\frac{-b \pm \sqrt{\text{negative number}}}{2a}$. When this number is positive, there are two real number solutions, $\frac{-b \pm \sqrt{\text{positive number}}}{2a}$. When this number is zero, there is one real zero: $\frac{-b \pm \sqrt{0}}{2a} = \frac{-b}{2a}$. For this reason, $b^2 - 4ac$ is called the *discriminant*. The polynomial function $f(x) = x^4 - 1$ can be factored using real numbers as $(x^2 - 1)(x^2 + 1) = (x - 1)(x + 1)(x^2 + 1)$. The factor $x^2 + 1$ is irreducible because it is factored with complex numbers as $(x - i)(x + i)$.

The graphs of some polynomials having irreducible quadratic factors need extra points plotted to get a more accurate graph. The graph in Figure 7-18 shows the graph of $f(x) = x^4 - 3x^2 - 4$ using our usual method—plotting the x-intercepts, a point to the left of the smallest x-intercept, a point between each consecutive pair of x-intercepts, and a point to the right of the largest x-intercept.

See what happens to the graph when we plot the points for $x = 1$ and $x = -1$. (See Figure 7-19.)

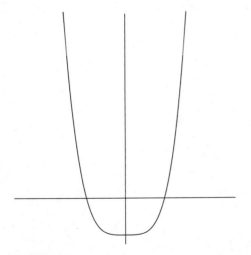

FIGURE 7-18

FIGURE 7-19

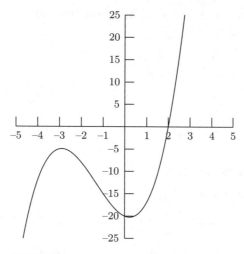

FIGURE 7-20

The graph of $f(x) = (x - 2)(x^2 + 6x + 10)$ is sketched in Figure 7-20. This graph has one real zero, 2, and two complex zeros, $-3 \pm i$.

You might have noticed that these graphs have several "turning around points" in addition to one or more x-intercepts. When this happens, we need calculus to find them.

The Fundamental Theorem of Algebra

By the *Fundamental Theorem of Algebra*, every polynomial of degree $n \geq 1$ has exactly n zeros (some might be counted more than once). Because $x = c$ is a zero implies $x - c$ is a factor; every polynomial can be completely factored in the form $a(x - c_n)(x - c_{n-1}) \ldots (x - c_1)$, where a is a real number and c_i is real or complex. Factors in the form $x - c$ are called *linear factors*. Factors such as $2x + 1$ can be written in the form $x - c$ by factoring 2: $2(x + \frac{1}{2})$ or $2[x - (-\frac{1}{2})]$.

To factor a polynomial completely, we need to first find its zeros. At times, we will use the Rational Zero Theorem, polynomial division, and the quadratic formula.

 EXAMPLE 7-22

Find all zeros, real and complex.

• $h(x) = x^4 - 16$

$$x^4 - 16 = (x^2 - 4)(x^2 + 4) = (x - 2)(x + 2)(x^2 + 4)$$

The real zeros are 2 and -2. We find the complex zeros by solving $x^2 + 4 = 0$.

$$x^2 + 4 = 0$$

$$x^2 = -4$$

$$x = \pm\sqrt{-4} = \pm 2i$$

The complex zeros are $\pm 2i$.

• $P(x) = x^4 + 6x^3 + 9x^2 - 6x - 10$

The possible rational zeros are ± 1, ± 2, ± 5, and ± 10. $P(1) = 0$.

$$
\begin{array}{r|rrrr}
1 & 1 & 6 & 9 & -6 & -10 \\
  &   & 1 & 7 & 16 & 10 \\
\hline
  & 1 & 7 & 16 & 10 & 0
\end{array}
$$

$P(x) = (x - 1)(x^3 + 7x^2 + 16x + 10)$

Because $x^3 + 7x^2 + 16x + 10$ has no sign changes, there are no positive zeros; $x = -1$ is a zero for $x^3 + 7x^2 + 16x + 10$.

$$
\begin{array}{r|rrrr}
-1 & 1 & 7 & 16 & 10 \\
   &   & -1 & -6 & -10 \\
\hline
   & 1 & 6 & 10 & 0
\end{array}
$$

$P(x) = (x - 1)(x + 1)(x^2 + 6x + 10)$

Solve $x^2 + 6x + 10 = 0$ to find the complex zeros.

$$x = \frac{-6 \pm \sqrt{6^2 - 4(1)(10)}}{2(1)} = \frac{-6 \pm \sqrt{-4}}{2}$$

$$= \frac{-6 \pm 2i}{2} = \frac{2(-3 \pm i)}{2} = -3 \pm i$$

The zeros are ± 1, $-3 \pm i$.

If we know that a complex number is a zero for a polynomial, we automatically know another zero—the complex conjugate is also a zero. This gives us a quadratic factor for the polynomial. Once we have this computed, we can use long division to find the quotient, which is another factor of the polynomial. Each time we factor a polynomial, we are closer to finding its zeros.

EXAMPLE 7-23

Find all zeros, real and complex.

- $f(x) = 3x^4 + x^3 + 17x^2 + 4x + 20$ and $x = 2i$ is a zero.

Because $x = 2i$ is a zero, its conjugate, $-2i$, is another zero. This tells us that two factors are $x - 2i$ and $x + 2i$.

$$(x - 2i)(x + 2i) = x^2 + 2ix - 2ix - 4i^2 = x^2 - 4(-1) = x^2 + 4$$

We divide $f(x)$ by $x^2 + 4 = x^2 + 0x + 4$.

$$
\begin{array}{r}
3x^2 + x + 5 \\
x^2 + 0x + 4 \overline{\big)\, 3x^4 + x^3 + 17x^2 + 4x + 20} \\
\underline{-(3x^4 + 0x^3 + 12x^2)} \\
x^3 + 5x^2 + 4x \\
\underline{-(x^3 + 0x^2 + 4x)} \\
5x^2 + 0x + 20 \\
\underline{-(5x^2 + 0x + 20)} \\
0
\end{array}
$$

$f(x) = (x^2 + 4)(3x^2 + x + 5)$

Solving $3x^2 + x + 5 = 0$, we get the solutions:

$$x = \frac{-1 \pm \sqrt{1^2 - 4(3)(5)}}{2(3)} = \frac{-1 \pm \sqrt{-59}}{6} = \frac{-1 \pm \sqrt{59}\,i}{6}$$

The zeros are $\pm 2i$, $\frac{-1 \pm \sqrt{59}\,i}{6}$.

- $h(x) = 2x^3 - 7x^2 + 170x - 246$, $x = 1 + 9i$ is a zero.

Because $x = 1 + 9i$ is a zero, we know that $x = 1 - 9i$ is also a zero. We also know that $x - (1 + 9i) = x - 1 - 9i$ and $x - (1 - 9i) = x - 1 + 9i$ are factors. We multiply these two factors.

$$(x - 1 - 9i)(x - 1 + 9i) = x^2 - x + 9ix - x + 1 - 9i - 9ix + 9i - 81i^2$$

$$= x^2 - 2x + 1 - 81(-1) = x^2 - 2x + 82$$

$$
\begin{array}{r}
2x-3 \\
x^2-2x+82\overline{\smash{\big)}\,2x^3-7x^2+170x-246} \\
\underline{-(2x^3-4x^2+164x)} \\
-3x^2+6x-246 \\
\underline{-(-3x^2+6x-246)} \\
0
\end{array}
$$

$h(x) = (2x - 3)(x^2 - 2x + 82)$

The zeros are $1 \pm 9i$ and $\frac{3}{2}$ (from $2x - 3 = 0$).

An interesting fact is that a polynomial having real coefficients can be factored as some combination of linear factors and irreducible quadratic factors, if we only wish to use real numbers in our factorization.

One consequence of the Fundamental Theorem of Algebra is that a polynomial of degree n has n zeros, though not necessarily n different zeros. For example, the polynomial $f(x) = (x - 2)^3 = (x - 2)(x - 2)(x - 2)$ has $x = 2$ as a zero three times. The number of times an x-value is a zero is called its *multiplicity*. In this example, $x = 2$ is a zero with multiplicity 3.

 EXAMPLE 7-24

- $f(x) = x^4(x + 3)^2(x - 6)$

  $x = 0$ is a zero with multiplicity 4 [We can think of x^4 as $(x - 0)^4$.]

  $x = -3$ is a zero with multiplicity 2

  $x = 6$ is a zero with multiplicity 1

Now, instead of finding the zeros for a given polynomial, we will find a polynomial with the given zeros. Because if we know the zeros, we will know the factors. Once we know the factors of a polynomial, we will pretty much know the polynomial.

 EXAMPLE 7-25

Find a polynomial with integer coefficients having the given degree and zeros.

- **Degree 3 with zeros 1, 2, and 5**

  Because $x = 1$ is a zero, $x - 1$ is a factor. Because $x = 2$ is a zero, $x - 2$ is a factor. And because $x = 5$ is a zero, $x - 5$ is a factor. Such a polynomial is of the form $a(x-1)(x-2)(x-5)$, where a is some nonzero number. We want to choose a so that the coefficients are integers.

$$a(x-1)(x-2)(x-5) = a(x-1)[(x-2)(x-5)]$$
$$= a(x-1)(x^2 - 7x + 10)$$
$$= a(x^3 - 7x^2 + 10x - x^2 + 7x - 10)$$
$$= a(x^3 - 8x^2 + 17x - 10)$$

Because the coefficients are already integers, we can let $a = 1$. One polynomial of degree 3 having integer coefficients and 1, 2, and 5 as zeros is $x^3 - 8x^2 + 17x - 10$.

• Degree 4 with zeros -3, $2 - 5i$, with -3 a zero of multiplicity 2

Because -3 is a zero of multiplicity 2, $(x + 3)^2 = x^2 + 6x + 9$ is a factor. Because $2 - 5i$ is a zero, $2 + 5i$ is another zero. Another factor of the polynomial is

$$[x - (2 - 5i)][x - (2 + 5i)]$$
$$= (x - 2 + 5i)(x - 2 - 5i)$$
$$= x^2 - 2x - 5ix - 2x + 4 + 10i + 5ix - 10i - 25i^2$$
$$= x^2 - 4x + 4 - 25(-1) = x^2 - 4x + 29$$

The polynomial has the form $a(x^2 + 6x + 9)(x^2 - 4x + 29)$, where a is any real number that makes all coefficients integers.

$$a(x^2 + 6x + 9)(x^2 - 4x + 29)$$
$$= a(x^4 - 4x^3 + 29x^2 + 6x^3 - 24x^2 + 174x + 9x^2 - 36x + 261)$$
$$= a(x^4 + 2x^3 + 14x^2 + 138x + 261)$$

Because the coefficients are already integers, we can let $a = 1$. One polynomial that satisfies the given conditions is $x^4 + 2x^3 + 14x^2 + 138x + 261$.

In the previous problems, there were infinitely many answers because a could be any integer. In the following problem, there is exactly one polynomial that satisfies the given conditions. This means that a is likely a number other than 1.

- Degree 3 with zeros -1, -2, and 4, where the coefficient for x is -20

$$a(x+1)(x+2)(x-4) = a(x+1)[(x+2)(x-4)]$$
$$= a(x+1)(x^2 - 2x - 8)$$
$$= a(x^3 - 2x^2 - 8x + x^2 - 2x - 8)$$
$$= a(x^3 - x^2 - 10x - 8)$$
$$= ax^3 - ax^2 - 10ax - 8a$$

Because the coefficient of x to be -20, we need $-10ax = -20x$. This gives us $a = 2$ (from $-10a = -20$). The polynomial that satisifies the conditions is $2x^3 - 2x^2 - 20x - 16$.

PRACTICE

For Problems 1 to 6, solve the equations and write complex solutions in the form $a + bi$, where a and b are real numbers.

1. $9x^2 + 4 = 0$
2. $6x^2 + 8x + 9 = 0$
3. $x^4 - 81 = 0$
4. $x^3 + 13x - 34 = 0$
5. $x^4 - x^3 + 8x^2 - 9x - 9 = 0$; $x = -3i$ is a solution
6. $x^3 - 5x^2 + 7x + 13 = 0$; $x = 3 - 2i$ is a solution

For Problems 7 to 10, find a polynomial with integer coefficients having the given conditions.

7. Degree 3 with zeros 0, -4, and 6
8. Degree 4 with zeros -1 and $6 - 7i$, where $x = -1$ has multiplicity 2
9. Degree 3, zeros 4, and ± 1, with leading coefficient 3
10. Degree 4 with zeros i and $4i$, with constant term -16
11. State each zero and its multiplicity for $f(x) = x^2(x + 4)(x + 9)^6(x - 5)^3$.

✔ SOLUTIONS

1.
$$9x^2 + 4 = 0$$
$$9x^2 = -4$$
$$x^2 = -\frac{4}{9}$$
$$x = \pm\sqrt{-\frac{4}{9}} = \pm\frac{2}{3}i = \frac{2}{3}i, \; -\frac{2}{3}i$$

2.
$$x = \frac{-8 \pm \sqrt{8^2 - 4(6)(9)}}{2(6)}$$
$$= \frac{-8 \pm \sqrt{-152}}{12} = \frac{-8 \pm 2\sqrt{38}\,i}{12}$$
$$= \frac{2(-4 \pm \sqrt{38}\,i)}{12} = \frac{-4 \pm \sqrt{38}\,i}{6}$$
$$= -\frac{4}{6} \pm \frac{\sqrt{38}}{6}i = -\frac{2}{3} \pm \frac{\sqrt{38}}{6}i$$
$$= -\frac{2}{3} + \frac{\sqrt{38}}{6}i, \; -\frac{2}{3} - \frac{\sqrt{38}}{6}i$$

3. $x^4 - 81 = (x^2 - 9)(x^2 + 9) = (x - 3)(x + 3)(x^2 + 9)$

$$x^2 + 9 = 0$$
$$x^2 = -9$$
$$x = \pm\sqrt{-9} = \pm3i$$

The solutions are ±3 and $\pm3i$.

4. $x = 2$ is a solution, so $x - 2$ is a factor of $x^3 + 13x - 34$. Using synthetic division, we can find the quotient, which is another factor.

$$
\begin{array}{r|rrrr}
2 & 1 & 0 & 13 & -34 \\
  &   & 2 & 4 & 34 \\
\hline
  & 1 & 2 & 17 & 0
\end{array}
$$

The quotient is $x^2 + 2x + 17$. We find the other solutions by solving $x^2 + 2x + 17 = 0$.

$$x = \frac{-2 \pm \sqrt{2^2 - 4(1)(17)}}{2(1)} = \frac{-2 \pm \sqrt{-64}}{2} = \frac{-2 \pm 8i}{2}$$

$$= \frac{2(-1 \pm 4i)}{2} = -1 \pm 4i$$

The solutions are 2 and $-1 \pm 4i$.

5. $x = -3i$ is a solution, so $x = 3i$ is a solution, also. One factor of $x^4 - x^3 + 8x^2 - 9x - 9$ is $(x - 3i)(x + 3i) = x^2 + 9 = x^2 + 0x + 9$.

$$
\begin{array}{r}
x^2 - x - 1 \\
x^2 + 0x + 9 \overline{\smash{\big)}\ x^4 - x^3 + 8x^2 - 9x - 9} \\
\underline{-(x^4 + 0x^3 + 9x^2)} \\
-x^3 - x^2 - 9x \\
\underline{-(-x^3 + 0x^2 - 9x)} \\
-x^2 + 0x - 9 \\
\underline{-(-x^2 + 0x - 9)} \\
0
\end{array}
$$

Solve $x^2 - x - 1 = 0$.

$$x = \frac{-(-1) \pm \sqrt{(-1)^2 - 4(1)(-1)}}{2(1)} = \frac{1 \pm \sqrt{5}}{2}$$

The solutions are $\pm 3i$ and $\frac{1 \pm \sqrt{5}}{2}$.

6. $x = 3 - 2i$ is a solution, so $x = 3 + 2i$ is also a solution. One factor of $x^3 - 5x^2 + 7x + 13$ is

$$[x - (3 - 2i)][x - (3 + 2i)]$$

$$= (x - 3 + 2i)(x - 3 - 2i)$$

$$= x^2 - 3x - 2ix - 3x + 9 + 6i + 2ix - 6i - 4i^2$$

$$= x^2 - 6x + 9 - 4(-1)$$

$$= x^2 - 6x + 13$$

$$x^2 - 6x + 13 \overline{\smash{\big)}\, x^3 - 5x^2 + 7x + 13}$$

$$\frac{x+1}{}$$

$$-(x^3 - 6x^2 + 13x)$$

$$x^2 - 6x + 13$$

$$-(x^2 - 6x + 13)$$

$$0$$

The solutions are $3 \pm 2i$ and -1.

7. One polynomial with integer coefficients, with degree 3 and zeros 0, -4, and 6 is

$$x(x+4)(x-6) = x(x^2 - 2x - 24) = x^3 - 2x^2 - 24x$$

8. One polynomial with integer coefficients, with degree 4 and zeros -1 and $6 - 7i$, where $x = -1$ has multiplicity 2 is

$$(x+1)^2[x-(6-7i)][x-(6+7i)]$$
$$= (x+1)^2(x-6+7i)(x-6-7i)$$
$$= [(x+1)(x+1)](x^2 - 6x - 7ix - 6x + 36 + 42i$$
$$+ 7ix - 42i - 49i^2)$$
$$= (x^2 + 2x + 1)(x^2 - 12x + 85)$$
$$= x^4 - 12x^3 + 85x^2 + 2x^3 - 24x^2 + 170x + x^2 - 12x + 85$$
$$= x^4 - 10x^3 + 62x^2 + 158x + 85$$

9. The factors are $x - 4$, $x - 1$, and $x + 1$.

$$a(x-4)(x-1)(x+1) = a(x-4)[(x-1)(x+1)]$$
$$= a(x-4)(x^2-1)$$
$$= a[(x-4)(x^2-1)]$$
$$= a(x^3 - 4x^2 - x + 4)$$
$$= ax^3 - 4ax^2 - ax + 4a$$

We want the leading coefficient to be 3, so $a = 3$. The polynomial that satisifies the conditions is $3x^3 - 12x^2 - 3x + 12$.

10. The factors are $x + i$, $x - i$, $x - 4i$, and $x + 4i$.

$$a(x + i)(x - i)(x - 4i)(x + 4i)$$
$$= a[(x + i)(x - i)][(x - 4i)(x + 4i)]$$
$$= a(x^2 + 1)(x^2 + 16)$$
$$= a(x^4 + 17x^2 + 16)$$
$$= ax^4 + 17ax^2 + 16a$$

We want $16a = -16$, so $a = -1$. The polynomial that satisifies the conditions is $-x^4 - 17x^2 - 16$.

11. $x = 0$ is a zero with multiplicity 2.

$x = -4$ is a zero with multiplicity 1.

$x = -9$ is a zero with multiplicity 6.

$x = 5$ is a zero with multiplicity 3.

Summary

In this chapter, we learned how to

- *Identify characteristics for the graph of a polynomial function.* From the leading term of a polymomial function (the term having x to its highest power), we know the end behavior for the graph. If the degree of the polynomial is even, both ends of the graph go up (when the leading coefficient is positive) or both ends go down (when the leading coefficient is negative). If the degree of the polynomial is odd, the graph goes down on the left and up on the right (when the leading coefficient is positive), or the graph goes up on the left and down on the right (when the leading coefficient is negative). If c is a real number, the graph has an x-intercept at $x = c$ for each factor of the form $x - c$.

- *Sketch the graph of a polynomial function.* We can sketch the graph of many polynomial functions by plotting the x-intercepts, a point between x-intercepts and a point outside the left-most and right-most x-intercept. We then draw a smooth curve through the points.

- *Perform polynomial division.* We learned how to find the quotient and remainder when dividing any two polynomials (except the zero polynomial). Long division works for any such divisor. When the divisor polynomial is in the form $x - c$, we can find the quotient and remainder much more easily with synthetic division.

- *Factor a polynomial using polynomial division.* If we know that $x = c$ is an x-intercept for the function's graph, then we know that $x - c$ is a factor of the polynomial. When dividing the polynomial by $x - c$, we get a remainder of zero, and we know that the quotient is another factor of the polynomial. We find the rest of the polynomial's zeros/factors by finding the zeros of the quotient.

- *Use the Rational Zeros Theorem, Rule of Signs, and the Upper and Lower Bounds Theorem to find zeros.* We cannot use polynomial division to factor a polynomial until we have a zero. We use the Rational Zero Theorem on polynomials with integer coefficients by constructing a list of rational numbers whose numerators divide the constant term and whose denominators divide the leading coefficient. We then check these candidates to see which, if any, is a zero. Descartes' Rule of Signs counts the possible number of real zeros. We use the Upper and Lower Bounds Theorem to find an interval on the x-axis that is guaranteed to contain every x-intercept.

- *Perform arithmetic on complex numbers.* We add/subtract two complex numbers by combining like terms. We multiply two complex numbers in the form $(a + bi)(c + di)$ using the FOIL method, replacing i^2 with -1, and combining like terms. We divide two complex numbers in the form $\frac{a+bi}{c+di}$ by multiplying the numerator and denominator by $c - di$ (the denominator's conjugate) and simplifying the numerator. The denominator is the real number $c^2 + d^2$.

- *Find complex solutions to quadratic equations.* Every quadratic equation, $ax^2 + bx + c = 0$, has a solution, but some of these solutions are complex. One way to find these solutions is to use the quadratic formula, $\frac{-b \pm \sqrt{b^2 - 4ac}}{2a}$. The solutions are complex if $b^2 - 4ac$ is negative.

- *Work with complex zeros of a polynomial.* Some polynomials have complex zeros. If a polynomial (with real coefficients) has a complex zero, then its conjugate is also a zero. The same fact for real zeros of a polynomial is true for complex zeros: $x = c$ is a zero means $x - c$ is a factor. We can find complex zeros for a polynomial function with polynomial division.

- *Find a polynomial with a given degree and given zeros.* If we are told the zeros of a polynomial function and its degree, then we know its factors and how many are there. By the Fundamental Theorem of Algebra, a polynomial of degree n has n zeros; therefore, it has n factors.

QUIZ

1. **The graph in Figure 7-21 is the graph of which polynomial function?**

   A. $P(x) = x(x-1)(x+3)$
      $= x^3 + 2x^2 - 3x$

   B. $P(x) = x^2(x-1)(x+3)$
      $= x^4 + 2x^3 - 3x^2$

   C. $P(x) = x(x+1)(x-3)$
      $= x^3 - 2x^2 - 3x$

   D. $P(x) = x^2(x+1)(x-3)$
      $= x^4 - 2x^3 - 3x^2$

2. **What are the x-intercepts for the graph of $f(x) = x(x-4)(x+5)$?**

   A. $0, 5, -4$

   B. $5, -4$

   C. $0, -5, 4$

   D. $-5, 4$

3. **According to the Rational Zero Theorem, which of the following is NOT a possible zero for the polynomial $3x^4 + 8x^3 - 5x^2 + 9x + 2$?**

   A. 2

   B. 3

   C. 1

   D. $-\frac{2}{3}$

4. **What is the remainder for $\frac{5x^3 - 6x^2 + 2x + 4}{x+3}$?**

   A. -191

   B. 91

   C. 65

   D. 29

5. **Find the product $(\frac{1}{2} - 3i)(4 + 2i)$.**

   A. $2 - 17i$

   B. $-1 + 11i$

   C. $8 - 11i$

   D. $-4 - 11i$

6. **Find the zeros for the polynomial function $y = x^3 - 2x^2 + 25x - 50$.**

   A. $5, \pm 2i$

   B. $-5, \pm 2i$

   C. $-2, \pm 5i$

   D. $2, \pm 5i$

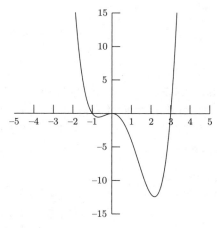

FIGURE 7-21

7. Completely factor the polynomial $x^4 + 8x^2 - 9$.

   A. $(x - i)(x + i)(x - 3)(x + 3)$ C. $(x - 1)(x + 1)(x - 3)(x + 3)$

   B. $(x - 3i)(x + 3i)(x - 1)(x + 1)$ D. $(x - 3i)(x + 3i)(x - i)(x + i)$

8. What is the quotient for $\frac{4x^3 - 2x^2 + 5x + 8}{x^2 + 2x - 3}$?

   A. $4x + 6$ C. $4x - 6$

   B. $4x - 10$ D. $4x + 10$

9. According to Descartes' Rule of Signs, how many positive zeros are there for the function $f(x) = x^5 + 3x^4 + 5x^3 + 6x^2 + x - 10$?

   A. 2 or 0   C. Exactly 1

   B. 5 or 3 or 1   D. It is impossible to tell without the graph.

10. Perform the division $\frac{4 - 9i}{1 + 2i}$.

   A. $-\frac{14}{5} - \frac{17}{5}i$ C. $\frac{22}{5} - \frac{1}{5}i$

   B. $\frac{22}{5} - \frac{17}{5}i$ D. $-\frac{14}{5} - \frac{1}{5}i$

11. Describe the end behavior for the graph of $y = -\frac{2}{3}x^5 + 4x^3 - 7x^2 + 8x + 15$.

   A. The graph goes up on the left and up on the right.

   B. The graph goes down on the left and down on the right.

   C. The graph goes down on the left and up on the right.

   D. The graph goes up on the left and down on the right.

12. Find a polynomial function having real coefficients of degree 4 and having zeros $1 - 3i$, 2, and -1.

   A. $y = x^4 - 3x^3 + 10x^2 - 6x - 20$ C. $y = x^4 + x^3 + 5x^2 - 13x - 18$

   B. $y = x^4 + x^3 + 6x^2 - 14x - 20$ D. $y = x^4 - 3x^3 + 9x^2 - 14x - 18$

13. Find the zeros for $2x^3 - 7x^2 - 9x + 6$.

   A. $\frac{1}{2}, \frac{3 \pm \sqrt{33}}{2}$ C. $3, \frac{2 \pm \sqrt{29}}{2}$

   B. $-\frac{1}{2}, \frac{-3 \pm \sqrt{33}}{2}$ D. $-3, \frac{-2 \pm \sqrt{29}}{2}$

14. According to the Rational Zeros Theorem, which interval on the x-axis contains *all* of the x-intercepts for the graph of $f(x) = x^3 - 16x^2 + 12x + 45$?

   A. Between $x = -1$ and $x = 16$ C. Between $x = -3$ and $x = 18$

   B. Between $x = -4$ and $x = 14$ D. Between $x = -1$ and $x = 21$

15. Solve the equation: $x^2 + 4x + 8 = 0$.

   A. $-2 \pm 2i$ C. $-4 \pm 2i$

   B. $2 \pm 2i$ D. $4 \pm 2i$

chapter **8**

Rational Functions

Rational functions are another major family of functions that you will see in calculus. The graph of many rational functions have one or more *asymptotes*. Learning about asymptotes will prepare you for infinite limits that you will study in calculus. We will learn about other functions having asymptotes in later chapters. As we have with other functions, we will learn how to sketch the graph of a rational function by plotting only a few points.

CHAPTER OBJECTIVES

In this chapter, you will

- Recognize characteristics of the graph of a rational function
- Find the intercepts for the graph of a rational function
- Find the asymptotes for the graph of a rational function
- Sketch the graph of a rational function

Introduction to Rational Functions

A *rational function* is a function that can be written as one polynomial divided by another.

$$r(x) = \frac{P(x)}{Q(x)} = \frac{a_n x^n + a_{n-1} x^{n-1} + \cdots + a_1 x + a_0}{b_m x^m + b_{m-1} x^{m-1} + \cdots + b_1 x + b_0}$$

Polynomial functions are a special kind of rational function whose denominator function is $Q(x) = 1$. While the graph of every polynomial function has exactly one y-intercept, the graph of a rational function might not have a y-intercept. If it has a y-intercept, we find it by evaluating the function at zero. The x-intercepts (if any) are the zeros of the numerator. The domain of a rational function is all real numbers except the zeros of the denominator.

Asymptotes

The graph of a rational function often comes in pieces. For every zero of the denominator, there is a break in the graph. If the function is reduced to lowest terms (the numerator and denominator have no common factors), then there is a *vertical asymptote* at these breaks. The graph rises (or falls) very fast near these asymptotes. The graph in Figure 8-1 is the graph of $f(x) = \frac{1}{x-1}$. It has a vertical asymptote at the line $x = 1$ because $x = 1$ is the zero of the denominator.

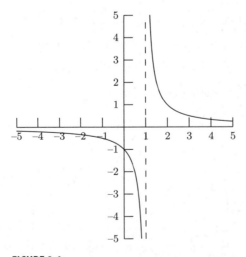

FIGURE 8-1

A vertical asymptote shows that the y-values get large when the x-values get close to a zero in the denominator. To see this, we evaluate $f(x) = \frac{1}{x-1}$ at $x = 0.99$ and $x = 1.01$, two x-values close to a zero in the denominator.

$$f(0.99) = \frac{1}{0.99 - 1} = -100 \qquad \text{and} \qquad f(1.01) = \frac{1}{1.01 - 1} = 100$$

If the graph flattens out for large values of x, then the graph has a *horizontal asymptote*. The graph in Figure 8-1 has the x-axis as its horizontal asymptote. A horizontal asymptote shows that as x gets very large, the y-values get very close to a fixed number. In the function $f(x) = \frac{1}{x-1}$, there is a horizontal asymptote at $y = 0$ (the x-axis). This means that as x gets large, the y-values get close to zero.

$$f(100) = \frac{1}{100 - 1} = \frac{1}{99} \approx 0.010101 \qquad \text{and}$$

$$f(-100) = \frac{1}{-100 - 1} = -\frac{1}{101} \approx -0.009901$$

Vertical asymptotes are easy to find—set the denominator equal to zero and solve for x. Whether or not a graph has a horizontal asymptote depends on the degree of the numerator and of the denominator.

- If the degree of the numerator is larger than the degree of the denominator, there is no horizontal asymptote.

- If the degree of the denominator is larger than the degree of the numerator, there is a horizontal asymptote at $y = 0$, which is the x-axis.

- If the degree of the numerator equals the degree of the denominator, there is a horizontal asymptote at $y = \frac{a_n}{b_m}$, where a_n is the leading coefficient of the numerator and b_m is the leading coefficient of the denominator.

We will see why these rules are true in Example 8-2.

EXAMPLE 8-1

Find the intercepts, vertical asymptotes, and horizontal asymptotes.

- $f(x) = \dfrac{x^2 - 16}{3x + 1}$

  Solving $3x + 1 = 0$, we get $x = -\frac{1}{3}$. The vertical line $x = -\frac{1}{3}$ is the vertical asymptote for this graph. There is no horizontal asymptote because the degree of the numerator, 2, is more than the degree of the denominator, 1. The x-intercepts are ± 4 (from $x^2 - 16 = 0$) and the y-intercept is $\frac{0^2 - 16}{3(0) + 1} = -16$.

• $g(x) = \dfrac{15}{x^2 - 4x - 5}$

The solutions to $x^2 - 4x - 5 = 0$ are $x = 5, -1$. This graph has two vertical asymptotes, the vertical lines $x = 5$ and $x = -1$. The x-axis is the horizontal asymptote because the degree of the numerator, 0, is less than the degree of the denominator, 2. (A reminder, the degree of a constant term is zero, $15 = 15x^0$.) There is no x-intercept because the numerator of this fraction is always 15, it is never zero. The y-intercept is $\frac{15}{0^2 - 4(0) - 5} = -3$.

• $f(x) = \dfrac{3x^2}{x^2 + 2}$

Because the equation $x^2 + 2 = 0$ has no real solutions, this graph has no vertical asymptote. There is a horizontal asymptote at $y = \frac{3}{1} = 3$ because the degree of the numerator and the degree of the denominator are the same. The x-intercept is zero (from $3x^2 = 0$). The y-intercept is $\frac{3(0)^2}{0^2 + 2} = \frac{0}{2} = 0$.

We now see why horizontal asymptotes depend on the degrees of the numerator and denominator. We use a technique that you will likely see in calculus. After identifying the highest power on x, we divide the numerator and denominator by x to this power. We then use the fact that $\frac{c}{x^n}$ (c is any real number) is very close to zero for large values of x. For example, if x is large, $\frac{1}{x^2}$ is very close to zero.

$$\frac{1}{(-100)^2} = 0.0001 \quad \text{and} \quad \frac{1}{100^2} = 0.0001$$

As x gets larger (in both the positive and negative directions), $\frac{1}{x^2}$ gets even closer to zero.

EXAMPLE 8-2

• $f(x) = \dfrac{3x^3 + 5x^2 + x - 6}{2x^4 + 8x^2 - 1}$

By our rule, we know that the x-axis, or the horizontal line $y = 0$, is a horizontal asymptote. Here is why. Because the highest power on x is 4, we multiply the fraction by $\dfrac{\frac{1}{x^4}}{\frac{1}{x^4}}$, which reduces to 1, so we are not changing the fraction.

$$\frac{3x^3 + 5x^2 + x - 6}{2x^4 + 8x^2 - 1} \cdot \frac{\frac{1}{x^4}}{\frac{1}{x^4}} = \frac{\frac{3x^3}{x^4} + \frac{5x^2}{x^4} + \frac{x}{x^4} - \frac{6}{x^4}}{\frac{2x^4}{x^4} + \frac{8x^2}{x^4} - \frac{1}{x^4}} = \frac{\frac{3}{x} + \frac{5}{x^2} + \frac{1}{x^3} - \frac{6}{x^4}}{2 + \frac{8}{x^2} - \frac{1}{x^4}}$$

For large values of x, the terms $\frac{3}{x}$, $\frac{5}{x^2}$, $\frac{1}{x^3}$, $\frac{6}{x^4}$, $\frac{8}{x^2}$, and $\frac{1}{x^4}$ are very close to zero, so for very large values of x,

$$\frac{\frac{3}{x} + \frac{5}{x^2} + \frac{1}{x^3} - \frac{6}{x^4}}{2 + \frac{8}{x^2} - \frac{1}{x^4}} \text{ is close to } \frac{0 + 0 + 0 - 0}{2 + 0 - 0} = \frac{0}{2} = 0.$$

• $g(x) = \dfrac{4x^3 + 8x^2 - 5x + 3}{9x^3 - x^2 + 8x - 2}$

The degree of the numerator equals the degree of the denominator, so the graph of this function has a horizontal asymptote at the line $y = \frac{4}{9}$. Here is why. Because the largest power on x is 3, we multiply the fraction by $\dfrac{\frac{1}{x^3}}{\frac{1}{x^3}}$.

$$\frac{4x^3 + 8x^2 - 5x + 3}{9x^3 - x^2 - 8x - 2} \cdot \frac{\frac{1}{x^3}}{\frac{1}{x^3}} = \frac{\frac{4x^3}{x^3} + \frac{8x^2}{x^3} - \frac{5x}{x^3} + \frac{3}{x^3}}{\frac{9x^3}{x^3} - \frac{x^2}{x^3} - \frac{8x}{x^3} - \frac{2}{x^3}} = \frac{4 + \frac{8}{x} - \frac{5}{x^2} + \frac{3}{x^3}}{9 - \frac{1}{x} - \frac{8}{x^2} - \frac{2}{x^3}}$$

For large values of x, $\dfrac{4 + \frac{8}{x} - \frac{5}{x^2} + \frac{3}{x^3}}{9 - \frac{1}{x} - \frac{8}{x^2} - \frac{2}{x^3}}$ is close to $\dfrac{4 + 0 - 0 + 0}{9 - 0 - 0 - 0} = \dfrac{4}{9}$.

These steps are not necessary to find the horizontal asymptotes, only the three rules given earlier in the chapter are.

We now put together our ability to find intercepts and asymptotes algebraically to match rational functions with their graphs. Also, the rational functions in Example 8-3 are either even or odd, so we can practice what we learned in Chapter 3 about the symmetry of even/odd functions.

EXAMPLE 8-3

Match the functions with the graphs in Figures 8-2 to 8-5.

• $f(x) = \dfrac{x}{x^2 - 4}$

The graph of $f(x)$ has an x- and y-intercept at $(0, 0)$ and has vertical asymptotes at $x = -2$, $x = 2$. The horizontal asymptote is $y = 0$ (the

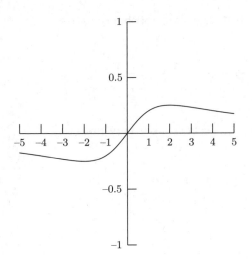

FIGURE 8-2

FIGURE 8-3

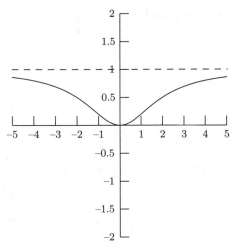

FIGURE 8-4

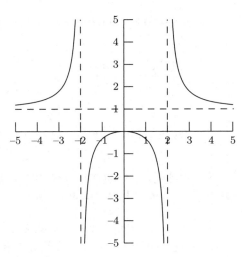

FIGURE 8-5

x-axis). Also the graph is symmetric with respect to the origin because the function is odd.

$$f(-x) = \frac{-x}{(-x)^2 - 4} = -\frac{x}{x^2 - 4} = -f(x)$$

The graph for this function is given in Figure 8-3.

- $g(x) = \dfrac{x^2}{x^2 - 4}$

The graph for this function also has its x- and y-intercept at $(0,0)$ and has vertical asymptotes at $x = -2$, $x = 2$. The horizontal asymptote is $y = 1$. The graph for $g(x)$ is symmetric with respect to the y-axis because $g(x)$ is an even function.

$$g(-x) = \frac{(-x)^2}{(-x)^2 - 4} = \frac{x^2}{x^2 - 4} = g(x)$$

The graph for $g(x)$ is in Figure 8-5.

- $r(x) = \dfrac{x}{x^2 + 4}$

The graph of $r(x)$ has its x- and y-intercept at $(0,0)$ but does not have any vertical asymptotes. It does have a horizontal asymptote at $y = 0$. The graph of $r(x)$ is symmetric with respect to the origin because $r(x)$ is an odd function.

$$r(-x) = \frac{-x}{(-x^2) + 4} = -\frac{x}{x^2 + 4} = -r(x)$$

The graph for $r(x)$ is in Figure 8-2.

- $h(x) = \dfrac{x^2}{x^2 + 4}$

This graph also has its x- and y-intercept at $(0,0)$ and does not have any vertical asymptotes. The graph has a horizontal asymptote at $y = 1$. Because the function is even, its graph is symmetric with respect to the y-axis.

$$h(-x) = \frac{(-x)^2}{(-x)^2 + 4} = \frac{x^2}{x^2 + 4} = h(x)$$

The graph for $h(x)$ is in Figure 8-4.

PRACTICE

Find the intercepts, vertical asymptotes, and horizontal asymptotes.

1. $f(x) = \dfrac{x + 2}{2x + 3}$

2. $g(x) = \dfrac{-3x}{x^2 + x - 20}$

3. $h(x) = \dfrac{x^2 - 1}{x^2 + 1}$

4. $R(x) = \dfrac{9x^2 - 1}{8x + 3}$

5. $f(x) = \dfrac{x^3 + 1}{x^2 + 4}$

6. $f(x) = \dfrac{2}{x^2}$

Match the function in Problems 7 to 10 with the graphs in Figures 8-6 to 8-9.

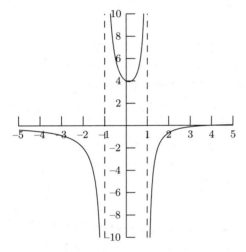

FIGURE 8-6

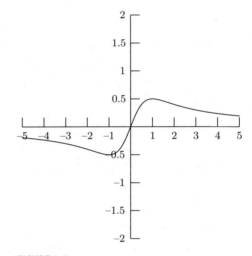

FIGURE 8-7

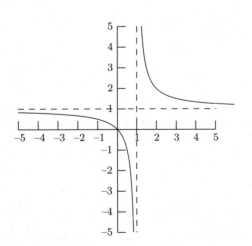

FIGURE 8-8

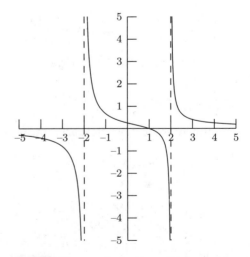

FIGURE 8-9

7. $y = \dfrac{x-1}{x^2-4}$

8. $r(x) = \dfrac{x-4}{x^2-1}$

9. $f(x) = \dfrac{x}{x-1}$

10. $R(x) = \dfrac{x}{x^2+1}$

 SOLUTIONS

1. The vertical asymptote is $x = -\frac{3}{2}$, from $2x + 3 = 0$. The horizontal asymptote is $y = \frac{1}{2}$ because the numerator and denominator have the same degree. The x-intercept is -2, from $x + 2 = 0$. The y-intercept is $\frac{0+2}{2(0)+3} = \frac{2}{3}$.

2. The vertical asymptotes are $x = -5$ and $x = 4$, from $x^2 + x - 20 = 0$. The horizontal asymptote is $y = 0$ because the denominator has the higher degree. The x-intercept is zero, from $-3x = 0$. The y-intercept is $\frac{-3(0)}{0^2+0-20} = \frac{0}{-20} = 0$.

3. There is no vertical asymptote because $x^2 + 1 = 0$ has no real solution. The horizontal asymptote is $y = \frac{1}{1} = 1$ because the numerator and denominator have the same degree. The x-intercepts are ± 1, from $x^2 - 1 = 0$. The y-intercept is $\frac{0^2-1}{0^2+1} = \frac{-1}{1} = -1$.

4. The vertical asymptote is $x = -\frac{3}{8}$, from $8x + 3 = 0$. There is no horizontal asymptote because the numerator has the higher degree. The x-intercepts are $\pm \frac{1}{3}$, from $9x^2 - 1 = 0$. The y-intercept is $\frac{9(0)^2-1}{8(0)+3} = \frac{-1}{3}$.

5. There is no vertical asymptote because $x^2 + 4 = 0$ has no real solution. There is no horizontal asymptote because the numerator has the higher degree. The x-intercept is -1, from $x^3 + 1 = 0$. The y-intercept is $\frac{0^3+1}{0^2+4} = \frac{1}{4}$.

6. The vertical asymptote is $x = 0$, from $x^2 = 0$. The horizontal asymptote $y = 0$ because the denominator has the higher degree. There is no x-intercept because the numerator is 2, never zero. There is no y-intercept because $\frac{2}{0^2}$ is not defined.

7. See Figure 8-9

8. See Figure 8-6

9. See Figure 8-8

10. See Figure 8-7

Sketching the Graph of a Rational Function

If the graph of a rational function has any asymptotes, we plot them with dashed lines. We then plot intercepts, if necessary and points that illustrate how fast the graph approaches any asymptote. To show how a graph behaves near a vertical asymptote, we plot a point to its left and to its right. To show how a graph behaves near a horizontal asymptote, we plot points for larger x-values (in both the postive and negative directions). When a graph has both horizontal and vertical asymptotes, we also plot points for a couple of mid-sized x-values.

EXAMPLE 8-4

Sketch the graph of the rational function.

• $f(x) = \dfrac{2x + 1}{x - 4}$

The x-intercept is $-\frac{1}{2}$, and the y-intercept is $-\frac{1}{4}$. The vertical asymptote is $x = 4$, and the horizontal asymptote is $y = 2$. We use dashed lines for the asymptotes and plot the points for $x = 3$, $x = 5$, $x = -10$, and $x = 10$ to show how the graph behaves near the asymptotes (see Figure 8-10).

It is not obvious what the graph looks like to the right of the vertical asymptote, so we plot a point for $x = 7$. We then draw a smooth curve through the points (see Figure 8-11).

• $g(x) = \dfrac{1}{x^2 + 1}$

There is no vertical asymptote because $x^2 + 1 = 0$ has no real solution. The x-axis is the horizontal asymptote. This graph has no x-intercept. The y-intercept is 1. We use $x = 5, -5$ to show the graph's horizontal asymptotic behavior. The function is even, so the left half is a reflection of the right half. We plot points for $x = 1, 2$. The y-values for $x = -1, -2$ are the same, so we plot these for points to the left of the y-axis (see Figure 8-12).

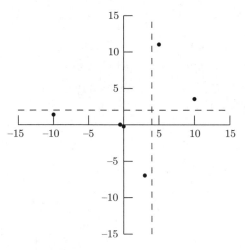

FIGURE 8-10

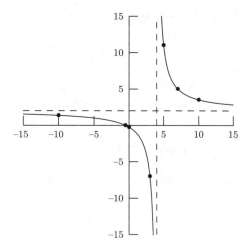

FIGURE 8-11

• $R(x) = \dfrac{x^2 + 1}{x^2 - 1}$

The vertical asymptotes are $x = -1$ and $x = 1$. The horizontal asymptote is $y = 1$. There is no x-intercept, and the y-intercept is -1. We use $x = 5$, -5 for the horizontal asymptote and $x = -0.9, 0.9, -1.1, 1.1$ for the vertical asymptotes. To get a better idea of what the graph looks like, we must plot other points. We use $x = 2$ and $x = -2$ (see Figure 8-13).

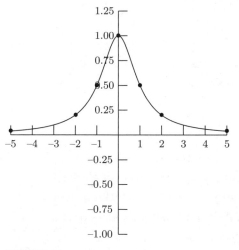

FIGURE 8-12

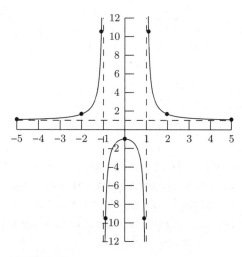

FIGURE 8-13

Slant Asymptotes

If the degree of the numerator is exactly one more than the degree of the denominator, then the graph has a *slant asymptote* (also called *oblique asymptote*). We can find the equation of a slant asymptote by performing polynomial division. The equation for the slant asymptote is "$y =$ quotient."

 EXAMPLE 8-5

Find an equation for the slant asymptote.

- $f(x) = \dfrac{4x^2 + 3x - 5}{x + 2}$

  When we divide $4x^2 + 3x - 5$ by $x + 2$, we get a quotient of $4x - 5$. The slant asymptote is the line $y = 4x - 5$.

$$
\begin{array}{r}
4x-5 \\
x+2 \overline{\smash{\big)}\ 4x^2+3x-5} \\
\underline{-(4x^2+8x)} \\
-5x-5 \\
\underline{-(-5x-10)} \\
5
\end{array}
$$

- $f(x) = \dfrac{x^3 + 2x^2 - 1}{x^2 + x + 2}$

$$
\begin{array}{r}
x+1 \\
x^2+x+2 \overline{\smash{\big)}\ x^3+2x^2+0x-1} \\
\underline{-(x^3+\ x^2+2x)} \\
x^2-2x-1 \\
\underline{-(x^2+\ x+2)} \\
-3x-3
\end{array}
$$

The slant asymptote is $y = x + 1$.

When sketching the graph of a rational function that has a slant asymptote, we can show the behavior of the graph near the slant asymptote by plotting points for larger x-values. We can tell if an x-value is large enough by checking their y-values in both the line and rational function. If they are fairly close, then the x-value is large enough.

EXAMPLE 8-6

Sketch the graph of rational function.

- $f(x) = \dfrac{x^2 + x - 6}{x + 2}$

The x-intercepts are -3 and 2. The y-intercept is -3. The vertical asymptote is $x = -2$.

$$
\begin{array}{r}
-2\,\big|\,\begin{array}{rrr} 1 & 1 & -6 \\ & -2 & 2 \end{array} \\
\hline
\begin{array}{rrr} 1 & -1 & -4 \end{array}
\end{array}
$$

The quotient is $x - 1$, so the slant asymptote is $y = x - 1$. We use $x = 10$ and $x = -10$ to show the graph's behavior near the slant asymptote. We also plot points for $x = -1$ and $x = -2.5$ for the vertical asymptote (see Figure 8-14).

- $h(x) = \dfrac{x^3}{x^2 - 1}$

The x-intercept is zero, and the y-intercept is zero, too. The vertical asymptotes are $x = -1$ and $x = 1$.

$$
\begin{array}{r}
x \\
x^2 + 0x - 1\,\big|\,\overline{\;x^3 + 0x^2 + 0x + 0\;} \\
\underline{-(x^3 + 0x^2 - x)} \\
x
\end{array}
$$

The quotient is x, so the slant asymptote is $y = x$. We plot points for $x = -5$ and $x = 5$ to show the graph's behavior near the slant asymptote, $x = -1.1, 1.1, -0.9, 0.9$ for the vertical asymptotes, and $x = -2, 2$ for in-between points (see Figure 8-15).

Still Struggling

The graph of a rational function can cross a horizontal asympote or a slant asymptote but never a vertical asymptote.

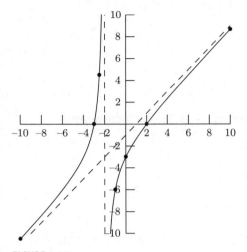

FIGURE 8-14

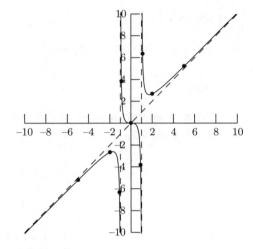

FIGURE 8-15

PRACTICE

Find the asymptotes and intercepts and sketch the graph.

1. $f(x) = \dfrac{1}{x+2}$

2. $g(x) = \dfrac{x}{x^2-1}$

3. $h(x) = \dfrac{2x-4}{x+2}$

4. Hint: Rewrite this function as one fraction.

$$f(x) = \dfrac{1}{x} + \dfrac{1}{x-2}$$

5. $f(x) = \dfrac{x^2+x-12}{x-2}$

SOLUTIONS

1. The asymptotes are $x = -2$ and $y = 0$ (the x-axis). There is no x-intercept. The y-intercept is $\frac{1}{2}$ (see Figure 8-16).

2. The asymptotes are $x = -1$, $x = 1$, and $y = 0$. The x-intercept and y-intercept are zero (see Figure 8-17).

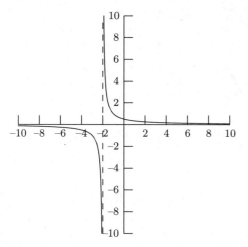

FIGURE 8-16

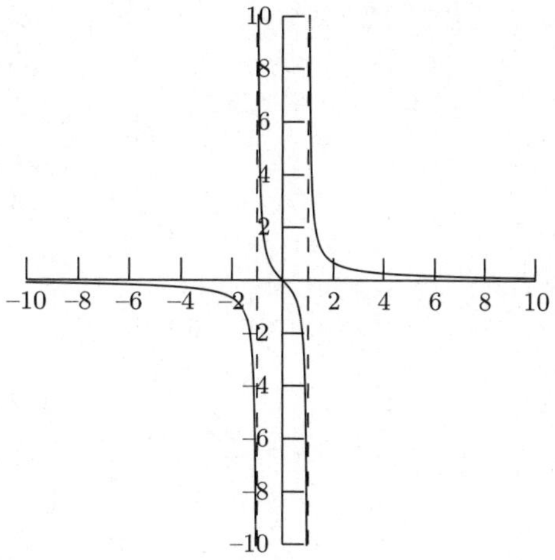

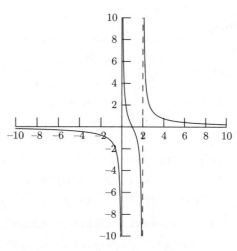

FIGURE 8-17

3. The asymptotes are $x = -2$ and $y = 2$. The x-intercept is 2, and the y-intercept is -2 (see Figure 8-18).

4. $f(x) = \dfrac{1}{x} + \dfrac{1}{x - 2} = \dfrac{1}{x} \cdot \dfrac{x - 2}{x - 2} + \dfrac{1}{x - 2} \cdot \dfrac{x}{x} = \dfrac{x - 2 + x}{x(x - 2)} = \dfrac{2x - 2}{x(x - 2)} = \dfrac{2x - 2}{x^2 - 2x}$

The asymptotes are $x = 0$, $x = 2$, and $y = 0$. The x-intercept is 1, and there is no y-intercept (see Figure 8-19).

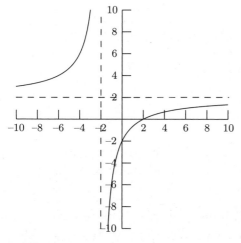

FIGURE 8-18

FIGURE 8-19

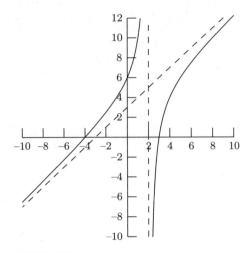

FIGURE 8-20

5. The vertical asymptote is $x = 2$. The x-intercepts are -4 and 3. The y-intercept is 6. We can use synthetic division to perform polynomial division to find the slant asymptote.

$$
\begin{array}{r|rrr}
2 & 1 & 1 & -12 \\
  &   & 2 & 6 \\
\hline
  & 1 & 3 & -6
\end{array}
$$

The quotient is $x + 3$, so the slant asymptote is $y = x + 3$ (see Figure 8-20).

Summary

Let $r(x) = \dfrac{P(x)}{Q(x)} = \dfrac{a_n x^n + a_{n-1} x^{n-1} + \cdots + a_1 x + a_0}{b_m x^m + b_{m-1} x^{m-1} + \cdots + b_1 x + b_0}$.

[Assume that $r(x)$ is written in lowest terms.]

In this chapter, we learned how to

- *Find the intercepts for the graph of a rational function.* The zeros of the numerator give us the x-intercepts, assuming any exist. We find the y-intercept (if it exists) by evaluating the function at $x = 0$.

- *Find the vertical asymptotes for the graph of a rational function.* The vertical asymptotes (if any exists) occur at the zeros of the denominator. As x gets closer to a vertical asymptote, its y-value gets larger.

- *Find the horizontal asymptote for the graph of a rational function.* If the degree of the numerator is the same as the degree of the denominator, the horizontal asymptote is $y = \frac{a_n}{b_m}$, the quotient of the leading coefficients of the numerator and denominator. If the denominator has the higher degree, the horizontal asymptote is the x-axis. If the numerator has the higher degree, the graph does not have a horizontal asymptote.

- *Find the slant asymptote for the graph of a rational function.* If the degree of the numerator is exactly one more than the degree of the denominator, the graph has a slant asymptote. We find the slant asymptote with polynomial division. The equation for the slant asymptote is "$y = $ quotient."

- *Sketch the graph of a rational function.* If the graph has any asymptotes, we plot them using dashed lines. If the graph has a horizontal asymptote or a slant asymptote, we plot a point for "larger" x-values (both positive and negative). For each vertical asymptote, we plot a point to its left and to its right. We also plot any intercepts. After plotting these, we often need to plot another few points.

QUIZ

1. Find the horizontal asymptote for the graph of $f(x) = \frac{x^2+4}{2x^2+1}$.

   A. $y = \frac{1}{2}$

   B. $y = 0$ (the x-axis)

   C. The graph does not have a horizontal asymptote.

   D. It is impossible to tell without the graph.

2. Find the horizontal asymptote for the graph of $f(x) = \frac{x+4}{2x^2+1}$.

   A. $y = \frac{1}{2}$

   B. $y = 0$ (the x-axis)

   C. The graph does not have a horizontal asymptote.

   D. It is impossible to tell without the graph.

3. Find the horizontal asymptote for the graph of $f(x) = \frac{x^3+4}{2x^2+1}$.

   A. $y = \frac{1}{2}$

   B. $y = 0$ (the x-axis)

   C. The graph does not have a horizontal asymptote.

   D. It is impossible to tell without the graph.

4. Find the vertical asymptote(s) for the graph of $r(x) = \frac{x-6}{x^2-x-6}$.

   A. $x = 6, x = 3, x = -2$

   B. $x = 6, x = -3, x = 2$

   C. $x = 3, x = -2$

   D. $x = -3, x = 2$

5. Find the vertical asymptote(s) for the graph of $y = \frac{x^2-16}{x^2+16}$.

   A. $x = 1$

   B. $x = -4, x = 4$

   C. The graph does not have a vertical asymptote.

   D. It is impossible to tell without the graph.

6. Find the slant asymptote for the graph of $r(x) = \frac{x^3+4x^2-6x+1}{x^2+x-3}$.

   A. $y = x + 3$

   B. $y = -6x + 10$

   C. The graph does not have a slant asymptote.

   D. It is impossible to tell without the graph.

7. Find the slant asymptote for the graph of $g(x) = \frac{x^2+x-3}{x^3+4x^2-6x+1}$.

   A. $y = x + 3$

   B. $y = -6x + 10$

   C. The graph does not have a slant asymptote.

   D. It is impossible to tell without the graph.

8. **Find the *x*-intercept(s) for the graph of $y = \frac{4}{x^2-25}$.**

   A. ±5

   B. 4

   C. 0

   D. The graph does not have an *x*-intercept.

9. **Find the *x*-intercept(s) for the graph of $y = \frac{4x}{x^2-25}$.**

   A. ±5

   B. 4

   C. 0

   D. The graph does not have an *x*-intercept.

10. **Find the *y*-intercept for the graph of $f(x) = \frac{10x-3}{x^2+6}$.**

    A. 10

    B. $-\frac{1}{2}$

    C. $\frac{3}{10}$

    D. The graph does not have a *y*-intercept.

11. **The graph of which function is given in Figure 8-21?**

    A. $y = \frac{(x+1)(x-5)}{(x-1)(x+4)} = \frac{x^2-4x-5}{x^2+3x-4}$

    B. $y = \frac{(x-1)(x+4)}{(x+1)(x-5)} = \frac{x^2+3x-4}{x^2-4x-5}$

    C. $y = \frac{(x+1)(x-4)}{(x-1)(x+5)} = \frac{x^2-3x-4}{x^2+4x-5}$

    D. $y = \frac{(x-1)(x+5)}{(x+1)(x-4)} = \frac{x^2+4x-5}{x^2-3x-4}$

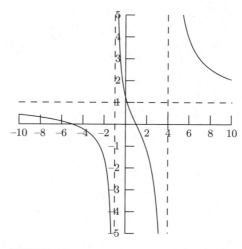

FIGURE 8-21

chapter 9

Exponential and Logarithmic Functions

Exponential functions and logarithmic functions show up in many professions. Their applications include the value of an asset (business), the population of a city (government), radioactive decay (physics), pH levels (chemistry), and earthquakes (geology). We will use what we learn in this chapter to solve some of these problem types. In addition to these applications, we will learn about exponents and logarithms—the domain and graph of their functions and solving equations involving them. We will also learn three properties of logarithms that will help us to rewrite logarithms. Using these properties to manipulate logarithms is good training for your work with formulas in calculus.

CHAPTER OBJECTIVES

In this chapter, you will

- Find the compound amount for an investment
- Sketch the graph of an exponential function
- Write an exponential equation in logarithmic form and vice versa

- Sketch the graph of a logarithmic function
- Find the domain of a logarithmic function
- Solve equations involving logarithms
- Solve equations involving exponents
- Solve applied problems involving exponents

Compound Growth

A quantity (such as a population, amount of money, or radiation level) changes *exponentially* if the growth or loss is a fixed percentage over a period of time. To see how this works, let us see how the value of an account grows over 4 years if $100 is deposited and earns 5% interest, compounded annually. *Compounded annually* means that the interest earned in the previous year earns interest.

After 1 year, $100 has grown to $100 + 0.05(100) = 100 + 5 = \$105$. In the second year, the original $100 earns 5% plus the $5 in interest earns 5% interest: $105 + (105)(0.05) = \$110.25$. Now this amount earns interest in the third year: $110.25 + (110.25)(0.05) = \$115.76$. Finally, this amount earns interest in the fourth year: $115.76 + (115.76)(0.05) = \$121.55$. If interest is not compounded, that is, the interest does not earn interest, the account would only be worth $120. The extra $1.55 is interest earned on interest.

Compound growth is not dramatic over the short run but it is over time. If $100 is left in an account earning 5% interest, compounded annually, for 20 years instead of 4 years, the difference between the compound growth and noncompound growth is a little more interesting. After 20 years, the compound amount is $265.33 compared to $200 for simple interest (noncompound growth). A graph of the growth of each type over 40 years is given in Figure 9-1. The line is the growth for simple interest, and the curve is the growth for compounded interest.

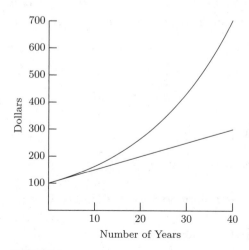

FIGURE 9-1

We can use a formula to compute the value of an account earning compounded interest. If P dollars is invested for t years, earning r interest rate, then it will grow to A dollars, where $A = P(1+r)^t$.

 **EXAMPLE 9-1**

Find the compound amount.

- **$5000, after 3 years, earning 6% interest, compounded annually**

  We use the formula $A = P(1+r)^t$: $P = 5000$, $r = 0.06$, and $t = 3$. We want to know A, the compound amount.

  $$A = 5000(1+0.06)^3 = 5000(1.06)^3 = 5000(1.191016) = 5955.08$$

  The compound amount is $5955.08.

- **$10,000 after 8 years, $7\frac{1}{4}$% interest, compounded annually**

  $$A = 10{,}000(1+0.0725)^8 = 10{,}000(1.0725)^8 \approx 10{,}000(1.7505656)$$

  $$\approx 17{,}505.66$$

  The compound amount is $17,505.66.

Many investments pay more often than once a year, some paying interest daily. Instead of using the annual interest rate, we use the interest rate per period, and instead of using the number of years, we use the number of periods. If there are n compounding periods per year, then the interest rate per period is $\frac{r}{n}$ and the total number of periods is nt. The compound amount formula becomes

$$A = P\left(1 + \frac{r}{n}\right)^{nt}$$

 **EXAMPLE 9-2**

Find the compound amount.

- **$5000, after 3 years, earning 6% annual interest**

  (a) **Compounded semiannually**

  (b) **Compounded monthly**

For (a), interest compounded semiannually means that it is compounded twice each year, so $n = 2$.

$$A = 5000\left(1 + \frac{0.06}{2}\right)^{2(3)} = 5000(1.03)^6 \approx 5000(1.194052) \approx 5970.26$$

The compound amount is $5970.26.

For (b), interest compounded monthly means that it is compounded 12 times each year, so $n = 12$.

$$A = 5000\left(1 + \frac{0.06}{12}\right)^{12(3)} = 5000(1.005)^{36} \approx 5000(1.19668) \approx 5983.40$$

The compound amount is $5983.40.

- $10,000, after 8 years, earning $7\frac{1}{4}\%$ annual interest, compounded weekly

   Interest that is paid weekly is paid 52 times each year, so $n = 52$.

$$A = 10,000\left(1 + \frac{0.0725}{52}\right)^{52(8)} \approx 10,000(1.001394231)^{416}$$

$$\approx 10,000(1.785317) \approx 17,853.17$$

The compound amount is $17,853.17.

Present Value

Suppose a couple wants to give their newborn grandson a gift of $50,000 on his 20th birthday. They can earn $7\frac{1}{2}\%$ interest, compounded annually. How much should they deposit now so that it grows to $50,000 in 20 years? To answer this question, we use the formula $A = P(1 + r)^t$, where we know that $A = 50,000$ but are looking for P.

$$50,000 = P(1 + 0.075)^{20}$$
$$= P(1.075)^{20}$$
$$\frac{50,000}{(1.075)^{20}} = P$$

The couple should deposit $11,770.66 now so that the investment grows to $50,000 in 20 years.

We say that $11,770.66 is the *present value* of $50,000 due in 20 years, earning $7\frac{1}{2}\%$ interest, compounded annually. The present value formula is

$P = A(1+r)^{-t}$, for interest compounded annually, and $P = A(1 + \frac{r}{n})^{-nt}$, for interest compounded n times per year.

 EXAMPLE 9-3

- Find the present value of $20,000 due in $8\frac{1}{2}$ years, earning 6% annual interest, compounded monthly.

$$P = 20{,}000\left(1 + \frac{0.06}{12}\right)^{-12(8.5)} = 20{,}000(1.005)^{-102} \approx 12{,}025.18$$

The present value is $12,025.18.

Continuous Compounding

The more often interest is compounded per year, the more interest is earned. $1000 earning 8% annual interest, compounded annually, is worth $1080 after 1 year. If interest is compounded quarterly, it is worth $1082.43 after 1 year. And if interest is compounded daily, it is worth $1083.28 after 1 year. What if interest is compounded each hour? Each second? It turns out that the most this investment could be worth (at 8% interest) is $1083.29, when interest is compounded each and every instant of time. During each instant of time, a tiny amount of interest is earned. This is called *continuous* compounding. The formula for the compound amount when interest is compounded continuously is $A = Pe^{rt}$, where A, P, r, and t are the same quantities as before. The letter e stands for a constant called Euler's number. It is approximately 2.718281828. You probably have an e or e^x key on your calculator. Although e is irrational, it can be approximated by rational numbers of the form $(1 + \frac{1}{m})^m$, where m is a large natural number. The larger m is, the better the approximation for e. If we make the substitution $m = \frac{n}{r}$ and use some algebra, we can see how $(1 + \frac{r}{n})^{nt}$ is very close to e^{rt}, for large values of n. If interest is compounded every minute, n would be 525,600, a rather large number!

EXAMPLE 9-4

- Find the compound amount of $5000 after 8 years, earning 12% annual interest, compounded continuously.

$$A = 5000e^{0.12(8)} = 5000e^{0.96} \approx 5000(2.611696) \approx 13{,}058.48$$

The compound amount is $13,058.48.

The compound growth formula for continuously compounded interest is used for other growth and decay problems. The general exponential growth model is $n(t) = n_0 e^{rt}$, where $n(t)$ replaces A and n_0 replaces P. Their meanings are the same—$n(t)$ is still the compound growth, and n_0 is still the beginning amount. The variable t represents time in this formula, although time is not always measured in years. The growth rate and t need to have the same unit of measure. If the growth rate is in days, then t needs to be in days. If the growth rate is in hours, then t needs to be in hours, and so on. If the "population" is getting smaller, then the formula is $n(t) = n_0 e^{-rt}$.

 EXAMPLE 9-5

- **The population of a city is estimated to be growing at the rate of 10% per year. In 2010, its population was 160,000. Estimate its population in the year 2015.**

  The year 2010 corresponds to $t = 0$, so the year 2015 corresponds to $t = 5$; n_0, the population in year $t = 0$, is 160,000. The population is growing at the rate of 10% per year, so $r = 0.10$. The formula $n(t) = n_0 e^{rt}$ becomes $n(t) = 160{,}000 e^{0.10t}$. We want to find $n(t)$ for $t = 5$.

  $$n(5) = 160{,}000 e^{0.10(5)} \approx 263{,}795$$

  The city's population is expected to be 264,000 in the year 2015 (estimates and projections are normally rounded off).

- **A county is losing population at the rate of 0.7% per year. If the population in 2011 is 1,000,000, what is it expected to be in the year 2018?**

  $n_0 = 1{,}000{,}000$, $t = 0$ in the year 2011, $t = 7$ in the year 2018, and $r = 0.007$. Because the county is losing population, we use the decay model: $n(t) = n_0 e^{-rt}$. The model for this county's population is $n(t) = 1{,}000{,}000 e^{-.007t}$. We want to find $n(t)$ for $t = 7$.

  $$n(7) = 1{,}000{,}000 e^{-.007(7)} \approx 952{,}181$$

  The population is expected to be 952,000 in the year 2018.

- **In an experiment, a culture of bacteria grew at the rate of 35% per hour. If 1000 bacteria were present at 10:00, how many were present at 10:45?**

  $n_0 = 1000$, $r = 0.35$, t is the number of hours after 10:00

The growth model becomes $n(t) = 1000e^{0.35t}$. We want to find $n(t)$ for 45 minutes, or $t = 0.75$ hours.

$$n(0.75) = 1000e^{0.35(0.75)} = 1000e^{0.2625} \approx 1300$$

At 10:45, there were approximately 1300 bacteria present in the culture.

PRACTICE

For Problems 1 to 6, find the compound amount.

1. Eight hundred dollars after 10 years, $6\frac{1}{2}\%$ interest, compounded annually

2. Twelve hundred dollars after 6 years, $9\frac{1}{2}\%$ interest, compounded annually

3. Eight hundred dollars after 10 years, earning $6\frac{1}{4}\%$ annual interest
   (a) Compounded quarterly
   (b) Compounded weekly

4. Nine thousand dollars after 5 years, earning $6\frac{3}{4}\%$ annual interest, compounded daily (assume 365 days per year)

5. Eight hundred dollars after 10 years, earning $6\frac{1}{2}\%$ annual interest, compounded continuously

6. Nine thousand dollars after 5 years, earning $6\frac{3}{4}\%$ annual interest, compounded continuously

7. Kia, a 20-year-old college student, opens a retirement account with $2000. If her account pays $8\frac{1}{4}\%$ interest, compounded annually, how much will this investment be worth when Kia reaches age 65?

8. The population of a city in the year 2012 is 2,000,000 and is expected to grow 1.5% per year. Estimate the city's population for the year 2022.

9. A construction company estimates that a piece of equipment is worth $150,000 when new. If it loses value continuously at the annual rate of 10%, what would be its value in 10 years?

10. Under certain conditions a culture of bacteria grows at the rate of about 200% per hour. If 8000 bacteria are present in a dish, how many are in the dish after 30 minutes?

11. Find the present value of $9000 due in 5 years, earning 7% annual interest, compounded annually.

12. **Find the present value of $50,000 due in 10 years, earning 4% annual interest, compounded quarterly.**

13. **Find the present value of $125,000 due in $4\frac{1}{2}$ years, earning $6\frac{1}{2}$% annual interest, compounded weekly.**

 SOLUTIONS

1. $A = 800(1 + 0.065)^{10} = 800(1.065)^{10} \approx 800(1.877137) \approx 1501.71$

    The compound amount is $1501.71.

2. $A = 1200(1 + 0.095)^6 = 1200(1.095)^6 \approx 1200(1.72379)$

    ≈ 2068.55

    The compound amount is $2068.55.

3. (a) $n = 4$

    $$A = 800\left(1 + \frac{0.0625}{4}\right)^{4(10)} = 800(1.015625)^{40} \approx 800(1.85924)$$

    $$\approx 1487.39$$

    The compound amount is $1487.39.

    (b) $n = 52$

    $$A = 800\left(1 + \frac{0.0625}{52}\right)^{52(10)} = 800(1.00120192)^{520}$$

    $$\approx 800(1.86754) \approx 1494.04$$

    The compound amount is $1494.04.

4. $n = 365$

    $$A = 9000\left(1 + \frac{0.0675}{365}\right)^{365(5)} \approx 9000(1.000184932)^{1825}$$

    $$\approx 9000(1.4013959) \approx 12{,}612.56$$

    The compound amount is $12,612.56.

5. $A = 800e^{0.065(10)} = 800e^{0.65} \approx 800(1.915540829) \approx 1532.43$

    The compound amount is $1532.43.

6. $A = 9000e^{0.0675(5)} = 9000e^{0.3375} \approx 9000(1.401439608)$

$\approx 12{,}612.96$

The compound amount is \$12,612.96.

7. $A = 2000(1 + 0.0825)^{45} = 2000(1.0825)^{45} \approx 2000(35.420585)$

$\approx 70{,}841.17$

The account will be worth \$70,841.17.

8. $n_0 = 2{,}000{,}000$, $r = 0.015$. The growth formula is $n(t) = 2{,}000{,}000e^{0.015t}$ and we want to find $n(t)$ when $t = 10$.

$$n(10) = 2{,}000{,}000e^{0.015(10)} \approx 2{,}323{,}668$$

The population in the year 2022 is expected to be about 2.3 million.

9. $n_0 = 150{,}000$, $r = 0.10$. We use the decay formula because value is being lost. The formula is $n(t) = 150{,}000e^{-0.10t}$. We want to find $n(t)$ when $t = 10$.

$$n(10) = 150{,}000e^{-0.10(10)} \approx 55{,}181.92$$

The equipment will be worth about \$55,000 after 10 years.

10. $n_0 = 8000$, $r = 2$. The growth formula is $n(t) = 8000e^{2t}$. We want to find $n(t)$ when $t = 0.5$.

$$n(0.5) = 8000e^{2(0.5)} \approx 21{,}746$$

About 21,700 bacteria are present after 30 minutes.

11. $P = 9000(1.07)^{-5} \approx 6416.88$

The present value is \$6416.88.

12. $P = 50{,}000\left(1 + \dfrac{0.04}{4}\right)^{-4(10)} = 50{,}000(1.01)^{-40} \approx 33{,}582.66$

The present value is \$33,582.66.

13. $P = 125{,}000 \left(1 + \dfrac{0.065}{52}\right)^{-52(4.5)} = 125{,}000(1.00125)^{-234}$

$\approx 93{,}316.45$

The present value is \$93,316.45.

The Exponential Function

A basic exponential function is of the form $f(x) = a^x$, where a is any positive number except 1. The graph of $f(x) = a^x$ comes in two shapes depending on whether $0 < a < 1$ (a is positive but smaller than 1) or $a > 1$. Figure 9-2 is the graph of $f(x) = (\tfrac{1}{2})^x$ and Figure 9-3 is the graph of $f(x) = 2^x$. Notice that the domain of an exponential function is all real numbers and that the graph of an exponential function has a horizontal asymptote.

We sketch the graph of $f(x) = a^x$ by plotting points for $x = -3$, $x = -2$, $x = -1$, $x = 0$, $x = 1$, $x = 2$, and $x = 3$. If a is too large or too small, points for $x = -3$ and $x = 3$ might be too awkward to graph because their y-values are too large or too close to zero. Before we begin sketching graphs, let us review the following exponent laws.

$$a^{-n} = \frac{1}{a^n} \qquad \left(\frac{1}{a}\right)^{-n} = a^n$$

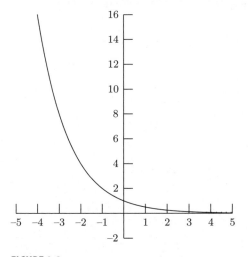

FIGURE 9-2   **FIGURE 9-3**

TABLE 9-1	
x	f(x)
−3	0.064 ($2.5^{-3} = \frac{1}{2.5^3}$)
−2	0.16 ($2.5^{-2} = \frac{1}{2.5^2}$)
−1	0.40 ($2.5^{-1} = \frac{1}{2.5}$)
0	1
1	2.5
2	6.25
3	15.625

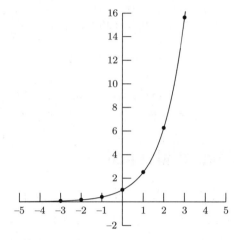

FIGURE 9-4

 EXAMPLE 9-6

Sketch the graph of the exponential function.

- $f(x) = 2.5^x$

    We begin with $x = -3,\ -2,\ -1,\ 0,\ 1,\ 2$, and 3 in a table of values (see Table 9-1). After computing the y-coordinates, we plot the points and draw the curve, see Figure 9-4.

- $g(x) = \left(\dfrac{1}{3}\right)^x$

    The points we plot are in Table 9-2 and the graph is sketched in Figure 9-5.

TABLE 9-2	
x	f(x)
−3	27 [$(\frac{1}{3})^{-3} = 3^3$]
−2	9 [$(\frac{1}{3})^{-2} = 3^2$]
−1	3 [$(\frac{1}{3})^{-1} = 3^1$]
0	1
1	0.33
2	0.11
3	0.037

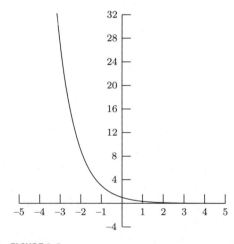

FIGURE 9-5

Transformations of the graphs of exponential functions behave in the same way as transformations of other functions.

 EXAMPLE 9-7

- The graph of $f(x) = -2^x$ is the graph of $y = 2^x$ reflected about the *x*-axis (flipped upside down). See Figure 9-6.

- The graph of $g(x) = 2^{-x}$ is the graph of $y = 2^x$ reflected about the *y*-axis (flipped sideways). See Figure 9-7.

- The graph of $h(x) = 2^{x+1}$ is the graph of $y = 2^x$ shifted to the left 1 unit. The point $(0, 1)$ has moved to $(-1, 1)$. See Figure 9-8.

- The graph of $F(x) = -3 + 2^x$ is the graph of $y = 2^x$ shifted down 3 units. The point $(0, 1)$ has moved to $(0, -2)$, and the horizontal asymptote has dropped to $y = -3$. See Figure 9-9.

 PRACTICE

Sketch the graph of the exponential function in Problems 1 to 3.

1. $f(x) = (\frac{3}{2})^x$

2. $g(x) = (\frac{2}{3})^x$

3. $h(x) = e^x$ (Use the *e* or e^x key on your calculator.)

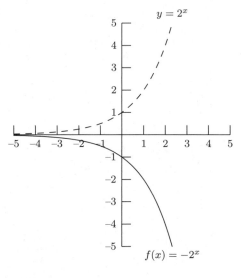

FIGURE 9-6

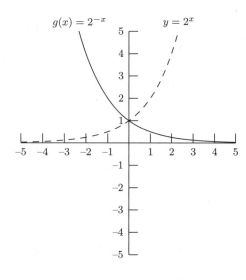

FIGURE 9-7

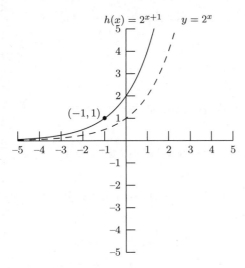

FIGURE 9-8

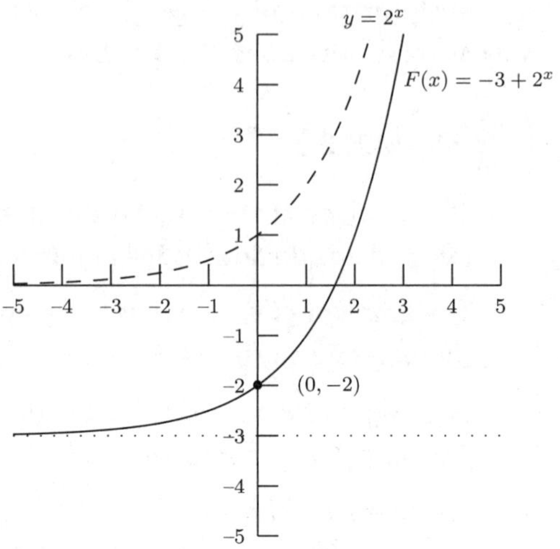

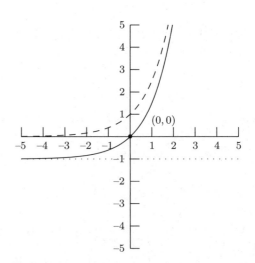

FIGURE 9-9

Match the function in Problems 4 to 7 with its graph in Figures 9-10 to 9-13. (The dashed graph is the graph of $y = 2.5^x$.)

4. $f(x) = 2.5^x - 1$

5. $g(x) = -2.5^x$

6. $G(x) = 2.5^{x+2}$

7. $R(x) = 2.5^{-x}$

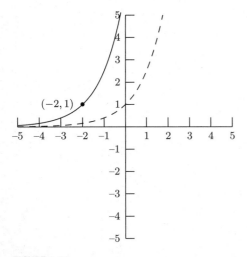

FIGURE 9-10

FIGURE 9-11

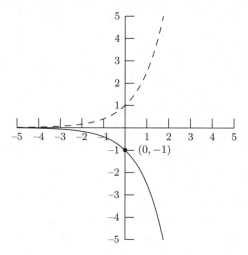

FIGURE 9-12

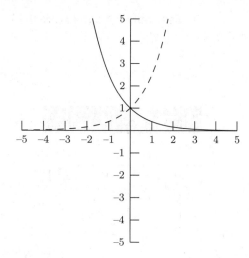

FIGURE 9-13

 SOLUTIONS

1. See Table 9-3 and Figure 9-14.

TABLE 9-3	
x	f(x)
−3	0.30 $[(\frac{3}{2})^{-3} = (\frac{2}{3})^3 = \frac{8}{27}]$
−2	0.44 $[(\frac{3}{2})^{-2} = (\frac{2}{3})^2 = \frac{4}{9}]$
−1	0.67 $[(\frac{3}{2})^{-1} = \frac{2}{3}]$
0	1
1	1.5
2	2.25
3	3.375

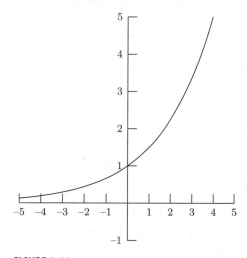

FIGURE 9-14

2. See Table 9-4 and Figure 9-15.

TABLE 9-4	
x	$f(x)$
−3	3.375 $[(\frac{2}{3})^{-3} = (\frac{3}{2})^3)]$
−2	2.25 $[(\frac{2}{3})^{-2} = (\frac{3}{2})^2]$
−1	1.5 $[(\frac{2}{3})^{-1} = \frac{3}{2}]$
0	1
1	0.67
2	0.44
3	0.30

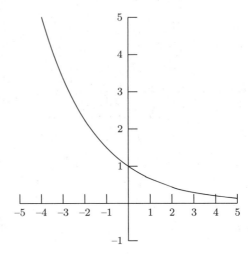

FIGURE 9-15

3. See Table 9-5 and Figure 9-16.

TABLE 9-5	
x	$f(x)$
−3	0.05
−2	0.14
−1	0.37
0	1
1	2.72
2	7.39
3	20.09

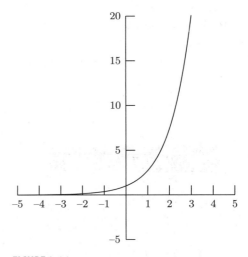

FIGURE 9-16

4. See Figure 9-11

5. See Figure 9-12

6. See Figure 9-10

7. See Figure 9-13

Logarithms

A common question for investors is, "How long will it take for my investment to double?" If $1000 is invested so that it earns 8% interest, compounded annually, how long will it take to grow to $2000? To answer the question using the compound growth formula, we need to solve for t in the equation $2000 = 1000(1.08)^t$. We divide both sides of the equation by 1000, giving us $2 = (1.08)^t$. Now what? It does not make sense to "take the tth root" of both sides. Instead, we need to use *logarithms*. In mathematical terms, the logarithm and exponent functions are inverses. Logarithms (or *logs*) are useful in solving many science and business problems.

The logarithmic equation $\log_a x = y$ is another way of writing the exponential equation $a^y = x$. Verbally, we say, "log base a of x is (or equals) y." For "$\log_a x$," we say, "log base a of x." Before we use logarithms to solve problems, we need to practice rewriting log equations in exponential form and exponential equations in log form.

 EXAMPLE 9-8

Rewrite the logarithmic equation in exponential form.

- $\log_3 9 = 2$

  The base of the logarithm is the base of the exponent, so 3 is raised to a power. The number that is equal to the log is the power, so the power on 3 is 2.

  $$\log_3 9 = 2 \text{ rewritten in exponential form is } 3^2 = 9$$

- $\log_2 \dfrac{1}{8} = -3$

  The base is 2 and the power is -3.

  $$2^{-3} = \frac{1}{8}$$

- $\log_9 3 = \dfrac{1}{2}$

  The base is 9 and the power is $\frac{1}{2}$.

  $$9^{1/2} = 3$$

Now we work in the other direction, rewriting exponential equations in logarithmic form. The equation $4^3 = 64$ written in logarithmic form is $\log_4 64 = 3$.

 EXAMPLE 9-9

- $3^4 = 81$

  The base of the logarithm is 3, and we are taking the log of 81. The equation rewritten in logarithmic form is $\log_3 81 = 4$.

- $a^3 = 4$

  The base is a, and we are taking the log of 4. The equation rewritten in logarithmic form is $\log_a 4 = 3$.

- $8^{(2/3)} = 4$

  The base is 8, and we are taking the log of 4. The equation rewritten in logarithmic form is $\log_8 4 = \frac{2}{3}$.

 PRACTICE

For Problems 1 to 5, rewrite the logarithmic equations in exponential form. For Problems 6 to 12, rewrite the exponential equations in logarithmic form.

1. $\log_4 16 = 2$

2. $\log_{100} 10 = \dfrac{1}{2}$

3. $\log_e 2 = 0.6931$

4. $\log_{(x+1)} 9 = 2$

5. $\log_7 \dfrac{1}{49} = -2$

6. $5^2 = 25$

7. $4^0 = 1$

8. $7^{-1} = \dfrac{1}{7}$

9. $125^{1/3} = 5$

10. $10^{-4} = 0.0001$

11. $e^{1/2} = 1.6487$

12. $8^x = 5$

✔ **SOLUTIONS**

1. $\log_4 16 = 2$ rewritten in exponential form is $4^2 = 16$

2. $\log_{100} 10 = \frac{1}{2}$ rewritten in exponential form is $100^{1/2} = 10$

3. $\log_e 2 = 0.6931$ rewritten in exponential form is $e^{0.6931} = 2$

4. $\log_{(x+1)} 9 = 2$ rewritten in exponential form is $(x + 1)^2 = 9$

5. $\log_7 \frac{1}{49} = -2$ rewritten in exponential form is $7^{-2} = \frac{1}{49}$

6. $5^2 = 25$ rewritten in logarithmic form is $\log_5 25 = 2$

7. $4^0 = 1$ rewritten in logarithmic form is $\log_4 1 = 0$

8. $7^{-1} = \frac{1}{7}$ rewritten in logarithmic form is $\log_7 \frac{1}{7} = -1$

9. $125^{1/3} = 5$ rewritten in logarithmic form is $\log_{125} 5 = \frac{1}{3}$

10. $10^{-4} = 0.0001$ rewritten in logarithmic form is $\log_{10} 0.0001 = -4$

11. $e^{1/2} = 1.6487$ rewritten in logarithmic form is $\log_e 1.6487 = \frac{1}{2}$

12. $8^x = 5$ rewritten in logarithmic form is $\log_8 5 = x$

Two Cancelation Properties

The first two logarithm properties we learn are the cancelation properties. They come directly from rewriting one form of an equation in the other form.

$$\log_a a^x = x \text{ and } a^{\log_a x} = x$$

When the bases of the exponent and logarithm are the same, they cancel, that is, they "undo" each other. Let us see why these properties are true. What would the expression $\log_a a^x$ be? We rewrite the equation "$\log_a a^x = ?$" as an exponential equation: $a^? = a^x$. Now we can see that "?" is x. This is why $\log_a a^x = x$. What would $a^{\log_a x}$ be? We rewrite "$a^{\log_a x} = ?$" in logarithmic form: $\log_a ? = \log_a x$, so "?" is x, and $a^{\log_a x} = x$.

▢ EXAMPLE 9-10

- $5^{\log_5 2}$

    The bases of the logarithm and exponent are both 5, so $5^{\log_5 2}$ simplifies to 2. Here are some other examples.

    - $10^{\log_{10} 8} = 8$ • $4^{\log_4 x} = x$ • $e^{\log_e 6} = 6$
    - $29^{\log_{29} 1} = 1$ • $\log_m m^r = r$ • $\log_7 7^{ab} = ab$

    Sometimes we need to use exponent properties before using the property $\log_a a^x = x$.

$$\sqrt[n]{a} = a^{1/n} \qquad \sqrt[n]{a^m} = a^{m/n} \qquad \frac{1}{a^m} = a^{-m}$$

EXAMPLE 9-11

- $\log_9 3 = \log_9 \sqrt{9} = \log_9 9^{1/2} = \dfrac{1}{2}$ • $\log_7 \dfrac{1}{49} = \log_7 \dfrac{1}{7^2}$
$$= \log_7 7^{-2} = -2$$

- $\log_{10} \sqrt[4]{10} = \log_{10} 10^{1/4} = \dfrac{1}{4}$ • $\log_{10} \sqrt[5]{100} = \log_{10} \sqrt[5]{10^2}$
$$= \log_{10} 10^{2/5} = \tfrac{2}{5}$$

Two types of logarithms occur frequently enough to have their own notation. They are $\log_e$ and $\log_{10}$. The notation for $\log_e$ is "ln" (pronounced "ell-in") and is called the *natural log*. The notation for $\log_{10}$ is "log" (no base is written) and is called the *common log*. The cancelation properties for these special logarithms are

$$\ln e^x = x \qquad e^{\ln x} = x \qquad \text{and} \qquad \log 10^x = x \qquad 10^{\log x} = x$$

EXAMPLE 9-12

- $e^4 = x - 1$ rewritten in log form is $\ln(x - 1) = 4$
- $10^x = 6$ rewritten in log form is $\log 6 = x$
- $\ln 2x = 25$ rewritten in exponent form is $e^{25} = 2x$
- $\log(2x - 9) = 4$ rewritten in exponent form is $10^4 = 2x - 9$

- $\ln e^{15} = 15$ • $10^{\log 5} = 5$
- $e^{\ln 14} = 14$ • $\log 10^{1/2} = \dfrac{1}{2}$
- $\ln e^{-4} = -4$ • $\log 10^{-4} = -4$

PRACTICE

1. Rewrite in logarithmic form: $e^{3x} = 4$
2. Rewrite in logarithmic form: $10^{x-1} = 15$
3. Rewrite in exponential form: $\ln 6 = x + 1$
4. Rewrite in exponential form: $\log 5x = 3$

Use logarithm and exponent properties to simplify the expression in Problems 5 to 24.

5. $9^{\log_9 3}$

6. $10^{\log_{10} 14}$

7. $5^{\log_5 x}$

8. $\log_{15} 15^2$

9. $\log_{10} 10^{-8}$

10. $\log_e e^x$

11. $\log_7 \sqrt{7}$

12. $\log_5 \dfrac{1}{5}$

13. $\log_3 \dfrac{1}{\sqrt{3}}$

14. $\log_4 \dfrac{1}{16}$

15. $\log_{25} \dfrac{1}{5}$

16. $\log_8 \dfrac{1}{2}$

17. $\log_{10} \sqrt{1000}$

18. $\ln e^5$

19. $\log 10^{\sqrt{x}}$

20. $10^{\log 9}$

21. $e^{\ln 6}$

22. $\log 10^{3x-1}$

23. $\ln e^{x+1}$

24. $\ln \dfrac{1}{e^3}$

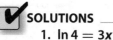

SOLUTIONS

1. $\ln 4 = 3x$

2. $\log 15 = x - 1$

3. $e^{x+1} = 6$

4. $10^3 = 5x$

5. $9^{\log_9 3} = 3$

6. $10^{\log_{10} 14} = 14$

7. $5^{\log_5 x} = x$

8. $\log_{15} 15^2 = 2$

9. $\log_{10} 10^{-8} = -8$

10. $\log_e e^x = x$

11. $\log_7 \sqrt{7} = \log_7 7^{1/2} = \dfrac{1}{2}$

12. $\log_5 \dfrac{1}{5} = \log_5 5^{-1} = -1$

13. $\log_3 \dfrac{1}{\sqrt{3}} = \log_3 \dfrac{1}{3^{1/2}} = \log_3 3^{-1/2} = -\dfrac{1}{2}$

14. $\log_4 \dfrac{1}{16} = \log_4 \dfrac{1}{4^2} = \log_4 4^{-2} = -2$

15. $\log_{25} \dfrac{1}{5} = \log_{25} \dfrac{1}{\sqrt{25}} = \log_{25} \dfrac{1}{25^{\frac{1}{2}}} = \log_{25} 25^{-1/2} = -\dfrac{1}{2}$

16. $2 = \sqrt[3]{8}$, so $\log_8 \dfrac{1}{2} = \log_8 \dfrac{1}{\sqrt[3]{8}} = \log_8 \dfrac{1}{8^{1/3}} = \log_8 8^{-1/3} = -\dfrac{1}{3}$

17. $1000 = 10^3$, so $\log_{10} \sqrt{1000} = \log_{10} \sqrt{10^3} = \log_{10} 10^{3/2} = \dfrac{3}{2}$

18. $\ln e^5 = 5$

19. $\log 10^{\sqrt{x}} = \sqrt{x}$

20. $10^{\log 9} = 9$

21. $e^{\ln 6} = 6$

22. $\log 10^{3x-1} = 3x - 1$

23. $\ln e^{x+1} = x + 1$

24. $\ln \dfrac{1}{e^3} = \ln e^{-3} = -3$

The Logarithmic Function

The logarithm function $g(x) = \log_a x$ is the inverse of the exponential function $f(x) = a^x$, so their graphs reflect each other across the line $y = x$. (See these graphs in Figure 9-17.) We can use what we know about the graph of an

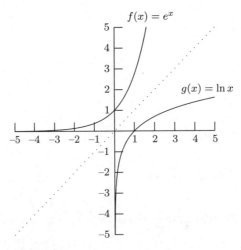

FIGURE 9-17

exponential function to sketch the graph of a logarithmic function. We rewrite the equation in exponential form and let the exponent (in this case, y) be the numbers $-3, -2, -1, 0, 1, 2,$ and 3.

 EXAMPLE 9-13

Sketch the graph of the logarithmic functions.

- $y = \log_2 x$

  Rewrite the equation in exponential form, $x = 2^y$, and let the exponent, y, be the numbers $-3, -2, -1, 0, 1, 2,$ and 3. The x-values for these points are computed in Table 9-6 and the graph is sketched in Figure 9-18.

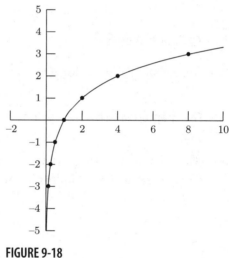

TABLE 9-6	
x	y
$\frac{1}{8}$	-3
$\frac{1}{4}$	-2
$\frac{1}{2}$	-1
1	0
2	1
4	2
8	3

FIGURE 9-18

- $y = \ln x$

  Rewritten in exponent form, this is $x = e^y$. Let $y = -3, -2, -1, 0, 1, 2,$ and 3. The y-values for these points are computed in Table 9-7 and the graph is sketched in Figure 9-19.

As long as a is larger than 1, all graphs for $f(x) = \log_a x$ look pretty much the same. The larger a is, the flatter the graph is to the right of $x = 1$. Knowing this and knowing how to graph transformations, we have a good idea of the graphs of many logarithmic functions.

TABLE 9-7	
x	**y**
0.05	−3
0.14	−2
0.37	−1
1	0
2.72	1
7.39	2
20.09	3

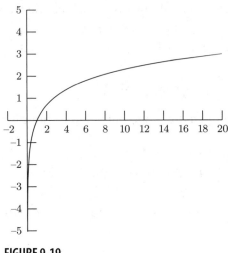

FIGURE 9-19

EXAMPLE 9-14

• The graph of $f(x) = \log_2(x - 2)$ is the graph of $y = \log_2 x$ shifted to the right 2 units.

• The graph of $f(x) = -5 + \log_3 x$ is the graph of $y = \log_3 x$ shifted down 5 units.

(The function $y = \log_a x$ is plotted with dashed graphs.) These transformations are sketched in Figures 9-20 and 9-21.

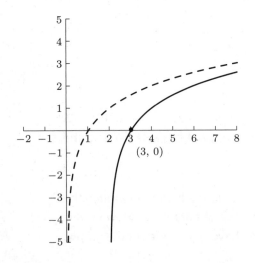

FIGURE 9-20

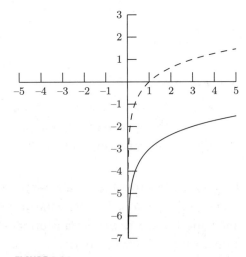

FIGURE 9-21

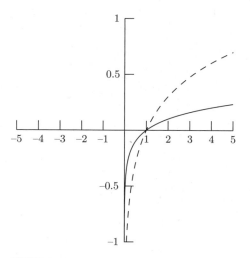

FIGURE 9-22   FIGURE 9-23

- $f(x) = \frac{1}{3} \log x$ is the graph of $y = \log x$ flattened vertically by a factor of one-third.

- The graph of $H(x) = \ln(-x)$ is the graph of $y = \ln x$ reflected across the y-axis. These transformations are sketched in Figures 9-22 and 9-23.

PRACTICE

Sketch the graph of the logarithmic function.

1. $y = \log_{1.5} x$
2. $y = \log_3 x$

Match the function in Problems 3 to 6 with its graph in Figures 9-24 to 9-27. [The dashed graph is the graph of $y = \log_2 x$. Hint: If the transformation involves vertical or horizontal shifting, the transformation of the point $(1, 0)$ is marked.]

3. $f(x) = -\log_2 x$
4. $g(x) = \log_2(x + 3)$
5. $h(x) = 3 + \log_2 x$
6. $P(x) = 2\log_2 x$

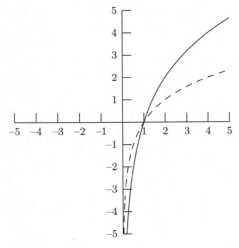

FIGURE 9-24

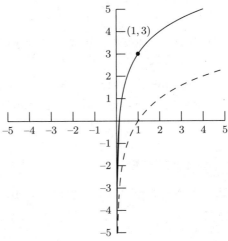

FIGURE 9-25

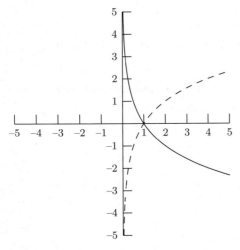

FIGURE 9-26

FIGURE 9-27

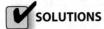SOLUTIONS

1. See Figure 9-28

2. See Figure 9-29

3. See Figure 9-26

4. See Figure 9-25

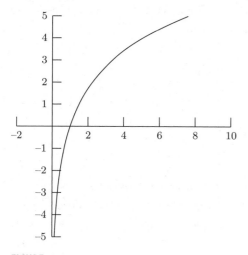

FIGURE 9-28

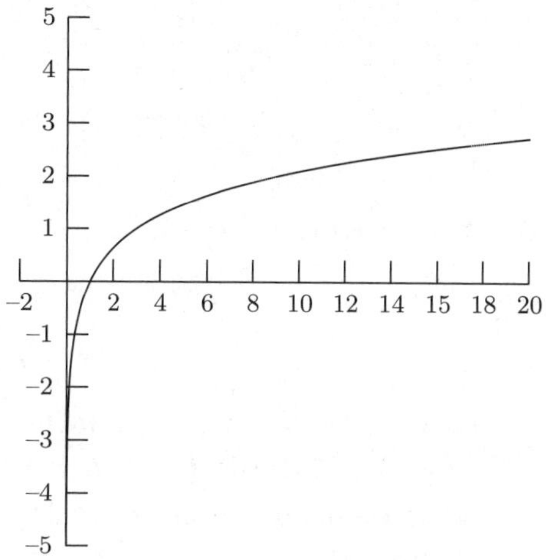

FIGURE 9-29

5. See Figure 9-27

6. See Figure 9-24

As you can see by these graphs, the domain of the function $f(x) = \log_a x$ is all positive real numbers, $(0, \infty)$. This means that we cannot take the log of zero or the log of a negative number. The reason is that a is a positive number, and raising a positive number to *any* power is always another positive number. We use this fact to find the domain of a logarithmic function algebraically.

EXAMPLE 9-15

Find the domain. Give your answers in interval notation.

- $f(x) = \log_5(2 - x)$

  Because we are taking the log of $2 - x$, $2 - x$ must be positive.

  $$2 - x > 0$$
  $$-x > -2$$
  $$x < 2$$

  The domain is $(-\infty, 2)$.

FIGURE 9-30

- $f(x) = \log(x^2 - x - 2)$

$$x^2 - x - 2 > 0$$

$$(x - 2)(x + 1) > 0$$

Put $x = 2$ and $x = -1$ on the number line and test to see where $(x - 2)$ $(x + 1) > 0$ is true. Once we have marked 2 and -1 on the number line, we test a point in each interval to see if the inequality is true or false, see Figure 9-30.

We want the "True" intervals, so the domain is $(-\infty, -1) \cup (2, \infty)$.

- $g(x) = \ln(x^2 + 1)$

Because $x^2 + 1$ is always positive, the domain is all real numbers, $(-\infty, \infty)$.

 PRACTICE

Find the domain. Give your answers in interval notation.

1. $f(x) = \ln(10 - 2x)$
2. $h(x) = \log(x^2 - 4)$
3. $f(x) = \log(x^2 + 4)$

 SOLUTIONS

1. Solve $10 - 2x > 0$. The domain is $x < 5$, $(-\infty, 5)$.

2. Solve $x^2 - 4 > 0$. From Figure 9-31, we see that the domain is $(-\infty, -2) \cup (2, \infty)$.

3. Because $x^2 + 4 > 0$ is always positive, the domain is all real numbers, $(-\infty, \infty)$.

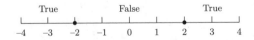

FIGURE 9-31

Equations Involving Exponents and Logarithms

Equations with exponents and logarithms come in many forms. Sometimes more than one strategy works to solve them. We first solve equations of the form "$\log_a$ = number" and "$\log_a = \log_a$." We solve an equation of the form "$\log_a$ = number" by rewriting the equation in exponential form.

 EXAMPLE 9-16

Solve the equation for x.

- $\log_3(x+1) = 4$

  Rewrite the equation in exponential form.

$$\log_3(x+1) = 4$$

$$3^4 = x + 1$$

$$81 = x + 1$$

$$80 = x$$

- $\log_2(3x - 4) = 5$

$$2^5 = 3x - 4 \qquad \text{Rewrite in exponential form.}$$

$$32 = 3x - 4$$

$$12 = x$$

The logarithms cancel for equations in the form "$\log_a = \log_a$" as long as the bases are the same. For example, the solution to the equation $\log_8 x = \log_8 10$ is $x = 10$. The cancelation law $a^{\log_a x} = x$ makes this work.

$$\log_8 x = \log_8 10$$

$$8^{\log_8 x} = 8^{\log_8 10}$$

$$x = 10 \qquad \text{(By a cancelation property)}$$

 EXAMPLE 9-17

Solve for x.

- $\log_6(x+1) = \log_6 2x$

$$\log_6(x+1) = \log_6 2x$$

$$x + 1 = 2x \qquad \text{The logs cancel.}$$

$$1 = x$$

- $\log 4 = \log(x - 1)$

$$\log 4 = \log(x - 1)$$
$$4 = x - 1 \quad \text{The logs cancel.}$$
$$5 = x$$

For some logarithmic equations, a solution might be extraneous. That is, such a solution is a solution to the rewritten equation but not to the original equation. We check them in the original equation to see which solutions are true solutions. In this book, you will be told when checking for extraneous solutions is necessary. In general, you should check all of your solutions.

EXAMPLE 9-18

Solve for x and check for extraneous solutions.

- $\log_2(x^2 + 3x - 10) = 3$

  We rewrite in exponential form: $2^3 = x^2 + 3x - 10$ and solve for x.

$$x^2 + 3x - 10 = 8$$
$$x^2 + 3x - 18 = 0$$
$$(x + 6)(x - 3) = 0$$

The solutions are $x = -6$ and $x = 3$. We check them in the original equation.

$$\log_2[(-6)^2 + 3(-6) - 10] = 3? \qquad \log_2[3^2 + 3(3) - 10] = 3?$$
$$\log_2 8 = 3 \text{ True} \qquad \log_2 8 = 3 \text{ True}$$

The solutions to the original equation are $x = -6$ and $x = 3$.

- $\log_5(x^2 + 5x - 4) = \log_5(x + 1)$

  The logs cancel leaving $x^2 + 5x - 4 = x + 1$.

$$x^2 + 5x - 4 = x + 1$$
$$x^2 + 4x - 5 = 0$$
$$(x + 5)(x - 1) = 0$$

The solutions are $x = -5$ and $x = 1$. We cannot allow $x = -5$ as a solution because $\log_5(-5 + 1)$ is not defined. We now check $x = 1$.

$$\log_5[1^2 + 5(1) - 4] = \log_5(1 + 1) \quad \text{is true}$$

The solution is $x = 1$.

 PRACTICE

Solve the equations for x.

1. $\log_7(2x + 1) = 2$
2. $\log_4(x + 6) = 2$
3. $\log 5x = 1$
4. $\log_2(8x - 1) = 4$

5. $\log_3(4x - 1) = \log_3 2$
6. $\log_2(3 - x) = \log_2 17$
7. $\ln 15x = \ln(x + 4)$
8. $\log \dfrac{x}{x - 1} = \log \dfrac{1}{2}$

9. $\ln(x^2 + x - 20) = \ln(3x + 4)$ (Check for extraneous solutions.)
10. $\log_4(2x^2 - 3x + 59) = 3$ (Check for extraneous solutions.)

SOLUTIONS

1.
$$\log_7(2x + 1) = 2$$
$$7^2 = 2x + 1$$
$$24 = x$$

2.
$$\log_4(x + 6) = 2$$
$$4^2 = x + 6$$
$$10 = x$$

3.
$$\log 5x = 1$$
$$10^1 = 5x$$
$$2 = x$$

4.

$$\log_2(8x - 1) = 4$$

$$2^4 = 8x - 1$$

$$\frac{17}{8} = x$$

5.

$$\log_3(4x - 1) = \log_3 2$$

$$4x - 1 = 2$$

$$x = \frac{3}{4}$$

6.

$$\log_2(3 - x) = \log_2 17$$

$$3 - x = 17$$

$$x = -14$$

7.

$$\ln 15x = \ln(x + 4)$$

$$15x = x + 4$$

$$x = \frac{4}{14} = \frac{2}{7}$$

8.

$$\log \frac{x}{x - 1} = \log \frac{1}{2}$$

$$\frac{x}{x - 1} = \frac{1}{2} \quad \text{Cross-multiply.}$$

$$2x = x - 1$$

$$x = -1$$

9.

$$\ln(x^2 + x - 20) = \ln(3x + 4)$$

$$x^2 + x - 20 = 3x + 4$$

$$x^2 - 2x - 24 = 0$$

$$(x - 6)(x + 4) = 0$$

The solutions are $x = 6$ and $x = -4$. Because $\ln[3(-4) + 4]$ is not defined, we only check $x = 6$ in the original equation.

$$\ln(6^2 + 6 - 20) = \ln[3(6) + 4] \quad \text{is true}$$

The only solution is $x = 6$.

10.

$$\log_4(2x^2 - 3x + 59) = 3$$

$$2x^2 - 3x + 59 = 4^3 \qquad (4^3 = 64)$$

$$2x^2 - 3x - 5 = 0$$

$$(2x - 5)(x + 1) = 0$$

We check the solutions $x = \frac{5}{2}$ and $x = -1$ in the original equation.

$$\log_4\left[2\left(\tfrac{5}{2}\right)^2 - 3\left(\tfrac{5}{2}\right) + 59\right] = 3? \qquad \log_4[2(-1)^2 - 3(-1) + 59] = 3?$$

$$\log_4 64 = 3 \text{ is true} \qquad \log_4 64 = 3 \text{ is true}$$

The solutions are $x = \frac{5}{2}$ and $x = -1$.

Strictly speaking, we only need to check that a solution is valid for the domain of every logarithm in the original equation.

Equations Involving Exponents

If an equation has a variable in an exponent, we use logarithms to solve it. For now, we solve exponential equations whose base is either e or 10. Once we have rewritten the equation in logarithmic form, we solve for the variable and then use a calculator to find approximate solutions.

EXAMPLE 9-19

Solve for *x*. Give solutions accurate to four decimal places.

• $e^{2x} = 3$

$$e^{2x} = 3 \qquad \text{Rewrite in logarithmic form.}$$

$$2x = \ln 3$$

$$x = \frac{\ln 3}{2}$$

$$x \approx \frac{1.0986}{2} \approx 0.5493$$

• $10^{x+1} = 9$

$$10^{x+1} = 9 \qquad \text{Rewrite in logarithmic form.}$$

$$x + 1 = \log 9$$

$$x = -1 + \log 9$$

$$x \approx -1 + 0.9542 \approx -0.0458$$

• $2500 = 1000e^{x-4}$

$$2500 = 1000e^{x-4} \qquad \text{Divide both sides by 1000 before rewriting}$$
$$\text{the equation.}$$

$$e^{x-4} = 2.5 \qquad \text{Rewrite in logarithmic form.}$$

$$x - 4 = \ln 2.5$$

$$x = 4 + \ln 2.5 \approx 4 + 0.9163 \approx 4.9163$$

PRACTICE

Solve for *x*. Give your solutions accurate to four decimal places.

1. $10^{3x} = 7$

2. $e^{2x+5} = 15$

3. $5000 = 2500e^{4x}$

4. $32 = 8 \cdot 10^{6x-4}$

5. $200 = 400e^{-0.06x}$

☑ **SOLUTIONS**

1.
$$10^{3x} = 7$$

$$3x = \log 7$$

$$x = \frac{\log 7}{3} \approx \frac{0.8451}{3} \approx 0.2817$$

2.
$$e^{2x+5} = 15$$

$$2x + 5 = \ln 15$$

$$2x = -5 + \ln 15$$

$$x = \frac{-5 + \ln 15}{2} \approx \frac{-5 + 2.7081}{2} \approx -1.1460$$

3.
$$5000 = 2500e^{4x}$$

$$\frac{5000}{2500} = e^{4x}$$

$$4x = \ln\left(\frac{5000}{2500}\right)$$

$$4x = \ln 2$$

$$x = \frac{\ln 2}{4} \approx \frac{0.6931}{4} \approx 0.1733$$

4.
$$32 = 8 \cdot 10^{6x-4} \qquad \textbf{Divide both sides by 8.}$$

$$4 = 10^{6x-4}$$

$$6x - 4 = \log 4$$

$$6x = 4 + \log 4$$

$$x = \frac{4 + \log 4}{6} \approx \frac{4 + 0.6021}{6} \approx 0.7670$$

5.
$$200 = 400e^{-0.06x}$$

$$\frac{1}{2} = e^{-0.06x}$$

$$-0.06x = \ln\left(\frac{1}{2}\right)$$

$$x = \frac{\ln(\frac{1}{2})}{-0.06} \approx \frac{-0.69315}{-0.06} \approx 11.5525$$

Three Important Logarithm Properties

The following three logarithm properties come directly from the exponent properties $a^m \cdot a^n = a^{m+n}$, $\frac{a^m}{a^n} = a^{m-n}$, and $a^{mn} = (a^m)^n$.

1. $\log_b mn = \log_b m + \log_b n$

2. $\log_b \dfrac{m}{n} = \log_b m - \log_b n$

3. $\log_b m^t = t\log_b m$

Let us see why Property 1 works. Let $x = \log_b m$ and $y = \log_b n$. Rewriting these equations in exponential form, we get $b^x = m$ and $b^y = n$. Multiplying m and n, we have $mn = b^x \cdot b^y = b^{x+y}$. Rewriting the equation $mn = b^{x+y}$ as a logarithmic equation, we get $\log_b mn = x + y$. Because $x = \log_b m$ and $y = \log_b n$, $\log_b mn = x + y$ becomes $\log_b mn = \log_b m + \log_b n$.

EXAMPLE 9-20

Use Property 1 to rewrite the logarithms.

- $\log_4 7x = \log_4 7 + \log_4 x$ • $\ln 15t = \ln 15 + \ln t$

- $\log_6 19t^2 = \log_6 19 + \log_6 t^2$ • $\log 100y^4 = \log 10^2 + \log y^4$

$$= 2 + \log y^4$$

- $\log_9 3 + \log_9 27$ • $\ln x + \ln \sqrt{y} = \ln x\sqrt{y}$

$$= \log_9 3(27) = \log_9 81 = 2$$

Use Property 2 to rewrite the logarithms.

- $\log\left(\dfrac{x}{4}\right) = \log x - \log 4$

- $\log_{15} 3 - \log_{15} 2 = \log_{15}\left(\dfrac{3}{2}\right)$

- $\log_4\left(\dfrac{4}{3}\right) = \log_4 4 - \log_4 3 = 1 - \log 3$

- $\ln\left(\dfrac{5}{x}\right) = \ln 5 - \ln x$

- $\ln 16 - \ln t = \ln \dfrac{16}{t}$

- $\log M_1 - \log M_0 = \log \dfrac{M_1}{M_0}$

 ## Still Struggling

When using Property 3, be careful not to include the "$\log_a$" symbol in the denominator.

The exponent property $\sqrt[n]{a^m} = a^{m/n}$ allows us to apply the third logarithm property to roots as well as to powers. The third logarithm property is especially useful in science and business applications.

 EXAMPLE 9-21

Use Property 3 to rewrite the logarithms.

- $\log_4 3^x = x\log_4 3$

- $\dfrac{1}{3}\ln t = \ln t^{1/3} = \ln \sqrt[3]{t}$

- $\log_6 \sqrt{2x} = \log_6(2x)^{1/2} = \dfrac{1}{2}\log_6 2x$

- $\log x^2 = 2\log x$

- $-3\log 8 = \log 8^{-3} = \log \dfrac{1}{8^3}$

- $\ln \sqrt[4]{t^3} = \ln t^{3/4} = \dfrac{3}{4}\ln t$

 PRACTICE

Use Property 1 to rewrite the logarithms in Problems 1 to 6. Use Property 2 to rewrite the logarithms in Problems 7 to 12. Use Property 3 to rewrite the logarithms in Problems 13 to 20.

1. $\ln 59t$

2. $\log 0.10y$

3. $\log_{30} 148x^2$

4. $\log_6 3 + \log_6 12$

5. $\log_5 9 + \log_5 10$

6. $\log 5 + \log 20$

7. $\log_4 \dfrac{10}{9x}$

8. $\log_2 \dfrac{7}{8}$

9. $\ln \dfrac{t}{4}$

10. $\log \dfrac{100}{x^2}$

11. $\log_7 2 - \log_7 4$

12. $\log_8 x - \log_8 3$

13. $\ln 5^x$

14. $\log_{12} \sqrt{3}$

15. $\log \sqrt{16x}$

16. $\log_5 6^{-t}$

17. $2 \log_8 3$

18. $(x + 6) \log_4 3$

19. $\log_{16} 10^{2x}$

20. $-2 \log_4 5$

✔ SOLUTIONS

1. $\ln 59t = \ln 59 + \ln t$

2. $\log 0.10y = \log 0.10 + \log y = \log 10^{-1} + \log y = -1 + \log y$

3. $\log_{30} 148x^2 = \log_{30} 148 + \log_{30} x^2$

4. $\log_6 3 + \log_6 12 = \log_6(3 \cdot 12) = \log_6 36 = \log_6 6^2 = 2$

5. $\log_5 9 + \log_5 10 = \log_5(9 \cdot 10) = \log_5 90$

6. $\log 5 + \log 20 = \log(5 \cdot 20) = \log 100 = \log 10^2 = 2$

7. $\log_4 \dfrac{10}{9x} = \log_4 10 - \log_4 9x$

8. $\log_2 \dfrac{7}{8} = \log_2 7 - \log_2 8 = \log_2 7 - \log_2 2^3 = (\log_2 7) - 3$

9. $\ln \dfrac{t}{4} = \ln t - \ln 4$

10. $\log \dfrac{100}{x^2} = \log 100 - \log x^2 = \log 10^2 - \log x^2 = 2 - \log x^2$

11. $\log_7 2 - \log_7 4 = \log_7 \dfrac{2}{4} = \log_7 \dfrac{1}{2}$

12. $\log_8 x - \log_8 3 = \log_8 \dfrac{x}{3}$

13. $\ln 5^x = x \ln 5$

14. $\log_{12} \sqrt{3} = \log_{12} 3^{1/2} = \dfrac{1}{2} \log_{12} 3$

15. $\log \sqrt{16x} = \log(16x)^{1/2} = \dfrac{1}{2}\log 16x$

16. $\log_5 6^{-t} = -t\log_5 6$

17. $2\log_8 3 = \log_8 3^2 = \log_8 9$

18. $(x+6)\log_4 3 = \log_4 3^{x+6}$

19. $\log_{16} 10^{2x} = 2x\log_{16} 10$

20. $-2\log_4 5 = \log_4 5^{-2} = \log_4 \dfrac{1}{5^2} = \log_4 \dfrac{1}{25}$

Using Multiple Properties

Sometimes we need to use several logarithm properties to rewrite more complicated logarithms. The hardest part of this process is to use the properties in the correct order. For example, which property should be used first on $\log \frac{x}{y^3}$? Do we first use the third property or the second property? We use the second property first. For the expression $\log(\frac{x}{y})^3$, we would use the third property first.

Going in the other direction, we need to use all three properties in the expression $\log_2 9 - \log_2 x + 3\log_2 y$. We need to use the second property to combine the first two terms.

$$\log_2 9 - \log_2 x + 3\log_2 y = \log_2 \frac{9}{x} + 3\log_2 y$$

We cannot use the first property on $\log_2 \frac{9}{x} + 3\log_2 y$ until we have used the third property to move the 3.

$$\log_2 \frac{9}{x} + 3\log_2 y = \log_2 \frac{9}{x} + \log_2 y^3 = \log_2 y^3 \frac{9}{x} = \log_2 \frac{9y^3}{x}$$

 EXAMPLE 9-22

Rewrite as a single logarithm.

- $\log_2 3x - 4\log_2 y$

    We need to use the third property to move the 4, and then we can use the second property.

$$\log_2 3x - 4\log_2 y = \log_2 3x - \log_2 y^4 = \log_2 \frac{3x}{y^4}$$

- $3 \log 4x + 2 \log 3 - 2 \log y$

$$3 \log 4x + 2 \log 3 - 2 \log y = \log(4x)^3 + \log 3^2 - \log y^2 \qquad \text{Property 3}$$
$$= \log 4^3 x^3 \cdot 3^2 - \log y^2 \qquad \text{Property 1}$$
$$= \log 576x^3 - \log y^2 = \log \frac{576x^3}{y^2} \quad \text{Property 2}$$

- $t \ln 4 + \ln 5$

$$t \ln 4 + \ln 5 = \ln 4^t + \ln 5 = \ln(5 \cdot 4^t) \qquad \text{(This is not } \ln 20^t.)$$

Expand each logarithm.

- $\ln \frac{3\sqrt{x}}{y^2}$

$$\ln \frac{3\sqrt{x}}{y^2} = \overbrace{\ln 3(x^{1/2}) - \ln y^2}^{\text{Property 2}} = \overbrace{\ln 3 + \ln x^{1/2} - \ln y^2}^{\text{Property 1}} = \overbrace{\ln 3 + \frac{1}{2} \ln x - 2 \ln y}^{\text{Property 3}}$$

- $\log_7 \frac{4}{10xy^2}$

$$\log_7 \frac{4}{10xy^2} = \log_7 4 - \log_7 10xy^2 = \log_7 4 - (\log_7 10 + \log_7 x + \log_7 y^2)$$
$$= \log_7 4 - (\log_7 10 + \log_7 x + 2 \log_7 y) \text{ or}$$
$$\log_7 4 - \log_7 10 - \log_7 x - 2 \log_7 y$$

PRACTICE

For Problems 1 to 5, rewrite each as a single logarithm. For Problems 6 to 10, expand each logarithm.

1. $2 \log x + 3 \log y$

2. $\log_6 2x - 2 \log_6 3$

3. $3 \ln t - \ln 4 + 2 \ln 5$

4. $t \ln 6 + 2 \ln 5$

5. $\frac{1}{2} \log x - 2 \log 2y + 3 \log z$

6. $\log \frac{4x}{y}$

7. $\ln \frac{6}{\sqrt{y}}$

8. $\log_4 \frac{10x}{\sqrt[3]{z}}$

9. $\ln \frac{\sqrt{4x}}{5y^2}$

10. $\log \sqrt{\frac{2y^3}{x}}$

✔ **SOLUTIONS**

1. $2\log x + 3\log y = \log x^2 + \log y^3 = \log x^2 y^3$

2. $\log_6 2x - 2\log_6 3 = \log_6 2x - \log_6 3^2$

$$= \log_6 2x - \log_6 9 = \log_6 \frac{2x}{9}$$

3. $$3\ln t - \ln 4 + 2\ln 5 = \ln t^3 - \ln 4 + \ln 5^2$$

$$= \ln \frac{t^3}{4} + \ln 25$$

$$= \ln 25\frac{t^3}{4} = \ln \frac{25t^3}{4}$$

4. $t\ln 6 + 2\ln 5 = \ln 6^t + \ln 5^2 = \ln[25(6^t)]$

5. $$\frac{1}{2}\log x - 2\log 2y + 3\log z = \log x^{1/2} - \log(2y)^2 + \log z^3$$

$$= \log x^{1/2} - \log 2^2 y^2 + \log z^3$$

$$= \log x^{1/2} - \log 4y^2 + \log z^3$$

$$= \log \frac{x^{1/2}}{4y^2} + \log z^3 = \log z^3\frac{x^{1/2}}{4y^2}$$

$$= \log \frac{z^3 x^{1/2}}{4y^2} \text{ or } \log \frac{z^3\sqrt{x}}{4y^2}$$

6. $\log \dfrac{4x}{y} = \log 4x - \log y = \log 4 + \log x - \log y$

7. $\ln \dfrac{6}{\sqrt{y}} = \ln 6 - \ln \sqrt{y} = \ln 6 - \ln y^{1/2} = \ln 6 - \dfrac{1}{2}\ln y$

8. $$\log_4 \frac{10x}{\sqrt[3]{z}} = \log_4 10x - \log_4 \sqrt[3]{z} = \log_4 10x - \log_4 z^{1/3}$$

$$= \log_4 10 + \log_4 x - \frac{1}{3}\log_4 z$$

9. $\ln \dfrac{\sqrt{4x}}{5y^2} = \ln \sqrt{4x} - \ln 5y^2 = \ln(4x)^{1/2} - \ln 5y^2$

$= \dfrac{1}{2} \ln 4x - (\ln 5 + \ln y^2) = \dfrac{1}{2}(\ln 4 + \ln x) - (\ln 5 + 2 \ln y)$

or $\dfrac{1}{2} \ln 4 + \dfrac{1}{2} \ln x - \ln 5 - 2 \ln y$

10. $\log \sqrt{\dfrac{2y^3}{x}} = \log \left(\dfrac{2y^3}{x} \right)^{1/2} = \dfrac{1}{2} \log \dfrac{2y^3}{x}$

$= \dfrac{1}{2}(\log 2y^3 - \log x) = \dfrac{1}{2}(\log 2 + \log y^3 - \log x)$

$= \dfrac{1}{2}(\log 2 + 3 \log y - \log x)$ or

$\dfrac{1}{2} \log 2 + \dfrac{3}{2} \log y - \dfrac{1}{2} \log x$

Solving Equations Using Logarithm Properties

With these logarithm properties we can solve more logarithm equations. We use these properties to rewrite equations either in the form "$\log_a = \log_a$" or in the form "$\log_a = $ number." When the equation is in the form "$\log_a = \log_a$," the logs cancel. When the equation is in the form "$\log_a = $ number," we rewrite the equation in exponential form. Instead of checking solutions in the original equation, we only need to make sure that the original logarithms are defined for the solutions.

EXAMPLE 9-23

- $\log_2(x - 5) + \log_2(x + 2) = 3$

    We use Property 1 to rewrite the equation in the form "$\log_a = $ number."

$\log_2(x - 5) + \log_2(x + 2) = 3$ Use Property 1.

$\log_2(x - 5)(x + 2) = 3$ Rewrite in exponential form.

$(x - 5)(x + 2) = 2^3$

$x^2 - 3x - 10 = 8$ This is a quadratic equation.

$x^2 - 3x - 18 = 0$

$(x - 6)(x + 3) = 0$

The solutions are $x = 6$ and $x = -3$. Because $\log_2(x + 2)$ is not defined for $x = -3$, the only solution is $x = 6$.

• $2\log_5(x + 1) - \log_5(x - 3) = \log_5 25$

We use Property 3 followed by Property 2 to rewrite the equation in the form "$\log_a = \log_a$."

$$2\log_5(x + 1) - \log_5(x - 3) = \log_5 25$$

$$\log_5(x + 1)^2 - \log_5(x - 3) = \log_5 25$$

$$\log_5 \frac{(x + 1)^2}{x - 3} = \log_5 25$$

$$\frac{(x + 1)^2}{x - 3} = 25$$

$$(x + 1)^2 = 25(x - 3)$$

$$(x + 1)(x + 1) = 25x - 75$$

$$x^2 + 2x + 1 = 25x - 75$$

$$x^2 - 23x + 76 = 0$$

$$(x - 4)(x - 19) = 0$$

Both $\log_5(x + 1)$ and $\log_5(x - 3)$ are defined for $x = 4$ and $x = 19$. The solutions are $x = 4$ and $x = 19$.

PRACTICE

Solve the equation for x.

1. $\log_3(2x + 1) + \log_3(x + 4) = 2$

2. $\ln(3x - 4) + \ln(x + 2) = \ln(2x + 1) + \ln(x + 2)$

3. $\log_2(5x + 1) - \log_2(x - 1) = 3$

4. $2\log_7(x + 1) = 2$

✅ SOLUTIONS

1. $\log_3(2x+1) + \log_3(x+4) = 2$ Use Property 1.

    $\log_3(2x+1)(x+4) = 2$ Rewrite in exponential form.

    $(2x+1)(x+4) = 3^2$

    $2x^2 + 9x + 4 = 9$

    $2x^2 + 9x - 5 = 0$

    $(2x-1)(x+5) = 0$

    Both $\log_3(2x+1)$ and $\log_3(x+5)$ are undefined for $x = -5$, so the only solution is $x = \frac{1}{2}$.

2. $\ln(3x-4) + \ln(x+2) = \ln(2x+1) + \ln(x+2)$ Use Property 1.

    $\ln(3x-4)(x+2) = \ln(2x+1)(x+2)$ The logs cancel.

    $(3x-4)(x+2) = (2x+1)(x+2)$

    $3x^2 + 2x - 8 = 2x^2 + 5x + 2$

    $x^2 - 3x - 10 = 0$

    $(x-5)(x+2) = 0$

    All of $\ln(3x-4)$, $\ln(x+2)$, and $\ln(x+2)$ are not defined for $x = -2$, so the only solution is $x = 5$.

3. $\log_2(5x+1) - \log_2(x-1) = 3$ Use Property 2.

    $\log_2 \dfrac{5x+1}{x-1} = 3$ Rewrite in exponential form.

    $\dfrac{5x+1}{x-1} = 2^3 = 8$ Cross-multiply.

    $5x+1 = 8(x-1)$

    $5x+1 = 8x-8$

    $x = 3$

4.

$$2\log_7(x+1) = 2 \qquad \text{Use Property 3.}$$

$$\log_7(x+1)^2 = 2 \qquad \text{Rewrite in exponential form.}$$

$$(x+1)^2 = 7^2$$

$$(x+1)(x+1) = 49$$

$$x^2 + 2x + 1 = 49$$

$$x^2 + 2x - 48 = 0$$

$$(x+8)(x-6) = 0$$

The only solution is $x = 6$ because $\log_7(x+1)$ is not defined at $x = -8$. We could have solved this problem in fewer steps if we had divided both sides by 2 in the first step, getting $\log_7(x+1) = 1$ in the second step.

The domains for $f(x) = \log(x-1)(x+2)$ and $g(x) = \log(x-1) + \log(x+2)$ are not the same, which *seems* to contradict the first logarithm property. Neither $\log(x-1)$ nor $\log(x+2)$ is defined for $x = -3$ because $-3 - 1$ and $-3 + 2$ are negative. But $\log(x-1)(x+2)$ *is* defined for $x = -3$ because $(-3 - 1)(-3 + 2)$ is *positive*. The domain of $f(x)$ includes x-values for which both $(x-1)$ and $(x+2)$ are negative.

The Change of Base Formula

There are countless bases for logarithms but calculators usually have only two logarithms—log and ln. How can we use our calculators to approximate $\log_2 5$? We can use the change of base formula but first, let us use logarithm properties to find this number. Let $x = \log_2 5$. Then $2^x = 5$. Take the common log of each side.

$$\log 2^x = \log 5 \qquad \text{Now use the third log property.}$$

$$x \log 2 = \log 5 \qquad \text{Divide both sides by the number } \log 2.$$

$$x = \frac{\log 5}{\log 2} \approx \frac{0.698970004}{0.301029996} \approx 2.321928095$$

This means that $2^{2.321928095}$ is very close to 5.

We just proved that $\log_2 5 = \frac{\log_{10} 5}{\log_{10} 2}$. Replace 2 with b, 5 with x, and 10 with a and we have the change of base formula.

$$\log_b x = \frac{\log_a x}{\log_a b}$$

This formula converts a logarithm with old base b to new base a. Usually, the new base is either e or 10.

 EXAMPLE 9-24

- Evaluate $\log_7 15$. Give your solution accurate to four decimal places.

    We use the change of base formula with both bases so that we can see it does not matter which base we choose.

$$\log_7 15 = \frac{\log 15}{\log 7} \approx \frac{1.176091259}{0.84509804} \approx 1.3917$$

$$\log_7 15 = \frac{\ln 15}{\ln 7} \approx \frac{2.708050201}{1.945910149} \approx 1.3917$$

The change of base formula can be used to solve equations such as $4^{2x+1} = 8$ by rewriting the equation in logarithmic form and then using the change of base formula. The equation becomes $\log_4 8 = 2x + 1$. Because $\log_4 8 = \frac{\ln 8}{\ln 4}$, the equation can be written as $2x + 1 = \frac{\ln 8}{\ln 4}$.

$$2x + 1 = \frac{\ln 8}{\ln 4}$$

$$2x = -1 + \frac{\ln 8}{\ln 4}$$

$$x = \frac{1}{2}\left(-1 + \frac{\ln 8}{\ln 4}\right) = \frac{1}{4}$$

EXAMPLE 9-25

- $8^x = \frac{1}{3}$

    Rewriting this in exponential form, we get $x = \log_8 \frac{1}{3}$. Now we can use the change of base formula.

$$x = \log_8 \frac{1}{3} = \frac{\ln \frac{1}{3}}{\ln 8} \approx -0.5283$$

 **PRACTICE**

Evaluate the logarithms. Give your solution accurate to four decimal places.

1. $\log_6 25$

2. $\log_{20} 5$

Solve the equation for *x*. Give your solutions accurate to four decimal places.

3. $3^{x+2} = 12$

4. $15^{3x-2} = 10$

5. $24^{3x+5} = 9$

 **SOLUTIONS**

1. $$\log_6 25 = \frac{\ln 25}{\ln 6} \approx \frac{3.218875825}{1.791759469} \approx 1.7965$$

$$= \frac{\log 25}{\log 6} \approx \frac{1.397940009}{0.7781525} \approx 1.7965$$

2. $$\log_{20} 5 = \frac{\ln 5}{\ln 20} \approx \frac{1.609437912}{2.995732274} \approx 0.5372$$

$$= \frac{\log 5}{\log 20} \approx \frac{0.698970004}{1.301029996} \approx 0.5372$$

3. Rewrite $3^{x+2} = 12$ in logarithmic form: $x + 2 = \log_3 12$

$$x + 2 = \log_3 12 \qquad \text{Use the change of base formula.}$$

$$= \frac{\ln 12}{\ln 3}$$

$$x = -2 + \frac{\ln 12}{\ln 3} \approx 0.2619$$

4. Rewrite $15^{3x-2} = 10$ in logarithmic form: $3x - 2 = \log_{15} 10$

$$3x - 2 = \log_{15} 10$$

$$= \frac{\ln 10}{\ln 15} \qquad \text{Use the change of base formula.}$$

$$3x = 2 + \frac{\ln 10}{\ln 15}$$

$$x = \frac{1}{3}\left(2 + \frac{\ln 10}{\ln 15}\right) \approx 0.9501$$

5. Rewrite $24^{3x+5} = 9$ in logarithmic form: $3x + 5 = \log_{24} 9$

$$3x + 5 = \log_{24} 9 \qquad \text{Use the change of base formula.}$$

$$= \frac{\ln 9}{\ln 24}$$

$$3x = -5 + \frac{\ln 9}{\ln 24}$$

$$x = \frac{1}{3}\left(-5 + \frac{\ln 9}{\ln 24}\right) \approx -1.4362$$

When both sides of an exponential equation have an exponent, we must use another method to solve for x. We take either the natural log or the common log of each side and then use the third logarithm property to move the exponents in front of the logarithm. Once we have used the third logarithm property, we perform the following steps to find x.

1. Distribute the logarithms.
2. Collect the x terms on one side of the equation and the non-x terms on the other side.
3. Factor x.
4. Divide both sides of the equation by x's coefficient (found in Step 3).

EXAMPLE 9-26

- $3^{2x} = 2^{x+1}$

We begin by taking the natural log of each side.

$$\ln 3^{2x} = \ln 2^{x+1}$$ 　　　　Use the third log property.

$$2x \ln 3 = (x + 1) \ln 2$$

$$2x \ln 3 = x \ln 2 + \ln 2$$ 　　　Distribute ln 2 over $(x + 1)$.

Now we want both terms with an x in them on one side of the equation and the term without x in it on the other side. This means that we move $x \ln 2$ to the left side of the equation.

$$2x \ln 3 - x \ln 2 = \ln 2$$ 　　　　Factor x on the left side.

$$x(2 \ln 3 - \ln 2) = \ln 2$$ 　　　Divide each side by $2 \ln 3 - \ln 2$.

$$x = \frac{\ln 2}{2 \ln 3 - \ln 2}$$ 　　　We are finished here.

$$x = \frac{\ln 2}{\ln \frac{9}{2}}$$ 　　　This is easier to calculate.

$$x \approx 0.4608$$

- $10^{x+4} = 6^{3x-1}$

Because one of the bases is 10, we use common logarithms. This will simplify some of the steps. We begin by taking the common log of both sides.

$$\log 10^{x+4} = \log 6^{3x-1}$$ 　　　The left side simplifies to $x + 4$.

$$x + 4 = \log 6^{3x-1}$$ 　　　Use the third log property.

$$x + 4 = (3x - 1) \log 6$$ 　　　Distribute $\log 6$ over $(3x - 1)$.

$$x + 4 = 3x \log 6 - \log 6$$ 　　　Collect x terms on one side.

$$x - 3x \log 6 = -4 - \log 6$$ 　　　Factor x on the left.

$$x(1 - 3 \log 6) = -4 - \log 6$$ 　　　Divide both sides by $1 - 3 \log 6$.

$$x = \frac{-4 - \log 6}{1 - 3 \log 6} = \frac{-4 - \log 6}{1 - \log 216} \approx 3.5806$$

PRACTICE

Solve the equation for *x*. Give your solutions accurate to four decimal places.

1. $4^x = 5^{x-1}$

2. $6^{2x} = 8^{3x-1}$

3. $10^{2-x} = 5^{x+3}$

 SOLUTIONS

1. Take the natural log of each side of $4^x = 5^{x-1}$.

$$\ln 4^x = \ln 5^{x-1} \qquad \text{Use the third log property.}$$

$$x \ln 4 = (x - 1) \ln 5$$

$$x \ln 4 = x \ln 5 - \ln 5 \qquad \text{This is Step 1.}$$

$$x \ln 4 - x \ln 5 = -\ln 5 \qquad \text{This is Step 2.}$$

$$x(\ln 4 - \ln 5) = -\ln 5 \qquad \text{This is Step 3.}$$

$$x = \frac{-\ln 5}{\ln 4 - \ln 5} \qquad \text{This is Step 4.}$$

$$\approx 7.2126$$

2. Take the natural log of each side of $6^{2x} = 8^{3x-1}$.

$$\ln 6^{2x} = \ln 8^{3x-1} \qquad \text{Use the third log property.}$$

$$2x \ln 6 = (3x - 1) \ln 8$$

$$2x \ln 6 = 3x \ln 8 - \ln 8 \qquad \text{This is Step 1.}$$

$$2x \ln 6 - 3x \ln 8 = -\ln 8 \qquad \text{This is Step 2.}$$

$$x(2 \ln 6 - 3 \ln 8) = -\ln 8 \qquad \text{This is Step 3.}$$

$$x = \frac{-\ln 8}{2 \ln 6 - 3 \ln 8} \qquad \text{This is Step 4.}$$

$$\approx 0.7833$$

3. Take the common log of each side of $10^{2-x} = 5^{x+3}$. This lets us use the cancelation fact that $\log 10^{2-x} = 2 - x$.

$$\log 10^{2-x} = \log 5^{x+3}$$

$$2 - x = (x + 3) \log 5$$

$$2 - x = x \log 5 + 3 \log 5 \qquad \text{This is Step 1.}$$

$$-x - x \log 5 = -2 + 3 \log 5 \qquad \text{This is Step 2.}$$

$$x(-1 - \log 5) = -2 + 3 \log 5 \qquad \text{This is Step 3.}$$

$$x = \frac{-2 + 3 \log 5}{-1 - \log 5} \qquad \text{This is Step 4.}$$

$$\approx -0.0570$$

Applications of Logarithm and Exponential Equations

Now that we can solve exponential and logarithmic equations, we can solve many applied problems. We need the compound growth formula for an investment earning interest rate r, compounded n times per year for t years, $A(t) = P(1 + \frac{r}{n})^{nt}$ and the exponential growth formula for a population growing at the rate of r per year for t years, $n(t) = n_0 e^{rt}$. In the problems in Example 9-27, we look for the time required for an investment to grow to a specified amount.

EXAMPLE 9-27

- How long will it take for $1000 to grow to $1500 if it earns 8% annual interest, compounded monthly?

In the formula $A(t) = P(1 + \frac{r}{n})^{nt}$, we know $A(t) = 1500$, $P = 1000$, $r = 0.08$, and $n = 12$. We do not know t.

$$1500 = 1000 \left(1 + \frac{0.08}{12}\right)^{12t}$$

We solve this equation for *t* and will round up to the nearest month.

$$1500 = 1000\left(1 + \frac{0.08}{12}\right)^{12t} \quad \text{Divide both sides by 1000.}$$

$$1.5 = \left(1 + \frac{0.08}{12}\right)^{12t}$$

$$1.5 = 1.00667^{12t} \qquad \text{Take the natural log of both sides.}$$

$$\ln 1.5 = \ln 1.00667^{12t} \qquad \text{Use the third log property.}$$

$$\ln 1.5 = 12t \ln 1.00667 \qquad \text{Divide both sides by 12 ln 1.00667.}$$

$$\frac{\ln 1.5}{12 \ln 1.00667} = t$$

$$t \approx 5.085$$

In 5 years and 1 month, the investment will grow to about $1500.

• How long will it take for an investment to double if it earns $6\frac{1}{2}$% annual interest, compounded daily?

An investment of $P doubles when it grows to $2P, so let $A(t) = 2P$ in the compound growth formula.

$$2P = P\left(1 + \frac{0.065}{365}\right)^{365t} \quad \text{Divide both sides by } P.$$

$$2 = \left(1 + \frac{0.065}{365}\right)^{365t}$$

$$2 = 1.000178^{365t} \qquad \text{Take the natural log of both sides.}$$

$$\ln 2 = \ln 1.000178^{365t} \qquad \text{Use the third log property.}$$

$$\ln 2 = 365t \ln 1.000178 \qquad \text{Divide both sides by 365 ln 1.000178.}$$

$$\frac{\ln 2}{365 \ln 1.000178} = t$$

$$t \approx 10.66$$

In about 10 years and 8 months, the investment will double.

PRACTICE

Give your answers rounded up to the nearest compounding period.

1. How long will it take for $2000 to grow to $40,000 if it earns 9% annual interest, compounded annually?

2. How long will it take for $5000 to grow to $7500 if it earns $6\frac{1}{2}$% annual interest, compounded weekly?

3. How long will it take for an investment to double if it earns $6\frac{1}{4}$% annual interest, compounded quarterly?

 SOLUTIONS

1.
$$40,000 = 2000(1 + 0.09)^t$$

$$20 = 1.09^t$$

$$\ln 20 = \ln 1.09^t$$

$$\ln 20 = t \ln 1.09$$

$$\frac{\ln 20}{\ln 1.09} = t$$

$$34.76 \approx t$$

The investment of $2000 will grow to $40,000 in 35 years.

2.
$$7500 = 5000 \left(1 + \frac{0.065}{52}\right)^{52t}$$

$$1.5 = 1.00125^{52t}$$

$$\ln 1.5 = \ln 1.00125^{52t}$$

$$\ln 1.5 = 52t \ln 1.00125$$

$$\frac{\ln 1.5}{52 \ln 1.00125} = t$$

$$t \approx 6.24$$

In 6 years and 13 weeks ($0.24 \times 52 = 12.48$ rounds up to 13), the investment of $5000 will grow to $7500.

3.

$$2P = P\left(1 + \frac{0.0625}{4}\right)^{4t}$$

$$2 = 1.015625^{4t}$$

$$\ln 2 = \ln 1.015625^{4t}$$

$$\ln 2 = 4t \ln 1.015625$$

$$\frac{\ln 2}{4 \ln 1.015625} = t$$

$$t \approx 11.18$$

In 11 years and 3 months (0.18 rounded up to the nearest quarter is 0.25, one quarter is 3 months), the investment will double.

The same method works with population models where the population (either of people, animals, insects, bacteria, etc.) grows or decays at a certain percent every period. We use the growth formula $n(t) = n_0 e^{rt}$. If the population is decreasing, we use the decay formula, $n(t) = n_0 e^{-rt}$. Because we will be working with the base e, instead of taking the log of both sides, we rewrite the equations in logarithmic form (this is equivalent to taking the natural log of both sides).

EXAMPLE 9-28

- A school district estimates that its student population will grow about 5% per year for the next 15 years. How long will it take the student population to grow from the current 8000 students to 12,000?

We solve for t in the equation $12{,}000 = 8000 e^{0.05t}$.

$$12{,}000 = 8000 e^{0.05t} \quad \text{Divide both sides by 8000.}$$

$$1.5 = e^{0.05t} \quad \text{Rewrite in logarithmic form.}$$

$$0.05t = \ln 1.5$$

$$t = \frac{\ln 1.5}{0.05} \approx 8.1$$

The population is expected to reach 12,000 in about 8 years.

- The population of a certain city in the year 2004 is about 650,000. If it is losing 2% of its population each year, when will the population decline to 500,000?

Because the population is declining, we use the formula $n(t) = n_0 e^{-rt}$. Solve for t in the equation $500{,}000 = 650{,}000e^{-0.02t}$.

$$500{,}000 = 650{,}000e^{-0.02t}$$

$$\frac{10}{13} = e^{-0.02t} \qquad \text{Rewrite in logarithmic form.}$$

$$-0.02t = \ln \frac{10}{13}$$

$$t = \frac{\ln \frac{10}{13}}{-0.02} \approx 13.1$$

The population is expected to drop to 500,000 around the year 2017.

- At 2:00, a culture contained 3000 bacteria. They are growing at the rate of 150% per hour. When will there be 5400 bacteria in the culture?

A growth rate of 150% per hour means that $r = 1.5$ and that t is measured in hours.

$$5400 = 3000e^{1.5t}$$

$$1.8 = e^{1.5t}$$

$$1.5t = \ln 1.8$$

$$t = \frac{\ln 1.8}{1.5} \approx 0.39$$

At about 2:24 ($0.39 \times 60 = 23.4$ minutes), there will be 5400 bacteria in the culture.

PRACTICE

1. In 2010, a rural area had 1800 birds of a certain species. If the bird population is increasing at the rate of 15% per year, when will it reach 3000?

2. In 2012, the population of a certain city was 2 million. If the city's population is declining at the rate of 1.8% per year, when will it fall to 1.5 million?

3. At 9:00, a petrie dish contained 5000 bacteria. The bacteria population is growing at the rate of 160% per hour. When will the dish contain 20,000 bacteria?

 SOLUTIONS

1.
$$3000 = 1800e^{0.15t}$$

$$\frac{5}{3} = e^{0.15t}$$

$$0.15t = \ln \frac{5}{3}$$

$$t = \frac{\ln \frac{5}{3}}{0.15} \approx 3.4$$

The bird population should reach 3000 in the year 2013.

2.
$$1.5 = 2e^{-0.018t}$$

$$0.75 = e^{-0.018t}$$

$$-0.018t = \ln 0.75$$

$$t = \frac{\ln 0.75}{-0.018} \approx 16$$

In the year 2028, the population will decline to 1.5 million.

3.
$$20,000 = 5000e^{1.6t}$$

$$4 = e^{1.6t}$$

$$1.6t = \ln 4$$

$$t = \frac{\ln 4}{1.6} \approx 0.87$$

At about 9:52 ($0.87 \times 60 = 52.2$ minutes), there will be 20,000 bacteria in the dish.

Finding the Growth Rate

We can find the growth rate of a population if we have reason to believe that it is growing exponentially (i.e., if it is growing at approximately the same percentage each year/day/hour) and if we know the population level at two different times. We use the first population level as n_0. Because we know another population level, we have a value for $n(t)$ and for t. This means that the equation $n(t) = n_0 e^{rt}$ has only one unknown, r. We can find r using natural logarithms in the same way we found t in the problems above.

 EXAMPLE 9-29

- **The population of a country is growing exponentially. In the year 2010, it was 10 million and in 2015, it was 12 million. What is the growth rate?**

  In the year $t = 0$ (2010), the population was 10 million, so $n_0 = 10$. The growth formula becomes $n(t) = 10e^{rt}$. When $t = 5$ (the year 2015), the population is 12 million, so $n(t) = 12$. We solve the equation $12 = 10e^{5r}$ for r.

  $$12 = 10e^{5r}$$

  $$1.2 = e^{5r}$$

  $$5r = \ln 1.2$$

  $$r = \frac{\ln 1.2}{5} \approx 0.036$$

  The country's population is growing at the rate of 3.6% per year.

- **Suppose a bacteria culture contains 2500 bacteria at 1:00 and at 1:30, there are 6000 bacteria. What is the hourly growth rate?**

  Because we are asked to find the hourly growth rate, t must be measured in hours and not in minutes. Initially, at $t = 0$, the population is 2500, so $n_0 = 2500$. Half an hour later, the population is 6000, so $t = 0.5$ and $n(t) = 6000$. We solve for r in the equation $6000 = 2500e^{0.5r}$.

  $$6000 = 2500e^{0.5r}$$

  $$2.4 = e^{0.5r}$$

  $$0.5r = \ln 2.4$$

  $$r = \frac{\ln 2.4}{0.5} \approx 1.75$$

  The bacteria are increasing at the rate of 175% per hour.

- A certain species of fish is introduced in a large lake. Wildlife biologists expect the fish's population to double every 4 months for the first few years. What is the annual growth rate?

If n_0 represents the fish's population when first put in the lake, then it will double to $2n_0$ after $t = 4$ months $= \frac{4}{12}$ years $= \frac{1}{3}$ years. The growth formula becomes $2n_0 = n_0e^{\frac{1}{3}r}$. This equation has two unknowns, n_0 and r, not one. But after we divide both sides of the equation by n_0, r becomes the only unknown.

$$2n_0 = n_0e^{\frac{1}{3}r}$$

$$2 = e^{\frac{1}{3}r}$$

$$\frac{1}{3}r = \ln 2$$

$$r = 3 \ln 2 \approx 2.08$$

The fish population is expected to grow at the rate of 208% per year.

 PRACTICE

1. The population of school children in a city grew from 125,000 to 200,000 in 5 years. Assuming exponential growth, find the annual growth rate for the number of school children.

2. A corporation that owns a chain of retail stores operated 500 stores in 2008 and 700 stores in 2011. Assuming that the number of stores is growing exponentially, what is its annual growth rate?

3. At 10:30, 1500 bacteria are present in a culture. At 11:00, 3500 are present. What is the hourly growth rate?

SOLUTIONS

1.
$$200,000 = 125,000e^{5r}$$

$$1.6 = e^{5r}$$

$$5r = \ln 1.6$$

$$r = \frac{\ln 1.6}{5} \approx 0.094$$

The population of school children grew at the rate of 9.4% per year.

2.
$$700 = 500e^{3r}$$
$$1.4 = e^{3r}$$
$$3r = \ln 1.4$$
$$r = \frac{\ln 1.4}{3} \approx 0.112$$

The number of stores is growing at the rate of 11.2% per year.

3.
$$3500 = 1500e^{0.5r}$$
$$\frac{7}{3} = e^{0.5r}$$
$$0.5r = \ln \frac{7}{3}$$
$$r = \frac{\ln \frac{7}{3}}{0.5} \approx 1.69$$

The bacteria are increasing at the rate of 169% per hour.

Radioactive Decay

Some radioactive substances decay at the rate of nearly 100% per year and others at nearly 0% per year. For this reason, we use the *half-life* of a radioactive substance to describe how fast its radioactivity decays. For example, bismuth-210 has a half-life of 5 days. After 5 days, 16 grams of bismuth-210 decays to 8 grams of bismuth-210 (and 8 grams of another substance); after 10 days, 4 grams remain, and after 15 days, only 2 grams remain. We can use logarithms and the half-life to find the rate of decay. We use the decay formula $n(t) = n_0 e^{-rt}$ in the following problems.

EXAMPLE 9-30

- **Find the daily decay rate of bismuth-210.**

  Because its half-life is 5 days, at $t = 5$, one-half of n_0 remains, so $n(t) = \frac{1}{2}n_0$.

$$\frac{1}{2}n_0 = n_0 e^{-5r} \qquad \text{Divide both sides by } n_0.$$

$$\frac{1}{2} = e^{-5r} \qquad \text{Rewrite in logarithmic form.}$$

$$-5r = \ln \frac{1}{2}$$

$$r = \frac{\ln \frac{1}{2}}{-5} \approx 0.1386$$

Bismuth-210 decays at the rate of 13.86% per day.

• The half-life of radium-226 is 1600 years. What is its annual decay rate?

$$\frac{1}{2}n_0 = n_0 e^{-1600r} \qquad \text{Divide both sides by } n_0.$$

$$\frac{1}{2} = e^{-1600r} \qquad \text{Rewrite in logarithmic form.}$$

$$-1600r = \ln \frac{1}{2}$$

$$r = \frac{\ln \frac{1}{2}}{-1600} \approx 0.000433$$

The decay rate for radium-226 is about 0.0433% per year.

In the same way we found the decay rate from the half-life, we can find the half-life from the decay rate. In the formula $\frac{1}{2}n_0 = n_0 e^{-rt}$, we know r and want to find t.

EXAMPLE 9-31

• Suppose a radioactive substance decays at the rate of 2.5% per hour. What is its half-life?

$$\frac{1}{2}n_0 = n_0 e^{-0.025t} \qquad \text{Divide both sides by } n_0.$$

$$\frac{1}{2} = e^{-0.025t} \qquad \text{Rewrite in logarithmic form.}$$

$$-0.025t = \ln \frac{1}{2}$$

$$t = \frac{\ln \frac{1}{2}}{-0.025} \approx 27.7$$

The half-life is 27.7 hours.

 **PRACTICE**

1. Suppose a substance has a half-life of 45 days. Find its daily decay rate.

2. The half-life of lead-210 is 22.3 years. Find its annual decay rate.

3. Suppose the half-life of a substance is 1.5 seconds. What is its decay rate per second?

4. Suppose a radioactive substance decays at the rate of 0.1% per day. What is its half-life?

5. A radioactive substance decays at the rate of 0.02% per year. What is its half-life?

SOLUTIONS

1.
$$\frac{1}{2}n_0 = n_0 e^{-45r}$$

$$\frac{1}{2} = e^{-45r}$$

$$-45r = \ln \frac{1}{2}$$

$$r = \frac{\ln \frac{1}{2}}{-45} \approx 0.0154$$

The decay rate is 1.5% per day.

2.
$$\frac{1}{2}n_0 = n_0 e^{-22.3r}$$

$$\frac{1}{2} = e^{-22.3r}$$

$$-22.3r = \ln \frac{1}{2}$$

$$r = \frac{\ln \frac{1}{2}}{-22.3} \approx 0.0311$$

The decay rate is 3.1% per year.

3.
$$\frac{1}{2}n_0 = n_0 e^{-1.5r}$$

$$\frac{1}{2} = e^{-1.5r}$$

$$-1.5r = \ln\frac{1}{2}$$

$$r = \frac{\ln\frac{1}{2}}{-1.5} \approx 0.462$$

The substance decays at the rate of 46.2% per second.

4.
$$\frac{1}{2}n_0 = n_0 e^{-0.001t}$$

$$\frac{1}{2} = e^{-0.001t}$$

$$-0.001t = \ln\frac{1}{2}$$

$$t = \frac{\ln\frac{1}{2}}{-0.001} \approx 693.1$$

The half-life is 693 days.

5.
$$\frac{1}{2}n_0 = n_0 e^{-0.0002t}$$

$$\frac{1}{2} = e^{-0.0002t}$$

$$-0.0002t = \ln\frac{1}{2}$$

$$t = \frac{\ln\frac{1}{2}}{-0.0002} \approx 3466$$

The half-life is about 3466 years.

All living things have carbon-14 in them. Once they die, the carbon-14 is not replaced and begins to decay. The half-life of carbon-14 is approximately 5700 years. This information is used to find the age of many archeological finds. We first find the annual decay rate for carbon-14 and then we answer some typical carbon-14 dating questions.

$$\frac{1}{2}n_0 = n_0 e^{-5700r}$$

$$\frac{1}{2} = e^{-5700r}$$

$$-5700r = \ln \frac{1}{2}$$

$$r = \frac{\ln \frac{1}{2}}{-5700} \approx 0.000121605$$

Carbon-14 decays at the rate of 0.012% per year.

EXAMPLE 9-32

- How long will it take for 80% of the carbon-14 to decay in an animal after it has died?

If 80% of the initial amount has decayed, then 20% remains, or $0.20n_0$.

$$0.20n_0 = n_0 e^{-0.00012t}$$

$$0.20 = e^{-0.00012t}$$

$$-0.00012t = \ln 0.20$$

$$t = \frac{\ln 0.20}{-0.00012} \approx 13,412$$

After about 13,400 years, 80% of the carbon-14 will have decayed.

- Suppose a bone is discovered and has 60% of its carbon-14. How old is the bone?

60% of its carbon-14 is $0.60n_0$.

$$0.60n_0 = n_0 e^{-0.00012t}$$

$$0.60 = e^{-0.00012t}$$

$$-0.00012t = \ln 0.60$$

$$t = \frac{\ln 0.60}{-0.00012} \approx 4257$$

The bone is about 4260 years old.

- Suppose an animal dies today. How much of its carbon-14 will remain after 250 years?

$$n(250) = n_0 e^{-0.00012(250)} \approx 0.97 n_0$$

About 97% of its carbon-14 will remain after 250 years.

PRACTICE

1. Suppose a piece of wood from an archeological dig is being carbon-14 dated, and found to have 70% of its carbon-14 remaining. Estimate the age of the piece of wood.

2. How long would it take for an object to lose 25% of its carbon-14?

3. Suppose a tree fell 400 years ago. How much of its carbon-14 remains?

SOLUTIONS

1.
$$0.70 n_0 = n_0 e^{-0.00012t}$$

$$0.70 = e^{-0.00012t}$$

$$-0.00012t = \ln 0.70$$

$$t = \frac{\ln 0.70}{-0.00012} \approx 2972$$

The wood is about 2970 years old.

2. An object has lost 25% of its carbon-14 when 75% of it remains.

$$0.75 n_0 = n_0 e^{-0.00012t}$$

$$0.75 = e^{-0.00012t}$$

$$-0.00012t = \ln 0.75$$

$$t = \frac{\ln 0.75}{-0.00012} \approx 2397$$

After about 2400 years, an object will lose 25% of its carbon-14.

3.
$$n(400) = n_0 e^{-0.00012(400)} \approx 0.953 n_0$$

About 95% of its carbon-14 remains after 400 years.

Summary

In this chapter, we learned how to

- *Compute the value of an account with compounded interest.* If $\$P$ earns r annual interest, compounded n times a year, the account is worth $A = P(1 + \frac{r}{n})^{nt}$ after t years. If interest is compounded continuously, the formula is $A = Pe^{rt}$, where $e \approx 2.718281828$ is an irrational number. A similar function, $n(t) = n_0 e^{rt}$, is used to model populations of people, bacteria, and other quantities whose numbers grow exponentially. If a population is declining, we use the formula $n(t) = n_0 e^{-rt}$.

- *Sketch the graph of an exponential function.* If $a > 1$, the graph of the exponential function $y = a^x$ rises to the right and approaches the x-axis on the left. If $0 < a < 1$, the graph rises to the left and approaches the x-axis on the right. We sketch the graph of this function by plotting points for $x = -3, -2, -1, 0, 1, 2, 3$. These values show how fast the graph rises and how fast it approaches the x-axis.

- *Rewrite exponential equations in logarithmic form.* The equation $a^x = y$ can be rewritten in logarithmic form as $\log_a y = x$ (and vice versa). Two special bases are base e and base 10: $\log_e x = \ln x$ and $\log_{10} x = \log x$.

- *Sketch the graph of a logarithmic function.* We sketch the graph of $y = \log_a x$ by rewriting the equation in exponential form and then plotting points for $y = -3, -2, -1, 0, 1, 2, 3$. The y-axis is the vertical asymptote and the graph either rises or falls to the right, depending on whether $a > 1$ or $0 < a < 1$. (In this book, we only sketched the graph for $a > 1$.)

- *Find the domain of a logarithmic function.* The domain of the function $y = \log_a[f(x)]$ is the solution to $f(x) > 0$. That is, we can only take a logarithm of a positive number.

- *Use cancelation properties to simplify logarithms.* We use two cancelation properties to solve equations: $\log_a a^x = x$ and $a^{\log_a x} = x$. When the bases of the exponent and logarithm are the same, the exponent and logarithm cancel ("undo") each other.

- *Use three properties of logarithms to rewrite logarithms.* Sometimes, we want to expand logarithms or to write a sum/difference of logarithms as a single logarithm. If $m > 0$ $n > 0$, then

1. $\log_a m + \log_a n = \log_a mn$
2. $\log_a m - \log_a n = \log_a \dfrac{m}{n}$
3. $\log_a m^t = t \log_a m$

We can use the third property to rewrite the logarithm of a root using the exponent property $\sqrt[n]{a^m} = a^{m/n}$.

- *Solve equations involving logarithms.* We solve equations in the form "$\log_a =$ number" by rewriting the equation in exponential form and then solving it. We solve the equation "$\log_a m = \log_a n$" by solving $m = n$. That is, the logs cancel each other. Sometimes, we must use properties of logarithms to rewrite an equation we are given in one of these two forms. Normally, we must check our solutions to make sure that they are valid for the logarithms in the original equation.

- *Use the change of base formula.* We can rewrite a logarithm in old base b as a logarithm in new base a. The formula is $\log_b x = \dfrac{\log_a x}{\log_a b}$.

- *Solve equations involving exponents.* If an equation has only one exponent containing a variable, we can solve the equation using the change of base formula. We algebraically solve for the term having the variable in the exponent, rewrite the equation using the change of base formula, and then solving for the unknown. If both sides of an equation have an exponent containing variable, we must use a different method (this method also works for only one variable in an exponent). We take a logarithm of each side (usually the natural log), use the third property of logarithms, and then algebraically solve for the variable.

- *Solve applied problems using logarithms.* We solved several different applied problems using logarithms. If we are looking for the length of time necessary for an investment to grow to a specified level, then we have $P(1 + \frac{r}{n})^{nt}$ in the equation, and t is unknown. Because this equation is an exponential equation, we solve it using one of the methods above. We solved various population problems involving either $n_0 e^{rt}$ or $n_0 e^{-rt}$. We solve these problems by rewriting the equations in logarithmic form, solving for t, and then using a calculator to approximate a solution. We used the quantity $n_0 e^{-rt}$ to solve problems involving radioactive decay. We solve these problems using the same strategy that we used for population problems.

QUIZ

1. Suppose $12,000 is invested earning 9% annual interest, compounded monthly. What will it be worth after 10 years?

   A. About $29,416

   B. About $28,408

   C. About $33,752

   D. About $35,166

2. What is the present value of $80,000 due in 12 years earning 7% interest, compounded annually?

   A. About $27,798

   B. About $40,668

   C. About $36,188

   D. About $35,521

3. Rewrite $\log_b x = z$ in exponential form.

   A. $b^z = x$

   B. $b^x = z$

   C. $x^b = z$

   D. $x^z = b$

4. Rewrite $9^y = s$ in logarithmic form.

   A. $\log_9 y = s$

   B. $\log_9 s = y$

   C. $\log_s 9 = y$

   D. $\log_y s = 9$

5. Rewrite $e^{x-4} = 15$ in exponential form.

   A. $\log_{15} x = e - 4$

   B. $\log_{x-4} 15 = e$

   C. $\ln 15 = x - 4$

   D. $\ln(x - 4) = 15$

6. $4^{\log_4 5x} = $ _____

   A. $5x$

   B. $\frac{1}{4}(5x)$

   C. 5^x

   D. 5^{4x}

7. $\ln e^{x-3} = $ _____

   A. $e - 3$

   B. $x - 3$

   C. -3

   D. $\ln(-3)$

8. Rewrite as a single logarithm: $3 \log_2 x + \log_2 y - 5 \log_2 z$.

   A. $\log_2 \frac{(xy)^3}{z^5}$

   B. $\frac{1}{5} \log_2 \frac{(xy)^3}{z}$

   C. $\log_2 \frac{x^3 y}{z^5}$

   D. $\log_2 \frac{3x+y}{5z}$

9. Expand the logarithm: $\log_6 \sqrt[5]{\frac{a^3 b}{z^2}}$.

   A. $\frac{1}{5} \cdot \frac{3\log_6 a + \log_6 b}{2\log_6 z}$

   B. $\sqrt[5]{\frac{3\log_6 a + \log_6 b}{2\log_6 z}}$

   C. $\frac{1}{5}(3\log_6 a + \log_6 b - 2\log_6 z)$

   D. $\frac{1}{5} \cdot \frac{\log_6 a^3 + \log_6 b}{\log z^3}$

10. Solve the equation for x: $\log_5(x + 3) = 2$.

    A. $-\frac{13}{5}$

    B. 7

    C. 29

    D. 22

11. Solve the equation for x: $\log_4 x + \log_4(x + 6) = 2$.

A. $-8, 2$ C. $8, -2$

B. 2   D. 8

12. Find the domain of the function $y = \ln(x - 6)$.

A. $(-6, \infty)$ C. $[0, \infty)$

B. $(0, \infty)$ D. $(6, \infty)$

13. Solve the equation for x: $5^{x+2} = 20$.

A. About 0.931   C. About 3.847

B. About -0.139 D. About -0.614

14. Solve the equation for x: $3^{2x} = 6^{x-1}$.

A. About -4.419 C. About 0.431

B. About -1.497 D. The equation has no solution.

15. About how long will it take for an investment to double if it earns 7% annual interest, compounded monthly?

A. About 3.44 years   C. About 10.24 years

B. About 6.88 years   D. About 9.93 years

16. Suppose the half-life of a substance is 50 years. What is its annual decay rate?

A. About 3.22%   C. About 1.39%

B. About 2.54%   D. About 1.73 %

17. The graph in Figure 9-32 is the graph of which function? (The dashed graph is the graph of $y = 3^x$.)

A. $y = 3^{x-2}$ C. $y = 3^x - 2$

B. $y = 3^{x+2}$ D. $y = 3^x + 2$

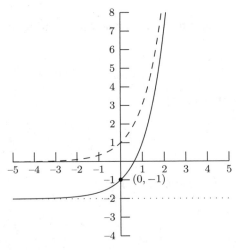

FIGURE 9-32

chapter 10

Systems of Equations and Inequalities

Most applied problems in calculus involve multiple equations. In this chapter, we learn how to solve multiple equations (called a *system*) both algebraically and with a graphing calculator. We also learn how to solve a system of inequalities, which involves shading regions in the plane. This will prepare you for finding the area of a region in the plane when you get to calculus. A region in the plane is the solution to an inequality or a system of inequalities.

CHAPTER OBJECTIVES

In this chapter, you will

- Solve a system of equations
- Graph the solution to an inequality
- Graph the solution to a system of inequalities
- Solve applied problems involving a system of equations

Systems of Linear Equations

A system of equations is a collection of two or more equations whose graphs might or might not intersect (share a common point or points). If the graphs do intersect, then we say that the solution to the system is the point or points where the graphs intersect. For example, the solution to the system

$$\begin{cases} x + y = 4 \\ 3x - y = 0 \end{cases}$$

is $(1, 3)$ because the point $(1, 3)$ is on both graphs. See Figure 10-1.

We say that $(1, 3)$ *satisfies* the system because if we let $x = 1$ and $y = 3$ in each equation, both are true.

$$x + y = 4 \qquad 1 + 3 = 4 \qquad \text{This is a true statement.}$$

$$3x - y = 0 \qquad 3(1) - 3 = 0 \qquad \text{This is a true statement.}$$

There are several methods for solving systems of equations. One of them is to sketch the graphs and seeing where, if anywhere, the graphs intersect. Even with a graphing calculator, though, these solutions might only be approximations. When the equations are lines, *matrices* can be used. Graphing calculators are useful for these, too. We learn two algebraic methods for solving systems in

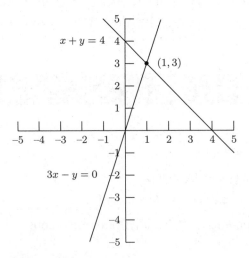

FIGURE 10-1

this chapter and two matrix methods in the next. One of the algebraic methods is *substitution* and the other is *elimination by addition*. Both methods work with many kinds of systems of equations, but we begin with systems of linear equations.

Substitution works by solving for one variable in one equation and making a substitution in the other equation. Usually, it does not matter which variable we use or which equation we begin with, but some choices are easier than others.

 EXAMPLE 10-1

Solve the systems of equations. Write the solution in the form of a point, (x, y).

- $\begin{cases} x + y = 5 \\ -2x + y = -1 \end{cases}$

We have four places to start.

1. Solve for x in the first equation: $x = 5 - y$
2. Solve for y in the first equation: $y = 5 - x$
3. Solve for x in the second equation: $x = \frac{1}{2} + \frac{1}{2}y$
4. Solve for y in the second equation: $y = 2x - 1$

The third option looks like the most troublesome option, so we use one of the others. We use the first option. Because $x = 5 - y$ came from the *first* equation, we substitute $5 - y$ for x in the *second* equation. Then $-2x + y = -1$ becomes $-2(5 - y) + y = -1$. Now we have one equation with a single variable.

$$-2(5 - y) + y = -1$$
$$-10 + 2y + y = -1$$
$$3y = 9$$
$$y = 3$$

We can find x by substituting $y = 3$ into any of the equations above. We know that $x = 5 - y$; so we use this.

$$x = 5 - 3 = 2$$

The solution is $x = 2$ and $y = 3$ or the point $(2, 3)$. It is a good idea to check the solution.

$$x + y = 5 \qquad 2 + 3 = 5 \qquad \text{This is true.}$$
$$-2x + y = 1 \qquad -2(2) + 3 = -1 \qquad \text{This is true.}$$

- $\begin{cases} 4x - y = 12 & \text{A} \\ 3x + y = 2 & \text{B} \end{cases}$

We solve for y in equation B: $y = 2 - 3x$. Next we substitute $2 - 3x$ for y in equation A and solve for x.

$$4x - y = 12$$
$$4x - (2 - 3x) = 12$$
$$4x - 2 + 3x = 12$$
$$7x = 14$$
$$x = 2$$

Now that we know $x = 2$, we substitute $x = 2$ in one of the above equations. We use $y = 2 - 3x$; $y = 2 - 3(2) = -4$. The solution is $x = 2$, $y = -4$, or $(2, -4)$. The graphs in Figure 10-2 verify that the solution $(2, -4)$ is on both lines.

- $\begin{cases} y = 4x + 1 & \text{A} \\ y = 3x + 2 & \text{B} \end{cases}$

Both equations are already solved for y; so all we need to do is to set them equal to each other.

$$\underset{\text{Equation A}}{4x + 1} = \underset{\text{Equation B}}{3x + 2}$$

$$x = 1$$

We could use either equation A or equation B to find y when $x = 1$. We use A: $y = 4x + 1 = 4(1) + 1 = 5$. The solution is $x = 1$ and $y = 5$, or $(1, 5)$. We can see from the graphs in Figure 10-3 that $(1, 5)$ is the solution to the system.

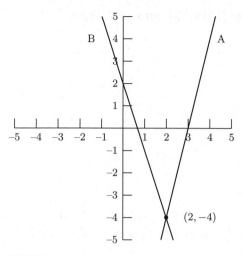

FIGURE 10-2

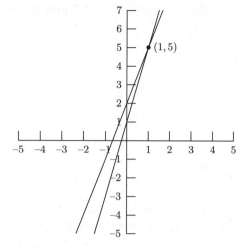

FIGURE 10-3

Solving a system of equations by substitution can be messy when none of the coefficients is 1. Fortunately, there is another way. We can always *add* the two equations to eliminate one of the variables. Sometimes, though, we need to multiply one or both equations by a number to make it work.

EXAMPLE 10-2

Solve the systems of equations. Write the solution in the form of a point, (*x, y*).

- $$\begin{cases} 2x - 3y = 16 & \text{A} \\ 5x + 3y = -2 & \text{B} \end{cases}$$

   We add the equations by adding like terms. Because we are adding $-3y$ to $3y$, the *y*-term cancels, leaving one equation with a single variable.

$$2x - 3y = 16$$
$$\underline{5x + 3y = -2}$$
$$7x + 0y = 14$$
$$x = 2$$

We can substitute $x = 2$ into either A or B to find y. We put $x = 2$ into A.

$$2x - 3y = 16$$
$$2(2) - 3y = 16$$
$$-3y = 12$$
$$y = -4$$

The solution is $(2, -4)$.

Sometimes we need to multiply one or both equations by some number or numbers so that one of the variables cancels. Multiplying both sides of *any* equation by a nonzero number never changes the solution.

EXAMPLE 10-3

Solve the system. Write the solution in the form of a point, (x, y).

- $$\begin{cases} 3x + 6y = -12 & \text{A} \\ 2x + 6y = -14 & \text{B} \end{cases}$$

Because the coefficients of y are the same, we only need to make one of them negative. Multiply either A or B by -1, and then add.

$$-3x - 6y = 12 \qquad -\text{A}$$
$$\underline{2x + 6y = -14 \qquad +\text{B}}$$
$$-x = -2$$
$$x = 2$$
$$3(2) + 6y = -12 \qquad \text{Put } x = 2 \text{ in A}$$
$$y = -3$$

The solution is $(2, -3)$.

- $$\begin{cases} 2x + 7y = 1 & \text{A} \\ 4x - 2y = 18 & \text{B} \end{cases}$$

Several options work. We could multiply A by -2 so that we could add $-4x$ (in -2A) to $4x$ in B. We could multiply A by 2 and multiply B by 7 so that we would add $14y$ (in 2A) to $-14y$ (in 7B). We could also divide B by -2 so that we would add $2x$ (in A) to $-2x$ (in $-\frac{1}{2}$B). We will add $-2A + B$.

$$-4x - 14y = -2 \qquad -2A$$

$$\underline{4x - 2y = 18} \qquad +B$$

$$-16y = 16$$

$$y = -1$$

$$2x + 7(-1) = 1 \qquad \text{Put } y = -1 \text{ in A}$$

$$x = 4$$

The solution is $(4, -1)$.

Both equations in each of the following systems need to be changed to eliminate one of the variables.

■ EXAMPLE 10-4

Solve the system. Write the solution in the form of a point, (x, y).

$$\bullet \quad \begin{cases} 8x - 5y = -2 & \text{A} \\ 3x + 2y = 7 & \text{B} \end{cases}$$

There are many options. Some are $3A - 8B$, $-3A + 8B$, and $2A + 5B$. We compute $2A + 5B$.

$$16x - 10y = -4 \qquad 2A$$

$$\underline{15x + 10y = 35} \qquad +5B$$

$$31x = 31$$

$$x = 1$$

$$8(1) - 5y = -2 \qquad \text{Put } x = 1 \text{ in A}$$

$$y = 2$$

The solution is $(1, 2)$.

$$\cdot \begin{cases} \dfrac{2}{3}x - \dfrac{1}{4}y = \dfrac{25}{72} & \text{A} \\[2mm] \dfrac{1}{2}x + \dfrac{2}{5}y = -\dfrac{1}{30} & \text{B} \end{cases}$$

First, we eliminate the fractions. The LCD for A is 72, and the LCD for B is 30.

$$48x - 18y = 25 \qquad 72\text{A}$$

$$15x + 12y = -1 \qquad 30\text{B}$$

Now we multiply the first equation by 2 and the second by 3, which eliminates y.

$$96x - 36y = 50$$

$$\underline{45x + 36y = -3}$$

$$141x = 47$$

$$x = \frac{47}{141} = \frac{1}{3}$$

$$96\left(\frac{1}{3}\right) - 36y = 50$$

$$y = -\frac{1}{2}$$

The solution is $\left(\frac{1}{3}, -\frac{1}{2}\right)$.

Applications of Systems of Equations

Systems of two linear equations can be used to solve many kinds of word problems. In these problems, two facts are given about two variables. Each pair of facts can be represented by a linear equation. This given facts give us a system of two equations with two variables.

EXAMPLE 10-5

- A movie theater charges $4 for each child's ticket and $6.50 for each adult's ticket. One night 200 tickets were sold, amounting to a total value of $1100 in ticket sales. How many of each type of ticket was sold?

Let x represent the number of child tickets sold and y, the number of adult tickets sold. One equation comes from the fact that a total of 200 adult and child tickets were sold, giving us $x + y = 200$. The other equation comes from the fact that the ticket revenue was $1100. The ticket revenue from selling x child tickets is $4x$, and the ticket revenue from selling y adult tickets is $6.50y$. Their sum is 1100 giving us $4x + 6.50y = 1100$.

$$\begin{cases} 4x + 6.50y = 1100 & \text{A} \\ x + y = 200 & \text{B} \end{cases}$$

We could use either substitution or addition to solve this system. Substitution is a little faster. We solve for x in B.

$$x = 200 - y$$

$$4(200 - y) + 6.50y = 1100 \qquad \text{Put } x = 200 - y \text{ into A}$$

$$800 - 4y + 6.50y = 1100$$

$$y = 120$$

$$x = 200 - y = 200 - 120 = 80$$

Eighty child tickets were sold, and 120 adult tickets were sold.

• A farmer had a soil test performed. He was told that his field needed 1080 pounds of Mineral A and 920 pounds of Mineral B. Two mixtures of fertilizers provide these minerals. Each bag of Brand I provides 25 pounds of Mineral A and 15 pounds of Mineral B. Each bag of Brand II provides 20 pounds of Mineral A and 20 pounds of Mineral B. How many bags of each brand should he buy?

Let x represent the number of bags of Brand I and y represent the number of bags of Brand II. Then the number of pounds of Mineral A he gets from x bags of Brand I is $25x$ and the number of pounds of Mineral B is $15x$. The number of pounds of Mineral A he gets from y bags of Brand II is $20y$ and the number of pounds of Mineral B is $20y$. He needs 1080 pounds of Mineral A; $25x$ pounds comes from Brand I and $20y$ comes from Brand II. This gives us the equation $25x + 20y = 1080$. He needs 920 pounds of Mineral B; $15x$ comes from Brand I and $20y$ comes from Brand II. This gives us the equation $15x + 20y = 920$.

$$\begin{cases} 25x + 20y = 1080 & \text{A} \\ 15x + 20y = 920 & \text{B} \end{cases}$$

We compute A − B.

$$25x + 20y = 1080 \qquad \text{A}$$
$$\underline{-15x - 20y = -920 \qquad -\text{B}}$$
$$10x = 160$$
$$x = 16$$
$$25(16) + 20y = 1080 \qquad \text{Put } x = 16 \text{ into A}$$
$$y = 34$$

He needs 16 bags of Brand I and 34 bags of Brand II.

- A furniture manufacturer has some discontinued fabric and trim in stock. It can use them on sofas and chairs. There are 160 yards of fabric and 110 yards of trim. Each sofa takes 6 yards of fabric and 4.5 yards of trim. Each chair takes 4 yards of fabric and 2 yards of trim. How many sofas and chairs should be produced in order to use all the fabric and trim?

Let x represent the number of sofas to be produced and y, the number of chairs. The manufacturer needs to use 160 yards of fabric; $6x$ are used on sofas and $4y$ yards on chairs. This gives us the equation $6x + 4y = 160$. There are 110 yards of trim, $4.5x$ yards will be used on the sofas and $2y$ on the chairs. This gives us the equation $4.5x + 2y = 110$.

$$\begin{cases} 6x + 4y = 160 & \text{F} \\ 4.5x + 2y = 110 & \text{T} \end{cases}$$

We compute F − 2T.

$$6x + 4y = 160 \qquad \text{F}$$
$$\underline{-9x - 4y = -220 \qquad -2\text{T}}$$
$$-3x = -60$$
$$x = 20$$
$$6(20) + 4y = 160 \qquad \text{Put } x = 20 \text{ into F}$$
$$y = 10$$

The manufacturer needs to produce 20 sofas and 10 chairs.

PRACTICE

For Problems 1 to 9, solve the systems of equations. Write the solution in the form of a point, (x, y).

1. $\begin{cases} 2x + 3y = 1 & \text{A} \\ x - 2y = -3 & \text{B} \end{cases}$

2. $\begin{cases} x + y = 3 & \text{A} \\ x + 4y = 0 & \text{B} \end{cases}$

3. $\begin{cases} -2x + 7y = 19 & \text{A} \\ 2x - 4y = -10 & \text{B} \end{cases}$

4. $\begin{cases} 15x - y = 9 & \text{A} \\ 2x + y = 8 & \text{B} \end{cases}$

5. $\begin{cases} -3x + 2y = 12 & \text{A} \\ 4x + 2y = -2 & \text{B} \end{cases}$

6. $\begin{cases} 6x - 5y = 1 & \text{A} \\ 3x - 2y = 1 & \text{B} \end{cases}$

7. $\begin{cases} 5x - 9y = -26 & \text{A} \\ 3x + 2y = 14 & \text{B} \end{cases}$

8. $\begin{cases} 7x + 2y = 1 & \text{A} \\ 2x + 3y = -7 & \text{B} \end{cases}$

9. $\begin{cases} \dfrac{3}{4}x + \dfrac{1}{5}y = \dfrac{23}{60} & \text{A} \\ \dfrac{1}{6}x - \dfrac{1}{4}y = -\dfrac{1}{9} & \text{B} \end{cases}$

10. A grocery store sells two different brands of milk. The price for the name brand is $3.50 per gallon, and the price for the store's brand is $2.25 per gallon. On one Saturday, 4500 gallons of milk were sold for sales of $12,875. How many of each brand were sold?

11. A gardener wants to add 39 pounds of Nutrient A and 16 pounds of Nutrient B to her garden. Each bag of Brand X provides 3 pounds of Nutrient A and 2 pounds of Nutrient B. Each bag of Brand Y provides 4 pounds of Nutrient A and 1 pound of Nutrient B. How many bags of each brand should she buy?

12. A clothing manufacturer has 70 yards of a certain fabric and 156 buttons in stock. It manufactures jackets and slacks that use this fabric and button. Each jacket requires $1\frac{1}{3}$ yards of fabric and 4 buttons. Each pair of slacks requires $1\frac{3}{4}$ yards of fabric and 3 buttons. How many jackets and pairs of slacks should the manufacturer produce to use all the available fabric and buttons?

 SOLUTIONS

1. Solve for x in B: $x = -3 + 2y$ and substitute this for x in A.

$$2x + 3y = 1$$
$$2(-3 + 2y) + 3y = 1$$
$$-6 + 4y + 3y = 1$$
$$7y = 7$$
$$y = 1 \qquad \text{Put } y = 1 \text{ in } x = -3 + 2y$$
$$x = -3 + 2(1) = -1$$

The solution is $(-1, 1)$.

2. Solve for x in B: $x = -4y$ and substitute this for x in A.

$$x + y = 3$$
$$-4y + y = 3$$
$$-3y = 3$$
$$y = -1 \qquad \text{Put } y = -1 \text{ in } x = -4y$$
$$x = -4(-1) = 4$$

The solution is $(4, -1)$.

3. We add A + B.

$$-2x + 7y = 19 \qquad \text{A}$$
$$\underline{2x - 4y = -10} \qquad +\text{B}$$
$$3y = 9$$
$$y = 3$$
$$-2x + 7(3) = 19 \qquad \text{Put } y = 3 \text{ in A}$$
$$x = 1$$

The solution is (1, 3).

4.
$$15x - y = 9 \qquad \text{A}$$
$$\underline{2x + y = 8} \qquad +\text{B}$$
$$17x = 17$$
$$x = 1$$
$$15(1) - y = 9 \qquad \text{Put } x = 1 \text{ in A}$$
$$y = 6$$

The solution is (1, 6).

5. We add −A + B.

$$3x - 2y = -12 \qquad -\text{A}$$
$$\underline{4x + 2y = -2} \qquad +\text{B}$$
$$7x = -14$$
$$x = -2$$
$$-3(-2) + 2y = 12 \qquad \text{Put } x = -2 \text{ in A}$$
$$y = 3$$

The solution is (−2, 3).

6. We compute A − 2B.

$$6x - 5y = 1 \qquad \text{A}$$

$$\underline{-6x + 4y = -2} \qquad \text{−2B}$$

$$-y = -1$$

$$y = 1$$

$$6x - 5(1) = 1 \qquad \text{Put } y = 1 \text{ in A}$$

$$x = 1$$

The solution is (1, 1).

7. We compute 3A − 5B.

$$15x - 27y = -78 \qquad \text{3A}$$

$$\underline{-15x - 10y = -70} \qquad \text{−5B}$$

$$-37y = -148$$

$$y = 4$$

$$5x - 9(4) = -26 \qquad \text{Put } y = 4 \text{ in A}$$

$$x = 2$$

The solution is (2, 4).

8. We compute 3A − 2B.

$$21x + 6y = 3 \qquad \text{3A}$$

$$\underline{-4x - 6y = 14} \qquad \text{−2B}$$

$$17x = 17$$

$$x = 1$$

$$7(1) + 2y = 1 \qquad \text{Put } x = 1 \text{ in A}$$

$$y = -3$$

The solution is (1, −3).

9. First we clear the fractions.

$$45x + 12y = 23 \quad 60A$$

$$6x - 9y = -4 \quad 36B$$

Now, we add three times the first to four times the second.

$$135x + 36y = 69$$

$$\underline{24x - 36y = -16}$$

$$159x = 53$$

$$x = \frac{53}{159} = \frac{1}{3}$$

$$45\left(\frac{1}{3}\right) + 12y = 23$$

$$y = \frac{2}{3}$$

The solution is $\left(\frac{1}{3}, \frac{2}{3}\right)$.

10. Let x represent the number of gallons of the name brand sold and y represent the number of gallons of the store brand sold. The total number of gallons sold is 4500, giving us $x + y = 4500$. Revenue from the name brand is $3.50x$ and is $2.25y$ for the store brand. Total revenue is \$12,875, giving us the equation $3.50x + 2.25y = 12,875$.

$$\begin{cases} x + y = 4500 \\ 3.50x + 2.25y = 12,875 \end{cases}$$

We use substitution.

$$x = 4500 - y$$

$$3.50(4500 - y) + 2.25y = 12,875$$

$$y = 2300$$

$$x = 4500 - y = 4500 - 2300 = 2200$$

The store sold 2200 gallons of the name brand and 2300 gallons of the store brand.

11. Let x represent the number of bags of Brand X and y, the number of bags of Brand Y. She gets $3x$ pounds of Nutrient A from x bags of Brand X and $4y$ pounds from y bags of Brand Y, so we need $3x + 4y = 39$. She gets $2x$ pounds of Nutrient B from x bags of Brand X and $1y$ pounds of Nutrient B from y bags of Brand Y, so we need $2x + y = 16$. We use substitution.

$$y = 16 - 2x$$

$$3x + 4(16 - 2x) = 39$$

$$x = 5$$

$$y = 16 - 2x = 16 - 2(5) = 6$$

The gardener needs to buy 5 bags of Brand X and 6 bags of Brand Y.

12. Let x represent the number of jackets to be produced and y the number of pairs of slacks. To use 70 yards of fabric, we need $1\frac{1}{3}x + 1\frac{3}{4}y = 70$. To use 156 buttons, we need $4x + 3y = 156$.

$$1\frac{1}{3}x + 1\frac{3}{4}y = 70 \qquad \text{Rewrite.}$$

$$\frac{4}{3}x + \frac{7}{4}y = 70 \qquad \text{F}$$

$$4x + 3y = 156 \qquad \text{B}$$

$$16x + 21y = 840 \qquad \text{12F}$$

$$\underline{-16x - 12y = -624 \qquad -4\text{B}}$$

$$9y = 216$$

$$y = 24$$

$$4x + 3(24) = 156$$

$$x = 21$$

The manufacturer should produce 21 jackets and 24 pairs of slacks.

Other Systems of Equations

Two lines in the plane either intersect in one point, are parallel, or are really the same line. Until now, our lines have intersected in one point. When solving a system of two linear equations that are parallel or are the same line, both variables cancel and we are left with a true statement such as "3 = 3" or a false statement such as "5 = 1." We have a true statement when the two lines are the same and a false statement when they are parallel.

 EXAMPLE 10-6

• $\begin{cases} 2x - 3y = 6 & \text{A} \\ -4x + 6y = 8 & \text{B} \end{cases}$

$$4x - 6y = 12 \qquad \text{2A}$$
$$\underline{-4x + 6y = 8} \qquad +\text{B}$$
$$0 = 20$$

This is a false statement, so the lines are parallel. They are sketched in Figure 10-4.

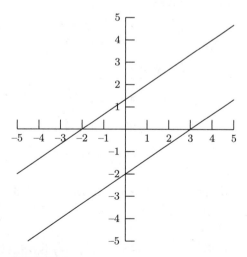

FIGURE 10-4

$$\bullet \begin{cases} y = \dfrac{2}{3}x - 1 \\ 2x - 3y = 3 \end{cases}$$

We use substitution.

$$2x - 3\left(\frac{2}{3}x - 1\right) = 3$$

$$2x - 2x + 3 = 3$$

$$0 = 0$$

Because $0 = 0$ is a true statement, these lines are the same.

When the system of equations is not a pair of lines, there could be no solutions, one solution, or more than one solution. The same methods used for pairs of lines work with other systems.

 EXAMPLE 10-7

$$\bullet \begin{cases} y = x^2 - 2x - 3 & \text{A} \\ 3x - y = 7 & \text{B} \end{cases}$$

Elimination by addition would not work to eliminate x^2 because B has no x^2 term to cancel x^2 in A. Solving for x in B and substituting it for x in A would work to eliminate x. Both addition and substitution work to eliminate y. We use addition to eliminate y.

$$y = x^2 - 2x - 3 \quad \text{A}$$
$$\underline{3x - y = 7 \qquad\qquad} \text{+B}$$
$$3x = x^2 - 2x + 4$$
$$0 = x^2 - 5x + 4$$
$$0 = (x - 1)(x - 4)$$

The solutions occur when $x = 1$ or $x = 4$. We need to find two y-values. We let $x = 1$ and $x = 4$ in A.

$$y = 1^2 - 2(1) - 3 = -4 \qquad (1, -4) \text{ is one solution.}$$
$$y = 4^2 - 2(4) - 3 = 5 \qquad (4, 5) \text{ is the other solution.}$$

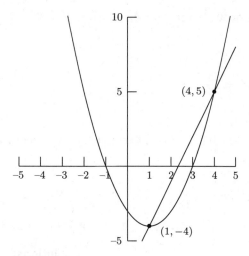

FIGURE 10-5

We can see from the graphs in Figure 10-5 that these solutions are correct.

$$\cdot \begin{cases} x^2 + y^2 = 25 & \textbf{A} \\ y = -\dfrac{1}{3}x^2 + 7 & \textbf{B} \end{cases}$$

We could solve for x^2 in A and substitute this in B. We cannot add the equations to eliminate y or y^2 because A does not have a y term to cancel y in B and B does not have a y^2 term to cancel y^2 in A. We move $-\frac{1}{3}x^2$ to the left side of B and multiply B by -3. Then we can add this to A to eliminate x^2.

$$\frac{1}{3}x^2 + y = 7 \qquad \textbf{B}$$

$$x^2 + y^2 = 25 \qquad \textbf{A}$$

$$\underline{-x^2 - 3y = -21 \qquad -3\textbf{B}}$$

$$y^2 - 3y = 4$$

$$y^2 - 3y - 4 = 0$$

$$(y - 4)(y + 1) = 0$$

The solutions occur when $y = 4, -1$. Put $y = 4, -1$ in A to find their x-values.

$$x^2 + 4^2 = 25$$

$$x^2 = 9$$

$$x = \pm 3 \qquad (-3, 4) \text{ and } (3, 4) \text{ are solutions.}$$

$$x^2 + (-1)^2 = 25$$

$$x^2 = 24$$

$$x = \pm\sqrt{24} = \pm 2\sqrt{6} \qquad (2\sqrt{6}, -1) \text{ and } (-2\sqrt{6}, -1)$$

$$\text{are solutions.}$$

• $\begin{cases} x^2 + y^2 = 4 & \text{A} \\ y = \dfrac{2}{x} & \text{B} \end{cases}$

Addition does not work on this system but substitution does. We substitute $y = \frac{2}{x}$ for y in A.

$$x^2 + \left(\frac{2}{x}\right)^2 = 4$$

$$x^2 + \frac{4}{x^2} = 4 \qquad \text{The LCD is } x^2$$

$$x^2 \left(x^2 + \frac{4}{x^2}\right) = x^2(4)$$

$$x^4 + 4 = 4x^2$$

$$x^4 - 4x^2 + 4 = 0$$

$$(x^2 - 2)(x^2 - 2) = 0$$

$$x^2 = 2$$

$$x = \pm\sqrt{2}$$

We use $x = \sqrt{2}$ and $x = -\sqrt{2}$ in $y = \frac{2}{x}$.

$$y = \frac{2}{\sqrt{2}} = \frac{2\sqrt{2}}{\sqrt{2}\sqrt{2}} = \frac{2\sqrt{2}}{2} = \sqrt{2}; \quad (\sqrt{2}, \sqrt{2}) \text{ is a solution.}$$

$$y = \frac{2}{-\sqrt{2}} = \frac{2\sqrt{2}}{-\sqrt{2}\sqrt{2}} = \frac{2\sqrt{2}}{-2} = -\sqrt{2}; \quad (-\sqrt{2}, -\sqrt{2}) \text{ is a solution.}$$

Solving a System of Equations with a Graphing Calculator

We can use the INTERSECT feature on a graphing calculator to solve a system of equations. This feature is located on the CALCULATE menu. The calculator finds an intersection point for the part of the graph that is displayed. The cursor marks the intersection point and its coordinates are displayed.

 EXAMPLE 10-8

- **Use a graphing calculator to solve the system.**

$$\begin{cases} y = 2x - 1 \\ x + y = 2 \end{cases}$$

We must enter both equations on the "Y = " Editor, so we solve the second equation for **y**. After entering $2x - 1$ and $-x + 2$ in the editor (see Figure 10-6), we plot the graph in the standard window. See Figure 10-7.

Go to the CALCULATE menu (second function on the TRACE key) and cursor to 5: intersect and press ENTER. (See Figure 10-8.) Press ENTER at the "First curve?" and "Second curve?" prompts. We can enter a guess at the "Guess?" prompt or we can ignore it by pressing ENTER. The calculator locates the intersection point. (See Figure 10-9.)

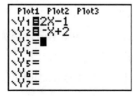

FIGURE 10-6

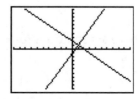

FIGURE 10-7

FIGURE 10-8

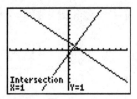

FIGURE 10-9

 PRACTICE

Solve the systems of equations. Write the solution in the form of a point, (x, y).

1. $\begin{cases} y = x^2 - 4 & \text{A} \\ x + y = 8 & \text{B} \end{cases}$

2. $\begin{cases} x^2 + y^2 + 6x - 2y = -5 & \text{A} \\ y = -2x - 5 & \text{B} \end{cases}$

3. $\begin{cases} x^2 - y^2 = 16 & \text{A} \\ x^2 + y^2 = 16 & \text{B} \end{cases}$

4. $\begin{cases} 4x^2 + y^2 = 5 & \text{A} \\ y = \dfrac{1}{x} & \text{B} \end{cases}$

 **SOLUTIONS**

1.
$$y = x^2 - 4 \qquad \text{A}$$
$$\underline{-x - y = -8 \qquad\qquad -\text{B}}$$
$$-x = x^2 - 12$$
$$0 = x^2 + x - 12 = (x + 4)(x - 3)$$

There are solutions for $x = -4$ and $x = 3$. Put these in A.

$$y = (-4)^2 - 4 = 12;\ (-4, 12) \text{ is a solution.}$$

$$y = 3^2 - 4 = 5;\ (3, 5) \text{ is a solution.}$$

2. **Substitute** $-2x - 5$ **for** y **in A.**

$$x^2 + (-2x - 5)^2 + 6x - 2(-2x - 5) = -5$$

$$x^2 + 4x^2 + 20x + 25 + 6x + 4x + 10 = -5$$

$$5x^2 + 30x + 40 = 0 \quad \text{Divide by 5}$$

$$x^2 + 6x + 8 = 0$$

$$(x + 4)(x + 2) = 0$$

There are solutions for $x = -4$ and $x = -2$. We put these in B instead of A because there is less computation to do in B.

$$y = -2(-4) - 5 = 3; \ (-4, 3) \text{ is a solution.}$$

$$y = -2(-2) - 5 = -1; \ (-2, -1) \text{ is a solution.}$$

3.
$$x^2 - y^2 = 16 \quad \text{A}$$

$$\underline{x^2 + y^2 = 16 \quad \ +\text{B}}$$

$$2x^2 = 32$$

$$x^2 = 16$$

$$x = \pm 4$$

Put $x = 4$ and $x = -4$ in A.

$$(-4)^2 - y^2 = 16 \qquad 4^2 - y^2 = 16$$

$$16 - y^2 = 16 \qquad 16 - y^2 = 16$$

$$y^2 = 0 \qquad \qquad y^2 = 0$$

$$y = 0 \qquad \qquad y = 0$$

The solutions are $(-4, 0)$ and $(4, 0)$.

4. Substitute $\frac{1}{x}$ for y in A.

$$4x^2 + \left(\frac{1}{x}\right)^2 = 5$$

$$x^2\left(4x^2 + \frac{1}{x^2}\right) = x^2(5)$$

$$4x^4 + 1 = 5x^2$$

$$4x^4 - 5x^2 + 1 = 0$$

$$(4x^2 - 1)(x^2 - 1) = 0$$

$$(2x - 1)(2x + 1)(x - 1)(x + 1) = 0$$

The solutions are $x = \pm\frac{1}{2}$ (from $2x - 1 = 0$ and $2x + 1 = 0$) and $x = \pm 1$. Put these in B.

$$y = \frac{1}{\frac{1}{2}} = 2; \ \left(\frac{1}{2}, 2\right) \text{ is a solution.}$$

$$y = \frac{1}{-\frac{1}{2}} = -2; \ \left(-\frac{1}{2}, -2\right) \text{ is a solution.}$$

$$y = \frac{1}{1} = 1; \ (1, 1) \text{ is a solution.}$$

$$y = \frac{1}{-1} = -1; \ (-1, -1) \text{ is a solution.}$$

Systems of Inequalities

The solution (if any) for a system of inequalities is usually a region in the plane. The solution to a polynomial inequality (the only kind in this book) is the region above or below the curve. To show the solution to an inequality graphically, we shade the region that is the solution. A solid boundary on the graph means that it is part of the solution and a dashed boundary indicates that it is not part of the solution. We will use the procedure in Table 10-1.

We begin with linear inequalities.

TABLE 10-1	Sketching the Solution to an Inequality

1. Sketch the graph of the equation, using a solid graph for "$\leq$" and "$\geq$" inequalities, and a dashed graph for "$<$" and "$>$" inequalities.
2. Determine which side of the graph to shade. First, choose *any* point not on the graph itself and use its coordinates in the inequality. If the coordinates make the inequality true, shade the side that contains the point. If the inequality is false, shade the other side, that is, the side that does *not* contain the point.

 EXAMPLE 10-9

• $2x + 3y \leq 6$

We sketch the line $2x + 3y = 6$, using a solid line because the inequality is "$\leq$." (See Figure 10-10.)

We always use the origin, $(0, 0)$ in our inequalities unless the graph goes through the origin. Does $x = 0$ and $y = 0$ make $2x + 3y \leq 6$ true? $2(0) + 3(0) \leq 6$ is a true statement, so we shade the side that has the origin. (See Figure 10-11.)

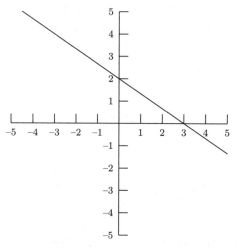

FIGURE 10-10

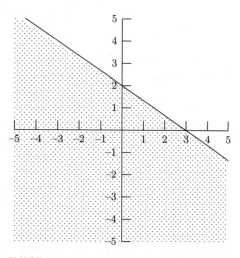

FIGURE 10-11

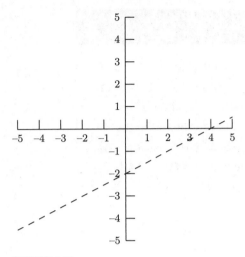

FIGURE 10-12

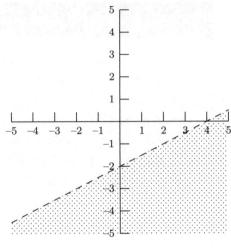

FIGURE 10-13

- $x - 2y > 4$

  We sketch the line $x - 2y = 4$ using a dashed line because the inequality is ">." (See Figure 10-12.)

  Now we need to decide which side of the line to shade. When we put $(0, 0)$ in $x - 2y > 4$, we get the false statement $0 - 2(0) > 4$. We need to shade the side of the line that does *not* have the origin. (See Figure 10-13.)

- $y < 3x$

  We use a dashed line to sketch the line $y = 3x$. Because the line goes through $(0, 0)$, we cannot use it to determine which side of the line to shade. This is because any point on the line makes the equality true. We want to know where the inequality is true. The point $(1, 0)$ is not on the line, so we can use it. $0 < 3(1)$ is true, so we shade the side of the line that has the point $(1, 0)$, which is the right side. (See Figure 10-14.)

- $x \geq -3$

  The line $x = -3$ is a vertical line through $x = -3$. Because we want $x \geq -3$, we shade to the right of the line. (See Figure 10-15.)

- $y < 2$

  The line $y = 2$ is a horizontal line at $y = 2$. Because we want $y < 2$, we shade below the line. (See Figure 10-16.)

Graphing the solution region for polynomial inequalities is done the same way—graph the equation, using a solid graph for "$\leq$" and "$\geq$" inequalities and a

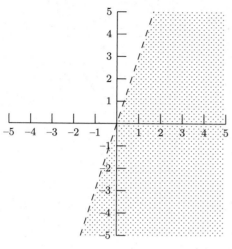

FIGURE 10-14

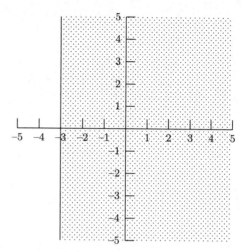

FIGURE 10-15

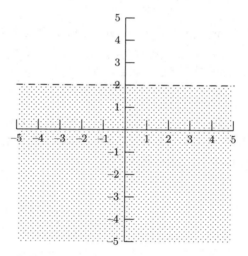

FIGURE 10-16

dashed graph for "<" and ">" inequalities, then checking a point to see which side of the graph to shade.

EXAMPLE 10-10

• $y \leq x^2 - x - 2$

The equation is $y = x^2 - x - 2 = (x - 2)(x + 1)$. The graph for this equation is a parabola. (See Figure 10-17.)

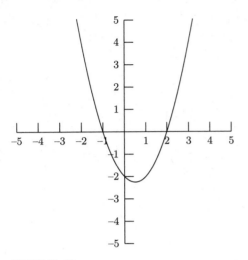

FIGURE 10-17

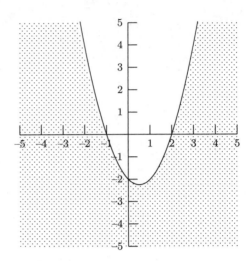

FIGURE 10-18

Because $(0, 0)$ is not on the graph, we can use it to decide which side to shade; $0 \leq 0^2 - 0 - 2$ is false, so we shade below the graph, the side that does not contain $(0, 0)$. (See Figure 10-18.)

- $y > (x + 2)(x - 2)(x - 4)$

When we check $(0, 0)$ in the inequality, we get the false statement $0 > (0 + 2)(0 - 2)(0 - 4) = 16$. We shade above the graph, the region that does not contain $(0, 0)$. (See Figure 10-19.)

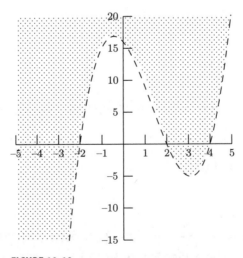

FIGURE 10-19

The solution (if there is one) to a system of two or more inequalities is the region that is part of each solution for the individual inequalities. For example, if we have a system of two inequalities and shade the solution to one inequality in blue and the other in yellow, then the solution to the system would be the region in green.

 EXAMPLE **10-11**

• $\begin{cases} x - y < 3 \\ x + 2y > 1 \end{cases}$

Sketch the solution for each inequality. The solution to $x - y < 3$ is the region shaded vertically. (See Figure 10-20.) The solution to $x + 2y > 1$ is the region shaded horizontally. (See Figure 10-21.)

The region that is in both solutions is above and between the lines. (See Figure 10-22.)

• $\begin{cases} y \leq 4 - x^2 \\ x - 7y \leq 4 \end{cases}$

The solution to $y \leq 4 - x^2$ is the region shaded vertically. The solution to $x - 7y \leq 4$ is the region shaded horizontally. (See Figure 10-23.) The

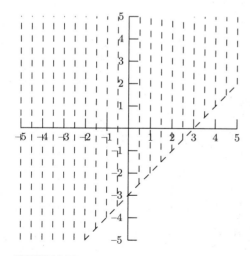

FIGURE 10-20

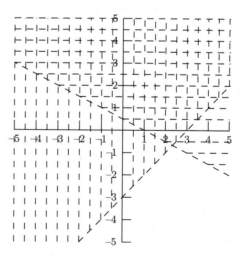

FIGURE 10-21

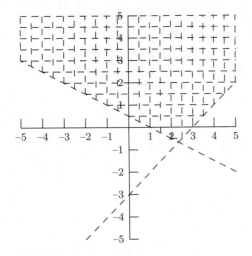

FIGURE 10-22

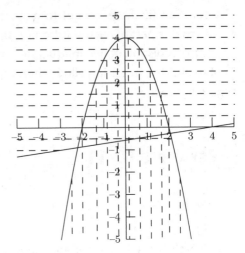

FIGURE 10-23

region that is in both solutions is above the line and inside the parabola. (See Figure 10-24.)

Because a solid graph indicates that points on the graph are also solutions, to be absolutely accurate, the correct solution uses dashed graphs for the part of the graphs that are not on the border of the shaded region. (See Figure 10-25.)

We will not quibble with this technicality here.

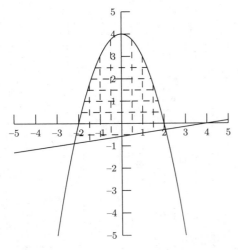

FIGURE 10-24

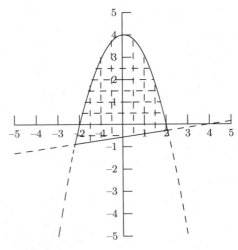

FIGURE 10-25

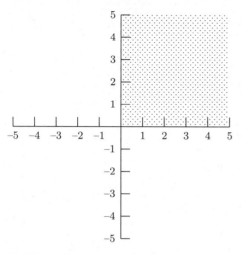

FIGURE 10-26

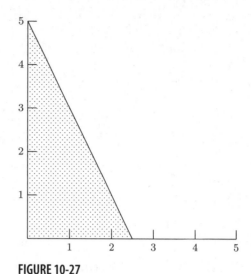

FIGURE 10-27

$$\bullet \begin{cases} 2x + y \leq 5 \\ x \geq 0 \\ y \geq 0 \end{cases}$$

The inequalities $x \geq 0$ and $y \geq 0$ mean that we only need the top right corner of the graph. These inequalities are common in word problems. (See Figure 10-26.)

The solution to the system is the region in the top right corner of the x-y plane below the line $2x + y = 5$. (See Figure 10-27.)

Some systems of inequalities have no solution. In the following example, the regions do not overlap, so there are no ordered pairs (points) that make both inequalities true.

EXAMPLE 10-12

$$\bullet \begin{cases} y \geq x^2 + 4 \\ x - y \geq 1 \end{cases}$$

See Figure 10-28.

It is easy to lose track of the solution for a system of three or more inequalities. There are a couple of things you can do to make it easier. First, make sure the

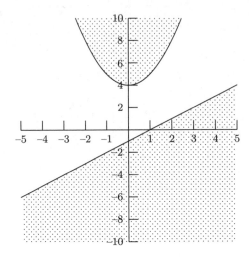

FIGURE 10-28

graph is large enough, using graph paper if possible. Second, shade the solution for each inequality in a different way, with different colors or shaded with horizontal, vertical, and slanted lines. The solution (if there is one) would be shaded in all different ways. You could also shade one region at a time, erasing the part of the previous region that is not part of the inequality.

EXAMPLE 10-13

$$\bullet \begin{cases} x + y \leq 4 \\ x \geq 1 \\ y \leq x \end{cases}$$

First we shade the solution for $x + y \leq 4$. (See Figure 10-29.)

The region for $x \geq 1$ is the right of the line $x = 1$, so we erase the region to the *left* of $x = 1$. (See Figure 10-30.)

The solution to $y \leq x$ is the region below the line $y = x$, so we erase the shading *above* the line $y = x$.

The shaded region in Figure 10-31 is the solution for the system.

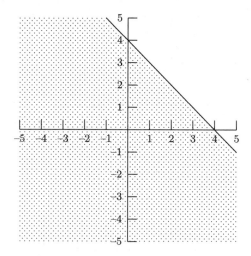

FIGURE 10-29

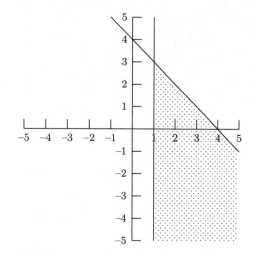

FIGURE 10-30

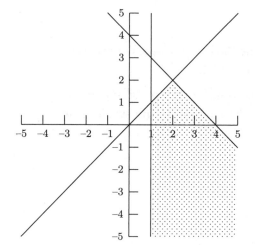

FIGURE 10-31

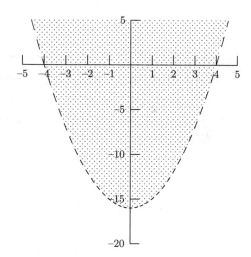

FIGURE 10-32

- $$\begin{cases} y > x^2 - 16 \\ x < 2 \\ y < -5 \\ -x + y < -8 \end{cases}$$

We begin with $y > x^2 - 16$. (See Figure 10-32.)

The solution to $x < 2$ is the region to the left of the line $x = 2$. We erase the shading to the right of $x = 2$. (See Figure 10-33.)

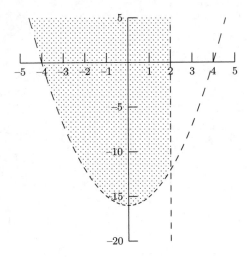

FIGURE 10-33

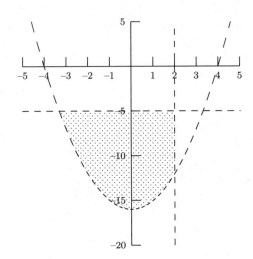

FIGURE 10-34

The solution to $y < -5$ is the region below the line $y = -5$. We erase the shading above the line $y = -5$. (See Figure 10-34.)

The solution to $-x + y < -8$ is the region below the line $-x + y = -8$, so we erase the shading above the line. The solution to the system is in Figure 10-35.

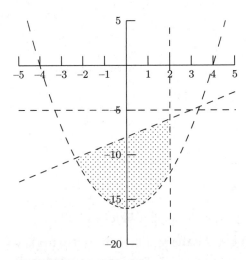

FIGURE 10-35

Graphing Inequalities on a Calculator

A graphing calculator can display the solution to an equality and even a system of inequalities. The calculator displays the region by shading it horizontally, vertically, or diagonally. We can access this feature on the "Y = " Editor.

 **EXAMPLE 10-14**

- Use a calculator to display the solution to $y \geq x^2$.

  After entering x^2 on the "Y = " Editor, cursor to the left and press ENTER twice. See Figure 10-36. (Notice the little triangle next to "$Y_1 =$." This is one of the two inequality symbols. The other symbol is a triangle facing the other direction, as you will see in Figure 10-38.) This shades the region above the graph. The region is displayed in Figure 10-37.

We can use a calculator to display the solution to a system of inequalities. The second inequality is shaded horizontally.

 **EXAMPLE 10-15**

- Use a graphing calculator to display the solution to the system.

$$\begin{cases} y \geq x^2 \\ y \leq 2x + 5 \end{cases}$$

  We already have the solution to $y \geq x^2$ plotted, so we only need to add the solution to $y \leq 2x + 5$. After entering $2x + 5$ in the "Y = " Editor, cursor to the left and press ENTER three times. (See Figure 10-38.) This shades the region below the graph. The solution to the second inequality is shaded horizontally, and the solution to the system is shaded both vertically and horizontally in Figure 10-39.

FIGURE 10-36

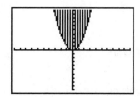

FIGURE 10-37

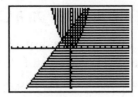

```
Plot1 Plot2 Plot3
\Y1◘X²
\Y2◘2X+5
\Y3=
\Y4=
\Y5=
\Y6=
\Y7=
```

FIGURE 10-38

FIGURE 10-39

 PRACTICE

Graph the solution.

1. $2x - 4y < 4$

2. $x > 1$

3. $y \leq -1$

4. $y \leq x^2 - 4$

5. $y > x^3$

6. $y < |x|$

7. $y \geq (x - 3)(x + 1)(x + 3)$

8. $\begin{cases} 2x - y \leq 6 \\ x \geq 3 \end{cases}$

9. $\begin{cases} y > x^2 + 2x - 3 \\ x + y < 5 \end{cases}$

10. $\begin{cases} 2x + 3y \geq 6 \\ x \geq 0 \\ y \geq 0 \end{cases}$

11. $\begin{cases} 2x + y \geq 1 \\ -x + 2y \leq 4 \\ 5x - 3y \leq 15 \end{cases}$

SOLUTIONS

1. See Figure 10-40.

2. See Figure 10-41.

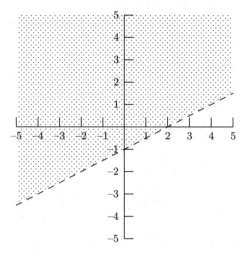

FIGURE 10-40

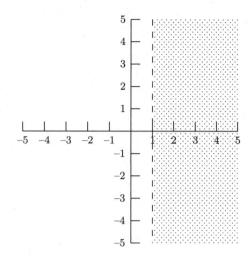

FIGURE 10-41

3. See Figure 10-42.

4. See Figure 10-43.

5. See Figure 10-44.

6. See Figure 10-45.

7. See Figure 10-46.

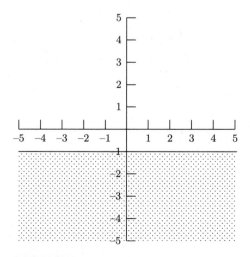

FIGURE 10-42

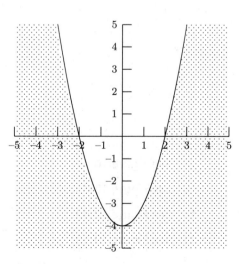

FIGURE 10-43

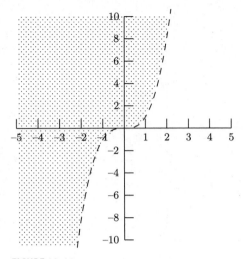

FIGURE 10-44

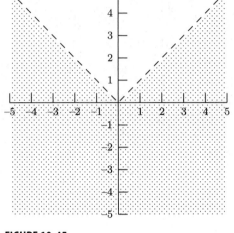

FIGURE 10-45

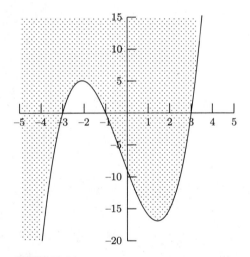

FIGURE 10-46

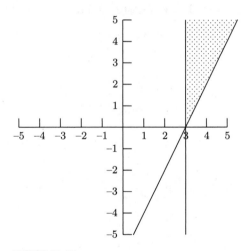

FIGURE 10-47

8. See Figure 10-47.

9. See Figure 10-48.

10. See Figure 10-49.

11. See Figure 10-50.

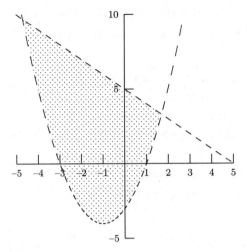

FIGURE 10-48

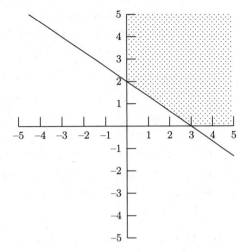

FIGURE 10-49

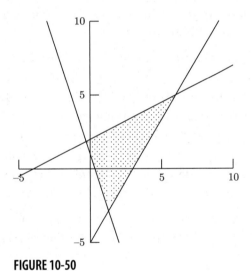

FIGURE 10-50

Summary

In this chapter, we learned how to

- *Solve a system of linear equations by substitution.* We can solve a system of linear equations by solving one of the equations for one of the variables and substituting this quantity into the other equation. This leaves us with one equation having a single unknown. We solve this equation for the unknown. We find the second unknown by putting this solution into any equation having both variables.

- *Solve a system of linear equations using elimination by addition.* Using elimination by addition, we add the equations, term by term, in such a way that the terms containing one of the variables add to zero, canceling this variable. Usually, we must multiply one equation or both equations by a number to make one of the coefficients the opposite of the other. Again, we are left with one equation having only one unknown. After solving this equation, we substitute the value into any equation having both variables to find the value of the second variable.

- *Solve other systems of equations.* We can use the same methods as above to solve systems of equations containing equations that are not linear. The main difference is that these systems might have multiple solutions.

- *Verify a solution graphically.* The solution to a system equations is any point (or points) that lies on both graphs.

- *Graph the solution to an inequality.* The solution to an inequality of the form $y < f(x)$, $y > f(x)$, $y \le f(x)$, or $y \ge f(x)$ is the region either above the curve or below the curve $y = f(x)$. If the inequality is $<$ or $>$, we use a dashed line/curve; and if the inequality is $\le$ or $\ge$, we use a solid line/curve. We can decide which side to shade by choosing a point not on the line/curve and testing it in the original inequality. If it makes the inequality true, we shade the side containing that point. If it makes the inequality false, we shade the side that does not contain the point.

- *Graph the solution to a system of inequalities.* The solution to a system of inequalities is the region (assuming it exists) that overlaps the solution to each inequality.

QUIZ

In some of the following problems, you will be asked to find quantities such as $x + 2y$ for a system of equations. Solve the system and put the solution in the formula. For example, if the solution is $x = 3$ and $y = 5$, then $x + 2y$ becomes $3 + 2(5) = 13$.

1. **Find $x + y$ for the system** $\begin{cases} 2x - 5y = 22 \\ 3x + 5y = -17 \end{cases}$.

    A. 5   C. The lines are the same.

    B. -3 D. The system has no solution.

2. **Find $x - y$ for the system** $\begin{cases} \frac{1}{3}x + y = 1 \\ x + 4y = 5 \end{cases}$.

    A. -5 C. The lines are the same.

    B. 2   D. The system has no solution.

3. **Find $2x + y$ for the system** $\begin{cases} \frac{2}{5}x + \frac{1}{2}y = 5 \\ x - 3y = -13 \end{cases}$.

    A. 16   C. The lines are the same.

    B. -4 D. The system has no solution.

4. **Find $x - 2y$ for the system** $\begin{cases} -\frac{2}{3}x + y = 1 \\ 2x - 3y = 6 \end{cases}$.

    A. -2 C. The lines are the same.

    B. 5   D. The system has no solution.

5. **Find $4x + 2y$ for the system** $\begin{cases} y = 4x + \frac{1}{2} \\ y = \frac{10}{3}x + 1 \end{cases}$.

    A. 10   C. The lines are the same.

    B. $\frac{5}{2}$ D. The system has no solution.

6. **Find $x + y$ for the system** $\begin{cases} 2x + y = 7 \\ y = -x^2 + 2x + 4 \end{cases}$.

    A. 5 and -3 C. 3 and 6

    B. 2 and -1 D. 4 and 6

7. **The graph in Figure 10-51 is the solution to which inequality?**

    A. $x - 2y \le 2$ C. $2x + y \le 2$

    B. $x - 2y < 2$ D. $2x + y < 2$

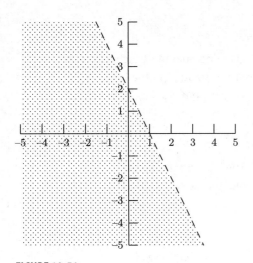

FIGURE 10-51   **FIGURE 10-52**

8. The graph in Figure 10-52 is the solution to which inequality?

   A. $y > \frac{1}{2}(x + 5)(x - 1)(x - 4)$ C. $y > \frac{1}{2}(x - 5)(x + 1)(x + 4)$

   B. $y < \frac{1}{2}(x + 5)(x - 1)(x - 4)$ D. $y < \frac{1}{2}(x - 5)(x + 1)(x + 4)$

9. The shaded region in Figure 10-53 is the solution to which system?

   A. $\begin{cases} y < x^2 + 4x \\ x \le 0 \\ 0 \le y \end{cases}$ C. $\begin{cases} y > x^2 + 4x \\ x \le 0 \\ y < 4 \end{cases}$

   B. $\begin{cases} y > x^2 + 4x \\ x \le 0 \\ 0 \le y < 4 \end{cases}$ D. $\begin{cases} y < x^2 + 4x \\ x \ge 0 \\ 0 \le y < 4 \end{cases}$

10. A grocery store sells regular bananas for $0.59 per pound and certified organic bananas for $1.19 per pound. One day, the store sold a total of 350 pounds of bananas for sales of $272.50. How many regular bananas were sold that day?

    A. 200 pounds   C. 240 pounds

    B. 220 pounds   D. 260 pounds

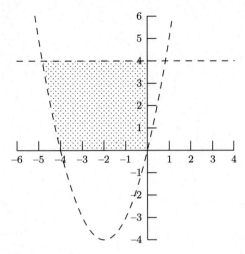

FIGURE 10-53

chapter 11

Matrices

Matrices have many applications. They are used in business (for linear programming), in physics and engineering (for work with vectors), and in mathematics. As a subject in mathematics, matrices are complex enough that some universities offer an entire course devoted to them. In this chapter, we are introduced to matrices and to one application—solving a system of linear equations.

CHAPTER OBJECTIVES

In this chapter, you will

- Perform arithmetic with matrices
- Find the inverse of a square matrix
- Use matrices to solve a system of equations
- Find the determinant of a square matrix

Much of our work with matrices is quite tedious. After learning how to use a calculator to quickly (and painlessly) work with matrices, you might wonder why you need to learn how to do these calculations by hand. There are two reasons. One is practical; some instructors do not permit calculators. Another reason is that some of the operations that you might do on matrices in other courses involve symbols, not numbers, so the calculator will not be very useful. Although you are not likely to see matrices in a first calculus course, you will work with them in multi-variate calculus (Calculus III) and in linear algebra.

Matrix Arithmetic

A matrix is an array of numbers or symbols made up of rows and columns. Matrices are used in science and business to represent several variables and relationships at once. For example, suppose there are three brands of fertilizer that provide different levels of three minerals that a gardener might need. The following matrix shows how much of each mineral is provided by each brand.

	Mineral A	Mineral B	Mineral C
Brand X	6	2	1
Brand Y	2	1	2
Brand Z	1	3	6

Matrix Arithmetic

The numbers in a matrix are called *cells* or *entries*. A matrix's size is given by the number of rows and columns it has. For example, a matrix that has two rows and three columns is called a 2×3 (pronounced "2 by 3") matrix. A matrix that has the same number of rows as columns is called a *square* matrix.

Two matrices must be of the same size before we can add them or find their difference. The sum of two or more matrices is the sum of their corresponding entries.

$$\begin{bmatrix} 2 & -1 \\ 3 & 4 \end{bmatrix} + \begin{bmatrix} 5 & 9 \\ 4 & 1 \end{bmatrix} = \begin{bmatrix} 2+5 & -1+9 \\ 3+4 & 4+1 \end{bmatrix} = \begin{bmatrix} 7 & 8 \\ 7 & 5 \end{bmatrix}$$

Subtract one matrix from another by subtracting their corresponding entries.

$$\begin{bmatrix} 2 & -1 \\ 3 & 4 \end{bmatrix} - \begin{bmatrix} 5 & 9 \\ 4 & 1 \end{bmatrix} = \begin{bmatrix} 2-5 & -1-9 \\ 3-4 & 4-1 \end{bmatrix} = \begin{bmatrix} -3 & -10 \\ -1 & 3 \end{bmatrix}$$

The *scalar product* of a matrix is a matrix whose entries are multiplied by a fixed number.

$$3 \begin{bmatrix} 6 & -4 \\ 2 & 1 \\ 5 & 0 \end{bmatrix} = \begin{bmatrix} 3 \cdot 6 & 3 \cdot (-4) \\ 3 \cdot 2 & 3 \cdot 1 \\ 3 \cdot 5 & 3 \cdot 0 \end{bmatrix} = \begin{bmatrix} 18 & -12 \\ 6 & 3 \\ 15 & 0 \end{bmatrix}$$

It might seem that matrix multiplication is carried out the same way addition and subtraction are—by multiplying their corresponding entries. This operation is not very useful. The matrix multiplication operation that is useful requires more work. Two matrices need not be of the same size, but the number of columns of the first matrix must be the same as the number of rows of the second matrix. This is because we find the entries of the product matrix by multiplying the rows of the first matrix by the columns of the second matrix. Here, we multiply a 3×3 matrix by a 3×2 matrix.

$$\begin{bmatrix} A & B & C \\ D & E & F \\ G & H & I \end{bmatrix} \cdot \begin{bmatrix} K & L \\ M & N \\ O & P \end{bmatrix} = \begin{bmatrix} \text{Row 1} \times \text{Column 1} & \text{Row 1} \times \text{Column 2} \\ \text{Row 2} \times \text{Column 1} & \text{Row 2} \times \text{Column 2} \\ \text{Row 3} \times \text{Column 1} & \text{Row 3} \times \text{Column 2} \end{bmatrix}$$

Row 1 of the first matrix is $A\,B\,C$ and Column 1 of the second matrix is $\begin{smallmatrix} K \\ M \\ O \end{smallmatrix}$. The first entry of the product matrix is Row 1 × Column 1, which is this sum.

$$
\begin{array}{ccc}
\text{Row 1} & & \text{Column 1} \\
A & \times & K \\
B & \times & M \\
+ \quad C & \times & O \\
\hline
\end{array}
$$

$$\begin{bmatrix} \text{Row 1} \times \text{Column 1} & \text{Row 1} \times \text{Column 2} \\ \text{Row 2} \times \text{Column 1} & \text{Row 2} \times \text{Column 2} \\ \text{Row 3} \times \text{Column 1} & \text{Row 3} \times \text{Column 2} \end{bmatrix}$$

$$= \begin{bmatrix} AK + BM + CO & AL + BN + CP \\ DK + EM + FO & DL + EN + FP \\ GK + HM + IO & GL + HN + IP \end{bmatrix}$$

EXAMPLE 11-1

Find the product.

$$\bullet \begin{bmatrix} 1 & -8 & 2 \\ 5 & 0 & -1 \\ 2 & 1 & 1 \end{bmatrix} \cdot \begin{bmatrix} 4 & -7 \\ -2 & 1 \\ 3 & 0 \end{bmatrix}$$

$$\begin{bmatrix} 1 \cdot 4 + (-8)(-2) + 2 \cdot 3 & 1(-7) + (-8)1 + 2 \cdot 0 \\ 5 \cdot 4 + 0(-2) + (-1)3 & 5(-7) + 0 \cdot 1 + (-1)0 \\ 2 \cdot 4 + 1(-2) + 1 \cdot 3 & 2(-7) + 1 \cdot 1 + 1 \cdot 0 \end{bmatrix} = \begin{bmatrix} 26 & -15 \\ 17 & -35 \\ 9 & -13 \end{bmatrix}$$

$$\bullet \begin{bmatrix} -6 & 2 \\ 7 & 1 \end{bmatrix} \cdot \begin{bmatrix} 4 & 1 & 0 \\ -3 & 5 & 2 \end{bmatrix}$$

$$\begin{bmatrix} -6 \cdot 4 + 2(-3) & -6 \cdot 1 + 2 \cdot 5 & -6 \cdot 0 + 2 \cdot 2 \\ 7 \cdot 4 + 1(-3) & 7 \cdot 1 + 1 \cdot 5 & 7 \cdot 0 + 1 \cdot 2 \end{bmatrix} = \begin{bmatrix} -30 & 4 & 4 \\ 25 & 12 & 2 \end{bmatrix}$$

An identity matrix is a square matrix with 1s on the main diagonal (from the upper left corner to the bottom right corner) and 0s everywhere else. The following are the 2 × 2 and 3 × 3 identity matrices.

$$\begin{bmatrix} 1 & 0 \\ 0 & 1 \end{bmatrix} \text{ and } \begin{bmatrix} 1 & 0 & 0 \\ 0 & 1 & 0 \\ 0 & 0 & 1 \end{bmatrix}$$

If we multiply any matrix by its corresponding identity matrix, the product is the original matrix.

$$\begin{bmatrix} 1 & 0 \\ 0 & 1 \end{bmatrix} \cdot \begin{bmatrix} 3 & 6 & -2 \\ 2 & 1 & 5 \end{bmatrix} = \begin{bmatrix} 1 \cdot 3 + 0 \cdot 2 & 1 \cdot 6 + 0 \cdot 1 & 1(-2) + 0 \cdot 5 \\ 0 \cdot 3 + 1 \cdot 2 & 0 \cdot 6 + 1 \cdot 1 & 0(-2) + 1 \cdot 5 \end{bmatrix}$$

$$= \begin{bmatrix} 3 & 6 & -2 \\ 2 & 1 & 5 \end{bmatrix}$$

Matrix multiplication is not commutative. Reversing the order of the multiplication usually gets a different matrix, even if the multiplication is possible.

The product

$$\begin{bmatrix} 1 & -3 \\ 2 & 4 \end{bmatrix} \cdot \begin{bmatrix} 0 & 1 \\ 2 & -1 \end{bmatrix} = \begin{bmatrix} 1 \cdot 0 + (-3)2 & 1 \cdot 1 + (-3)(-1) \\ 2 \cdot 0 + 4 \cdot 2 & 2 \cdot 1 + 4(-1) \end{bmatrix} = \begin{bmatrix} -6 & 4 \\ 8 & -2 \end{bmatrix}$$

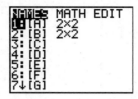

FIGURE 11-1

is not the same as the product

$$\begin{bmatrix} 0 & 1 \\ 2 & -1 \end{bmatrix} \cdot \begin{bmatrix} 1 & -3 \\ 2 & 4 \end{bmatrix} = \begin{bmatrix} 0 \cdot 1 + 1 \cdot 2 & 0(-3) + 1 \cdot 4 \\ 2 \cdot 1 + (-1)2 & 2(-3) + (-1)4 \end{bmatrix} = \begin{bmatrix} 2 & 4 \\ 0 & -10 \end{bmatrix}.$$

Matrix Arithmetic with a Calculator

The matrix features on a graphing calculator can save us a lot of time on matrix calculations. For now, we learn how to enter a matrix on the calculator and how to add/subtract and to find the product of two matrices. We enter a matrix on the EDIT screeen of the MATRIX menu (second function on the x^{-1} key). See Figure 11-1. Cursor to EDIT and press ENTER. After you enter the matrix's size, the calculator displays a matrix with the appropriate number of entries. Input each entry, pressing ENTER after each one. Once you have finished entering the matrix, return to the main screen by pressing ''QUIT'' (press the 2nd key followed by the MODE key). To enter a second matrix, cursor down to 2:[B] on the EDIT screen.

EXAMPLE 11-2

• Find the sum $\begin{bmatrix} 8 & -5 \\ 3 & 1 \end{bmatrix} + \begin{bmatrix} -2 & 7 \\ 2 & 0 \end{bmatrix}$.

We enter the first matrix as 1:[A] and the second as 2:[B] on the EDIT menu. See Figures 11-2 and 11-3.

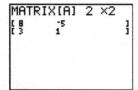

FIGURE 11-2

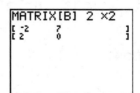

FIGURE 11-3

$$[A]+[B]$$
$$[[6\ 2]$$
$$[5\ 1]]$$

FIGURE 11-4

$$[A]*[B]$$
$$[[-26\ 56]$$
$$[-4\ 21]]$$

FIGURE 11-5

To find the sum, go to the MATRIX menu and press ENTER. (This pastes matrix [A] on the CALCULATE screen.) Press the + key and return to the MATRIX menu, cursor down to 2:[B] and press ENTER twice. This will display the sum. See Figure 11-4.

• Find the product $\begin{bmatrix} 8 & -5 \\ 3 & 1 \end{bmatrix} \cdot \begin{bmatrix} -2 & 7 \\ 2 & 0 \end{bmatrix}$.

We already have these matrices entered in the calculator, so we only need to find the product. Go to the MATRIX menu and press ENTER, press the × key, return to the MATRIX menu, cursor to 2:[B] and press ENTER twice. See Figure 11-5.

PRACTICE

Compute the following.

1. $\begin{bmatrix} 4 & 0 & -2 \\ 1 & 1 & 5 \end{bmatrix} - \begin{bmatrix} -3 & -2 & 2 \\ 6 & -4 & 3 \end{bmatrix}$

2. $5\begin{bmatrix} 3 & -6 \\ 2 & 4 \end{bmatrix}$

3. $\begin{bmatrix} 2 & -5 \\ 3 & 8 \end{bmatrix} \cdot \begin{bmatrix} 1 & 4 & -1 \\ 0 & -1 & 2 \end{bmatrix}$

4. $\begin{bmatrix} 1 & 0 & 3 \\ 2 & 1 & 0 \\ 3 & 1 & -2 \end{bmatrix} \cdot \begin{bmatrix} 4 & 2 & 1 \\ 1 & -3 & 1 \\ 3 & 6 & 2 \end{bmatrix}$

 SOLUTIONS

1. $\begin{bmatrix} 4-(-3) & 0-(-2) & -2-2 \\ 1-6 & 1-(-4) & 5-3 \end{bmatrix} = \begin{bmatrix} 7 & 2 & -4 \\ -5 & 5 & 2 \end{bmatrix}$

2. $$\begin{bmatrix} 5\cdot 3 & 5\cdot(-6) \\ 5\cdot 2 & 5\cdot 4 \end{bmatrix} = \begin{bmatrix} 15 & -30 \\ 10 & 20 \end{bmatrix}$$

3. $$\begin{bmatrix} 2\cdot 1+(-5)0 & 2\cdot 4+(-5)(-1) & 2(-1)+(-5)2 \\ 3\cdot 1+8\cdot 0 & 3\cdot 4+8(-1) & 3(-1)+8\cdot 2 \end{bmatrix}$$
$$= \begin{bmatrix} 2 & 13 & -12 \\ 3 & 4 & 13 \end{bmatrix}$$

4.

$$\begin{bmatrix} 1\cdot 4+0\cdot 1+3\cdot 3 & 1\cdot 2+0(-3)+3\cdot 6 & 1\cdot 1+0\cdot 1+3\cdot 2 \\ 2\cdot 4+1\cdot 1+0\cdot 3 & 2\cdot 2+1(-3)+0\cdot 6 & 2\cdot 1+1\cdot 1+0\cdot 2 \\ 3\cdot 4+1\cdot 1+(-2)3 & 3\cdot 2+1(-3)+(-2)6 & 3\cdot 1+1\cdot 1+(-2)2 \end{bmatrix}$$
$$= \begin{bmatrix} 13 & 20 & 7 \\ 9 & 1 & 3 \\ 7 & -9 & 0 \end{bmatrix}$$

Row Operations and Inverses

We use *row operations* to solve systems of equations and to find the multiplicative inverse of a matrix. These operations are similar to the elimination by addition method studied in Chapter 10. For instance, we can switch the order of the rows, multiply every entry in one row by a nonzero number, and we can replace a row with the sum of two rows. For now, we will multiply each entry in a row by a nonzero number and add two rows together. Our aim is to make a particular entry a zero. For example, in the matrix $\begin{bmatrix} 1 & -3 & 2 \\ 4 & 1 & 6 \end{bmatrix}$, we might want to change the entry with a 4 in it to 0. To do so, we can multiply the first row (Row 1) by -4 and add it to the second row (Row 2).

$$-4\,\text{Row 1}=-4(1 \quad -3 \quad 2)=-4 \quad 12 \quad -8$$

$$\begin{array}{lrrr} -4\,\text{Row 1} & -4 & 12 & -8 \\ +\,\text{Row 2} & 4 & 1 & 6 \\ \hline \text{New Row 2} & 0 & 13 & -2 \end{array}$$

The matrix becomes $\begin{bmatrix} 1 & -3 & 2 \\ 0 & 13 & -2 \end{bmatrix}$.

EXAMPLE 11-3

- Using Row 2 and Row 3, change the entry with a 3 in it on the second row to 0.

$$\begin{bmatrix} 1 & 8 & 5 \\ -2 & 1 & 3 \\ 1 & 0 & 4 \end{bmatrix}$$

When adding the rows together, we need the last entry in each column to be the opposites. If we multiply Row 2 by -4 and Row 3 by 3, we would be adding $-4(3)$ to $3(4)$ to get zero. Multiplying Row 2 by 4 and Row 3 by -3 also works.

$$
\begin{array}{rccccccc}
-4 \text{ Row 2} & = & -4(-2) & -4(1) & -4(3) & = & 8 & -4 & -12 \\
+3 \text{ Row 3} & = & 3(1) & 3(0) & 3(4) & = & 3 & 0 & 12 \\
\hline
& & & & \text{New Row 2} & & 11 & -4 & 0
\end{array}
$$

The new matrix is $\begin{bmatrix} 1 & 8 & 5 \\ 11 & -4 & 0 \\ 1 & 0 & 4 \end{bmatrix}$.

Our first use for row operations is to find the inverse of a matrix (if it has one). If we multiply a matrix by its inverse, we get the corresponding identity matrix. For example, the inverse of $\begin{bmatrix} 1 & -2 \\ -1 & 4 \end{bmatrix}$ is the matrix $\begin{bmatrix} 2 & 1 \\ \frac{1}{2} & \frac{1}{2} \end{bmatrix}$ because their product is the 2×2 identity matrix.

$$\begin{bmatrix} 1 & -2 \\ -1 & 4 \end{bmatrix} \cdot \begin{bmatrix} 2 & 1 \\ \frac{1}{2} & \frac{1}{2} \end{bmatrix} = \begin{bmatrix} 1 & 0 \\ 0 & 1 \end{bmatrix}$$

To find the inverse of $\begin{bmatrix} A & B \\ C & D \end{bmatrix}$, we first need to write the *augmented* matrix. An augmented matrix for this method has the original matrix on the left and the identity matrix on the right.

$$\left[\begin{array}{cc|cc} A & B & 1 & 0 \\ C & D & 0 & 1 \end{array}\right]$$

We use row operations to change the left half of the matrix to the 2×2 identity matrix. The inverse matrix becomes the right half of the augmented matrix in Step 6.

Step 1 Use row operations to make the **C** entry a 0 for the new Row 2.

Step 2 Use row operations to make the **B** entry a 0 for the new Row 1.

Step 3 Write the next matrix.

Step 4 Divide Row 1 by the **A** entry.

Step 5 Divide Row 2 by the **D** entry.

Step 6 Write the new matrix. The inverse matrix is the right half of this matrix.

 EXAMPLE 11-4

Find the inverse matrix.

$$\bullet \begin{bmatrix} 1 & -2 \\ -1 & 4 \end{bmatrix}$$

The augmented matrix is $\begin{bmatrix} 1 & -2 & | & 1 & 0 \\ -1 & 4 & | & 0 & 1 \end{bmatrix}$.

Step 1 We want to change -1, the **C** entry, to 0.

Row 1	1	−2	1	0
+ Row 2	−1	4	0	1
New Row 2	0	2	1	1

Step 2 We want to change -2, the **B** entry, to 0.

2 Row 1	2	−4	2	0
+ Row 2	−1	4	0	1
New Row 1	1	0	2	1

Step 3

$$\begin{bmatrix} 1 & 0 & | & 2 & 1 \\ 0 & 2 & | & 1 & 1 \end{bmatrix}$$

Step 4 This step is not necessary because dividing Row 1 by 1, the **A** entry, does not change any of its entries.

Step 5 Divide Row 2 by 2, the **D** entry. $\frac{1}{2}(0 \quad 2 \quad 1 \quad 1) = 0 \quad 1 \quad \frac{1}{2} \quad \frac{1}{2}$.

Step 6

$$\begin{bmatrix} 1 & 0 & | & 2 & 1 \\ 0 & 1 & | & \frac{1}{2} & \frac{1}{2} \end{bmatrix}$$

The inverse matrix is $\begin{bmatrix} 2 & 1 \\ \frac{1}{2} & \frac{1}{2} \end{bmatrix}$.

Finding the inverse of a 3×3 matrix takes a few more steps. Again, we begin by writing the augmented matrix.

$$\begin{bmatrix} A & B & C \\ D & E & F \\ G & H & I \end{bmatrix} \longrightarrow \begin{bmatrix} A & B & C & | & 1 & 0 & 0 \\ D & E & F & | & 0 & 1 & 0 \\ G & H & I & | & 0 & 0 & 1 \end{bmatrix}$$

We use row operations to turn the left half of the augmented matrix into the 3×3 identity matrix. There are many methods for getting from the first matrix to the last. The method outlined below always works, assuming the matrix has an inverse.

Step 1 Use Row 1 and Row 2 to make the *D* entry to 0 for new Row 2.

Step 2 Use Row 1 and Row 3 to make the *G* entry to 0 for new Row 3.

Step 3 Write the next matrix. $\begin{bmatrix} \text{Old Row 1} \\ \text{New Row 2} \\ \text{New Row 3} \end{bmatrix}$.

Step 4 Use Row 1 and Row 2 to make the *B* entry a 0 for new Row 1.

Step 5 Use Row 2 and Row 3 to make the *H* entry a 0 for new Row 3.

Step 6 Write the next matrix. $\begin{bmatrix} \text{New Row 1} \\ \text{Old Row 2} \\ \text{New Row 3} \end{bmatrix}$.

Step 7 Use Row 1 and Row 3 to make the *C* entry a 0 for new Row 1.

Step 8 Use Row 2 and Row 3 to make the *F* entry a 0 for new Row 2.

Step 9 Write the next matrix. $\begin{bmatrix} \text{New Row 1} \\ \text{New Row 2} \\ \text{Old Row 3} \end{bmatrix}$.

Step 10 Divide Row 1 by *A*, Row 2 by *E*, and Row 3 by *I*. The inverse is the right half of the augmented matrix.

EXAMPLE 11-5

• Find the inverse matrix.

$$\begin{bmatrix} 1 & 0 & -1 \\ 2 & 2 & 3 \\ 4 & -2 & 1 \end{bmatrix}$$

The augmented matrix is $\begin{bmatrix} 1 & 0 & -1 & | & 1 & 0 & 0 \\ 2 & 2 & 3 & | & 0 & 1 & 0 \\ 4 & -2 & 1 & | & 0 & 0 & 1 \end{bmatrix}$.

Step 1 Use Row 1 and Row 2 to make the *D* entry a 0 by computing −2 Row 1 + Row 2.

−2 Row 1	−2	0	2	−2	0	0
+ Row 2	2	2	3	0	1	0
New Row 2	0	2	5	−2	1	0

Step 2 Use Row 1 and Row 3 to make the *G* entry a 0 by computing −4 Row 1 + Row 3.

−4 Row 1	−4	0	4	−4	0	0
+ Row 3	4	−2	1	0	0	1
New Row 3	0	−2	5	−4	0	1

Step 3

$$\begin{bmatrix} 1 & 0 & -1 & | & 1 & 0 & 0 \\ 0 & 2 & 5 & | & -2 & 1 & 0 \\ 0 & -2 & 5 & | & -4 & 0 & 1 \end{bmatrix}$$

Step 4 This step is not necessary because the *B* entry is already 0. New Row 1 is old Row 1.

Step 5 Use Row 2 and Row 3 to make the *H* entry a 0 by computing Row 2 + Row 3.

Row 2	0	2	5	−2	1	0
+ Row 3	0	−2	5	−4	0	1
New Row 3	0	0	10	−6	1	1

Step 6

$$\begin{bmatrix} 1 & 0 & -1 & | & 1 & 0 & 0 \\ 0 & 2 & 5 & | & -2 & 1 & 0 \\ 0 & 0 & 10 & | & -6 & 1 & 1 \end{bmatrix}$$

Step 7 Use Row 1 and Row 3 to make the *C* entry a 0 by computing 10 Row 1 + Row 3.

10 Row 1	10	0	−10	10	0 0
+ Row 3	0	0	10	−6	1 1
New Row 1	10	0	0	4	1 1

Step 8 Use Row 2 and Row 3 to make the *F* entry a 0 by computing −2 Row 2 + Row 3.

−2 Row 2	0	−4	−10	4	−2 0
+ Row 3	0	0	10	−6	1 1
New Row 2	0	−4	0	−2	−1 1

Step 9

$$\begin{bmatrix} 10 & 0 & 0 & | & 4 & 1 & 1 \\ 0 & -4 & 0 & | & -2 & -1 & 1 \\ 0 & 0 & 10 & | & -6 & 1 & 1 \end{bmatrix}$$

Step 10 Divide Row 1 by 10, Row 2 by −4, and Row 3 by 10 to get the next matrix.

$$\begin{bmatrix} 1 & 0 & 0 & | & \frac{2}{5} & \frac{1}{10} & \frac{1}{10} \\ 0 & 1 & 0 & | & \frac{1}{2} & \frac{1}{4} & -\frac{1}{4} \\ 0 & 0 & 1 & | & -\frac{3}{5} & \frac{1}{10} & \frac{1}{10} \end{bmatrix}$$ The inverse matrix is $$\begin{bmatrix} \frac{2}{5} & \frac{1}{10} & \frac{1}{10} \\ \frac{1}{2} & \frac{1}{4} & -\frac{1}{4} \\ -\frac{3}{5} & \frac{1}{10} & \frac{1}{10} \end{bmatrix}.$$

• Find the inverse matrix.

$$\begin{bmatrix} 6 & 0 & 2 \\ 1 & -1 & 0 \\ 0 & 1 & 1 \end{bmatrix}$$

The augmented matrix is $$\begin{bmatrix} 6 & 0 & 2 & | & 1 & 0 & 0 \\ 1 & -1 & 0 & | & 0 & 1 & 0 \\ 0 & 1 & 1 & | & 0 & 0 & 1 \end{bmatrix}.$$

Step 1 Use Row 1 and Row 2 to make the 1 entry a 0.

Row 1	6	0	2	1	0	0
+(−6) Row 2	−6	6	0	0	−6	0
New Row 2	0	6	2	1	−6	0

Step 2 This step is not necessary because 0 is already in the **G** entry. New Row 3 is old Row 3.

Step 3

$$\begin{bmatrix} 6 & 0 & 2 & | & 1 & 0 & 0 \\ 0 & 6 & 2 & | & 1 & -6 & 0 \\ 0 & 1 & 1 & | & 0 & 0 & 1 \end{bmatrix}$$

Step 4 This step is not necessary because the **B** entry is already 0. New Row 1 is old Row 1.

Step 5 Use Row 2 and Row 3 to make the 1 entry a 0.

Row 2	0	6	2	1	−6	0
+(−6) Row 3	0	−6	−6	0	0	−6
New Row 3	0	0	−4	1	−6	−6

Step 6

$$\begin{bmatrix} 6 & 0 & 2 & | & 1 & 0 & 0 \\ 0 & 6 & 2 & | & 1 & -6 & 0 \\ 0 & 0 & -4 & | & 1 & -6 & -6 \end{bmatrix}$$

Step 7 Use Row 1 and Row 3 to make 2, the **C** entry, a 0.

2 Row 1	12	0	4	2	0	0
+ Row 3	0	0	−4	1	−6	−6
New Row 1	12	0	0	3	−6	−6

Step 8 Use Row 2 and Row 3 to make 2, the **F** entry, a 0.

2 Row 2	0	12	4	2	−12	0
+ Row 3	0	0	−4	1	−6	−6
New Row 2	0	12	0	3	−18	−6

Step 9

$$\left[\begin{array}{ccc|ccc} 12 & 0 & 0 & 3 & -6 & -6 \\ 0 & 12 & 0 & 3 & -18 & -6 \\ 0 & 0 & -4 & 1 & -6 & -6 \end{array}\right]$$

Step 10 Divide Row 1 and Row 2 by 12 and Row 3 by -4.

$$\left[\begin{array}{ccc|ccc} 1 & 0 & 0 & \frac{1}{4} & -\frac{1}{2} & -\frac{1}{2} \\ 0 & 1 & 0 & \frac{1}{4} & -\frac{3}{2} & -\frac{1}{2} \\ 0 & 0 & 1 & -\frac{1}{4} & \frac{3}{2} & \frac{3}{2} \end{array}\right]$$ The inverse matrix is $\left[\begin{array}{ccc} \frac{1}{4} & -\frac{1}{2} & -\frac{1}{2} \\ \frac{1}{4} & -\frac{3}{2} & -\frac{1}{2} \\ -\frac{1}{4} & \frac{3}{2} & \frac{3}{2} \end{array}\right].$

- Use a calculator to find the inverse matrix $\begin{bmatrix} 8 & -5 \\ 3 & 1 \end{bmatrix}$.

  We already have this matrix entered as matrix [A] from a previous example. Here, we find its inverse. Go to the MATRIX menu and press ENTER. Now, press the x^{-1} key, followed by ENTER. See Figure 11-6. We can convert these entries to fractions by pressing the MATH key and then the ENTER key twice. See Figure 11-7.

 PRACTICE

Find the inverse matrix.

1. $\begin{bmatrix} 1 & -1 \\ 2 & 3 \end{bmatrix}$

2. $\begin{bmatrix} -3 & 5 & 1 \\ 1 & 1 & -2 \\ 2 & -1 & 6 \end{bmatrix}$

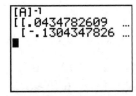

FIGURE 11-6

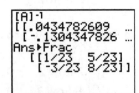

FIGURE 11-7

✔ SOLUTIONS

1. $\begin{bmatrix} 1 & -1 & | & 1 & 0 \\ 2 & 3 & | & 0 & 1 \end{bmatrix}$

Step 1

$$\begin{array}{lrrrr} -2\text{ Row 1} & -2 & 2 & -2 & 0 \\ +\text{ Row 2} & 2 & 3 & 0 & 1 \\ \hline \text{New Row 2} & 0 & 5 & -2 & 1 \end{array}$$

Step 2

$$\begin{array}{lrrrr} 3\text{ Row 1} & 3 & -3 & 3 & 0 \\ +\text{ Row 2} & 2 & 3 & 0 & 1 \\ \hline \text{New Row 1} & 5 & 0 & 3 & 1 \end{array}$$

Step 3

$$\begin{bmatrix} 5 & 0 & | & 3 & 1 \\ 0 & 5 & | & -2 & 1 \end{bmatrix}$$

Step 4 Divide Row 1 by 5.

Step 5 Divide Row 2 by 5.

Step 6

$$\begin{bmatrix} 1 & 0 & | & \frac{3}{5} & \frac{1}{5} \\ 0 & 1 & | & -\frac{2}{5} & \frac{1}{5} \end{bmatrix}$$

The inverse matrix is $\begin{bmatrix} \frac{3}{5} & \frac{1}{5} \\ -\frac{2}{5} & \frac{1}{5} \end{bmatrix}$.

2. $\begin{bmatrix} -3 & 5 & 1 & | & 1 & 0 & 0 \\ 1 & 1 & -2 & | & 0 & 1 & 0 \\ 2 & -1 & 6 & | & 0 & 0 & 1 \end{bmatrix}$

Step 1

Row 1	−3	5	1	1	0	0
+3 Row 2	3	3	−6	0	3	0
New Row 2	0	8	−5	1	3	0

Step 2

2 Row 1	−6	10	2	2	0	0
+3 Row 3	6	−3	18	0	0	3
New Row 3	0	7	20	2	0	3

Step 3

$$\begin{bmatrix} -3 & 5 & 1 & | & 1 & 0 & 0 \\ 0 & 8 & -5 & | & 1 & 3 & 0 \\ 0 & 7 & 20 & | & 2 & 0 & 3 \end{bmatrix}$$

Step 4

8 Row 1	−24	40	8	8	0	0
+(−5) Row 2	0	−40	25	−5	−15	0
New Row 1	−24	0	33	3	−15	0

Step 5

−7 Row 2	0	−56	35	−7	−21	0
+8 Row 3	0	56	160	16	0	24
New Row 3	0	0	195	9	−21	24

Step 6

$$\begin{bmatrix} -24 & 0 & 33 & | & 3 & -15 & 0 \\ 0 & 8 & -5 & | & 1 & 3 & 0 \\ 0 & 0 & 195 & | & 9 & -21 & 24 \end{bmatrix}$$

To make the numbers smaller, replace Row 1 with $\frac{1}{3}$ Row 1 and Row 3 with $\frac{1}{3}$ Row 3.

$$\begin{bmatrix} -8 & 0 & 11 & | & 1 & -5 & 0 \\ 0 & 8 & -5 & | & 1 & 3 & 0 \\ 0 & 0 & 65 & | & 3 & -7 & 8 \end{bmatrix}$$

Step 7

65 Row 1	−520	0	715	65	−325	0
+(−11) Row 3	0	0	−715	−33	77	−88
New Row 1	−520	0	0	32	−248	−88

Step 8

13 Row 2	0	104	−65	13	39	0
+ Row 3	0	0	65	3	−7	8
New Row 2	0	104	0	16	32	8

Step 9

$$\begin{bmatrix} -520 & 0 & 0 & | & 32 & -248 & -88 \\ 0 & 104 & 0 & | & 16 & 32 & 8 \\ 0 & 0 & 65 & | & 3 & -7 & 8 \end{bmatrix}.$$

Step 10 Divide Row 1 by −520, Row 2 by 104, and Row 3 by 65.

$$\begin{bmatrix} 1 & 0 & 0 & | & -\frac{4}{65} & \frac{31}{65} & \frac{11}{65} \\ 0 & 1 & 0 & | & \frac{2}{13} & \frac{4}{13} & \frac{1}{13} \\ 0 & 0 & 1 & | & \frac{3}{65} & -\frac{7}{65} & \frac{8}{65} \end{bmatrix}$$

The inverse matrix is $\begin{bmatrix} -\frac{4}{65} & \frac{31}{65} & \frac{11}{65} \\ \frac{2}{13} & \frac{4}{13} & \frac{1}{13} \\ \frac{3}{65} & -\frac{7}{65} & \frac{8}{65} \end{bmatrix}.$

Matrices and Systems of Equations

There are three algebraic ways that we can use matrices to solve a system of linear equations. Two of them are covered in this book. Solving systems using the first of these methods is very much like finding inverses. We begin with a 2×2 system (two equations and two variables) and an augmented matrix of the form $\begin{bmatrix} A & B & | & E \\ C & D & | & F \end{bmatrix}$. A, B, C, and D are the coefficients of x and y in the equations and E and F are the constant terms. We use the same row operations above to change this matrix to one of the forms $\begin{bmatrix} 1 & 0 & | & number \\ 0 & 1 & | & number \end{bmatrix}$. The numbers in the last column are the solution.

 EXAMPLE 11-6

Solve the system using matrices.

$$\begin{cases} 2x - 3y = 17 \\ -x + y = -7 \end{cases}$$

The coefficients 2, −3, −1, and 1 are the entries in the left side of the matrix. The constant terms 17 and −7 are the entries on the right side of the matrix. The augmented matrix is $\begin{bmatrix} 2 & -3 & | & 17 \\ -1 & 1 & | & -7 \end{bmatrix}$.

Step 1 We want −1, the **C** entry, to be 0.

Row 1	2	−3	17
+2 Row 2	−2	2	−14
New Row 2	0	−1	3

Step 2 We want −3, the **B** entry, to be 0.

Row 1	2	−3	17
+3 Row 2	−3	3	−21
New Row 1	−1	0	−4

Step 3

$$\begin{bmatrix} -1 & 0 & | & -4 \\ 0 & -1 & | & 3 \end{bmatrix}$$ This row represents the equation $-1x + 0y = -4$.
This row represents the equation $0x + (-1)y = 3$.

Step 4 Divide Row 1 by −1.

Step 5 Divide Row 2 by −1.

Step 6

$$\begin{bmatrix} 1 & 0 & | & 4 \\ 0 & 1 & | & -3 \end{bmatrix}$$
This row represents the equation $1x + 0y = 4$.
This row represents the equation $0x + 1y = -3$.

The solution is $x = 4$ and $y = -3$.

Begin solving a 3 × 3 system (three equations and three variables) by writing the augmented matrix $\begin{bmatrix} A & B & C & | & J \\ D & E & F & | & K \\ G & H & I & | & L \end{bmatrix}$. Using the same steps we used to find the inverse of a matrix, we want to change this matrix to one of the forms $\begin{bmatrix} 1 & 0 & 0 & | & number \\ 0 & 1 & 0 & | & number \\ 0 & 0 & 1 & | & number \end{bmatrix}$. The numbers in the fourth column are the solution.

 EXAMPLE 11-7

Solve the system using matrices.

$$\begin{cases} x + 3z = 3 \\ -x + y - z = 5 \\ 2x + y = -2 \end{cases}$$

The augmented matrix is $\begin{bmatrix} 1 & 0 & 3 & | & 3 \\ -1 & 1 & -1 & | & 5 \\ 2 & 1 & 0 & | & -2 \end{bmatrix}$.

Step 1 Use Row 1 and Row 2 to change the D entry to 0.

Row 1	1	0	3	3
+ Row 2	−1	1	−1	5
New Row 2	0	1	2	8

Step 2 Use Row 1 and Row 3 to change the G entry to 0.

−2 Row 1	−2	0	−6	−6
+ Row 3	2	1	0	−2
New Row 3	0	1	−6	−8

Step 3

$$\begin{bmatrix} 1 & 0 & 3 & | & 3 \\ 0 & 1 & 2 & | & 8 \\ 0 & 1 & -6 & | & -8 \end{bmatrix}$$

Step 4 Because the *B* entry is already 0, this step is not necessary. New Row 1 is old Row 1.

Step 5 Use Row 2 and Row 3 to change the *H* entry to 0.

−Row 2	0	−1	−2	−8
+ Row 3	0	1	−6	−8
New Row 3	0	0	−8	−16

Step 6

$$\begin{bmatrix} 1 & 0 & 3 & | & 3 \\ 0 & 1 & 2 & | & 8 \\ 0 & 0 & -8 & | & -16 \end{bmatrix}$$

Step 7 Use Row 1 and Row 3 to make the *C* entry a 0.

8 Row 1	8	0	24	24
+3 Row 3	0	0	−24	−48
New Row 1	8	0	0	−24

Step 8 Use Row 2 and Row 3 to make the *F* entry a 0.

4 Row 2	0	4	8	32
+ Row 3	0	0	−8	−16
New Row 2	0	4	0	16

Step 9

$$\begin{bmatrix} 8 & 0 & 0 & | & -24 \\ 0 & 4 & 0 & | & 16 \\ 0 & 0 & -8 & | & -16 \end{bmatrix}$$

Step 10 Divide Row 1 by 8, Row 2 by 4, and Row 3 by −8.

$$\begin{bmatrix} 1 & 0 & 0 & | & -3 \\ 0 & 1 & 0 & | & 4 \\ 0 & 0 & 1 & | & 2 \end{bmatrix}$$ The solution is $x = -3$, $y = 4$, and $z = 2$.

The second method we use to solve systems of equations involves finding the inverse of a matrix and multiplying the two matrices. We begin by creating the coefficient matrix and the constant matrix for the system.

$$\begin{cases} Ax + By = E \\ Cx + Dy = F \end{cases}$$

The coefficient matrix is $\begin{bmatrix} A & B \\ C & D \end{bmatrix}$ and the coefficient matrix is $\begin{bmatrix} E \\ F \end{bmatrix}$. We find the inverse of the coefficient matrix and multiply the inverse by the coefficient matrix. The product matrix consists of one column of two numbers. These two numbers are the solution to the system.

EXAMPLE 11-8

Solve the system using matrices.

- $$\begin{cases} -2x + y = -7 \\ x - 3y = 1 \end{cases}$$

The coefficient matrix and the constant matrix are $\begin{bmatrix} -2 & 1 \\ 1 & -3 \end{bmatrix}$ and $\begin{bmatrix} -7 \\ 1 \end{bmatrix}$, respectively. We begin with the inverse of the coefficient matrix.

$$\begin{bmatrix} -2 & 1 & | & 1 & 0 \\ 1 & -3 & | & 0 & 1 \end{bmatrix}$$

Row 1	−2	1	1	0		3 Row 1	−6	3	3	0
+2 Row 2	2	−6	0	2	and	+ Row 2	1	−3	0	1
New Row 2	0	−5	1	2		New Row 1	−5	0	3	1

The next matrix is $\begin{bmatrix} -5 & 0 & | & 3 & 1 \\ 0 & -5 & | & 1 & 2 \end{bmatrix}$. We need to divide Row 1 and Row 2 by −5.

$$\begin{bmatrix} 1 & 0 & | & -\frac{3}{5} & -\frac{1}{5} \\ 0 & 1 & | & -\frac{1}{5} & -\frac{2}{5} \end{bmatrix}$$ The inverse matrix is $\begin{bmatrix} -\frac{3}{5} & -\frac{1}{5} \\ -\frac{1}{5} & -\frac{2}{5} \end{bmatrix}$.

Multiply the inverse matrix by the coefficient matrix.

$$\begin{bmatrix} -\frac{3}{5} & -\frac{1}{5} \\ -\frac{1}{5} & -\frac{2}{5} \end{bmatrix} \cdot \begin{bmatrix} -7 \\ 1 \end{bmatrix} = \begin{bmatrix} -\frac{3}{5} \cdot (-7) + \left(-\frac{1}{5}\right) \cdot 1 \\ -\frac{1}{5} \cdot (-7) + \left(-\frac{2}{5}\right) \cdot 1 \end{bmatrix} = \begin{bmatrix} 4 \\ 1 \end{bmatrix}$$

The solution is $x = 4$ and $y = 1$.

The strategy is the same for a 3×3 system of equations.

$$\begin{cases} Ax + By + Cz = J \\ Dx + Ey + Fz = K \\ Gx + Hy + Iz = L \end{cases}$$

The coefficient matrix and the constant matrix are

$$\begin{bmatrix} A & B & C \\ D & E & F \\ G & H & I \end{bmatrix} \text{ and } \begin{bmatrix} J \\ K \\ L \end{bmatrix}.$$

We find the inverse matrix of the coefficient matrix and multiply it by the constant matrix.

 EXAMPLE 11-9

Solve the system using matrices.

$$\begin{cases} -3x + 2y + z = 3 \\ 2x + y - z = 5 \\ -y + 2z = -3 \end{cases}$$

The coefficient matrix and constant matrix are $\begin{bmatrix} -3 & 2 & 1 \\ 2 & 1 & -1 \\ 0 & -1 & 2 \end{bmatrix}$ and $\begin{bmatrix} 3 \\ 5 \\ -3 \end{bmatrix}$, respectively. We begin with the inverse of the coefficient matrix.

$$\begin{bmatrix} -3 & 2 & 1 & | & 1 & 0 & 0 \\ 2 & 1 & -1 & | & 0 & 1 & 0 \\ 0 & -1 & 2 & | & 0 & 0 & 1 \end{bmatrix}$$

$$
\begin{array}{lrrrrrr}
2\,\text{Row 1} & -6 & 4 & 2 & 2 & 0 & 0 \\
+3\,\text{Row 2} & 6 & 3 & -3 & 0 & 3 & 0 \\
\hline
\text{New Row 2} & 0 & 7 & -1 & 2 & 3 & 0
\end{array}
$$

New Row 3 is old Row 3. The next matrix is

$$
\left[\begin{array}{rrr|rrr}
-3 & 2 & 1 & 1 & 0 & 0 \\
0 & 7 & -1 & 2 & 3 & 0 \\
0 & -1 & 2 & 0 & 0 & 1
\end{array}\right].
$$

$$
\begin{array}{lrrrrrr}
7\,\text{Row 1} & -21 & 14 & 7 & 7 & 0 & 0 \\
+(-2)\,\text{Row 2} & 0 & -14 & 2 & -4 & -6 & 0 \\
\hline
\text{New Row 1} & -21 & 0 & 9 & 3 & -6 & 0
\end{array}
$$

$$
\begin{array}{lrrrrrr}
\text{Row 2} & 0 & 7 & -1 & 2 & 3 & 0 \\
+7\,\text{Row 3} & 0 & -7 & 14 & 0 & 0 & 7 \\
\hline
\text{New Row 3} & 0 & 0 & 13 & 2 & 3 & 7
\end{array}
$$

The next matrix is
$$
\left[\begin{array}{rrr|rrr}
-21 & 0 & 9 & 3 & -6 & 0 \\
0 & 7 & -1 & 2 & 3 & 0 \\
0 & 0 & 13 & 2 & 3 & 7
\end{array}\right].
$$

$$
\begin{array}{lrrrrrr}
13\,\text{Row 1} & -273 & 0 & 117 & 39 & -78 & 0 \\
+(-9)\,\text{Row 3} & 0 & 0 & -117 & -18 & -27 & -63 \\
\hline
\text{New Row 1} & -273 & 0 & 0 & 21 & -105 & -63
\end{array}
$$

$$
\begin{array}{lrrrrrr}
13\,\text{Row 2} & 0 & 91 & -13 & 26 & 39 & 0 \\
+\,\text{Row 3} & 0 & 0 & 13 & 2 & 3 & 7 \\
\hline
\text{New Row 2} & 0 & 91 & 0 & 28 & 42 & 7
\end{array}
$$

The next matrix is
$$
\left[\begin{array}{rrr|rrr}
-273 & 0 & 0 & 21 & -105 & -63 \\
0 & 91 & 0 & 28 & 42 & 7 \\
0 & 0 & 13 & 2 & 3 & 7
\end{array}\right].
$$

Divide Row 1 by -273, Row 2 by 91, and Row 3 by 13.

$$
\left[\begin{array}{rrr|rrr}
1 & 0 & 0 & -\frac{1}{13} & \frac{5}{13} & \frac{3}{13} \\
0 & 1 & 0 & \frac{4}{13} & \frac{6}{13} & \frac{1}{13} \\
0 & 0 & 1 & \frac{2}{13} & \frac{3}{13} & \frac{7}{13}
\end{array}\right]
$$

```
MATRIX[A] 3 ×3
[ 4    0    -1    ]
[ 3    1    2     ]
[ 0    -2   1     ]
```

FIGURE 11-8

```
MATRIX[B] 3 ×1■
[ 7          ]
[ 3.         ]
[ 11         ]
```

FIGURE 11-9

```
[A]⁻¹* [B]
          [[2 ]
           [-5]
           [1 ]]
```

FIGURE 11-10

Multiply the inverse matrix by the constant matrix.

$$\begin{bmatrix} -\frac{1}{13} & \frac{5}{13} & \frac{3}{13} \\ \frac{4}{13} & \frac{6}{13} & \frac{1}{13} \\ \frac{2}{13} & \frac{3}{13} & \frac{7}{13} \end{bmatrix} \cdot \begin{bmatrix} 3 \\ 5 \\ -3 \end{bmatrix} = \begin{bmatrix} 3\left(-\frac{1}{13}\right) + 5\left(\frac{5}{13}\right) + (-3)\frac{3}{13} \\ 3\left(\frac{4}{13}\right) + 5\left(\frac{6}{13}\right) + (-3)\left(\frac{1}{13}\right) \\ 3\left(\frac{2}{13}\right) + 5\left(\frac{3}{13}\right) + (-3)\left(\frac{7}{13}\right) \end{bmatrix} = \begin{bmatrix} 1 \\ 3 \\ 0 \end{bmatrix}$$

The solution is $x = 1$, $y = 3$, and $z = 0$.

- Use a graphing calculator to solve the system $\begin{cases} 4x + 0y - z = 7 \\ 3x + y + 2z = 3 \\ 0x - 2y + z = 11 \end{cases}$.

We use the second method to solve this system. Enter the coefficient matrix as 1:[A] on the calculator and the coefficient matrix as matrix 2:[B]. See Figures 11-8 and 11-9.

The product $[A]^{-1} \times [B]$ gives us the solution. See Figure 11-10.

The solution is $x = 2$, $y = -5$, and $z = 1$.

PRACTICE

1. Use the first method to solve the system.

$$\begin{cases} -5x + 2y + 3z = -8 \\ x + y - z = -5 \\ 2x + y + 3z = 23 \end{cases}$$

2. Use the first method to solve the system.

$$\begin{cases} 6x + 2z = -12 \\ x - y = -3 \\ y + z = 1 \end{cases}$$

3. Use the second method to solve the system.

$$\begin{cases} x + z = 6 \\ 3x - y + 2z = 17 \\ 6x + y - z = 5 \end{cases}$$

 SOLUTIONS

1. The augmented matrix is $\begin{bmatrix} -5 & 2 & 3 & | & -8 \\ 1 & 1 & -1 & | & -5 \\ 2 & 1 & 3 & | & 23 \end{bmatrix}$.

Row 1	−5	2	3	−8
+5 Row 2	5	5	−5	−25
New Row 2	0	7	−2	−33

2 Row 1	−10	4	6	−16
+5 Row 3	10	5	15	115
New Row 3	0	9	21	99

The next matrix is $\begin{bmatrix} -5 & 2 & 3 & | & -8 \\ 0 & 7 & -2 & | & -33 \\ 0 & 9 & 21 & | & 99 \end{bmatrix}$.

7 Row 1	−35	14	21	−56
+(−2) Row 2	0	−14	4	66
New Row 1	−35	0	25	10

9 Row 2	0	63	−18	−297
+(−7) Row 3	0	−63	−147	−693
New Row 3	0	0	−165	−990

The next matrix is $\begin{bmatrix} -35 & 0 & 25 & | & 10 \\ 0 & 7 & -2 & | & -33 \\ 0 & 0 & -165 & | & -990 \end{bmatrix}$.

We can make the numbers in Row 1 and Row 3 smaller by dividing Row 1 by 5 and Row 3 by −165.

$$\begin{bmatrix} -7 & 0 & 5 & | & 2 \\ 0 & 7 & -2 & | & -33 \\ 0 & 0 & 1 & | & 6 \end{bmatrix}$$

$$
\begin{array}{lrrrr}
\text{Row 1} & -7 & 0 & 5 & 2 \\
+(-5)\ \text{Row 3} & 0 & 0 & -5 & -30 \\
\hline
\text{New Row 1} & -7 & 0 & 0 & -28
\end{array}
\qquad
\begin{array}{lrrrr}
\text{Row 2} & 0 & 7 & -2 & -33 \\
+2\ \text{Row 3} & 0 & 0 & 2 & 12 \\
\hline
\text{New Row 2} & 0 & 7 & 0 & -21
\end{array}
$$

The next matrix is $\begin{bmatrix} -7 & 0 & 0 & | & -28 \\ 0 & 7 & 0 & | & -21 \\ 0 & 0 & 1 & | & 6 \end{bmatrix}$. Divide Row 1 by -7 and Row 2 by 7.

$\begin{bmatrix} 1 & 0 & 0 & | & 4 \\ 0 & 1 & 0 & | & -3 \\ 0 & 0 & 1 & | & 6 \end{bmatrix}$ The solution is $x = 4$, $y = -3$, and $z = 6$.

2. The augmented matrix is $\begin{bmatrix} 6 & 0 & 2 & | & -12 \\ 1 & -1 & 0 & | & -3 \\ 0 & 1 & 1 & | & 1 \end{bmatrix}$.

$$
\begin{array}{lrrrr}
\text{Row 1} & 6 & 0 & 2 & -12 \\
+(-6)\ \text{Row 2} & -6 & 6 & 0 & 18 \\
\hline
\text{New Row 2} & 0 & 6 & 2 & 6
\end{array}
$$

New Row 3 is old Row 3. The next matrix is $\begin{bmatrix} 6 & 0 & 2 & | & -12 \\ 0 & 6 & 2 & | & 6 \\ 0 & 1 & 1 & | & 1 \end{bmatrix}$.

$$
\begin{array}{lrrrr}
\text{Row 2} & 0 & 6 & 2 & 6 \\
+(-6)\ \text{Row 3} & 0 & -6 & -6 & -6 \\
\hline
\text{New Row 3} & 0 & 0 & -4 & 0
\end{array}
$$

New Row 1 is old Row 1. The next matrix is $\begin{bmatrix} 6 & 0 & 2 & | & -12 \\ 0 & 6 & 2 & | & 6 \\ 0 & 0 & -4 & | & 0 \end{bmatrix}$.

$$
\begin{array}{lrrrr}
\text{Row 1} & 6 & 0 & 2 & -12 \\
+\frac{1}{2}\ \text{Row 3} & 0 & 0 & -2 & 0 \\
\hline
\text{New Row 1} & 6 & 0 & 0 & -12
\end{array}
\qquad
\begin{array}{lrrrr}
\text{Row 2} & 0 & 6 & 2 & 6 \\
+\frac{1}{2}\ \text{Row 3} & 0 & 0 & -2 & 0 \\
\hline
\text{New Row 2} & 0 & 6 & 0 & 6
\end{array}
$$

The next matrix is $\begin{bmatrix} 6 & 0 & 0 & | & -12 \\ 0 & 6 & 0 & | & 6 \\ 0 & 0 & -4 & | & 0 \end{bmatrix}$. Divide Row 1 and Row 2 by 6 and Row 3 by −4.

$\begin{bmatrix} 1 & 0 & 0 & | & -2 \\ 0 & 1 & 0 & | & 1 \\ 0 & 0 & 1 & | & 0 \end{bmatrix}$ The solution is $x = -2$, $y = 1$, and $z = 0$.

3. The augmented matrix is $\begin{bmatrix} 1 & 0 & 1 & | & 1 & 0 & 0 \\ 3 & -1 & 2 & | & 0 & 1 & 0 \\ 6 & 1 & -1 & | & 0 & 0 & 1 \end{bmatrix}$.

−3 Row 1	−3	0	−3	−3	0	0
+ Row 2	3	−1	2	0	1	0
New Row 2	0	−1	−1	−3	1	0

−6 Row 1	−6	0	−6	−6	0	0
+ Row 3	6	1	−1	0	0	1
New Row 3	0	1	−7	−6	0	1

The next matrix is $\begin{bmatrix} 1 & 0 & 1 & | & 1 & 0 & 0 \\ 0 & -1 & -1 & | & -3 & 1 & 0 \\ 0 & 1 & -7 & | & -6 & 0 & 1 \end{bmatrix}$.

Row 2	0	−1	−1	−3	1	0
+ Row 3	0	1	−7	−6	0	1
New Row 3	0	0	−8	−9	1	1

New Row 1 is old Row 1. The next matrix is

$\begin{bmatrix} 1 & 0 & 1 & | & 1 & 0 & 0 \\ 0 & -1 & -1 & | & -3 & 1 & 0 \\ 0 & 0 & -8 & | & -9 & 1 & 1 \end{bmatrix}$.

8 Row 1	8	0	8	8	0	0
+ Row 3	0	0	−8	−9	1	1
New Row 1	8	0	0	−1	1	1

−8 Row 2	0	8	8	24	−8	0
+ Row 3	0	0	−8	−9	1	1
New Row 2	0	8	0	15	−7	1

The next matrix is $\begin{bmatrix} 8 & 0 & 0 & | & -1 & 1 & 1 \\ 0 & 8 & 0 & | & 15 & -7 & 1 \\ 0 & 0 & -8 & | & -9 & 1 & 1 \end{bmatrix}$. Divide Row 1 and Row 2 by 8 and Row 3 by -8.

$$\begin{bmatrix} 1 & 0 & 0 & | & -\frac{1}{8} & \frac{1}{8} & \frac{1}{8} \\ 0 & 1 & 0 & | & \frac{15}{8} & -\frac{7}{8} & \frac{1}{8} \\ 0 & 0 & 1 & | & \frac{9}{8} & -\frac{1}{8} & -\frac{1}{8} \end{bmatrix}$$

The inverse matrix is $\begin{bmatrix} -\frac{1}{8} & \frac{1}{8} & \frac{1}{8} \\ \frac{15}{8} & -\frac{7}{8} & \frac{1}{8} \\ \frac{9}{8} & -\frac{1}{8} & -\frac{1}{8} \end{bmatrix}$.

Multiply the inverse matrix by the coefficient matrix $\begin{bmatrix} 6 \\ 17 \\ 5 \end{bmatrix}$.

$$\begin{bmatrix} -\frac{1}{8} & \frac{1}{8} & \frac{1}{8} \\ \frac{15}{8} & -\frac{7}{8} & \frac{1}{8} \\ \frac{9}{8} & -\frac{1}{8} & -\frac{1}{8} \end{bmatrix} \cdot \begin{bmatrix} 6 \\ 17 \\ 5 \end{bmatrix} = \begin{bmatrix} 6\left(-\frac{1}{8}\right) + 17\left(\frac{1}{8}\right) + 5\left(\frac{1}{8}\right) \\ 6\left(\frac{15}{8}\right) + 17\left(-\frac{7}{8}\right) + 5\left(\frac{1}{8}\right) \\ 6\left(\frac{9}{8}\right) + 17\left(-\frac{1}{8}\right) + 5\left(-\frac{1}{8}\right) \end{bmatrix} = \begin{bmatrix} 2 \\ -3 \\ 4 \end{bmatrix}$$

The solution is $x = 2$, $y = -3$, and $z = 4$.

The Determinant of a Matrix

The last computation we learn is finding a matrix's *determinant*. Although we do not use the determinant here, it is used in vector mathematics courses, some theoretical algebra courses, and in algebra courses that cover Cramer's rule (used to solve systems of linear equations). An interesting fact about determinants is that a square matrix has an inverse only when its determinant is a nonzero number.

The usual notation for a determinant is to enclose the matrix using two vertical bars instead of two brackets. The determinant for the matrix $\begin{bmatrix} A & B \\ C & D \end{bmatrix}$ is $\begin{vmatrix} A & B \\ C & D \end{vmatrix}$. Finding the determinant for a 2×2 matrix is not hard.

$$\begin{vmatrix} A & B \\ C & D \end{vmatrix} = AD - BC$$

EXAMPLE 11-10

Find the determinant.

- $\begin{vmatrix} 4 & -3 \\ 5 & 2 \end{vmatrix} = 4(2) - (-3)(5) = 23$

We find the determinant of larger matrices by breaking down the larger matrix into several 2×2 submatrices. For larger matrices, there are numerous formulas for computing their determinants. Some of them come from *expanding the matrix* along each row and each column. This means that we multiply the entries in a row or a column by the determinant of a smaller matrix. This smaller matrix comes from deleting the row and column where an entry is in. When working with a 3×3 matrix, these submatrices are 2×2 matrices.

Suppose we choose to expand the following matrix along the first row.

$$\begin{bmatrix} A & B & C \\ D & E & F \\ G & H & I \end{bmatrix}$$

We multiply the *A* entry by the submatrix obtained by removing the first row *A B C* and the first column $\begin{smallmatrix} A \\ D \\ G \end{smallmatrix}$. This leaves us with the matrix $\begin{bmatrix} - & - & - \\ - & E & F \\ - & H & I \end{bmatrix}$.

Our first calculation is:

$$A\begin{vmatrix} E & F \\ H & I \end{vmatrix} = A(EI - FH)$$

Similarly, when we use entry *B*, we need to remove the first row *A B C* and the second column $\begin{smallmatrix} B \\ E \\ H \end{smallmatrix}$. This leaves us with $\begin{vmatrix} D & F \\ G & I \end{vmatrix}$. There is a complication— the signs on the entries must alternate when we perform these expansions. For our matrix, the signs alternate beginning with *A* not changing, but *B* and *D* changing.

$$\begin{matrix} A & -B & C \\ -D & E & -F \\ G & -H & I \end{matrix}$$

For our 3×3 matrix, the expansion along the first row looks like this.

$$A \begin{vmatrix} E & F \\ H & I \end{vmatrix} - B \begin{vmatrix} D & F \\ G & I \end{vmatrix} + C \begin{vmatrix} D & E \\ G & H \end{vmatrix}$$

$$= A(EI - FH) - B(DI - FG) + C(DH - EG)$$

The expansion along the second column looks like this.

$$-B \begin{vmatrix} D & F \\ G & I \end{vmatrix} + E \begin{vmatrix} A & C \\ G & I \end{vmatrix} - H \begin{vmatrix} A & C \\ D & F \end{vmatrix}$$

$$= -B(DI - FG) + E(AI - CG) - H(AF - CD)$$

EXAMPLE 11-11

* Find the determinant for $\begin{bmatrix} 4 & 1 & -3 \\ 2 & 0 & 4 \\ -2 & 2 & 1 \end{bmatrix}$.

We use two calculations, along Row 2 and Column 3. By Row 2 we have

$$-2 \begin{vmatrix} 1 & -3 \\ 2 & 1 \end{vmatrix} + 0 \begin{vmatrix} 4 & -3 \\ -2 & 1 \end{vmatrix} - 4 \begin{vmatrix} 4 & 1 \\ -2 & 2 \end{vmatrix}$$

$$= -2[1 \cdot 1 - (-3)2] + 0[4 \cdot 1 - (-3)(-2)] - 4[4 \cdot 2 - 1(-2)] = -54.$$

By Column 3 we have

$$-3 \begin{vmatrix} 2 & 0 \\ -2 & 2 \end{vmatrix} - 4 \begin{vmatrix} 4 & 1 \\ -2 & 2 \end{vmatrix} + 1 \begin{vmatrix} 4 & 1 \\ 2 & 0 \end{vmatrix}$$

$$= -3[2 \cdot 2 - 0(-2)] - 4[4 \cdot 2 - 1(-2)] + 1(4 \cdot 0 - 1 \cdot 2) = -54$$

* Use a calculator to find the determinant for $\begin{bmatrix} 5 & -8 \\ 3 & 2 \end{bmatrix}$.

Begin by entering the matrix as 1:[A] on the EDIT menu. Go to the main screen ("QUIT") and return to the MATRIX menu. Cursor to MATH and press ENTER to select "1:det(," the determinant function. See Figure 11-11. Return to the MATRIX menu and press ENTER to paste [A] into the determinant. Press ENTER again to calculate the determinant. See Figure 11-12.

FIGURE 11-11

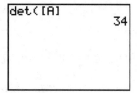

FIGURE 11-12

The method for finding the determinant for larger matrices is the same except that there are more levels of work.

$$\begin{bmatrix} A & B & C & D \\ E & F & G & H \\ I & J & K & L \\ M & N & O & P \end{bmatrix}$$

Expanding this matrix along Row 1 gives us

$$A\begin{vmatrix} F & G & H \\ J & K & L \\ N & O & P \end{vmatrix} - B\begin{vmatrix} E & G & H \\ I & K & L \\ M & O & P \end{vmatrix} + C\begin{vmatrix} E & F & H \\ I & J & L \\ M & N & P \end{vmatrix} - D\begin{vmatrix} E & F & G \\ I & J & K \\ M & N & O \end{vmatrix}.$$

Each of these four determinants must be computed using the previous method for a 3 × 3 matrix.

 PRACTICE

Find the determinant.

1. $\begin{bmatrix} -8 & 1 & 3 \\ 2 & 5 & 0 \\ 6 & -4 & 2 \end{bmatrix}$

 SOLUTION

1. Exanding this matrix along Row 2, we have

$$-2\begin{vmatrix} 1 & 3 \\ -4 & 2 \end{vmatrix} + 5\begin{vmatrix} -8 & 3 \\ 6 & 2 \end{vmatrix} - 0\begin{vmatrix} -8 & 1 \\ 6 & -4 \end{vmatrix}$$

$$= -2[1 \cdot 2 - 3(-4)] + 5(-8 \cdot 2 - 3 \cdot 6) - 0[(-8)(-4) - 1 \cdot 6]$$

$$= -198$$

Summary

In this chapter, we learned how to

- *Perform arithmetic with matrices.* We add or subtract two matrices by adding/subtracting their corresponding entries. The scalar multiple of a matrix by a real number a is the matrix with each entry multiplied by a. Finding the product of two matrices is more involved. The entries in the rows of the first matrix are multiplied by the entries in the columns of the second matrix to find the entries of the product matrix. For example,

$$\begin{bmatrix} A & B & C \\ D & E & F \\ G & H & I \end{bmatrix} \cdot \begin{bmatrix} K & L \\ M & N \\ O & P \end{bmatrix} = \begin{bmatrix} \text{Row 1} \times \text{Column 1} & \text{Row 1} \times \text{Column 2} \\ \text{Row 2} \times \text{Column 1} & \text{Row 2} \times \text{Column 2} \\ \text{Row 3} \times \text{Column 1} & \text{Row 3} \times \text{Column 2} \end{bmatrix}.$$

- *Use row operations to find the inverse of a square matrix.* The identity for matrix multiplication is a square matrix with 1s on the diagonal from top left to bottom right and 0s everywhere else. The inverse of a square matrix is another square matrix so that the product of the two matrices is the identity matrix (for their size). We find the identity matrix by *augmenting* the original matrix with the identity matrix. We use row operations similar to those we learned in Chapter 10 to change the left side of the augmented matrix to the identity matrix. The right side of the final augmented matrix is the inverse matrix.

- *Use matrices to solve systems of linear equations.* We learned two matrix methods for solving a system of linear equations. The first method is similar to the method used to find the inverse of a matrix. We create the coefficient matrix and augment it with the constant terms. Using row operations, we change the left side of the matrix to the identity matrix. The right side of the final matrix is the solution to the system. For the other method, we create two matrices. Matrix A is the coefficient matrix and Matrix B is the constant matrix. The entries in the product matrix $A^{-1} \times B$ are the solution to the system.

- *Find the determinant of a square matrix.* There are many different ways of finding the determinant of a square matrix. We choose any row (or column). For each entry in the row (or column), we delete the row and column containing the entry. This creates a submatrix. We find the determinant of each submatrix and multiply this number by the entry (or its negative) of the original matrix. The sum of these is the determinant.

QUIZ

1. $\begin{bmatrix} 2 & 9 & 6 \\ -1 & 2 & 3 \end{bmatrix} - \begin{bmatrix} 8 & -4 & -5 \\ 6 & 1 & 0 \end{bmatrix} =$

   A. $\begin{bmatrix} 10 & 5 & 1 \\ 5 & 3 & 3 \end{bmatrix}$

   B. $\begin{bmatrix} -6 & 5 & 1 \\ -7 & 1 & 3 \end{bmatrix}$

   C. $\begin{bmatrix} -6 & 13 & 11 \\ -5 & 1 & 3 \end{bmatrix}$

   D. $\begin{bmatrix} -6 & 13 & 11 \\ -7 & 1 & 3 \end{bmatrix}$

2. $\begin{bmatrix} 3 & 6 \\ -1 & 0 \end{bmatrix} \cdot \begin{bmatrix} 1 & 4 & 1 \\ 0 & 1 & 5 \end{bmatrix} =$

   A. $\begin{bmatrix} 3 & 18 & 33 \\ -1 & -4 & 5 \end{bmatrix}$

   B. $\begin{bmatrix} 3 & 18 & 30 \\ -1 & -4 & 5 \end{bmatrix}$

   C. $\begin{bmatrix} 3 & 18 & 33 \\ -1 & -4 & -1 \end{bmatrix}$

   D. The product does not exist.

3. $\begin{bmatrix} \frac{1}{2} & -1 \\ 3 & 4 \end{bmatrix} \cdot \begin{bmatrix} 2 & 6 \\ -8 & 1 \end{bmatrix} =$

   A. $\begin{bmatrix} 19 & 22 \\ -1 & 12 \end{bmatrix}$

   B. $\begin{bmatrix} 9 & 2 \\ -26 & 22 \end{bmatrix}$

   C. $\begin{bmatrix} 1 & -6 \\ -24 & 4 \end{bmatrix}$

   D. The product does not exist.

4. **Find the determinant for the matrix** $\begin{bmatrix} 12 & -1 \\ 3 & \frac{1}{4} \end{bmatrix}$.

   A. 3

   B. −4

   C. 5

   D. 6

5. **Find the determinant for the matrix** $\begin{bmatrix} 2 & 1 & 0 \\ -2 & 0 & 3 \\ 3 & 5 & -1 \end{bmatrix}$.

   A. −23

   B. 41

   C. 37

   D. −19

6. Find the inverse of the matrix $\begin{bmatrix} 2 & -1 \\ 3 & 4 \end{bmatrix}$.

A. $\begin{bmatrix} \frac{1}{2} & -1 \\ \frac{1}{3} & \frac{1}{4} \end{bmatrix}$

C. $\begin{bmatrix} \frac{4}{11} & \frac{1}{11} \\ -\frac{3}{11} & \frac{2}{11} \end{bmatrix}$

B. $\begin{bmatrix} -\frac{1}{2} & 1 \\ -\frac{1}{3} & -\frac{1}{4} \end{bmatrix}$

D. $\begin{bmatrix} \frac{4}{5} & -\frac{1}{5} \\ \frac{3}{5} & -\frac{2}{5} \end{bmatrix}$

7. Find the inverse of the matrix $\begin{bmatrix} 0 & 2 & 1 \\ 3 & 4 & 6 \\ 0 & 2 & -1 \end{bmatrix}$.

A. $\begin{bmatrix} -\frac{4}{3} & \frac{1}{3} & \frac{2}{3} \\ \frac{1}{4} & 0 & \frac{1}{4} \\ \frac{1}{2} & 0 & -\frac{1}{2} \end{bmatrix}$

C. $\begin{bmatrix} -\frac{2}{11} & \frac{1}{11} & \frac{4}{11} \\ \frac{15}{22} & -\frac{1}{11} & \frac{3}{22} \\ -\frac{4}{11} & \frac{2}{11} & -\frac{3}{11} \end{bmatrix}$

B. $\begin{bmatrix} \frac{2}{3} & \frac{1}{3} & -\frac{4}{3} \\ \frac{1}{4} & 0 & \frac{1}{4} \\ -\frac{1}{2} & 0 & \frac{1}{2} \end{bmatrix}$

D. $\begin{bmatrix} -\frac{14}{15} & \frac{1}{3} & -\frac{8}{15} \\ \frac{2}{5} & 0 & -\frac{1}{5} \\ \frac{1}{5} & 0 & \frac{2}{5} \end{bmatrix}$

Use a matrix method to solve the system in Problems 8 to 10.

8. What is $x + y$ for the system $\begin{cases} -4x + 3y = -10 \\ x - 5y = 11 \end{cases}$?

A. −1   B. 4   C. −3   D. 2

9. What is $x + y + z$ for the system $\begin{cases} x - 2y + 5z = 13 \\ -3x + 4y - z = 11 \\ 3x + 3y + z = 10 \end{cases}$?

A. 5   B. 6   C. 7   D. 8

10. What is $x + y + z$ for the system $\begin{cases} 2x - 5y + z = -15 \\ x + y - z = 6 \\ -3x + 2y + 2z = -1 \end{cases}$?

A. 0   B. 1   C. 2   D. 3

chapter 12

Conic Sections

A *conic section* is a shape made when a slice is made through a cone. The study of conic sections began over two thousand years ago and we use their properties today. Planets in our solar system move around the sun in elliptical orbits. The cross section of many reflecting surfaces is in the shape of a parabola. In fact, all of the conic sections have useful reflecting properties.

CHAPTER OBJECTIVES

In this chapter, you will

- Give the definition for a conic section
- Determine features of the graph of a conic section from its equation
- Find an equation for a conic section from its graph
- Sketch the graph of an ellipse and a hyperbola
- Find the eccentricity of an ellipse
- Find different forms for the equation of a conic section

In this chapter, we will work with three conic sections—parabolas, ellipses (including circles), and hyperbolas. We will learn the usual—how to recognize features of a conic section from its equation and how to sketch their graphs. Because conic sections are common shapes in physics and mathematics, you will work with them in calculus.

Parabolas

In Chapter 6, we learned how to sketch the graph of a parabola when its equation is in the form $y = a(x - h)^2 + k$ or $y = ax^2 + bx + c$. Now we will learn the formal definition for a parabola and another form for its equation.

> A parabola is the set of all points whose distance to a fixed point and a to fixed line are the same.

The fixed point is the *focus*. The fixed line is the *directrix*. For example, the focus for the parabola $y = -\frac{1}{2}x^2 - 3x + 2$ is $(-3, 6)$, and the directrix is the horizontal line $y = 7$. The point $(0, 2)$ is on the parabola. Its distance from the line $y = 7$ is 5. Its distance from the focus $(-3, 6)$ is also 5. Let us see this both graphically (see Figure 12-1) and with the distance formula.

$$\sqrt{(-3 - 0)^2 + (6 - 2)^2} = \sqrt{25} = 5$$

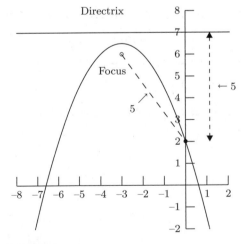

FIGURE 12-1

TABLE 12-1

$(x-h)^2 = 4p(y-k)$	$(y-k)^2 = 4p(x-h)$
The vertex is (h, k).	The vertex is (h, k).
The parabola opens up if p is positive and down if p is negative.	The parabola opens to the right if p is positive and to the left if p is negative.
The focus is $(h, k+p)$.	The focus is $(h+p, k)$.
The directrix is $y = k - p$.	The directrix is $x = h - p$.
The axis of symmetry is $x = h$.	The axis of symmetry is $y = k$.

The new form for a parabola that opens vertically is $(x-h)^2 = 4p(y-k)$. The vertex is still at (h, k), but when the equation is in this form, we can use p to find the focus and the equation for the directrix. The focus is the point $(h, k+p)$, and the directrix is the horizontal line $y = k - p$. The form for the equation for a parabola that opens horizontally is $(y-k)^2 = 4p(x-h)$. The focus for a parabola that opens horizontally is the point $(h+p, k)$, and the directrix is the vertical line $x = h - p$. This information is summarized in Table 12-1 and in Figures 12-2 and 12-3.

In the following examples, we are asked to match the equation to its graph. The vertex for each parabola is at $(0, 0)$. We can decide which graph goes to which equation either by finding the focus or the directrix for the equation and finding which graph has this focus or directrix.

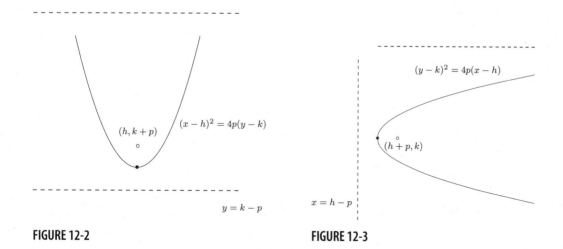

FIGURE 12-2   **FIGURE 12-3**

EXAMPLE 12-1

Match the graphs in Figures 12-4 to 12-7 with their equations.

- $x^2 = 6y$

    The equation is in the form $(x - h)^2 = 4p(y - k)$, so the parabola opens up or down. We have $p = \frac{3}{2}$ (from $6 = 4p$). Now we know three things—that the parabola opens up (because p is positive), that the focus is $(h, k + p) = (0, 0 + \frac{3}{2}) = (0, \frac{3}{2})$, and the directrix is $y = -\frac{3}{2}$ (from $h - p = 0 - \frac{3}{2}$). The graph that behaves this way is in Figure 12-6.

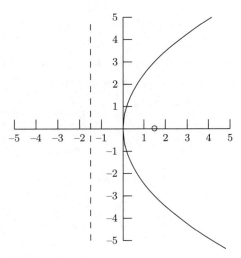

FIGURE 12-4

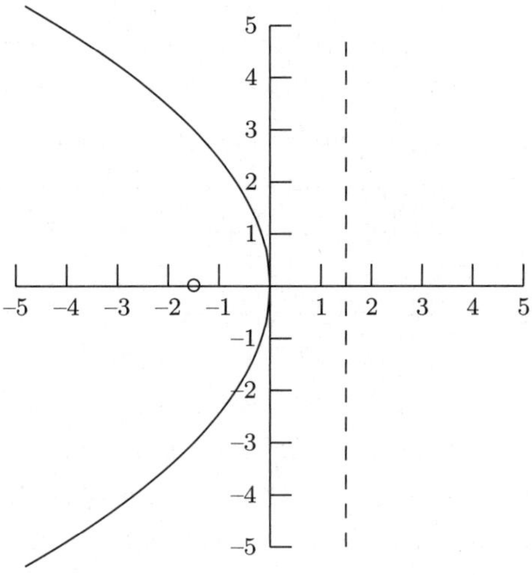

FIGURE 12-5

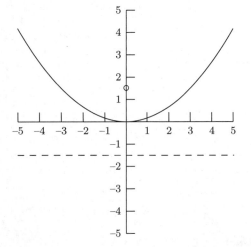

FIGURE 12-6

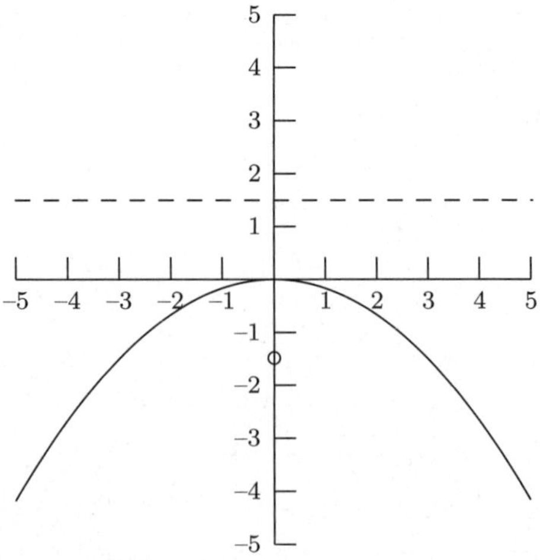

FIGURE 12-7

- $y^2 = 6x$

  The equation is in the form $(y - k)^2 = 4p(x - h)$, so the parabola opens to the left or to the right. We have $p = \frac{3}{2}$ (from $6 = 4p$). Now we know that the parabola opens to the right, the focus is $(h + p, k) = (0 + \frac{3}{2}, 0) = (\frac{3}{2}, 0)$, and the directrix is $x = -\frac{3}{2}$ (from $h - p = 0 - \frac{3}{2}$). The graph for this equation is in Figure 12-4.

- $y^2 = -6x$

  The equation is in the form $(y - k)^2 = 4p(x - h)$, so the parabola opens to the left or to the right. We have $p = -\frac{3}{2}$ (from $-6 = 4p$). The parabola opens to the left, the focus is $(h + p, k) = (0 + (-\frac{3}{2}, 0)) = (-\frac{3}{2}, 0)$, and the directrix is $x = \frac{3}{2}$ [from $h - p = 0 - (-\frac{3}{2})$]. The graph for this equation is in Figure 12-5.

- $x^2 = -6y$

  The equation is in the form $(x - h)^2 = 4p(y - k)$, so the parabola opens up or down. We have $p = -\frac{3}{2}$ (from $-6 = 4p$). The parabola opens down, the focus is $(h, k + p) = (0, 0 + (-\frac{3}{2})) = (0, -\frac{3}{2})$, and the directrix is $y = \frac{3}{2}$ [from $k - p = 0 - (-\frac{3}{2})$]. The graph for this equation is in Figure 12-7.

We now use the information in Table 12-1 to find the vertex, focus, directrix, and whether the parabola opens up, down, to the left, or to the right on parabolas whose vertex is not the origin.

EXAMPLE 12-2

Find the vertex, focus, and directrix. Determine if the parabola opens up, down, to the left, or to the right.

- $(x - 3)^2 = 4(y - 2)$

  This equation is in the form $(x - h)^2 = 4p(y - k)$. Because $h = 3$ and $k = 2$, the vertex is $(3, 2)$. Once we have p, we can find the focus and directrix and how the parabola opens. Because $4 = 4p$, we have $p = 1$. The parabola opens up because p is positive, the focus is $(h, k + p) = (3, 2 + 1) = (3, 3)$, and the directrix is $y = 1$ (from $y = k - p = 2 - 1 = 1$).

- $(y + 1)^2 = 8(x - 3)$

  The equation is in the form $(y - k)^2 = 4p(x - h)$. The vertex is $(3, -1)$, $p = 2$ (from $8 = 4p$); the parabola opens to the right; the focus is

$(h + p, k) = (3 + 2, -1) = (5, -1)$; and the directrix is $x = 1$ (from $x = h - p = 3 - 2 = 1$).

If we know any two of the vertex, focus, and directrix, we can find an equation for the parabola. From the information given, we first decide which form to use. Knowing the directrix is the fastest way to decide this. If the directrix is a horizontal line ($y = number$), then the equation is $(x - h)^2 = 4p(y - k)$. If the directrix is a vertical line ($x = number$), then the equation is $(y - k)^2 = 4p(x - h)$. If we do not have the directrix, we look at the coordinates of the vertex and focus. Either both the x-coordinates are same or both the y-coordinates are same. If both the x-coordinates are same, the parabola opens up or down, so we use the form $(x - h)^2 = 4p(y - k)$. If both the y-coordinates are same, the parabola opens to the side. We use the form $(y - k)^2 = 4p(x - h)$. Once we have decided which form to use, we might need algebra to find h, k, and p. For example, if we know the focus is $(2, -1)$ and the directrix is $x = 6$, then we know $h - p = 6$, $h + p = 2$, and $k = -1$. The equations $h - p = 6$ and $h + p = 2$ form a system of equations.

$$h - p = 6$$
$$h + p = 2$$
$$\overline{}$$
$$2h = 8$$
$$h = 4$$
$$4 - p = 6 \qquad \text{Let } h = 4 \text{ in } h - p = 6$$
$$p = -2$$

Now that we have all the three numbers and the form, we are ready to write the equation: $(y + 1)^2 = -8(x - 4)$.

EXAMPLE 12-3

Find an equation for the parabola.

- The directrix is $y = 2$, and the vertex is $(3, 1)$.

  Because the directrix is a horizontal line, the equation we want is $(x - h)^2 = 4p(y - k)$. The vertex is $(3, 1)$, giving us $h = 3$ and $k = 1$. From $y = k - p$ and $y = 2$, we have $1 - p = 2$, making $p = -1$. The equation is $(x - 3)^2 = -4(y - 1)$.

- The focus is $(4, -2)$, and the vertex is $(0, -2)$.

    The y-coordinates are same; so this parabola opens to the side, and the equation we need is $(y - k)^2 = 4p(x - h)$. The vertex is $(h, k) = (0, -2)$, giving us $h = 0$ and $k = -2$. The focus is $(h + p, k) = (4, -2)$. From this we have $h + p = 0 + p = 4$, making $p = 4$. The equation is $(y + 2)^2 = 16x$.

- See Figure 12-8.

    The directrix is the vertical line $x = -1$, and the focus is $(3, 2)$. Because the parabola opens to the right, the form we use is $(y - k)^2 = 4p(x - h)$. From the focus we have $(h + p, k) = (3, 2)$, so $h + p = 3$ and $k = 2$. The directrix is $x = -1$ and $x = h - p$, so $h - p = -1$.

$$h - p = -1$$
$$h + p = 3$$
$$\overline{}$$
$$2h = 2$$
$$h = 1$$
$$1 + p = 3 \qquad \text{Let } h = 1 \text{ in } h + p = 3$$
$$p = 2$$

The equation is $(y - 2)^2 = 8(x - 1)$.

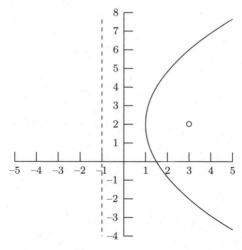

FIGURE 12-8

PRACTICE

1. Identify the vertex, focus, and directrix for $(y - 5)^2 = 10(x - 1)$.

2. Identify the vertex, focus, and directrix for $(x + 6)^2 = -\frac{1}{2}(y - 4)$.

3. Find an equation for the parabola that has the directrix $y = -2$ and focus $(4, 10)$.

For Problems 4 to 6, match the equation with its graph in Figures 12-9 to 12-11.

4. $x^2 = -8(y + 1)$

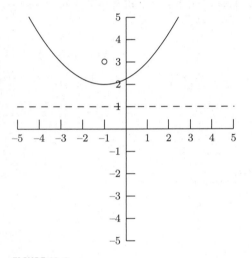

FIGURE 12-9

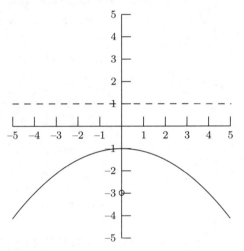

FIGURE 12-10

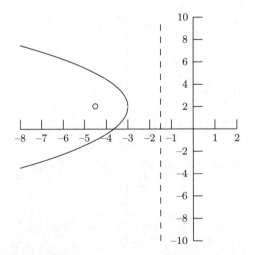

FIGURE 12-11

5. $(x + 1)^2 = 4(y - 2)$

6. $(y - 2)^2 = -6(x + 3)$

 SOLUTIONS

1. $h = 1$, $k = 5$, and $p = \frac{5}{2}$ (from $4p = 10$). The vertex is $(1, 5)$, the focus is $(h + p, k) = (1 + \frac{5}{2}, 5) = (\frac{7}{2}, 5)$, and the directrix is $x = -\frac{3}{2}$ (from $h - p = 1 - \frac{5}{2}$).

2. $h = -6$, $k = 4$, and $p = -\frac{1}{8}$ (from $4p = -\frac{1}{2}$). The vertex is $(-6, 4)$, the focus is $(h, k + p) = (-6, 4 + (-\frac{1}{8})) = (-6, \frac{31}{8})$, and the directrix is $y = \frac{33}{8}$ [from $k - p = 4 - (-\frac{1}{8})$].

3. We want to use the equation $(x - h)^2 = 4p(y - k)$. The focus is $(h, k + p)$, so $h = 4$ and $k + p = 10$. The directrix is $y = k - p$, so $k - p = -2$.

$$k + p = 10$$
$$\underline{k - p = -2}$$
$$2k = 8$$
$$k = 4$$
$$4 + p = 10 \qquad \text{Let } k = 4 \text{ in } k + p = 10$$
$$p = 6$$

The equation is $(x - 4)^2 = 24(y - 4)$.

4. See Figure 12-10.

5. See Figure 12-9.

6. See Figure 12-11.

Ellipses

Most ellipses look like flattened circles. Usually one diameter is longer than the other. In Figure 12-12, the horizontal diameter is longer than the vertical diameter. In Figure 12-13, the vertical diameter is longer than the horizontal diameter. The longer diameter is the *major axis*, and the shorter diameter is the

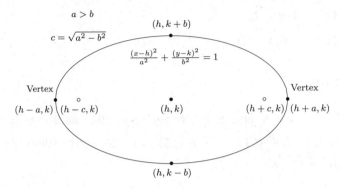

FIGURE 12-12

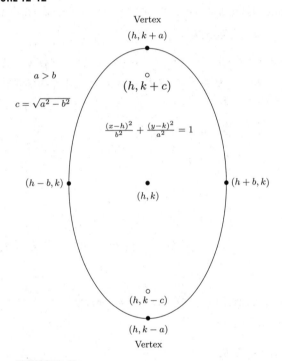

FIGURE 12-13

minor axis. An ellipse has seven important points—the center, two endpoints of the major axis (the vertices), two endpoints of the minor axis, and two points along the major axis called the *foci* (plural for *focus*). When the equation of an ellipse is in standard form,

$$\frac{(x-h)^2}{a^2} + \frac{(y-k)^2}{b^2} = 1 \text{ or } \frac{(x-h)^2}{b^2} + \frac{(y-k)^2}{a^2} = 1,$$

we can find these points without much trouble.

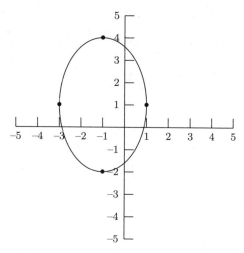

FIGURE 12-14

If all we want to do is to sketch the graph, we only need to plot the endpoints of the diameters and draw a rounded curve connecting them. For example, if we want to sketch the graph of $\frac{(x+1)^2}{4} + \frac{(y-1)^2}{9} = 1$, $a = 3$, $b = 2$, $h = -1$, and $k = 1$. According to Figure 12-13, the diameters have coordinates $(-1-2, 1) = (-3, 1)$, $(-1+2, 1) = (1, 1)$, $(-1, 1+3) = (-1, 4)$, and $(-1, 1-3) = (-1, -2)$, see Figure 12-14.

Like the definition of a parabola, the definition of the ellipse involves distance.

> *An ellipse is the set of all points for which the sum of their distances to two fixed points (the foci) is constant.*

For example, the foci for $\frac{x^2}{25} + \frac{y^2}{9} = 1$ are $(-4, 0)$ and $(4, 0)$. If we take any point on this ellipse and calculate its distance to $(-4, 0)$ and to $(4, 0)$ and add these numbers, the sum is 10. Two points on this ellipse are $(0, 3)$ and $\left(\frac{5}{3}, \sqrt{8}\right)$.

$$\overbrace{\sqrt{(-4-0)^2 + (0-3)^2}}^{\text{Distance from }(0,3)\text{ to }(-4,0)} + \overbrace{\sqrt{(4-0)^2 + (0-3)^2}}^{\text{Distance from }(0,3)\text{ to }(4,0)}$$

$$= \sqrt{16+9} + \sqrt{16+9} = \sqrt{25} + \sqrt{25} = 5 + 5 = 10$$

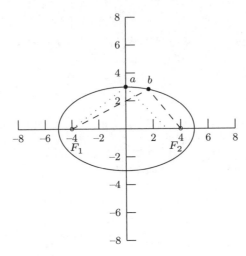

FIGURE 12-15

and

$$\overbrace{\text{Distance from } (5/3, \sqrt{8}) \text{ to } (-4, 0)}\qquad\overbrace{\text{Distance from } (5/3, \sqrt{8}) \text{ to } (4, 0)}$$

$$\sqrt{\left(-4 - \frac{5}{3}\right)^2 + (0 - \sqrt{8})^2} + \sqrt{\left(4 - \frac{5}{3}\right)^2 + (0 - \sqrt{8})^2}$$

$$= \sqrt{\frac{289}{9} + 8} + \sqrt{\frac{49}{9} + 8} = \sqrt{\frac{361}{9}} + \sqrt{\frac{121}{9}} = \frac{19}{3} + \frac{11}{3} = 10$$

If we connect any point on the graph to each focus, F_1 and F_2, the sum of the two lengths is 10. See Figure 12-15.

In the next set of problems, we are given an equation for an ellipse. From the equation, we can find h, k, a, and b. With these numbers and the information in Figures 12-12 or 12-13, we can find the center, foci, and vertices.

EXAMPLE 12-4

Find the center, foci, and vertices for the ellipse.

- $$\frac{(x - 3)^2}{16} + \frac{(y + 5)^2}{25} = 1$$

From the equation, we see that $h = 3$, $k = -5$, a^2 and b^2 are 4^2 and 5^2, but which is a and which is b? The larger number is a, so $a = 5$ and $b = 4$.

This makes $c = \sqrt{a^2 - b^2} = \sqrt{25 - 16} = 3$. We use the information in Figure 12-13 because the larger denominator is under $(y - k)^2$.

Center: $(h, k) = (3, -5)$

Foci: $(h, k - c) = (3, -5 - 3) = (3, -8)$ and $(h, k + c) = (3, -5 + 3) = (3, -2)$

Vertices: $(h, k - a) = (3, -5 - 5) = (3, -10)$ and $(h, k + a) = (3, -5 + 5) = (3, 0)$

- $\dfrac{x^2}{16} + (y - 2)^2 = 1$

To make it easier to find h, k, a, and b, we rewrite the equation.

$$\frac{(x - 0)^2}{16} + \frac{(y - 2)^2}{1} = 1$$

Now we can see that $h = 0$, $k = 2$, $a = 4$, $b = 1$, $c = \sqrt{a^2 - b^2} = \sqrt{16 - 1} = \sqrt{15}$. Because the larger denominator is under $(x - 0)^2$, we use the information in Figure 12-12.

Center: $(h, k) = (0, 2)$

Foci: $(h - c, k) = (0 - \sqrt{15}, 2) = (-\sqrt{15}, 2)$ and $(h + c, k) = (0 + \sqrt{15}, 2) = (\sqrt{15}, 2)$

Vertices: $(h - a, k) = (0 - 4, 2) = (-4, 2)$ and $(h + a, k) = (0 + 4, 2) = (4, 2)$

Now that we can find this important information from an equation of an ellipse, we are ready to match ellipses with their equations.

▮ EXAMPLE 12-5

Match the equations with the graphs in Figures 12-16 to 12-18.

- $\dfrac{x^2}{4} + \dfrac{y^2}{9} = 1$

The larger denominator is under y^2, so we use the information in Figure 12-13. Because $a = 3$, we look for a graph with vertices $(0, 3)$ and $(0, -3)$. This graph is in Figure 12-17.

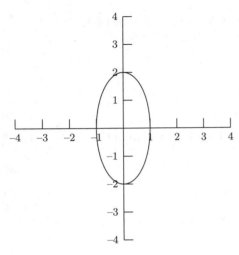

FIGURE 12-16

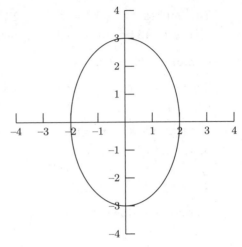

FIGURE 12-17

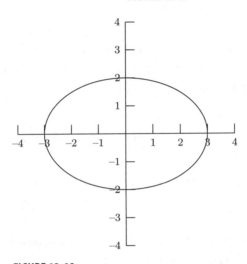

FIGURE 12-18

- $\dfrac{x^2}{9} + \dfrac{y^2}{4} = 1$

  The larger denominator is under x^2, so we use the information in Figure 12-12. Because $a = 3$, the vertices are $(-3, 0)$ and $(3, 0)$. This graph is in Figure 12-18.

- $x^2 + \dfrac{y^2}{4} = 1$

  The larger denominator is under y^2, so we use the information in Figure 12-13. Because $a = 2$, the vertices are $(0, 2)$ and $(0, -2)$. This graph is in Figure 12-16.

With as few as three points, we can find an equation for an ellipse. Using the formulas in Figures 12-12 and 12-13 and some algebra, we can find $h, k, a,$ and $b.$

 EXAMPLE 12-6

Find an equation for the ellipse.

- The vertices are $(-4, 2)$ and $(6, 2)$, and $(1, 5)$ is a point on the graph.

  The y-coordinates are the same, so the major axis (the larger diameter) is horizontal, which means we use the information in Figure 12-12. The vertices are $(h - a, k)$ and $(h + a, k)$, so $h - a = -4$ and $h + a = 6$, and $k = 2.$

$$h - a = -4$$
$$h + a = 6$$
$$\overline{}$$
$$2h = 2$$
$$h = 1$$
$$1 - a = -4 \qquad \text{Let } h = 1 \text{ in } h - a = -4$$
$$a = 5$$

So far we know

$$\frac{(x - 1)^2}{25} + \frac{(y - 2)^2}{b^2} = 1$$

Because $(1, 5)$ is on the graph, $\frac{(1-1)^2}{25} + \frac{(5-2)^2}{b^2} = 1$. Solving this equation for b, we find that $b = 3$. The equation is

$$\frac{(x - 1)^2}{25} + \frac{(y - 2)^2}{9} = 1$$

- The foci are $(-4, -10)$ and $(-4, 14)$, and $(-4, 15)$ is a vertex.

  The x-values of foci are the same, so the major axis is vertical. This tells us that we use the information in Figure 12-13.

$(h, k - c) = (-4, -10)$ and $(h, k + c) = (-4, 14)$, so $h = -4$, $k - c = -10$, and $k + c = 14$.

$$k - c = -10$$
$$k + c = 14$$
$$\overline{}$$
$$2k = 4$$
$$k = 2$$
$$2 - c = -10 \qquad \text{Let } k = 2 \text{ in } k - c = -10$$
$$c = 12$$

Because $(-4, 15)$ is a vertex, $k + a = 15$, so $2 + a = 15$ and $a = 13$. All that remains is to find b. Let $a = 13$ and $c = 12$ in $c = \sqrt{a^2 - b^2}$: $12 = \sqrt{13^2 - b^2}$. Solving this for b, gives us $b = 5$. The equation is

$$\frac{(x + 4)^2}{25} + \frac{(y - 2)^2}{169} = 1$$

The *eccentricity* of an ellipse is a number that measures how flat it is. The formula is $e = \frac{c}{a}$. This number ranges between 0 and 1. The closer to 1 the eccentricity of an ellipse is, the flatter it is. If $e = \frac{c}{a} = 0$, then the ellipse is a circle. In a circle, the center and foci are all the same point, and a and b are the same number. For example, $\frac{(x-5)^2}{9} + \frac{(y-4)^2}{9} = 1$ is a circle with center $(5, 4)$ and radius $\sqrt{9} = 3$. Usually we see equations of circles in the form $(x - h)^2 + (y - k)^2 = r^2$.

EXAMPLE 12-7

Find the ellipse's eccentricity.

- $\frac{x^2}{9} + \frac{y^2}{25} = 1$; $a = 5$, $b = 3$, $c = \sqrt{25 - 9} = 4$, and $e = \frac{c}{a} = \frac{4}{5}$

- $\frac{(x + 8)^2}{144} + \frac{(y + 6)^2}{169} = 1$; $a = 13$, $b = 12$, $c = \sqrt{169 - 144} = 5$, and $e = \frac{c}{a} = \frac{5}{13}$

This ellipse is more rounded than the first because e is closer to zero.

PRACTICE

1. Identify the center, foci, vertices, and eccentricity for

$$\frac{x^2}{169} + \frac{(y-10)^2}{25} = 1$$

2. Identify the center, foci, vertices, and eccentricity for

$$\frac{(x+9)^2}{20^2} + \frac{(y+2)^2}{29^2} = 1$$

3. Identify the center and radius for the circle

$$\frac{(x+6)^2}{49} + \frac{(y-1)^2}{49} = 1$$

For Problems 4 to 7, match the equation with the graph in Figures 12-19 to 12-22.

4. $\dfrac{(x-1)^2}{16} + \dfrac{(y-2)^2}{25} = 1$

5. $\dfrac{x^2}{144} + \dfrac{y^2}{169} = 1$

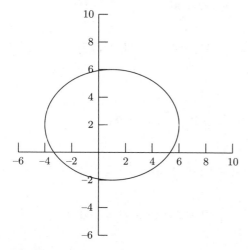

FIGURE 12-19

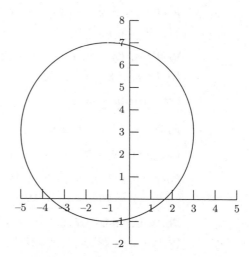

FIGURE 12-20

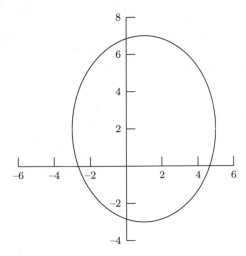

FIGURE 12-21

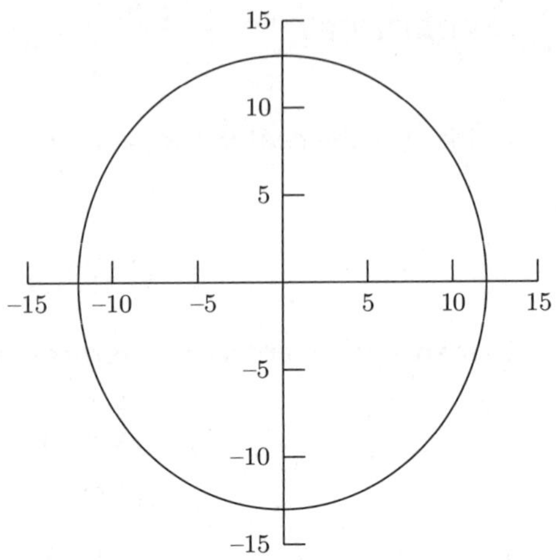

FIGURE 12-22

6. $\dfrac{(x+1)^2}{16} + \dfrac{(y-3)^2}{16} = 1$

7. $\dfrac{(x-1)^2}{25} + \dfrac{(y-2)^2}{16} = 1$

✔ SOLUTIONS

1. $h = 0, k = 10, a = 13, b = 5, c = \sqrt{a^2 - b^2} = \sqrt{169 - 25} = 12$

   Center: $(0, 10)$

   Foci: $(h - c, k) = (0 - 12, 10) = (-12, 10)$ and $(h + c, k) = (0 + 12, 10) = (12, 10)$

   Vertices: $(h - a, k) = (0 - 13, 10) = (-13, 10)$ and $(h + a, k) = (0 + 13, 10) = (13, 10)$

   Eccentricity: $\dfrac{c}{a} = \dfrac{12}{13}$

2. $h = -9, k = -2, a = 29, b = 20, c = \sqrt{29^2 - 20^2} = 21$

   Center: $(-9, -2)$

   Foci: $(h, k - c) = (-9, -2 - 21) = (-9, -23)$ and $(h, k + c) = (-9, -2 + 21) = (-9, 19)$

   Vertices: $(h, k - a) = (-9, -2 - 29) = (-9, -31)$ and $(h, k + a) = (-9, -2 + 29) = (-9, 27)$

   Eccentricity: $\dfrac{c}{a} = \dfrac{21}{29}$

3. The center is $(-6, 1)$, and the radius is 7.

4. See Figure 12-21.

5. See Figure 12-22.

6. See Figure 12-20.

7. See Figure 12-19.

Hyperbolas

The last conic section is the hyperbola. Hyperbolas are formed when a slice is made through both parts of a double cone. The graph of a hyperbola comes in two pieces called *branches*. Like ellipses, hyperbolas have a center, two foci, and two vertices. Hyperbolas also have two slant asymptotes. The definition of a hyperbola involves the distance between points on the graph and the two foci.

> A hyperbola is the set of all points such as the difference between the distance between the point and the fixed points (the foci) is constant.

For example, the foci for $\frac{x^2}{9} - \frac{y^2}{16} = 1$ are $(-5, 0)$ and $(5, 0)$. For any point P on the hyperbola, the distance between P and one focus minus the distance between P and the other focus is 6. Two points on the hyperbola are $(6, \sqrt{48})$ and $(12, \sqrt{240})$.

$$\overbrace{\sqrt{(-5-6)^2 + (0-\sqrt{48})^2}}^{\text{Distance from } (6, \sqrt{48}) \text{ to } (-5, 0)} - \overbrace{\sqrt{(5-6)^2 + (0-\sqrt{48})^2}}^{\text{Distance from } (6, \sqrt{48}) \text{ to } (5, 0)}$$

$$= \sqrt{121 + 48} - \sqrt{1 + 48} = 13 - 7 = 6$$

and

$$\overbrace{\sqrt{(-5-12)^2 + (0-\sqrt{240})^2}}^{\text{Distance from } (12, \sqrt{240}) \text{ to } (-5, 0)} - \overbrace{\sqrt{(5-12)^2 + (0-\sqrt{240})^2}}^{\text{Distance from } (12, \sqrt{240}) \text{ to } (5, 0)}$$

$$= \sqrt{289 + 240} = \sqrt{49 + 240} = 23 - 17 = 6$$

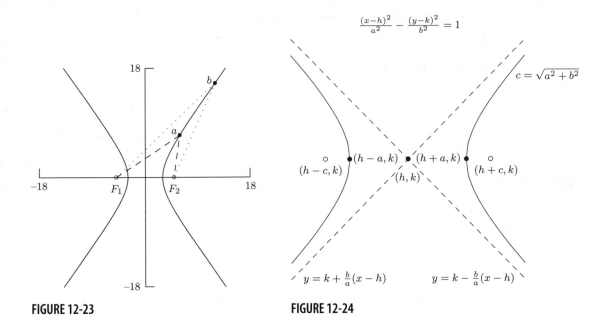

FIGURE 12-23

FIGURE 12-24

If we choose any point on the hyperbola and connect it to each focus, F_1 and F_2, the difference in the lengths of these line segments is 6. See Figure 12-23. Equations of hyperbolas come in one of the two forms.

$$\frac{(x-h)^2}{a^2} - \frac{(y-k)^2}{b^2} = 1 \text{ or } \frac{(y-k)^2}{a^2} - \frac{(x-h)^2}{b^2} = 1$$

If the x^2 term is positive, one branch opens to the left and the other to the right. If the y^2 term is positive, one branch opens up and the other down. The standard forms for these graphs are in Figures 12-24 and 12-25.

We can sketch a hyperbola by plotting the vertices and sketching the asymptotes, using dashed lines. We should also plot two points to the left and two points to the right of each vertex to show how fast the graph approaches the asymptotes.

EXAMPLE 12-8

- Sketch the graph for $\frac{y^2}{4} - x^2 = 1$.

    Because y^2 is positive, we use the information in Figure 12-25. The center is $(0, 0)$, $a = 2$, and $b = 1$. The vertices are $(h, k + a) = (0, 0 + 2) = (0, 2)$ and $(h, k - a) = (0, 0 - 2) = (0, -2)$. The asymptote equations are $y = k - \frac{a}{b}(x - h)$ and $y = k + \frac{a}{b}(x - h)$. Using our numbers for

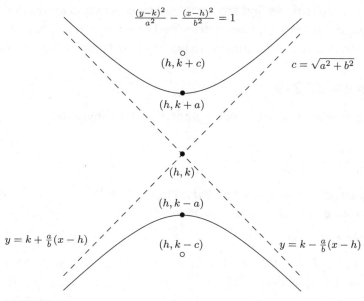

$$\frac{(y-k)^2}{a^2} - \frac{(x-h)^2}{b^2} = 1$$

$(h, k+c)$

$c = \sqrt{a^2 + b^2}$

$(h, k+a)$

(h, k)

$(h, k-a)$

$y = k + \frac{a}{b}(x - h)$

$(h, k-c)$

$y = k - \frac{a}{b}(x - h)$

FIGURE 12-25

h, k, a, and *b*, we have *y* = −2*x* and *y* = 2*x*. We use *x* = 4 and *x* = −4 for our extra points. If we let *x* = 4 or *x* = −4, we get two *y*-values, ±$\sqrt{68}$. These give us four more points: (4, $\sqrt{68}$), (4, −$\sqrt{68}$), (−4, $\sqrt{68}$), and (−4, −$\sqrt{68}$). After sketching the asymptotes as dashed lines and plotting these points, we draw the branches through these points (see Figure 12-26).

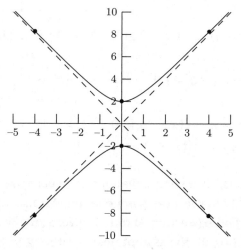

FIGURE 12-26

In the next problems, we find the center, vertices, foci, and asymptotes for the given hyperbolas. Once we have determined whether x^2 is positive or y^2 is positive, we can decide which formulas to use, those in Figure 12-24 or 12-25.

 EXAMPLE 12-9

Find the center, vertices, foci, and asymptotes for the hyperbola.

- $$\frac{(x+7)^2}{36} - \frac{(y+4)^2}{64} = 1$$

Because x^2 is positive, we use the information in Figure 12-24. $h = -7$, $k = -4$, $a = 6$, $b = 8$, $c = \sqrt{36 + 64} = 10$

Center: $(-7, -4)$

Vertices: $(h - a, k) = (-7 - 6, -4) = (-13, -4)$ and $(h + a, k) = (-7 + 6, -4) = (-1, -4)$

Foci: $(h - c, k) = (-7 - 10, -4) = (-17, -4)$ and $(h + c, k) = (-7 + 10, -4) = (3, -4)$

Asymptotes: $y = k - \frac{b}{a}(x - h) = -4 - \frac{8}{6}(x + 7) = -\frac{4}{3}x - \frac{40}{3}$ and $y = k + \frac{b}{a}(x - h) = -4 + \frac{8}{6}(x + 7) = \frac{4}{3}x + \frac{16}{3}$

- $$\frac{y^2}{144} - \frac{(x-1)^2}{25} = 1$$

Because y^2 is positive, we use the information in Figure 12-25. $h = 1$, $k = 0$, $a = 12$, $b = 5$, $c = \sqrt{144 + 25} = 13$

Center: $(1, 0)$

Vertices: $(h, k - a) = (1, 0 - 12) = (1, -12)$ and $(h, k + a) = (1, 0 + 12) = (1, 12)$

Foci: $(h, k - c) = (1, 0 - 13) = (1, -13)$ and $(h, k + c) = (1, 0 + 13) = (1, 13)$

Asymptotes: $y = k - \frac{a}{b}(x - h) = 0 - \frac{12}{5}(x - 1) = -\frac{12}{5}x + \frac{12}{5}$ and $y = k + \frac{a}{b}(x - h) = 0 + \frac{12}{5}(x - 1) = \frac{12}{5}x - \frac{12}{5}$

In the next problems, we match equations of hyperbolas with their graphs. Being able to identify the vertices is not enough. We also use the equations of the asymptotes to find b (we know a from the vertices). Because the center of each hyperbola is at $(0, 0)$, the asymptotes are either $y = \frac{a}{b}x$ and $y = -\frac{a}{b}x$ or $y = \frac{b}{a}x$ and $y = -\frac{b}{a}x$.

▢ EXAMPLE **12-10**

Match the equation with its graph in Figures 12-27 to 12-30.

- $\dfrac{x^2}{4} - \dfrac{y^2}{4} = 1$

  The vertices are $(-2, 0)$ and $(2, 0)$. The slopes of the asymptotes are -1 and 1. The graph is in Figure 12-28.

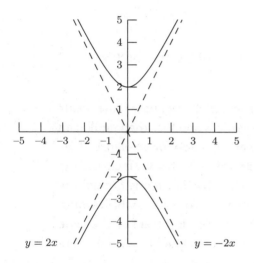

FIGURE 12-27

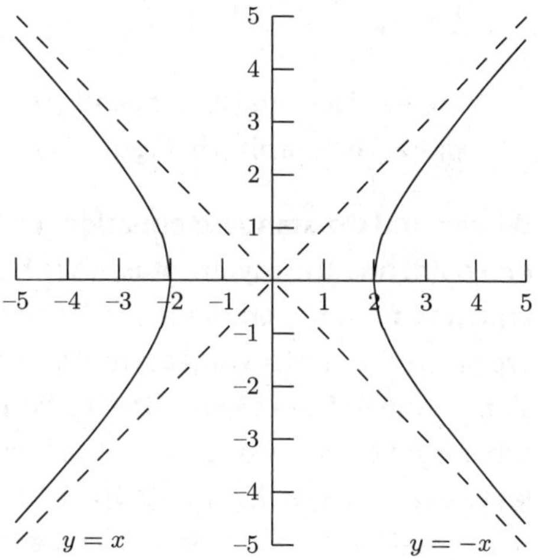

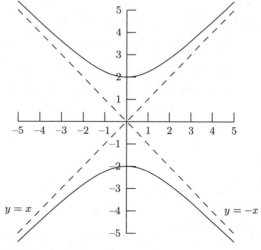

FIGURE 12-28

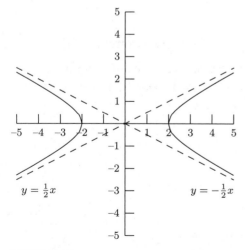

FIGURE 12-29

FIGURE 12-30

- $\dfrac{x^2}{4} - y^2 = 1$

  The vertices are $(-2, 0)$ and $(2, 0)$. The slopes of the asymptotes are $-\frac{1}{2}$ and $\frac{1}{2}$. The graph is in Figure 12-29.

- $\dfrac{y^2}{4} - \dfrac{x^2}{4} = 1$

  The vertices are $(0, -2)$ and $(0, 2)$. The slopes of the asymptotes are -1 and 1. The graph is in Figure 12-30.

- $\dfrac{y^2}{4} - x^2 = 1$

  The vertices are $(0, -2)$ and $(0, 2)$. The slopes of the asymptotes are -2 and 2. The graph is in Figure 12-27.

We can find the standard equation for a hyperbola when we know some points or a point and the asymptotes. If we have the vertices and foci, then finding an equation for a hyperbola is similar to finding an equation for an ellipse. If we are given the vertices and asymptotes or foci and asymptotes, we must use the slope of one of the asymptotes to find either a or b (we know one but not the other from the vertices or foci). The first thing we need to decide is which formulas to use—those in Figure 12-24 or 12-25. If the vertices or foci are on the same horizontal line (the y-coordinates are the same), we use Figure 12-24. If they are on the same vertical line (the x-coordinates are the same), we use Figure 12-25.

 EXAMPLE 12-11

Find an equation for the hyperbola.

- The vertices are $(3, -1)$ and $(3, 7)$ and $y = \frac{4}{3}x - 1$ is an asymptote.

  The vertices are on the same vertical line, so we use the information in Figure 12-25. The vertices are $(h, k - a) = (3, -1)$ and $(h, k + a) = (3, 7)$. This gives us $h = 3$, $k - a = -1$, and $k + a = 7$.

$$
\begin{array}{r}
k + a = 7 \\
k - a = -1 \\
\hline
2k = 6 \\
k = 3 \\
\end{array}
$$

$3 + a = 7$ Let $k = 3$ in $k + a = 7$

$a = 4$

The center is $(3, 3)$ and $a = 4$. Once we have b, we are done. The slope of one of the asymptotes in Figure 12-25 is $\frac{a}{b}$; so we have $\frac{a}{b} = \frac{4}{b} = \frac{4}{3}$, so $b = 3$. The equation is

$$\frac{(y - 3)^2}{16} - \frac{(x - 3)^2}{9} = 1$$

• The vertices are $(-8, 5)$ and $(4, 5)$, and the foci are $(-12, 5)$ and $(8, 5)$.

The vertices and foci are on the same horizontal line, so we use the information in Figure 12-24. The vertices are $(h - a, k) = (-8, 5)$ and $(h + a, k) = (4, 5)$. Now we know $k = 5$ and we have the system $h - a = -8$ and $h + a = 4$.

$$
\begin{aligned}
h - a &= -8 \\
h + a &= 4 \\
\hline
2h &= -4 \\
h &= -2 \\
-2 - a &= -8 \qquad \text{Let } h = -2 \text{ in } h - a = -8 \\
a &= 6
\end{aligned}
$$

A focus is $(h - c, k) = (-2 - c, 5) = (-12, 5)$, which gives us $-2 - c = -12$. Now we see that $c = 10$, so we can put this and $a = 6$ in $c = \sqrt{a^2 + b^2}$ to find b.

$$10 = \sqrt{36 + b^2}$$

$$100 = 36 + b^2$$

$$8 = b$$

The equation is

$$\frac{(x + 2)^2}{36} - \frac{(y - 5)^2}{64} = 1$$

PRACTICE

1. Find the center, vertices, foci, and asymptotes for

$$\frac{y^2}{16} - \frac{(x - 5)^2}{9} = 1$$

2. Find the center, vertices, foci, and asymptotes for

$$\frac{(x+8)^2}{49} - \frac{(y+6)^2}{576} = 1$$

3. Find an equation for the hyperbola having vertices $(-4, 2)$ and $(12, 2)$ and foci $(-6, 2)$ and $(14, 2)$.

4. Find an equation for the hyperbola having vertices $(-8, 0)$ and $(-4, 0)$ and with an asymptote $y = \frac{1}{2}x + 3$.

In Problems 5 to 7, match the graphs in Figures 12-31 to 12-33 with their equations.

5. $(y-1)^2 - (x-1)^2 = 1$

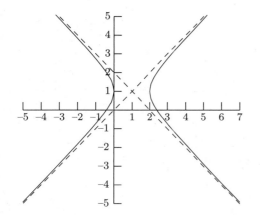

FIGURE 12-31

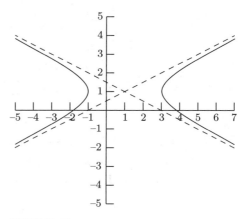

FIGURE 12-32

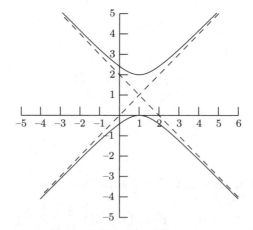

FIGURE 12-33

6. $(x-1)^2 - (y-1)^2 = 1$

7. $\dfrac{(x-1)^2}{4} - (y-1)^2 = 1$

✔ SOLUTIONS

1. $h = 5$, $k = 0$, $a = 4$, $b = 3$, and $c = \sqrt{16+9} = 5$

Center: $(5, 0)$

Vertices: $(h, k-a) = (5, 0-4) = (5, -4)$ and $(h, k+a) = (5, 0+4) = (5, 4)$

Foci: $(h, k-c) = (5, 0-5) = (5, -5)$ and $(h, k+c) = (5, 0+5) = (5, 5)$

Asymptotes: $y = k - \frac{a}{b}(x-h) = 0 - \frac{4}{3}(x-5) = -\frac{4}{3}x + \frac{20}{3}$ and

$y = k + \frac{a}{b}(x-h) = 0 + \frac{4}{3}(x-5) = \frac{4}{3}x - \frac{20}{3}$

2. $h = -8$, $k = -6$, $a = 7$, $b = 24$, and $c = \sqrt{49+576} = 25$

Center: $(-8, -6)$

Vertices: $(h-a, k) = (-8-7, -6) = (-15, -6)$ and $(h+a, k) = (-8+7, -6) = (-1, -6)$

Foci: $(h-c, k) = (-8-25, -6) = (-33, -6)$ and $(h+c, k) = (-8+25, -6) = (17, -6)$

Asymptotes: $y = k - \frac{b}{a}(x-h) = -6 - \frac{24}{7}(x+8) = -\frac{24}{7}x - \frac{234}{7}$

and $y = k + \frac{b}{a}(x-h) = -6 + \frac{24}{7}(x+8) = \frac{24}{7}x + \frac{150}{7}$

3. The vertices are $(-4, 2)$ and $(12, 2)$, which gives us $(h-a, k) = (-4, 2)$ and $(h+a, k) = (12, 2)$.

$$h - a = -4$$
$$h + a = 12$$
$$\overline{}$$
$$2h = 8$$
$$h = 4$$
$$4 - a = -4 \qquad \text{Let } h = 4 \text{ in } h - a = -4$$
$$a = 8$$

A focus is $(-6, 2)$, which gives us $(h - c, k) = (-6, 2)$ and $h - c = 4 - c = -6$. Solving $4 - c = -6$ gives us $c = 10$. We can find b by letting $a = 8$ and $c = 10$ in $c = \sqrt{a^2 + b^2}$.

$$c = \sqrt{a^2 + b^2}$$

$$10 = \sqrt{64 + b^2}$$

$$100 = 64 + b^2$$

$$6 = b$$

The equation is $\frac{(x-4)^2}{64} - \frac{(y-2)^2}{36} = 1$.

4. $(h - a, k) = (-8, 0)$ and $(h + a, k) = (-4, 0)$, so $k = 0$ and we have the following system.

$$h - a = -8$$

$$h + a = -4$$

$$\overline{}$$

$$2h = -12$$

$$h = -6$$

$$-6 - a = -8 \qquad \text{Let } h = -6 \text{ in } h - a = -8$$

$$a = 2$$

The slope of an asymptote is $\frac{1}{2}$, so $\frac{b}{a} = \frac{b}{2} = \frac{1}{2}$ and $b = 1$. The equation is $\frac{(x+6)^2}{4} - y^2 = 1$.

5. See Figure 12-33.

6. See Figure 12-31.

7. See Figure 12-32.

Equations in Other Forms

In order to use some graphing calculators to plot the graph of a conic section, you might have to enter it as two separate functions. For example, the graph of $y^2 = x$ could be entered as $y = \sqrt{x}$ and $y = -\sqrt{x}$. To use a graphing calculator to graph a conic section that is not a function, we solve its equation for y. When taking the square root of both sides, we use a "$\pm$" symbol on one of the sides. It is this sign that gives us two separate equations.

 EXAMPLE 12-12

Solve for y.

$$\bullet \; (y-1)^2 + \frac{(x+3)^2}{9} = 1$$

$$(y-1)^2 + \frac{(x+3)^2}{9} = 1$$

$$(y-1)^2 = 1 - \frac{(x+3)^2}{9}$$

$$y - 1 = \pm\sqrt{1 - \frac{(x+3)^2}{9}}$$

$$y = 1 \pm \sqrt{1 - \frac{(x+3)^2}{9}}$$

$$y = 1 + \sqrt{1 - \frac{(x+3)^2}{9}}, \; y = 1 - \sqrt{1 - \frac{(x+3)^2}{9}}$$

The equations for this ellipse are shown in Figure 12-34 and its graph is shown in Figure 12-35. The window is $-8 \le x \le 2$ and $-2 \le y \le 8$.

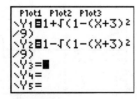

FIGURE 12-34

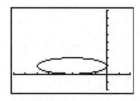

FIGURE 12-35

- $\dfrac{x^2}{9} - \dfrac{(y+2)^2}{4} = 1$

$$\dfrac{x^2}{9} - \dfrac{(y+2)^2}{4} = 1$$

$$-\dfrac{(y+2)^2}{4} = 1 - \dfrac{x^2}{9}$$

$$\dfrac{(y+2)^2}{4} = -1 + \dfrac{x^2}{9}$$

$$(y+2)^2 = 4\left(-1 + \dfrac{x^2}{9}\right)$$

$$y + 2 = \pm\sqrt{4\left(-1 + \dfrac{x^2}{9}\right)}$$

$$y = -2 \pm \sqrt{4\left(-1 + \dfrac{x^2}{9}\right)}$$

$$y = -2 + \sqrt{4\left(-1 + \dfrac{x^2}{9}\right)}, \ y = -2 - \sqrt{4\left(-1 + \dfrac{x^2}{9}\right)}$$

See Figure 12-36 for the equations entered into the "Y =" Editor and its graph in Figure 12-37. It is plotted in the window $-15 \le x \le 15$ and $-15 \le y \le 15$.

The TI-84 has a CONICS application. If it is loaded on your calculator, you can access the application on the APPS menu. For example, you can use this feature to plot the graph of an ellipse. Choose the ELLIPSE option and the appropriate orientation. Once you have this, fill in h, k, a, and b and then press GRAPH. (See Figures 12-38 and 12-39.)

FIGURE 12-36

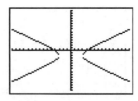

FIGURE 12-37

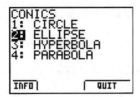

FIGURE 12-38   FIGURE 12-39

Equations of conic sections do not always come in the convenient forms we have been using. Sometimes they come in the general form $Ax^2 + Bxy + Cy^2 + Dx + Ey + F = 0$. When A and C are equal (and $B = 0$), the graph is a circle. If A and C are positive and not equal (and $B = 0$), the graph is an ellipse. If A and C have different signs (and $B = 0$), the graph is a hyperbola. If only one of A or C is nonzero (and $B = 0$), the graph is a parabola. There are some conic sections whose entire graph is one point. These are called *degenerate conics*. We can rewrite an equation in the general form in the standard form (the form we have been using) by completing the square.

EXAMPLE 12-13

Rewrite the equation in standard form.

- $x^2 - 2x - 4y = 11$

  Because there is no y^2 term, the graph of this equation is a parabola that opens up or down. The standard equation is $(x - h)^2 = 4p(y - k)$. We need the x terms on one side of the equation and the other terms on the other side.

  $$x^2 - 2x - 4y = 11$$
  $$x^2 - 2x = 4y + 11$$
  $$x^2 - 2x + \left(\frac{2}{2}\right)^2 = 4y + 11 + \left(\frac{2}{2}\right)^2$$
  $$x^2 - 2x + 1 = 4y + 12$$
  $$(x - 1)^2 = 4(y + 3)$$

- $-9x^2 + 16y^2 - 18x - 160y + 247 = 0$

  Because the signs on x^2 and y^2 are different, the graph of this equation is a hyperbola. The standard form for this equation is $\frac{(y-k)^2}{a^2} - \frac{(x-h)^2}{b^2} = 1$.

$$-9x^2 + 16y^2 - 18x - 160y + 247 = 0$$

$$16y^2 - 160y - 9x^2 - 18x = -247$$

$$16(y^2 - 10y) - 9(x^2 + 2x) = -247$$

$$16\left[y^2 - 10y + \left(\frac{10}{2}\right)^2\right] - 9\left[x^2 + 2x + \left(\frac{2}{2}\right)^2\right] = -247 + 16\left(\frac{10}{2}\right)^2 - 9\left(\frac{2}{2}\right)^2$$

$$16(y-5)^2 - 9(x+1)^2 = 144$$

$$\frac{16(y-5)^2}{144} - \frac{9(x+1)^2}{144} = \frac{144}{144}$$

$$\frac{(y-5)^2}{9} - \frac{(x+1)^2}{16} = 1$$

PRACTICE

1. Solve for y.

$$\frac{y^2}{4} - \frac{(x-3)^2}{9} = 1$$

2. Solve for y.

$$\frac{(x+10)^2}{25} + \frac{(y+3)^2}{25} = 1$$

3. Rewrite the equation in standard form: $36x^2 + 9y^2 - 216x - 72y + 144 = 0$.

SOLUTIONS

1.

$$\frac{y^2}{4} - \frac{(x-3)^2}{9} = 1$$

$$\frac{y^2}{4} = 1 + \frac{(x-3)^2}{9}$$

$$y^2 = 4\left[1 + \frac{(x-3)^2}{9}\right]$$

$$y = \pm\sqrt{4\left[1 + \frac{(x-3)^2}{9}\right]}$$

2. $$\frac{(x+10)^2}{25} + \frac{(y+3)^2}{25} = 1$$

$$\frac{(y+3)^2}{25} = 1 - \frac{(x+10)^2}{25}$$

$$(y+3)^2 = 25\left[1 - \frac{(x+10)^2}{25}\right]$$

$$y+3 = \pm\sqrt{25\left[1 - \frac{(x+10)^2}{25}\right]}$$

$$y = -3 \pm \sqrt{25\left[1 - \frac{(x+10)^2}{25}\right]}$$

3. $$36x^2 + 9y^2 - 216x - 72y + 144 = 0$$

$$36x^2 - 216x + 9y^2 - 72y = -144$$

$$36(x^2 - 6x) + 9(y^2 - 8y) = -144$$

$$36(x^2 - 6x + 9) + 9(y^2 - 8y + 16) = -144 + 36(9) + 9(16)$$

$$36(x-3)^2 + 9(y-4)^2 = 324$$

$$\frac{36(x-3)^2}{324} + \frac{9(y-4)^2}{324} = \frac{324}{324}$$

$$\frac{(x-3)^2}{9} + \frac{(y-4)^2}{36} = 1$$

Summary

In this chapter, we learned how to

- *Give the formal definition for the parabola, ellipse, and hyperbola.* All of these definitions come from the distance between a point on the graph and two features of its graph: the focus and the directrix for a parabola and the two foci for an ellipse and a hyperbola.

- *Identify features for a parabola from its equation.* When the equation for a parabola is in standard form, $(x-h)^2 = 4p(y-k)$ or $(y-k)^2 = 4p(x-h)$, we can identify the directrix, the focus, and the vertex for its graph.

We know whether or not the parabola opens up/down or left/right. Also, if we have enough information about a parabola (e.g., the focus and the directrix), we can determine its equation.

- *Identify features for an ellipse from its equation.* When the equation for an ellipse is in standard form, $\frac{(x-h)^2}{a^2} + \frac{(y-k)^2}{b^2} = 1$ or $\frac{(x-h)^2}{b^2} + \frac{(y-k)^2}{a^2} = 1$ (for $a > b$), we can identify the length of its major axis and minor axis as well as the location of the center, foci, and vertices. This information helps us to sketch the graph with little trouble. Also, if we know some of these features, we can determine an equation for the ellipse.

- *Sketch an ellipse.* We plot the endpoints of the major and minor axis and draw a curve through them.

- *Compute the eccentricity of an ellipse.* The eccentricity ranges between 0 and 1. The closer e is to 1, the flatter the ellipse. If $e = 0$, then the ellipse is, in fact, a circle. The formula is $e = \frac{c}{a}$, where $c = \sqrt{a^2 - b^2}$.

- *Identify features for a hyperbola from its equation.* When the equation is in standard form, $\frac{(x-h)^2}{a^2} - \frac{(y-k)^2}{b^2} = 1$ or $\frac{(y-k)^2}{a^2} - \frac{(x-h)^2}{b^2} = 1$, we can identify the equations of the asymptotes and the location of the center, vertices, and foci.

- *Sketch a hyperbola.* We sketch a hyperbola by plotting the vertices and the asymptotes, using dashed lines. We should also plot two points to the left and two points to the right of each vertex.

- *Solve an equation in standard form for y.* Solving an equation for y allows us to use a graphing calculator to plot its graph. Some graphing calculators can plot the graph of a conic section when its equation is in standard form.

- *Write the equation of a conic in standard form.* If the equation of a conic section comes in the general form, $Ax^2 + Bxy + Cy^2 + Dx + Ey + F = 0$ (with $B = 0$), we can complete the square to rewrite the equation in standard form.

QUIZ

1. What is the directrix for the parabola $(y - 10)^2 = 12(x + 1)$?

   A. $y = -2$ B. $y = -4$ C. $x = -2$ D. $x = -4$

2. What is the focus for the parabola $(y - 10)^2 = 12(x + 1)$?

   A. $(4, 10)$ B. $(2, 10)$ C. $(10, 4)$ D. $(10, 2)$

3. What are the vertices for the ellipse $\frac{(x+8)^2}{49} + \frac{(y-5)^2}{625} = 1$?

   A. $(-8, -20)$ and $(-8, 30)$ C. $(-15, 5)$ and $(-1, 5)$

   B. $(8, -20)$ and $(8, 30)$ D. $(15, 5)$ and $(1, 5)$

4. What are the foci for the ellipse $\frac{(x+8)^2}{49} + \frac{(y-5)^2}{625} = 1$?

   A. $(-33, 3)$ and $(17, 5)$ C. $(-8, -19)$ and $(-8, 29)$

   B. $(-33, -5)$ and $(17, -5)$ D. $(8, -19)$ and $(8, 29)$

5. Which line is an asymptote for the hyperbola $\frac{(y-8)^2}{9} - (x - 3)^2 = 1$?

   A. $y = 3x - 21$ B. $y = 3x - 1$ C. $y = \frac{1}{3}x + \frac{16}{3}$ D. $y = \frac{1}{3}x + 7$

6. What are the center and radius for the circle $(x - 4)^2 + (y - 6)^2 = 9$?

   A. The center is $(4, 6)$, and the   C. The center is $(-4, -6)$, and the
      radius is 3.   radius is 3.

   B. The center is $(4, 6)$, and the   D. The center is $(4, -6)$, and the
      radius is 9.   radius is 9.

7. Solve for y: $\frac{(x+2)^2}{4} + \frac{(y-1)^2}{9} = 1$.

   A. $y = -1 \pm 3\sqrt{\dfrac{(x+2)^2}{4} - 1}$ C. $y = -1 \pm 3\sqrt{1 - \dfrac{(x+2)^2}{4}}$

   B. $y = 1 \pm 3\sqrt{\dfrac{(x+2)^2}{4} - 1}$ D. $y = 1 \pm 3\sqrt{1 - \dfrac{(x+2)^2}{4}}$

8. The graph in Figure 12-40 is the graph of which equation?

   A. $y^2 = -12x$ B. $y^2 = 12x$ C. $x^2 = 12y$ D. $x^2 = -12x$

9. Rewrite the equation in standard form: $x^2 + 10x + 9y^2 - 54y + 97 = 0$.

   A. $\dfrac{(x+5)^2}{4} + \dfrac{(y-3)^2}{9} = 1$ C. $(x+5)^2 + \dfrac{(y-3)^2}{9} = 1$

   B. $(x+5)^2 + \dfrac{(y-3)^2}{4} = 1$ D. $\dfrac{(x+5)^2}{9} + (y-3)^2 = 1$

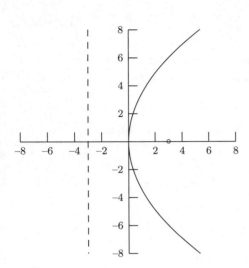

FIGURE 12-40   FIGURE 12-41

10. **Which of the following is an equation for the hyperbola with center $(4, 1)$ and with asymptote $y = 3x - 11$.**

A. $\dfrac{(x-4)^2}{4} - \dfrac{(y-1)^2}{36} = 1$

C. $\dfrac{(x-1)^2}{4} - \dfrac{(y-4)^2}{36} = 1$

B. $\dfrac{(x-4)^2}{36} - \dfrac{(y-1)^2}{4} = 1$

D. $\dfrac{(x-1)^2}{36} - \dfrac{(y-4)^2}{4} = 1$

11. **Find an equation for the ellipse with vertices $(4, 0)$ and $(4, 10)$ and with a focus at $(4, 2)$.**

A. $\dfrac{(x-5)^2}{16} + \dfrac{(y-4)^2}{25} = 1$

C. $\dfrac{(x-4)^2}{16} + \dfrac{(y-5)^2}{25} = 1$

B. $\dfrac{(x-5)^2}{25} + \dfrac{(y-4)^2}{9} = 1$

D. $\dfrac{(x-4)^2}{25} + \dfrac{(y-5)^2}{9} = 1$

12. **The equation in Figure 12-41 is the graph of which equation?**

A. $\dfrac{y^2}{4} - \dfrac{x^2}{9} = 1$

C. $\dfrac{x^2}{4} - \dfrac{y^2}{9} = 1$

B. $\dfrac{y^2}{9} - \dfrac{x^2}{4} = 1$

D. $\dfrac{x^2}{9} - \dfrac{y^2}{4} = 1$

chapter **13**

Trigonometry

Trigonometry has been used for over two thousand years to solve many real-world problems, among them are surveying, navigating, and problems in engineering. Another important use is analytic—the trigonometric functions and their graphs are important in many mathematics courses. Understanding trigonometry will help you in every course in the calculus sequence (Calculus I, II, III, and differential equations) as well as in courses in physics and engineering.

CHAPTER OBJECTIVES

In this chapter, you will

- Determine when a point is on the unit circle
- Work with angles measured in degrees and in radians
- Evaluate trigonometric functions
- Sketch the graph of sine and cosine functions
- Recognize graphs of the other trigonometric functions
- Solve right triangles
- Evaluate inverse trigonometric functions
- Use the Law of Sines and the Law of Cosines to solve triangles
- Work with trigonometric formulas

The Unit Circle

Although trigonometry was developed from the study of triangles, calculus students work mostly with trigonometric functions, which are based on the *unit circle*. You might recall from Chapter 12 that the equation for a circle centered at (h, k) with radius r is $(x - h)^2 + (y - k)^2 = r^2$. The unit circle is centered at $(0, 0)$ and has radius 1, so its equation is $x^2 + y^2 = 1$. Because the trigonometric functions are based on points on the unit circle, we begin our study of trigonometry with these points.

A point (a, b) is on the unit circle if its coordinates make the equation $x^2 + y^2 = 1$ true. For example, $(\frac{3}{5}, \frac{4}{5})$ is on the unit circle because $(\frac{3}{5})^2 + (\frac{4}{5})^2 = \frac{9}{25} + \frac{16}{25} = \frac{25}{25} = 1$.

 EXAMPLE 13-1

Verify the fact that the points are on the unit circle.

- $\left(\dfrac{15}{17}, \dfrac{8}{17} \right)$

- $\left(\dfrac{\sqrt{11}}{6}, -\dfrac{5}{6} \right)$

- $(0, -1)$

$\left(\dfrac{15}{17} \right)^2 + \left(\dfrac{8}{17} \right)^2$

$\left(\dfrac{\sqrt{11}}{6} \right)^2 + \left(-\dfrac{5}{6} \right)^2$

$0^2 + (-1)^2$

$= \dfrac{225}{289} + \dfrac{64}{289} = \dfrac{289}{289} = 1$

$= \dfrac{11}{36} + \dfrac{25}{36} = \dfrac{36}{36} = 1$

$= 0 + 1 = 1$

If we know one coordinate for a point on the unit circle and the sign of the other coordinate, we can use algebra to find the other coordinate. We substitute the coordinate we know in $x^2 + y^2 = 1$ and then solve for the other.

 EXAMPLE 13-2

Find the missing coordinate for the indicated points in Figure 13-1.

- For **A**, we know $x = \frac{1}{2}$ and that y is positive, so we solve the following for y.

$$\left(\frac{1}{2} \right)^2 + y^2 = 1$$

$$\frac{1}{4} + y^2 = 1 \qquad \text{Subtract } \frac{1}{4} \text{ from each side.}$$

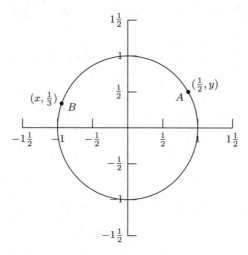

FIGURE 13-1

$$y^2 = \frac{3}{4} \qquad \text{Take the } \textit{positive} \text{ square root on the right.}$$

$$y = \sqrt{\frac{3}{4}} = \frac{\sqrt{3}}{2}$$

- For **B**, we know $y = \frac{1}{3}$ and that **x** is negative.

$$x^2 + \left(\frac{1}{3}\right)^2 = 1$$

$$x^2 + \frac{1}{9} = 1 \qquad \text{Subtract } \frac{1}{9} \text{ from each side.}$$

$$x^2 = \frac{8}{9} \qquad \text{Take the } \textit{negative} \text{ square root on the right.}$$

$$x = -\sqrt{\frac{8}{9}} = -\frac{\sqrt{8}}{3} = -\frac{2\sqrt{2}}{3}$$

Angles

Angles have two sides, the initial side and the terminal side. On the unit circle, the initial side is the positive part of the x-axis. The terminal side is the side that rotates, see Figure 13-2.

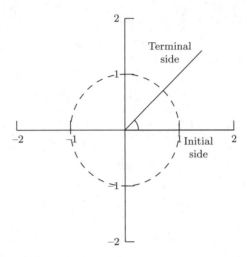

FIGURE 13-2

A positive angle rotates counterclockwise, ↶. A negative angle rotates clockwise, ↷. Angles on the unit circle are often measured in *radians*. Radian measure is based on the circumference of the unit circle, $C = 2\pi r$. The radius is 1, so $2\pi r = 2\pi$. An angle that rotates all the way around the circle is 2π radians, half-way around is π radians, one-third the way is $\frac{1}{3}(2\pi) = \frac{2\pi}{3}$ radians, and so on. The relationship 2π radians = $360°$ gives us two equations.

$$\frac{\pi}{180} \text{ radians} = 1° \quad \text{and} \quad \frac{180°}{\pi} = 1 \text{ radian}$$

These equations help us to convert radian measure to degrees and degree measure to radians. We can convert radians to degrees by multiplying the angle by $\frac{180}{\pi}$ and degrees to radians by multiplying the angle by $\frac{\pi}{180}$.

EXAMPLE 13-3

- Convert $\frac{4\pi}{5}$ radians to degree measure.

  Because we are going from radians to degrees, we multiply the angle by $\frac{180}{\pi}$.

$$\frac{4\pi}{5} \cdot \frac{180}{\pi} = 144°$$

- Convert $\frac{5\pi}{6}$ radians to degree measure.

$$\frac{5\pi}{6} \cdot \frac{180}{\pi} = 150°$$

- Convert $48°$ to radian measure.

Because we are going from degrees to radians, we multiply the angle by $\frac{\pi}{180}$.

$$48 \cdot \frac{\pi}{180} = \frac{4\pi}{15} \text{ radians}$$

- Convert $-72°$ to radian measure.

$$-72 \cdot \frac{\pi}{180} = -\frac{2\pi}{5} \text{ radians}$$

Two angles are *coterminal* if their terminal sides are the same. For example, the terminal sides of the angles $300°$ and $-60°$ are the same. See Figure 13-3.

Two angles are coterminal if their difference is a multiple of $360°$ or 2π radians. In the example above, the difference of $300°$ and $-60°$ is $300° - (-60°) = 360°$.

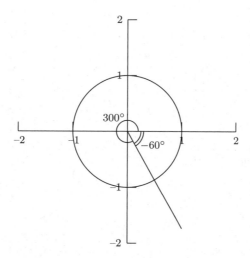

FIGURE 13-3

EXAMPLE 13-4

Determine whether or not the angles are coterminal.

- 18° and 738°

  Is the difference between 18° and 738° a multiple of 360°? $738° - 18° = 720°$, $720° = 2 \cdot 360°$; so the angles are coterminal.

- −170° and 350°

  $350° - (-170°) = 350° + 170° = 520°$ and 520° is not a multiple of 360°; so the angles are not coterminal.

- $\frac{\pi}{8}$ radians and $-\frac{7\pi}{8}$ radians

  Is the difference of $\frac{\pi}{8}$ and $-\frac{7\pi}{8}$ a multiple of 2π?

  $$\frac{\pi}{8} - \left(-\frac{7\pi}{8}\right) = \frac{8\pi}{8} = \pi \text{ radians}$$

  Because π radians is not a multiple of 2π radians, the angles are not coterminal.

Every angle, θ (the Greek letter *theta*), has a *reference angle*, $\bar{\theta}$, associated with it. The reference angle is the smallest angle between the terminal side of the angle and the *x*-axis. A reference angle is between zero and $\frac{\pi}{2}$ radians, or 0° and 90°. The reference angle for all of the angles shown in Figures 13-4 to 13-7 is $\frac{\pi}{6}$.

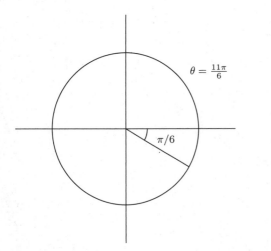

FIGURE 13-4

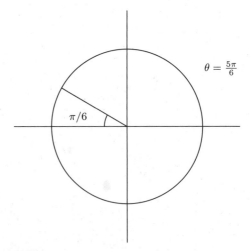

FIGURE 13-5

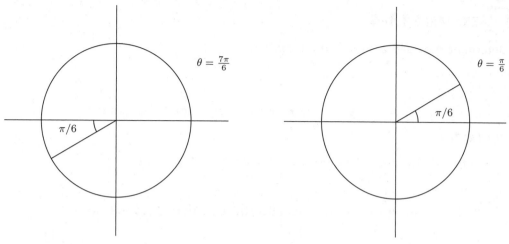

FIGURE 13-6   **FIGURE 13-7**

The *xy* plane is divided into four quadrants. The trigonometric functions of angles in the different quadrants have different signs. It is important to be familiar with the signs of the trigonometric functions in the different quadrants. One reason is that formulas have $\pm$ signs in them, and the sign of $+$ or $-$ depends on the quadrant that contains the angle. Before we find reference angles, let us become familiar with the quadrants in the *xy* plane. A summary of facts about the four quadrants is shown in Figure 13-8.

Quadrant II	Quadrant I
Angles between $\pi/2$ and π	Angles between 0 and $\pi/2$
x is negative and y is positive	x is positive and y is positive
Quadrant III	Quadrant IV
Angles between π and $3\pi/2$	Angles between $3\pi/2$ and 2π
x is negative and y is negative	x is positive and y is negative

FIGURE 13-8

EXAMPLE 13-5

Determine the quadrant that contains point.

- $(5, -3)$

  $x = 5$ is positive, and $y = -3$ is negative; the point is in Quadrant IV.

- $(4, 7)$

  Both $x = 4$ and $y = 7$ are positive; the point is in Quadrant I.

- $(-1, -6)$

  Both $x = -1$ and $y = -6$ are negative; the point is in Quadrant III.

- $(-2, 10)$

  $x = -2$ is negative and $y = 10$ is positive; the point is in Quadrant II.

Below is an outline for finding the reference angle.

1. If the angle is not between zero radians and 2π radians, find an angle between these two angles by adding or subtracting a multiple of 2π. Call this angle θ.

2. If θ is in Quadrant I, θ is its own reference angle.

3. If θ is in Quadrant II, the reference angle is $\pi - \theta$.

4. If θ is in Quadrant III, the reference angle is $\theta - \pi$.

5. If θ is in Quadrant IV, the reference angle is $2\pi - \theta$.

EXAMPLE 13-6

Find the reference angle.

- $\theta = \dfrac{9\pi}{8}$

  This angle is in Quadrant III (bigger than π but smaller than $\frac{3\pi}{2}$), so $\bar{\theta} = \frac{9\pi}{8} - \pi = \frac{\pi}{8}$.

- $\theta = \dfrac{7\pi}{3}$

  This angle is not between zero and 2π, so we need to add or subtract some multiple of 2π so that we do have an angle between zero and 2π.

The coterminal angle we need is $\frac{7\pi}{3} - 2\pi = \frac{7\pi}{3} - \frac{6\pi}{6} = \frac{\pi}{3}$; $\frac{\pi}{3}$ is its own reference angle because it is in Quadrant I, so $\bar{\theta} = \frac{\pi}{3}$.

• $\theta = \dfrac{5\pi}{7}$

This angle is in Quadrant II (between $\frac{\pi}{2}$ and π), so $\bar{\theta} = \pi - \frac{5\pi}{7} = \frac{7\pi}{7} - \frac{5\pi}{7} = \frac{2\pi}{7}$.

• $\theta = -\dfrac{2\pi}{3}$

This angle is not between zero and 2π. It is coterminal with $2\pi + (-\frac{2\pi}{3}) = \frac{6\pi}{3} - \frac{2\pi}{3} = \frac{4\pi}{3}$. The angles are in Quadrant III, so $\bar{\theta} = \frac{4\pi}{3} - \pi = \frac{4\pi}{3} - \frac{3\pi}{3} = \frac{\pi}{3}$.

Trigonometric Functions

There are six trigonometric functions, but all of them are written in terms of the main functions—sine and/or cosine. Although trigonometry was developed to solve problems involving triangles, there is a very close relationship between sine and cosine and the unit circle. Suppose an angle θ is given. The x-coordinate of the point on the unit circle for θ is cosine of the angle (written $\cos \theta$). The y-coordinate of the point is sine of the angle (written $\sin \theta$). For example, suppose the point determined by the angle θ is $(\frac{3}{5}, \frac{4}{5})$. Then $\cos \theta = \frac{3}{5}$ and $\sin \theta = \frac{4}{5}$. See Figure 13-9.

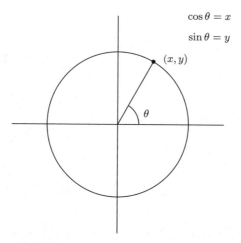

$\cos \theta = x$

$\sin \theta = y$

(x, y)

θ

FIGURE 13-9

EXAMPLE 13-7

Find $\sin \theta$ and $\cos \theta$ for the points in Figures 13-10 and 13-11.

- Because the point determined by θ is $\left(-\frac{1}{2}, \frac{\sqrt{3}}{2}\right)$, we have $\sin \theta = \frac{\sqrt{3}}{2}$ and $\cos \theta = -\frac{1}{2}$.

- Because the point determined by θ is $\left(-\frac{3}{4}, -\frac{\sqrt{7}}{4}\right)$, we have $\sin \theta = -\frac{\sqrt{7}}{4}$ and $\cos \theta = -\frac{3}{4}$.

Let us see what happens to the equation for the unit circle, $x^2 + y^2 = 1$, when we replace x with $\cos \theta$ and y with $\sin \theta$. These changes give us the equation to $\cos^2 \theta + \sin^2 \theta = 1$ [$\cos^2 \theta$ means $(\cos \theta)^2$ and $\sin^2 \theta$ means $(\sin \theta)^2$]. This important equation is called a *Pythagorean Identity*. It allows us to find $\cos \theta$ if we know $\sin \theta$ and $\sin \theta$ if we know $\cos \theta$. Solving this equation for $\cos \theta$ gives us $\cos \theta = \pm\sqrt{1 - \sin^2 \theta}$. Solving it for $\sin \theta$ gives us $\sin \theta = \pm\sqrt{1 - \cos^2 \theta}$. For example, if we know $\sin \theta = \frac{1}{2}$, we can find $\cos \theta$.

$$\cos \theta = \pm\sqrt{1 - \sin^2 \theta} = \pm\sqrt{1 - \left(\frac{1}{2}\right)^2} = \pm\sqrt{\frac{3}{4}} = \pm\frac{\sqrt{3}}{2}$$

Is $\cos \theta = \frac{\sqrt{3}}{2}$ or $-\frac{\sqrt{3}}{2}$? We cannot answer this without knowing where θ is. If we know that θ is in Quadrants I or IV, then $\cos \theta = \frac{\sqrt{3}}{2}$ because cosine is positive in Quadrants I and IV. If we know that θ is in Quadrant II or III, then $\cos \theta = -\frac{\sqrt{3}}{2}$ because cosine is negative in Quadrants II and III.

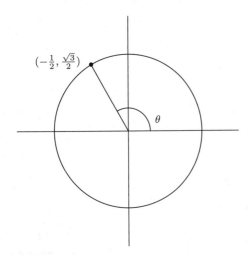

FIGURE 13-10

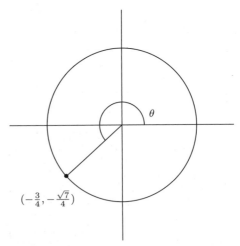

FIGURE 13-11

EXAMPLE 13-8

Find $\sin \theta$ and $\cos \theta$.

- The terminal point for θ is $\left(-\frac{12}{13}, y\right)$, and θ is in Quadrant II.

$\cos \theta = -\frac{12}{13}$

$$\text{Is } \sin \theta = \sqrt{1 - \left(-\frac{12}{13}\right)^2} \quad \text{or} \quad -\sqrt{1 - \left(-\frac{12}{13}\right)^2} \, ?$$

Because the **y**-values in Quadrant II are positive, $\sin \theta$ is positive.

$$\sin \theta = \sqrt{1 - \left(-\frac{12}{13}\right)^2} = \sqrt{\frac{25}{169}} = \frac{5}{13}$$

- The terminal point for θ is $\left(x, -\frac{1}{9}\right)$, and θ is in Quadrant III.

Both sine and cosine are negative in Quadrant III, so we take the negative square root. Using $\sin \theta = -\frac{1}{9}$, we have

$$\cos \theta = -\sqrt{1 - \left(-\frac{1}{9}\right)^2} = -\sqrt{\frac{80}{81}} = -\frac{4\sqrt{5}}{9}$$

The values for sine and cosine of the following angles should be memorized: $0, \frac{\pi}{6}, \frac{\pi}{4}, \frac{\pi}{3}$, and $\frac{\pi}{2}$. See Figure 13-12.

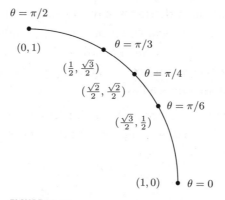

FIGURE 13-12

TABLE 13-1   Special Angles and Their Quadrants

	θ	$\cos\theta$	$\sin\theta$		θ	$\cos\theta$	$\sin\theta$
	0	1	0		π	-1	0
Quadrant I	$\frac{\pi}{6}$	$\frac{\sqrt{3}}{2}$	$\frac{1}{2}$	Quadrant III	$\pi+\frac{\pi}{6}=\frac{7\pi}{6}$	$-\frac{\sqrt{3}}{2}$	$-\frac{1}{2}$
Quadrant I	$\frac{\pi}{4}$	$\frac{\sqrt{2}}{2}$	$\frac{\sqrt{2}}{2}$	Quadrant III	$\pi+\frac{\pi}{4}=\frac{5\pi}{4}$	$-\frac{\sqrt{2}}{2}$	$-\frac{\sqrt{2}}{2}$
Quadrant I	$\frac{\pi}{3}$	$\frac{1}{2}$	$\frac{\sqrt{3}}{2}$	Quadrant III	$\pi+\frac{\pi}{3}=\frac{4\pi}{3}$	$-\frac{1}{2}$	$-\frac{\sqrt{3}}{2}$
	$\frac{\pi}{2}$	0	1		$\frac{3\pi}{2}$	0	-1
Quadrant II	$\pi-\frac{\pi}{3}=\frac{2\pi}{3}$	$-\frac{1}{2}$	$\frac{\sqrt{3}}{2}$	Quadrant IV	$2\pi-\frac{\pi}{3}=\frac{5\pi}{3}$	$\frac{1}{2}$	$-\frac{\sqrt{3}}{2}$
Quadrant II	$\pi-\frac{\pi}{4}=\frac{3\pi}{4}$	$-\frac{\sqrt{2}}{2}$	$\frac{\sqrt{2}}{2}$	Quadrant IV	$2\pi-\frac{\pi}{4}=\frac{7\pi}{4}$	$\frac{\sqrt{2}}{2}$	$-\frac{\sqrt{2}}{2}$
Quadrant II	$\pi-\frac{\pi}{6}=\frac{5\pi}{6}$	$-\frac{\sqrt{3}}{2}$	$\frac{1}{2}$	Quadrant IV	$2\pi-\frac{\pi}{6}=\frac{11\pi}{6}$	$\frac{\sqrt{3}}{2}$	$-\frac{1}{2}$

All of these angles are also reference angles in the other three quadrants. You should either memorize or be able to quickly compute them. The information is in Table 13-1.

The other trigonometric functions are tangent (tan), cotangent (cot), secant (sec), and cosecant (csc). All of them can be written as a ratio with sine, cosine, or both.

$$\tan\theta=\frac{\sin\theta}{\cos\theta}=\frac{y}{x} \qquad \cot\theta=\frac{\cos\theta}{\sin\theta}=\frac{x}{y} \qquad \sec\theta=\frac{1}{\cos\theta}=\frac{1}{x}$$

$$\csc\theta=\frac{1}{\sin\theta}=\frac{1}{y}$$

Sine and cosine can be evaluated at any angle. This is not true for the other trigonometric functions. For example, $\tan\frac{\pi}{2}=\frac{\sin\pi/2}{\cos\pi/2}$ and $\sec\frac{\pi}{2}=\frac{1}{\cos\pi/2}$ are not defined because $\cos\frac{\pi}{2}=0$. We can find all six trigonometric functions for an angle θ if we either know both coordinates of its terminal point or one coordinate and the quadrant where θ lies.

Before we begin the next set of problems, let us review a shortcut that saves some computation for $\tan\theta$. A compound fraction of the form $\frac{a/b}{c/b}$ simplifies to $\frac{a}{c}$.

$$\frac{\frac{a}{b}}{\frac{c}{b}}=\frac{a}{b}\div\frac{c}{b}=\frac{a}{b}\cdot\frac{b}{c}=\frac{a}{c}$$

EXAMPLE 13-9

- $\dfrac{\frac{1}{8}}{\frac{5}{8}} = \dfrac{1}{5}$

- $\dfrac{-\frac{2}{3}}{\frac{1}{3}} = -\dfrac{2}{1} = -2$

- $\dfrac{\frac{4}{7}}{\frac{2}{7}} = \dfrac{4}{2} = 2$

- $\dfrac{\frac{1}{9}}{-\frac{5}{9}} = -\dfrac{1}{5}$

Find all six trigonometric functions for θ.

- The terminal point for θ is $\left(\frac{24}{25}, \frac{7}{25}\right)$

$$\cos\theta = \frac{24}{25} \qquad\qquad \sin\theta = \frac{7}{25}$$

$$\sec\theta = \frac{25}{24} \qquad\qquad \csc\theta = \frac{25}{7}$$

$$\tan\theta = \frac{\frac{7}{25}}{\frac{24}{25}} = \frac{7}{24} \qquad \cot\theta = \frac{24}{7}$$

- $\theta = \dfrac{\pi}{3}$

$$\cos\theta = \frac{1}{2} \qquad\qquad \sin\theta = \frac{\sqrt{3}}{2}$$

$$\sec\theta = 2 \qquad\qquad \csc\theta = \frac{2}{\sqrt{3}} = \frac{2\sqrt{3}}{3}$$

$$\tan\theta = \frac{\frac{\sqrt{3}}{2}}{\frac{1}{2}} = \frac{\sqrt{3}}{1} = \sqrt{3} \qquad \cot\theta = \frac{1}{\sqrt{3}} = \frac{\sqrt{3}}{3}$$

- $\theta = \dfrac{5\pi}{6}$

$$\cos\theta = -\frac{\sqrt{3}}{2} \qquad\qquad \sin\theta = \frac{1}{2}$$

$$\sec\theta = -\frac{2}{\sqrt{3}} = -\frac{2\sqrt{3}}{3} \qquad\qquad \csc\theta = 2$$

$$\tan\theta = \frac{\frac{1}{2}}{-\frac{\sqrt{3}}{2}} = -\frac{1}{\sqrt{3}} = -\frac{\sqrt{3}}{3} \qquad \cot\theta = -\sqrt{3}$$

- The **x**-coordinate for θ is $\frac{2}{5}$, and θ is in Quadrant IV.

$$\cos\theta = \frac{2}{5} \qquad\qquad \sin\theta = -\sqrt{1 - \left(\frac{2}{5}\right)^2} = -\frac{\sqrt{21}}{5}$$

$$\sec\theta = \frac{5}{2} \qquad\qquad \csc\theta = -\frac{5}{\sqrt{21}} = -\frac{5\sqrt{21}}{21}$$

$$\tan\theta = \frac{-\frac{\sqrt{21}}{5}}{\frac{2}{5}} = -\frac{\sqrt{21}}{2} \qquad \cot\theta = -\frac{2}{\sqrt{21}} = -\frac{2\sqrt{21}}{21}$$

PRACTICE

1. The point $\left(-\frac{2}{5}, y\right)$ is on the unit circle, and **y** is positive. Find **y**.

2. Find the reference angle for $\frac{11\pi}{9}$.

3. Are the angles $143°$ and $-217°$ coterminal?

4. The terminal point for **t** is $\left(\frac{7}{25}, -\frac{24}{25}\right)$. Find the six trigonometric functions for **t**.

5. Evaluate $\tan\frac{\pi}{6}$.

SOLUTIONS

1. $\left(-\frac{2}{5}\right)^2 + y^2 = 1$ Substitute $-\frac{2}{5}$ for **x** in $x^2 + y^2 = 1$.

   $\frac{4}{25} + y^2 = 1$ Subtract $\frac{4}{25}$ from each side.

   $y^2 = \frac{21}{25}$ Take the positive square root.

   $y = \sqrt{\frac{21}{25}} = \frac{\sqrt{21}}{5}$

2. Subtract π to get a positive angle between 0 and $\frac{\pi}{2}$.

   $$\bar{\theta} = \frac{11\pi}{9} - \frac{9\pi}{9} = \frac{2\pi}{9}$$

3. **Yes, the difference between them is a multiple of 360°: 143° − (−217°) = 360°.**

4. $\sin t = -\dfrac{24}{25}$ $\cos t = \dfrac{7}{25}$ $\tan t = -\dfrac{24}{7}$

   $\csc t = -\dfrac{25}{24}$ $\sec t = \dfrac{25}{7}$ $\cot t = -\dfrac{7}{24}$

5. $\tan \dfrac{\pi}{6} = \dfrac{\sin \frac{\pi}{6}}{\cos \frac{\pi}{6}} = \dfrac{\frac{1}{2}}{\frac{\sqrt{3}}{2}} = \dfrac{1}{\sqrt{3}} = \dfrac{\sqrt{3}}{3}$

Graphs of Trigonometric Functions

The graph of a trigonometric function is a record of each cycle around the unit circle. Each cycle is called a *period*. For the function $f(x) = \sin x$, x is the angle and $f(x)$ is the y-coordinate of the terminal point determined by the angle x. In the function $g(x) = \cos x$, $g(x)$ is the x-coordinate of the terminal point determined by the angle x. For example, the point determined by the angle $\frac{\pi}{6}$ is $(\frac{\sqrt{3}}{2}, \frac{1}{2})$, so $f(\frac{\pi}{6}) = \sin \frac{\pi}{6} = \frac{1}{2}$ and $g(\frac{\pi}{6}) = \cos \frac{\pi}{6} = \frac{\sqrt{3}}{2}$. We now sketch the graph of $f(x) = \sin x$, using the points in Table 13-2.

The graph in Figure 13-13 is two *periods* from the entire graph. This pattern repeats itself in both directions. Each period begins and ends at every multiple

TABLE 13-2

x	$\sin x$	Plot This Point
-2π	$\sin(-2\pi) = 0$	$(-2\pi, 0)$
$-\frac{3\pi}{2}$	$\sin(-\frac{3\pi}{2}) = 1$	$(-\frac{3\pi}{2}, 1)$
$-\pi$	$\sin(-\pi) = 0$	$(-\pi, 0)$
$-\frac{\pi}{2}$	$\sin(-\frac{\pi}{2}) = -1$	$(-\frac{\pi}{2}, -1)$
0	$\sin 0 = 0$	$(0, 0)$
$\frac{\pi}{2}$	$\sin \frac{\pi}{2} = 1$	$(\frac{\pi}{2}, 1)$
π	$\sin \pi = 0$	$(\pi, 0)$
$\frac{3\pi}{2}$	$\sin \frac{3\pi}{2} = -1$	$(\frac{3\pi}{2}, -1)$
2π	$\sin 2\pi = 0$	$(2\pi, 0)$

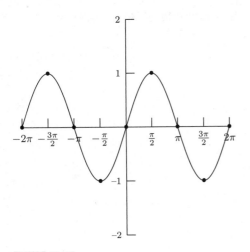

FIGURE 13-13

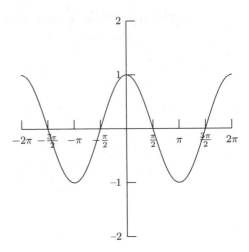

FIGURE 13-14

of 2π: ... , $(-2\pi, 0)$, $(0, 2\pi)$, $(2\pi, 4\pi)$, ... The graph between zero and 2π represents sine on the first positive cycle around the unit circle, between 2π and 4π represents the second positive cycle, and between zero and -2π represents the first negative cycle.

The graph for $g(x) = \cos x$ behaves in the same way. In fact, the graph of $g(x)$ is the graph of $f(x)$ shifted horizontally $\frac{\pi}{2}$ units. (We will see why this is true when we work with right triangles.) The graph for $g(x) = \cos x$ is shown in Figure 13-14.

From their graphs, we can tell that $f(x) = \sin x$ is an odd function $[\sin(-x) = -\sin x]$, and $g(x) = \cos x$ is even $[\cos(-x) = \cos x]$. We can also see that their domain is all x- and their range is all y-values between -1 and 1.

The graphs of $f(x) = \sin x$ and $g(x) = \cos x$ can be shifted up or down, left or right, and stretched or compressed in the same way as other graphs. The graphs of $y = c + \sin x$ and $y = c + \cos x$ are shifted up or down. The graphs of $y = a \sin x$ and $y = a \cos x$ are vertically stretched or compressed, and the graphs of $y = \sin(x - b)$ and $y = \cos(x - b)$ are shifted horizontally.

EXAMPLE 13-10

The dashed graph in Figures 13-15 to 13-18 is one period of the graph of $f(x) = \sin x$, and the solid graphs are transformations. Match the functions with their graphs.

- $y = 3 \sin\left(x + \dfrac{\pi}{3}\right)$

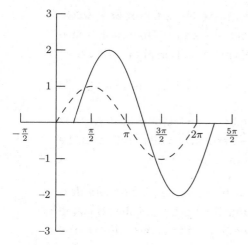

FIGURE 13-15

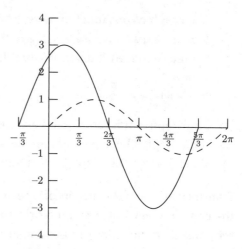

FIGURE 13-16

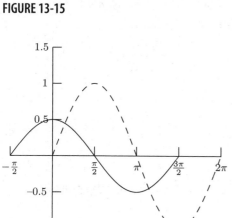

FIGURE 13-17

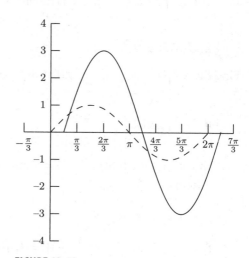

FIGURE 13-18

The graph of this function is vertically stretched by a factor of 3, so we look for a graph whose y-values are between −3 and 3. The graph is also shifted to the left $\frac{\pi}{3}$ units. The graph for this function is in Figure 13-16.

- $y = 3\sin\left(x - \dfrac{\pi}{6}\right)$

The graph of this function is also vertically stretched by a factor of three, but it is shifted to the right $\frac{\pi}{6}$ units. The graph for this function is in Figure 13-18.

- $y = \dfrac{1}{2}\sin\left(x + \dfrac{\pi}{2}\right)$

The graph of this function is vertically compressed by a factor of $\frac{1}{2}$, so we look for a graph whose *y*-values are between $-\frac{1}{2}$ and $\frac{1}{2}$. The graph is also shifted to the left $\frac{\pi}{2}$ units. The graph for this function is in Figure 13-17.

- $y = 2 \sin\left(x - \dfrac{\pi}{4}\right)$

The graph of this function is vertically stretched by a factor of 2, so we look for a graph whose *y*-values are between -2 and 2. It is also shifted to the right $\frac{\pi}{4}$ units. The graph for this function is in Figure 13-15.

Transformations of the graphs of sine and cosine have names. The *amplitude* is the degree of vertical stretching or compressing. The horizontal shift is called the *phase shift*. Horizontal stretching or compressing changes the length of the period. For functions of the form $y = a \sin[k(x - b)]$ and $y = a \cos[k(x - b)]$, $|a|$ is the graph's amplitude, *b* is its phase shift, and $\frac{2\pi}{k}$ is its period.

EXAMPLE 13-11

Find the amplitude, period, and phase shift.

- $y = \overset{a}{-4} \sin\left[\overset{k}{2}\left(x - \overset{b}{\dfrac{\pi}{3}}\right)\right]$

  The amplitude is $|a| = -4| = 4$, the period is $\frac{2\pi}{k} = \frac{2\pi}{2} = \pi$, and the phase shift is $b = \frac{\pi}{3}$.

- $y = -\cos\left(x + \dfrac{\pi}{2}\right)$

  The amplitude is $|a| = -1| = 1$, the period is $\frac{2\pi}{k} = \frac{2\pi}{1} = 2\pi$, and the phase shift is $b = -\frac{\pi}{2}$.

- $y = \dfrac{1}{2} \cos\left(2x + \dfrac{2\pi}{3}\right)$

  The amplitude is $|\frac{1}{2}| = \frac{1}{2}$. In order for us to find *k* and *b* for the period and phase shift, we need to write the function in the form $y = a \cos[k(x - b)]$. We must factor 2 from $2x + \frac{2\pi}{3}$.

  $$2x + \frac{2\pi}{3} = 2 \cdot x + 2 \cdot \frac{\pi}{3} = 2\left(x + \frac{\pi}{3}\right)$$

  The function can be written as $y = \frac{1}{2} \cos[2(x + \frac{\pi}{3})]$. The period is $\frac{2\pi}{k} = \frac{2\pi}{2} = \pi$, and the phase shift is $k = -\frac{\pi}{3}$.

Sketching the Graphs of Sine and Cosine

We can sketch one period of the graphs of sine and cosine or any of its transformations by plotting five key points. These points for $y = \sin x$ and $y = \cos x$ are $x = 0$, $\frac{\pi}{2}$, π, $\frac{3\pi}{2}$, and 2π. These points are the x-intercepts and the vertices (where $y = 1$ or -1). For the functions $y = a\sin[k(x - b)]$ and $y = a\cos[k(x - b)]$, these points are shifted to b, $b + \frac{\pi}{2k}$, $b + \frac{\pi}{k}$, $b + \frac{3\pi}{2k}$, and $b + \frac{2\pi}{k}$.

 EXAMPLE 13-12

Sketch one period of the graph for the function.

- $y = -3\cos\dfrac{1}{2}x$

   After plotting five points (computed in Table 13-3), we draw a curve through them (see Figure 13-19).

TABLE 13-3

x	$-3\cos\left(\frac{1}{2}x\right)$	Plot This Point
$b = 0$	$-3\cos\frac{1}{2}(0) = -3\cos 0 = -3$	$(0, -3)$
$b + \frac{\pi}{2k} = 0 + \frac{\pi}{2(\frac{1}{2})} = 0 + \pi = \pi$	$-3\cos\frac{1}{2}(\pi) = -3\cos\frac{\pi}{2} = 0$	$(\pi, 0)$
$b + \frac{\pi}{k} = 0 + \frac{\pi}{\frac{1}{2}} = 0 + 2\pi = 2\pi$	$-3\cos\frac{1}{2}(2\pi) = -3\cos\pi = 3$	$(2\pi, 3)$
$b + \frac{3\pi}{2k} = 0 + \frac{3\pi}{2(\frac{1}{2})} = 0 + 3\pi = 3\pi$	$-3\cos\frac{1}{2}(3\pi) = -3\cos\frac{3\pi}{2} = 0$	$(3\pi, 0)$
$b + \frac{2\pi}{k} = 0 + \frac{2\pi}{\frac{1}{2}} = 0 + 4\pi = 4\pi$	$-3\cos\frac{1}{2}(4\pi) = -3\cos 2\pi = -3$	$(4\pi, -3)$

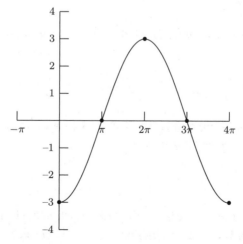

FIGURE 13-19

TABLE 13-4

x	$5\sin[3(x+\frac{\pi}{6})]$	Plot This Point
$b=-\frac{\pi}{6}$	$5\sin 3(-\frac{\pi}{6}+\frac{\pi}{6})=5\sin 0=0$	$(-\frac{\pi}{6},0)$
$b+\frac{\pi}{2k}=-\frac{\pi}{6}+\frac{\pi}{2(3)}=0$	$5\sin 3(0+\frac{\pi}{6})=5\sin\frac{\pi}{2}=5$	$(0,5)$
$b+\frac{\pi}{k}=-\frac{\pi}{6}+\frac{\pi}{3}=\frac{\pi}{6}$	$5\sin 3(\frac{\pi}{6}+\frac{\pi}{6})=5\sin\pi=0$	$(\frac{\pi}{6},0)$
$b+\frac{3\pi}{2k}=-\frac{\pi}{6}+\frac{3\pi}{2(3)}=\frac{\pi}{3}$	$5\sin 3(\frac{\pi}{3}+\frac{\pi}{6})=5\sin\frac{3\pi}{2}=-5$	$(\frac{\pi}{3},-5)$
$b+\frac{2\pi}{k}=-\frac{\pi}{6}+\frac{2\pi}{3}=\frac{\pi}{2}$	$5\sin 3(\frac{\pi}{2}+\frac{\pi}{6})=5\sin 2\pi=0$	$(\frac{\pi}{2},0)$

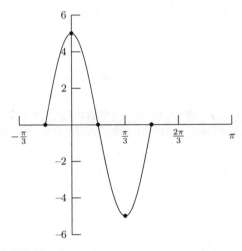

FIGURE 13-20

- $y=5\sin\left(3x+\dfrac{\pi}{2}\right)$

    We need to write the function in the form $y=a\sin[k(x-b)]$ so that we can find k and b.

$$3x+\frac{\pi}{2}=3x+\frac{3}{3}\cdot\frac{\pi}{2}=3\cdot x+3\cdot\frac{\pi}{6}=3\left(x+\frac{\pi}{6}\right)$$

    Once we compute the points (see Table 13-4), we can plot them and sketch the graph (see Figure 13-20).

PRACTICE

For Problems 1 to 3, match the function with its graph in Figures 13-21 to 13-23. The dashed graph is the graph of one period of $y=\cos x$. The solid graph is the graph of one period of a transformation.

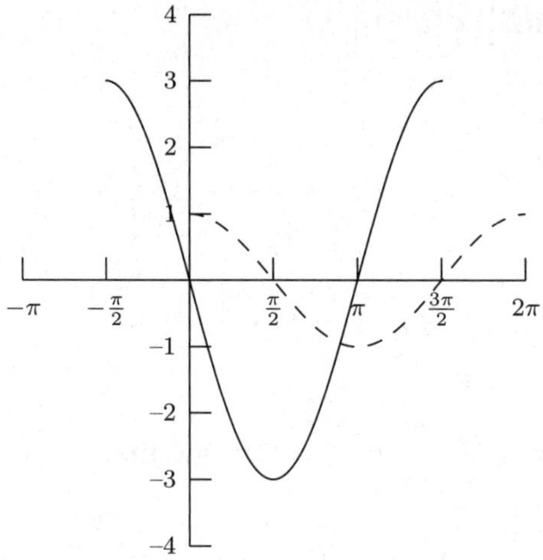

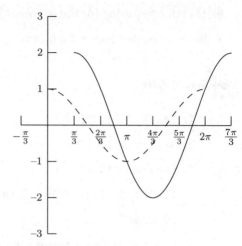

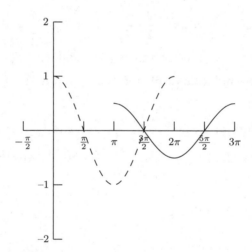

FIGURE 13-21

FIGURE 13-22

FIGURE 13-23

1. $y = 2\cos\left(x - \dfrac{\pi}{3}\right)$

2. $y = 3\cos\left(x + \dfrac{\pi}{2}\right)$

3. $y = \dfrac{1}{2}\cos(x - \pi)$

4. Find the amplitude, period, and phase shift for $y = -3\cos[\frac{2}{3}(x - \frac{\pi}{4})]$.

5. Find the amplitude, period, and phase shift for $y = 6\sin(2x - \frac{\pi}{2})$.

6. Sketch one period for the graph of $y = 3\cos[\frac{1}{2}(x + \frac{\pi}{4})]$.

7. Sketch one period for the graph of $y = -1 + 2\sin(x - \frac{\pi}{3})$.

SOLUTIONS

1. See Figure 13-22.

2. See Figure 13-21.

3. See Figure 13-23.

4. The amplitude is $|-3| = 3$, the period is $\frac{2\pi}{\frac{2}{3}} = 2\pi \cdot \frac{3}{2} = 3\pi$, and the phase shift is $b = \frac{\pi}{4}$.

5. In order to find k and b, we need to write the function in the form $y = a\sin[k(x - b)]$.

$$2x - \frac{\pi}{2} = 2x - \frac{2}{2} \cdot \frac{\pi}{2} = 2 \cdot x - 2 \cdot \frac{\pi}{4} = 2\left(x - \frac{\pi}{4}\right)$$

The function can be written as $y = 6\sin[2(x - \frac{\pi}{4})]$. Now we can see that the amplitude is $|6| = 6$, the period is $\frac{2\pi}{2} = \pi$, and the phase shift is $\frac{\pi}{4}$.

6. Plot points for $x = -\frac{\pi}{4}, \frac{3\pi}{4}, \frac{7\pi}{4}, \frac{11\pi}{4}$, and $\frac{15\pi}{4}$, see Figure 13-24.

7. Plot points for $x = \frac{\pi}{3}, \frac{5\pi}{6}, \frac{4\pi}{3}, \frac{11\pi}{6}$, and $\frac{7\pi}{3}$, see Figure 13-25.

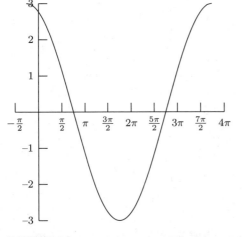

FIGURE 13-24

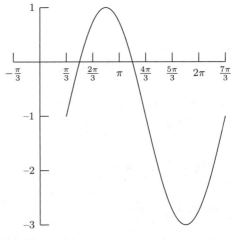

FIGURE 13-25

Graphs for Other Trigonometric Functions

Because $\csc x = \frac{1}{\sin x}$, the graph of $y = \csc x$ has a vertical asymptote everywhere $y = \sin x$ has an x-intercept (where $\sin x = 0$). Because $\sec x = \frac{1}{\cos x}$, the graph of $y = \sec x$ has a vertical asymptote everywhere $y = \cos x$ has an x-intercept. The period for $y = \csc x$ and $y = \sec x$ is 2π. The graph for $y = \csc x$ is shown in Figure 13-26, and the graph for $y = \sec x$ is shown in Figure 13-27.

The domain for $y = \csc x$ is all real numbers except for the zeros of $\sin x$, $x \neq \ldots, -2\pi, -\pi, 0, \pi, 2\pi, \ldots$. The range is $(-\infty, -1] \cup [1, \infty)$. The domain for $y = \sec x$ is all real numbers except for the zeros of $\cos x$, $x \neq \ldots, -\frac{3\pi}{2}, -\frac{\pi}{2}, \frac{\pi}{2}, \frac{3\pi}{2}, \ldots$. The range is $(-\infty, -1] \cup [1, \infty)$. Because $y = \sin x$ is an odd function, $y = \csc x$ is also an odd function. Because $y = \cos x$ is an even function, $y = \sec x$ is also an even function.

We can sketch the graphs of $y = \csc x$ and $y = \sec x$ using the graphs of $y = \sin x$ and $y = \cos x$ as guides. We sketch the vertical asymptotes as well as the graphs of $y = \sin x$ or $y = \cos x$ using dashed graphs.

The graph of $y = \sin x$ is given in Figure 13-28. We plot the vertical asymptotes for $y = \csc x$ with dashed lines at every x-intercept of $y = \sin x$.

The maximum/minimum for each piece on the graph of $y = \csc x$ is also a minimum/maximum for $y = \sin x$, see Figure 13-29.

We now plot a point to the left and right of each maximum/minimum (staying inside the vertical asymptotes) to show how fast the graph gets close to the vertical asymptotes.

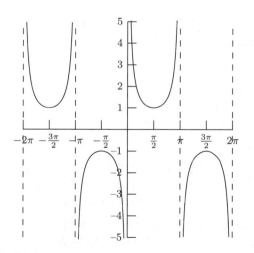

FIGURE 13-26   **FIGURE 13-27**

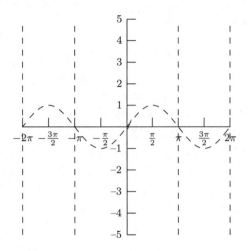

FIGURE 13-28

FIGURE 13-29

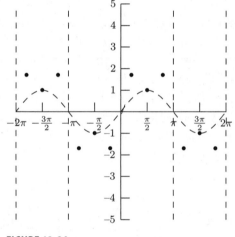

FIGURE 13-30

x	csc x
-1.8π	1.7
-1.2π	1.7
-0.8π	-1.7
-0.2π	-1.7
0.2π	1.7
0.8π	1.7
1.2π	-1.7
1.8π	-1.7

TABLE 13-5

The points are computed in Table 13-5 and plotted in Figure 13-30.

Now we can draw ∪ or ∩ through the points, staying within the asymptotes, see Figure 13-31.

These steps also work for the graph of $y = \sec x$.

The period for the functions $y = \tan x$ and $y = \cot x$ is π instead of 2π as it is with the other trigonometric functions. These graphs also have vertical asymptotes. The graph of $y = \tan x = \frac{\sin x}{\cos x}$ has a vertical asymptote at each zero of $y = \cos x$. The graph of $y = \cot x = \frac{\cos x}{\sin x}$ has a vertical asymptote at each zero of $y = \sin x$. The graph of $y = \tan x$ is in Figure 13-32, and the graph of $y = \cot x$ is in Figure 13-33.

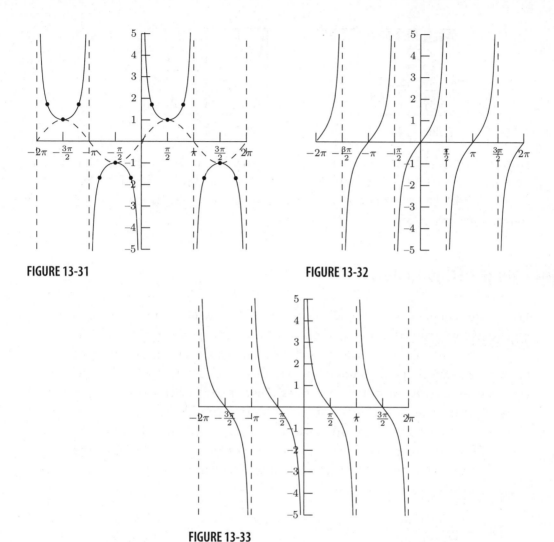

FIGURE 13-31

FIGURE 13-32

FIGURE 13-33

The domain for $y = \tan x$ is all real numbers except the zeros of $y = \cos x$, $x \neq \ldots, -\frac{3\pi}{2}, -\frac{\pi}{2}, \frac{\pi}{2}, \frac{3\pi}{2}, \ldots$. The domain for $y = \cot x$ is all real numbers except for the zeros of $y = \sin x$, $x \neq \ldots, -2\pi, -\pi, 0, \pi, 2\pi, \ldots$. The range for both $y = \tan x$ and $y = \cot x$ is all real numbers. Both are odd functions.

The transformations of these are similar to those of the other trigonometric functions. For functions of the form $y = a\csc[k(x-b)]$ and $y = a\sec[k(x-b)]$, the period is $\frac{2\pi}{k}$, and the phase shift is b. For functions of the form $y = a\tan[k(x-b)]$ and $y = a\cot[k(x-b)]$, the period is $\frac{\pi}{k}$, and the phase shift is b. The term *amplitude* only applies to the sine and cosine functions.

Many calculators have a special trigonometric window to display the graph of a trigonometric function. This window for the TI-84® is $-2\pi \leq x \leq 2\pi$

FIGURE 13-34

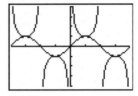

FIGURE 13-35

(with a scale of $\frac{\pi}{2}$) and $-4 \le y \le 4$ (with a scale of 1). To access this window, press the ZOOM key and cursor to "7:ZTrig" and press ENTER. (See Figure 13-34.) The graphs of $y = \sin x$ and $y = \csc x$ (entered as $y = \frac{1}{\sin x}$) are shown in Figure 13-35.

Right Triangle Trigonometry

Using trigonometry to solve triangles is one of the oldest forms of mathematics. One of its most powerful uses is to measure distances—the height of a tree or building, the distance between earth and the moon, or the dimensions of a plot of land. The trigonometric ratios below are the same as before with the unit circle; only the labels are different. We begin with right triangles.

In a right triangle, one angle measures 90° and the sum of the other angles is also 90°. The side opposite the 90° angle is the *hypotenuse*. The other sides are the *legs*. If we let θ represent one of the acute angles, then one of the legs is the side opposite θ, and the other side is adjacent to θ. The trigonometric ratios are based on the lengths of these sides (see Figure 13-36).

$$\sin \theta = \frac{\text{Opposite}}{\text{Hypotenuse}} \qquad \cos \theta = \frac{\text{Adjacent}}{\text{Hypotenuse}} \qquad \tan \theta = \frac{\text{Opposite}}{\text{Adjacent}}$$

$$\csc \theta = \frac{\text{Hypotenuse}}{\text{Opposite}} \qquad \sec \theta = \frac{\text{Hypotenuse}}{\text{Adjacent}} \qquad \cot \theta = \frac{\text{Adjacent}}{\text{Opposite}}$$

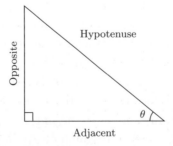

FIGURE 13-36

Using the Pythagorean Theorem, we arrive at the same Pythagorean Identity we found earlier.

$$\text{Opposite}^2 + \text{Adjacent}^2 = \text{Hypotenuse}^2 \quad \text{Divide both sides by Hypotenuse}^2.$$

$$\left(\frac{\text{Opposite}}{\text{Hypotenuse}}\right)^2 + \left(\frac{\text{Adjacent}}{\text{Hypotenuse}}\right)^2 = \left(\frac{\text{Hypotenuse}}{\text{Hypotenuse}}\right)^2$$

$$\sin^2\theta + \cos^2\theta = 1$$

From this equation, we get two other Pythagorean Identities, one from dividing both sides of the equation by $\sin^2\theta$, and the other by dividing both sides by $\cos^2\theta$.

$$\left(\frac{\sin\theta}{\sin\theta}\right)^2 + \left(\frac{\cos\theta}{\sin\theta}\right)^2 = \left(\frac{1}{\sin\theta}\right)^2, \text{ so } 1 + \cot^2\theta = \csc^2\theta$$

$$\left(\frac{\sin\theta}{\cos\theta}\right)^2 + \left(\frac{\cos\theta}{\cos\theta}\right)^2 = \left(\frac{1}{\cos\theta}\right)^2, \text{ so } \tan^2\theta + 1 = \sec^2\theta$$

EXAMPLE 13-13

• Find all six trigonometric ratios, for θ, in the triangle in Figure 13-37.

$$\sin\theta = \frac{\text{Opposite}}{\text{Hypotenuse}} = \frac{3}{5} \qquad \cos\theta = \frac{\text{Adjacent}}{\text{Hypotenuse}} = \frac{4}{5}$$

$$\tan\theta = \frac{\text{Opposite}}{\text{Adjacent}} = \frac{3}{4} \qquad \csc\theta = \frac{\text{Hypotenuse}}{\text{Opposite}} = \frac{5}{3}$$

$$\sec\theta = \frac{\text{Hypotenuse}}{\text{Adjacent}} = \frac{5}{4} \qquad \cot\theta = \frac{\text{Adjacent}}{\text{Opposite}} = \frac{4}{3}$$

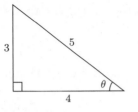

FIGURE 13-37

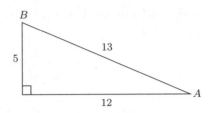

FIGURE 13-38

- Find sin *A*, cos *B*, sec *A*, csc *B*, tan *A*, and cot *B* for the triangle in Figure 13-38.

  The hypotenuse is 13, the side opposite ∠*A* is 5, so sin $A = \frac{5}{13}$. The side adjacent to ∠*B* is 5, so cos $B = \frac{5}{13}$. The other ratios are sec $A = \frac{13}{12}$, csc $B = \frac{13}{12}$, tan $A = \frac{5}{12}$, and cot $B = \frac{5}{12}$.

The side opposite ∠*A* is the side adjacent to ∠*B*, and the side adjacent to ∠*A* is opposite ∠*B*. This is why sine and cosine, secant and cosecant, and tangent and cotangent are *cofunctions*. Because ∠*A* + ∠*B* = 90°, we have ∠*B* = 90° − ∠*A*. These facts give us the following cofunction relationships.

$$\sin A = \cos B = \cos(90° − A) \qquad \cos A = \sin B = \sin(90° − A)$$

$$\tan A = \cot B = \cot(90° − A) \qquad \csc A = \sec B = \sec(90° − A)$$

$$\sec A = \csc B = \csc(90° − A) \qquad \cot A = \tan B = \tan(90° − A)$$

Because 90° = $\frac{\pi}{2}$ radians, we have another set of cofunction relationships.

$$\sin A = \cos B = \cos\left(\frac{\pi}{2} − A\right) \qquad \cos A = \sin B = \sin\left(\frac{\pi}{2} − A\right)$$

$$\tan A = \cot B = \cot\left(\frac{\pi}{2} − A\right) \qquad \csc A = \sec B = \sec\left(\frac{\pi}{2} − A\right)$$

$$\sec A = \csc B = \csc\left(\frac{\pi}{2} − A\right) \qquad \cot A = \tan B = \tan\left(\frac{\pi}{2} − A\right)$$

Solving Right Triangles

To "solve a triangle" means to find all the three angles and lengths of all the three sides. For now, we solve right triangles. Later, after covering inverse trigonometric functions, we can solve other triangles. When solving right triangles, we use the Pythagorean Theorem as well as the fact that the sum of the two acute angles is $90°$. Except for the angles $30°$, $45°$, and $60°$, we need a calculator. The calculator should be in degree mode. Also, there are probably no keys for secant, cosecant, and cotangent, so you need to use the reciprocal key, marked either $\frac{1}{x}$ or x^{-1}. The keys marked $\sin^{-1}$, $\cos^{-1}$, and $\tan^{-1}$ are used to evaluate inverse functions covered in the next section.

 EXAMPLE 13-14

- **Solve the triangle in Figure 13-39.**

  The side opposite the angle $30°$ is 3, so $\sin 30° = \frac{3}{c}$. We know that $\sin 30° = \frac{1}{2}$. This gives us an equation to solve.

  $$\frac{1}{2} = \frac{3}{c}$$

  $$c = 6$$

  We could use trigonometry to find the third side, but it is usually easier to use the Pythagorean Theorem.

  $$a^2 + 3^2 = 6^2 \qquad\qquad A = 90° - B$$

  $$a^2 = 36 - 9 = 27 \qquad\qquad = 90° - 30°$$

  $$a = \sqrt{27} = 3\sqrt{3} \qquad\qquad = 60°$$

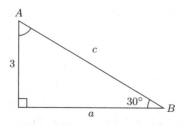

FIGURE 13-39

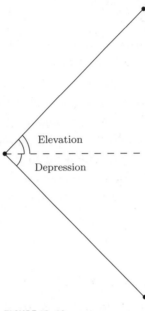

FIGURE 13-40

In some applications of right triangles, we are given the angle of *elevation* or *depression* to an object. The angle of elevation is the measure of upward rotation. The angle of depression is the measure of the downward rotation (see Figure 13-40).

EXAMPLE 13-15

- A person is standing 300 feet from the base of a five-story building. He estimates that the angle of elevation to the top of the building is 63°. Approximately how tall is the building?

We need to find *b* for the triangle in Figure 13-41.

We could use either of the ratios that use the opposite and adjacent sides, tangent (opposite/adjacent) and cotangent (adjacent/opposite). We use tangent.

$$\tan 63° = \frac{\text{Opposite}}{\text{Adjacent}} = \frac{b}{300}$$

This gives us the equation $\tan 63° = \frac{b}{300}$. When we solve for *b*, we have $b = 300 \tan 63° \approx (300)\,1.9626 \approx 588.78$. The building is about 589 feet tall.

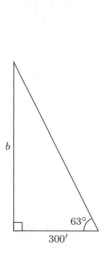

FIGURE 13-41

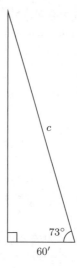

FIGURE 13-42

- A guy wire is 60 feet from the base of a tower. The angle of elevation to the top of the tower along the wire is 73°. How long is the wire?

We need to find **c** for the triangle in Figure 13-42.

We could use either cosine (adjacent/hypotenuse) or secant (hypotenuse/adjacent). Using cosine, we have $\cos 73° = \frac{60}{c}$. Solving this equation for **c** gives us $c = \frac{60}{\cos 73°} \approx \frac{60}{0.2924} \approx 205$. The wire is about 205 feet long.

PRACTICE

1. Find all six trigonometric ratios, for θ, in the triangle in Figure 13-43.

2. Solve the triangle in Figure 13-44.

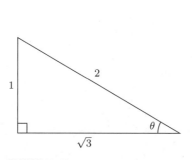

FIGURE 13-43

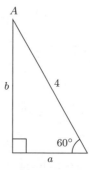

FIGURE 13-44

3. A plane is flying at an altitude of 5000 feet. The angle of elevation to the plane from a car traveling on a highway is about 38.7°. How far apart are the plane and car?

 **SOLUTIONS**

1. $\sin \theta = \dfrac{1}{2}$ $\cos \theta = \dfrac{\sqrt{3}}{2}$ $\tan \theta = \dfrac{1}{\sqrt{3}} = \dfrac{\sqrt{3}}{3}$

   $\csc \theta = 2$ $\sec \theta = \dfrac{2}{\sqrt{3}} = \dfrac{2\sqrt{3}}{3}$ $\cot \theta = \sqrt{3}$

2. We could use any of the ratios involving the hypotenuse. We use cosine: $\cos 60° = \frac{a}{4}$. Since $\cos 60° = \frac{1}{2}$, we have $\frac{1}{2} = \frac{a}{4}$. Solving for *a* gives us *a* = 2.

   $$2^2 + b^2 = 4^2 \qquad \text{Use } a = 2, c = 4 \text{ in the Pythagorean Theorem.}$$

   $$b = \sqrt{4^2 - 2^2} = \sqrt{12} = 2\sqrt{3}$$

   $$\angle A = 90° - 60° = 30°$$

3. We need to find *c* in the triangle in Figure 13-45, so we use sine.

   $$\sin 38.7° = \frac{5000}{c}$$

   $$c = \frac{5000}{\sin 38.7°} \approx \frac{5000}{0.6252} \approx 7997$$

   The plane and car are about 8000 feet apart.

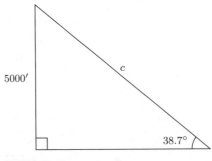

FIGURE 13-45

Inverse Trigonometric Functions

Only one-to-one functions have inverses, and the trigonometric functions are certainly not one-to-one. But we can limit their domains and force them to be one-to-one. Limiting the sine function to the interval from $x = -\frac{\pi}{2}$ to $x = \frac{\pi}{2}$ makes $f(x) = \sin x$ a one-to-one function. The graph in Figure 13-46 passes the Horizontal Line Test.

The domain of this function is $[-\frac{\pi}{2}, \frac{\pi}{2}]$, and the range is $[-1, 1]$. If we limit the cosine function to the interval from $x = 0$ to $x = \pi$, we have another one-to-one function. Its graph is shown in Figure 13-47. The domain of this function is $[0, \pi]$, and the range is $[-1, 1]$.

By limiting the tangent function from $x = -\frac{\pi}{2}$ to $x = \frac{\pi}{2}$, $f(x) = \tan x$ is one-to-one. Its domain is $(-\frac{\pi}{2}, \frac{\pi}{2})$, and its range is all real numbers. The graph of this function is in Figure 13-48.

There are two notations for inverse trigonometric functions. One uses "-1," as an exponent and the other uses the letters arc. For example, the inverse sine function is noted as $\sin^{-1}$ or arcsin. Remember that for any function $f(x)$ and its inverse $f^{-1}(x)$, $f[f^{-1}(x)] = x$ and $f^{-1}[f(x)] = x$. In other words, a function evaluated at its inverse "cancels" itself.

$$\cos^{-1}\left(\cos\frac{\pi}{3}\right) = \frac{\pi}{3} \qquad \sin\left(\sin^{-1}\frac{1}{4}\right) = \frac{1}{4}$$

$$\tan(\tan^{-1}1) = 1 \qquad \tan^{-1}\left(\tan\frac{\pi}{5}\right) = \frac{\pi}{5}$$

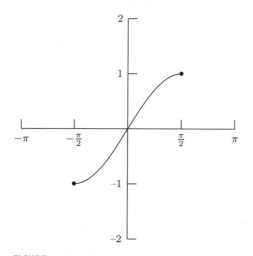

FIGURE 13-46

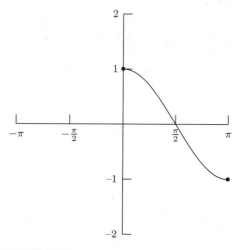

FIGURE 13-47

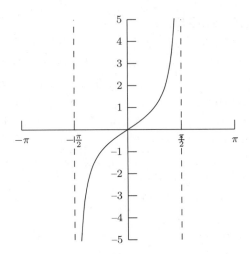

FIGURE 13-48

The x- and y-values are reversed for inverse functions. For example, if $(4, 9)$ is a point on the graph of $f(x)$, then $(9, 4)$ is a point on the graph of $f^{-1}(x)$. This means that the y-values for the inverse trigonometric functions are angles. Though we need to use a calculator to evaluate most of these functions, we can find a few of them without a calculator. For $\cos^{-1} \frac{1}{2}$, ask yourself what angle (between 0 and π) has a cosine of $\frac{1}{2}$? Because $\cos \frac{\pi}{3} = \frac{1}{2}$, $\cos^{-1} \frac{1}{2} = \frac{\pi}{3}$. When evaluating inverse trigonometric functions, we need to keep in mind what their range is. The domain of $f(x) = \sin(x)$ is $[-\frac{\pi}{2}, \frac{\pi}{2}]$ (Quadrants I and IV), so the range of $y = \sin^{-1} x$ is $[-\frac{\pi}{2}, \frac{\pi}{2}]$. The domain of $f(x) = \cos x$ is $[0, \pi]$, so the range of $y = \cos^{-1} x$ is $[0, \pi]$ (Quadrants I and II). And the domain of $f(x) = \tan x$ is $(-\frac{\pi}{2}, \frac{\pi}{2})$, so the range of $y = \tan^{-1} x$ is $(-\frac{\pi}{2}, \frac{\pi}{2})$ (Quadrants I and IV).

EXAMPLE 13-16

Evalulate the inverse trigonometric functions.

- $\sin^{-1} \dfrac{\sqrt{2}}{2}$

  Because $\sin \frac{\pi}{4} = \frac{\sqrt{2}}{2}$, $\sin^{-1} \frac{\sqrt{2}}{2} = \frac{\pi}{4}$.

- $\tan^{-1} \sqrt{3}$

  Because $\tan \frac{\pi}{3} = \sqrt{3}$, $\tan^{-1} \sqrt{3} = \frac{\pi}{3}$.

- $\cos^{-1}(-1)$

  $\cos^{-1}(-1) = \pi$ because $\cos \pi = -1$.

- $\tan^{-1}\left(\dfrac{1}{3}\right)$

  None of the important angles between $-\frac{\pi}{2}$ and $\frac{\pi}{2}$ has a tangent of $\frac{1}{3}$, so we need to use a calculator to get an approximation: $\tan^{-1}(\frac{1}{3}) \approx 0.32175$ radians.

- $\sin^{-1}\left(\cos\dfrac{\pi}{6}\right)$

  $\cos\frac{\pi}{6} = \frac{\sqrt{3}}{2}$, so we need to replace $\cos\frac{\pi}{6}$ with $\frac{\sqrt{3}}{2}$. This gives us $\sin^{-1}\frac{\sqrt{3}}{2}$. Because $\sin\frac{\pi}{3} = \frac{\sqrt{3}}{2}$, $\sin^{-1}\frac{\sqrt{3}}{2} = \frac{\pi}{3}$.

- $\cos[\tan^{-1}(-1)]$

  What angle in the interval $(-\frac{\pi}{2}, \frac{\pi}{2})$ has a tangent of -1? That would be $-\frac{\pi}{4}$, so $\tan^{-1}(-1) = -\frac{\pi}{4}$.

  $$\cos[\tan^{-1}(-1)] = \cos\left(-\frac{\pi}{4}\right) = \frac{\sqrt{2}}{2}$$

In the next set of problems, we use right triangles to find the exact value of expressions like $\cos(\sin^{-1}\frac{2}{3})$. We begin by letting $\sin^{-1}\frac{2}{3} = \theta$. We can think of $\sin^{-1}\frac{2}{3} = \theta$ as $\sin\theta = \frac{2}{3}$. This allows us to use $\frac{\text{Opposite}}{\text{Hypotenuse}}$ to represent $\frac{2}{3}$. We create a right triangle with acute angle θ, where the side opposite θ is 2, and the hypotenuse is 3. See Figure 13-49.

We want $\cos\theta$. We have the hypotenuse. We use the Pythagorean Theorem to find x: $x^2 + 2^2 = 3^2$. This gives us $x = \sqrt{5}$ and $\cos\theta = \frac{\sqrt{5}}{3}$. Now we have $\cos(\sin^{-1}\frac{2}{3}) = \cos\theta = \frac{\sqrt{5}}{3}$.

EXAMPLE 13-17

Construct a triangle to evaluate the expression.

- $\sin\left(\tan^{-1}\dfrac{4}{5}\right)$

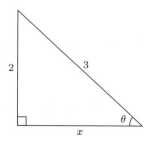

FIGURE 13-49

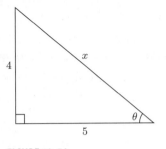

FIGURE 13-50   FIGURE 13-51

Let $\tan^{-1}\frac{4}{5} = \theta$, so $\tan\theta = \frac{4}{5}$. We want a right triangle where the side opposite to θ is 4 and the side adjacent to θ is 5, see Figure 13-50.

Solving $4^2 + 5^2 = x^2$ gives us $x = \sqrt{16 + 25} = \sqrt{41}$.

$$\sin\theta = \frac{4}{\sqrt{41}} = \frac{4\sqrt{41}}{41}, \text{ so } \sin\left(\tan^{-1}\frac{4}{5}\right) = \sin\theta = \frac{4\sqrt{41}}{41}$$

We use inverse trigonometric functions to solve right triangles when we are given one acute angle and the length of one side. We can also use them to solve right triangles when we only have the lengths of two sides.

 EXAMPLE 13-18

- Solve the triangle in Figure 13-51.

    We need to find the side opposite θ or the hypotenuse. If we want to find the side opposite θ, we can use $\tan 30° = \frac{1}{\sqrt{3}}$. If we want to find the hypotenuse, we can use $\cos 30° = \frac{\sqrt{3}}{2}$.

$$\cos 30° = \frac{5}{h} \qquad\qquad \tan 30° = \frac{y}{5}$$

$$\frac{\sqrt{3}}{2} = \frac{5}{h} \qquad\qquad \frac{1}{\sqrt{3}} = \frac{y}{5}$$

$$h = 5 \cdot \frac{2}{\sqrt{3}} = \frac{10\sqrt{3}}{3} \qquad\qquad y = \frac{5}{\sqrt{3}} = \frac{5\sqrt{3}}{3}$$

The third angle is $90° - 30° = 60°$.

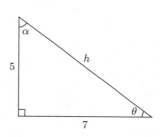

FIGURE 13-52   FIGURE 13-53

- Solve the triangle in Figure 13-52. When rounding is necessary, give your solutions accurate to one decimal place.

$$\sin 40° = \frac{y}{10} \qquad\qquad \cos 40° = \frac{x}{10}$$

$$y = 10\sin 40° \approx 6.4 \qquad x = 10\cos 40° \approx 7.7$$

The third angle is $90° - 40° = 50°$.

- Solve the triangle in Figure 13-53. When rounding is necessary, give your solutions accurate to one decimal place.

$$5^2 + 7^2 = h^2 \qquad\qquad \tan\theta = \frac{5}{7}$$

$$h = \sqrt{25 + 49} = \sqrt{74} \qquad \theta = \tan^{-1}\frac{5}{7} \approx 35.5°$$

$$\alpha \approx 90° - 35.5° \approx 54.5°$$

- A 30-foot ladder is leaning against a wall. The top of the ladder is 24 feet above the ground. What angle does the ladder make with the ground? See Figure 13-54.

$$\sin\theta = \frac{24}{30}, \text{ so } \theta = \sin^{-1}\frac{24}{30} \approx 53.1°$$

- Find x, the height of the triangle in Figure 13-55.

By viewing the triangle as two separate right triangles, the height of the triangle is the length of one of the legs of the separate triangles. We only need to use one of them. See Figure 13-56.

$$\sin 45° = \frac{x}{\sqrt{2}}, \text{ so } x = \sqrt{2}\sin 45° = \sqrt{2}\left(\frac{1}{\sqrt{2}}\right) = 1$$

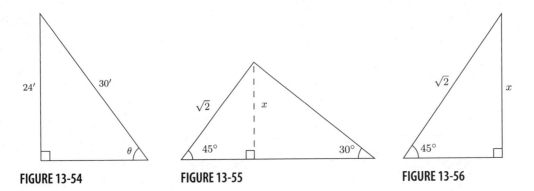

FIGURE 13-54   FIGURE 13-55   FIGURE 13-56

The Law of Sines and the Law of Cosines

We can solve other triangles using inverse trigonometric functions and the Law of Sines and/or the Law of Cosines. Although all triangles can be solved, sometimes we are given information that is true about more than one triangle or about a triangle that cannot exist. In the following problems, we use the labels in the triangles in Figures 13-57 and 13-58. The angles are A, B, and C. The sides opposite these angles are a, b, and c, respectively.

We cannot solve a triangle if all we know are the three angles because two triangles can be *similar*, that is having the same angles but different sizes. Also, we might be given an angle with the side opposite the angle and another side that makes two triangles true. For example, suppose we are told to find a triangle where $\angle A = 21°$, $a = 3$, and $b = 8$. There are *two* triangles that satisfy these conditions.

Triangle 1	Triangle 2
$\angle A = 21°$	$\angle A = 21°$
$\angle B \approx 72.9°$	$\angle B \approx 107.1°$
$\angle C \approx 86.1°$	$\angle C \approx 52°$
$a = 3$	$a = 3$
$b = 8$	$b = 8$
$c \approx 8.4$	$c \approx 6.6$

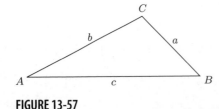

FIGURE 13-57

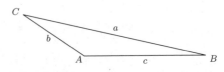

FIGURE 13-58

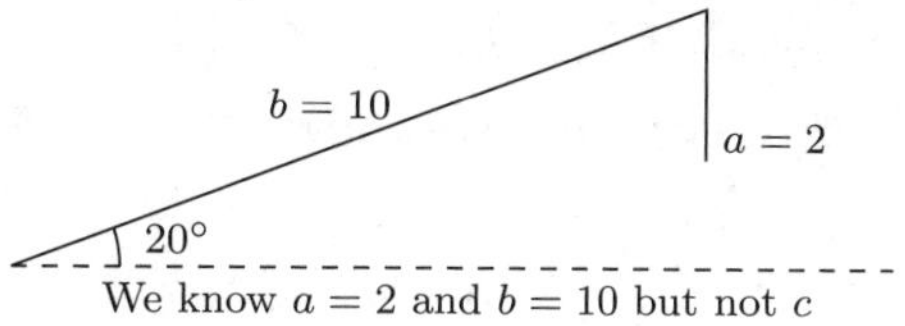

We know $a = 2$ and $b = 10$ but not c

FIGURE 13-59

There are two triangles when $b \sin A < a < b$. If we have another number in addition to A, a, and b, then there will only be one triangle.

As an example of a triangle that cannot exist, let $\angle A = 20°$, $b = 10$, and $a = 2$. As you can see in Figure 13-59, a is too short to close the triangle. This happens when $a < b \sin A$.

We can use the Law of Sines to solve a triangle if we know two sides and one of the angles opposite one of these sides or two angles and one side (if we know two angles, then we know all three because their sum is 180°). If we do not have this information, the Law of Cosines works. We can use the Law of Cosines when we have two sides and any angle or when we have all three sides.

Here is the Law of Sines.

$$\frac{\sin A}{a} = \frac{\sin B}{b} = \frac{\sin C}{c}$$

This is really three separate equations.

$$\frac{\sin A}{a} = \frac{\sin B}{b} \qquad \frac{\sin B}{b} = \frac{\sin C}{c} \qquad \frac{\sin A}{a} = \frac{\sin C}{c}$$

Here is the Law of Cosines.

$$a^2 = b^2 + c^2 - 2bc \cos A \quad \text{or} \quad b^2 = a^2 + c^2 - 2ac \cos B \quad \text{or}$$
$$c^2 = a^2 + b^2 - 2ab \cos C$$

EXAMPLE 13-19

Solve the triangle. When rounding is necessary, give your solutions accurate to one decimal place.

- $\angle A = 30°$, $\angle B = 70°$, and $a = 5$

  We use the Law of Sines because we know an angle, A, and the side opposite it, a.

  $$\frac{\sin A}{a} = \frac{\sin B}{b} \text{ becomes } \frac{\sin 30°}{5} = \frac{\sin 70°}{b}$$

  $$\frac{\sin 30°}{5} = \frac{\sin 70°}{b}$$

  $$\frac{\frac{1}{2}}{5} \approx \frac{0.9397}{b} \qquad \left(\sin 30° = \frac{1}{2}, \ \sin 70° \approx 0.9397 \right)$$

  $$b \approx 10(0.9397) \approx 9.4$$

  Now we use $\frac{\sin A}{a} = \frac{\sin C}{c}$ to find c. ($\angle C = 180° - 30° - 70° = 80°$)

  $$\frac{\sin 30°}{5} = \frac{\sin 80°}{c}$$

  $$\frac{\frac{1}{2}}{5} \approx \frac{0.9848}{c}$$

  $$c \approx 10(0.9848) \approx 9.8$$

- $a = 5$, $b = 8$, and $c = 12$

  There is not enough information to get one equation with one variable using the Law of Sines, so we use the Law of Cosines. We can begin with any angle.

  $$a^2 = b^2 + c^2 - 2bc \cos A$$

  $$5^2 = 8^2 + 12^2 - 2(8)(12) \cos A$$

  $$-183 = -192 \cos A$$

  $$\frac{61}{64} = \cos A, \text{ so } A = \cos^{-1} \frac{61}{64} \approx 17.6°$$

We can use either the Law of Sines or the Law of Cosines to find $\angle B$. The Law of Sines is a little easier.

$$\frac{\sin A}{a} = \frac{\sin B}{b}$$

$$\frac{\sin 17.6°}{5} = \frac{\sin B}{8}$$

$$\sin B = \frac{8 \sin 17.6°}{5} \approx 0.484$$

$$B \approx \sin^{-1} 0.484 \approx 28.9°$$

$$\angle C \approx 180° - 17.6° - 28.9° \approx 133.5°$$

- See Figure 13-60.

  We will call the 120° angle A, then $b = 10$ and $c = 6$. (It does not matter which side is b and which side is c, as long as we do not label either one of them a.) There is not enough information to use the Law of Sines, so we use the Law of Cosines.

$$a^2 = b^2 + c^2 - 2bc \cos A$$

$$a^2 = 10^2 + 6^2 - 2(10)(6) \cos 120°$$

$$a^2 = 136 - 120(-0.5)$$

$$a^2 = \sqrt{196}, \text{ so } a = \sqrt{196} = 14$$

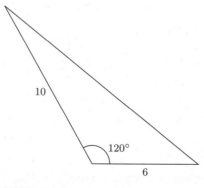

10

120°

6

FIGURE 13-60

We can use either the Law of Sines or the Law of Cosines to find $\angle B$ or $\angle C$. We use the Law of Sines to find $\angle B$.

$$\frac{\sin 120°}{14} = \frac{\sin B}{10}$$

$$\frac{\sqrt{3}}{2} \cdot \frac{10}{14} = \sin B \qquad \left(\sin 120° = \frac{\sqrt{3}}{2} \right)$$

$$B = \sin^{-1} \left(\frac{10\sqrt{3}}{28} \right) \approx \sin^{-1} 0.6186 \approx 38.2°$$

$$\angle C \approx 180° - 120° - 38.2° \approx 21.8°$$

Still Struggling

Only use the Pythagorean Theorem ($a^2 + b^2 = c^2$) on *right* triangles. This equation is not true for other triangles.

PRACTICE

When rounding is necessary, give solutions accurate to one decimal place. The angles for Problems 1 to 6 are in radians.

1. $\cos^{-1} \left(\cos \frac{\pi}{8} \right)$

2. $\tan(\tan^{-1} -1)$

3. $\cos^{-1} \frac{1}{2}$

4. $\sin^{-1} \frac{1}{2}$

5. $\tan^{-1} 0$

6. $\sin^{-1} 0.9$

7. Solve the triangle in Figure 13-61.

8. A 20-foot ladder is leaning against a wall. The base of the ladder is 4 feet from the wall. What angle is formed by the ground and the ladder?

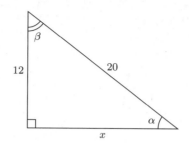

FIGURE 13-61

9. Solve the triangle: $\angle A = 42°$, $a = 11$, and $b = 6$.

10. Find all three angles for the triangle whose sides are 6, 8, and 10.

11. A plane is flying over a highway at an altitude of 6000 feet. A blue car is traveling on a highway in front of the plane and a white car is on the highway behind the plane. The angle of elevation from the blue car to the plane is 45°. If the cars are 2 miles apart, how far is the plane from each car? (Hint: Consider the triangle formed by the cars and plane as two right triangles that share a leg.)

✔ **SOLUTIONS**

1. $\frac{\pi}{8}$ radians

2. -1 radian

3. $\frac{\pi}{3}$ radians

4. $\frac{\pi}{6}$ radians

5. 0 radian

6. Approximately 1.1 radians

7. $\qquad \sin\alpha = \dfrac{12}{20} = \dfrac{3}{5} \qquad\qquad\qquad x^2 + 12^2 = 20^2$

$\qquad\qquad \alpha = \sin^{-1}\dfrac{3}{5} \approx 36.9° \qquad\qquad x^2 = 400 - 144$

$\qquad\qquad\qquad \beta \approx 90° - 36.9° \approx 53.1° \qquad\qquad x = \sqrt{256} = 16$

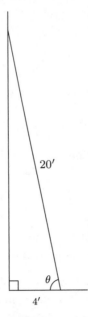

20′

θ

4′

FIGURE 13-62

8. See Figure 13-62.

$$\cos \theta = \frac{4}{20} = \frac{1}{5}$$

$$\theta = \cos^{-1} \frac{1}{5} \approx 78.5°$$

9. We use the Law of Sines twice.

$$\frac{\sin 42°}{11} = \frac{\sin B}{6}$$

$$\sin B = \frac{6}{11} \sin 42° \approx 0.365$$

$$B \approx \sin^{-1} 0.365 \approx 21.4°$$

$$C \approx 180° - 21.4° - 42° \approx 116.6°$$

$$\frac{\sin 42°}{11} = \frac{\sin 116.6°}{c}$$

$$c \approx \frac{11 \sin 116.6°}{\sin 42°} \approx 14.7$$

10. Let $a = 6$, $b = 8$, and $c = 10$. We first use the Law of Cosines to find $\angle A$. Then we use the Law of Sines to find $\angle B$.

$$a^2 = b^2 + c^2 - 2bc \cos A$$

$$6^2 = 8^2 + 10^2 - 2(8)(10) \cos A$$

$$-128 = -160 \cos A$$

$$\frac{4}{5} = \cos A$$

$$A = \cos^{-1} \frac{4}{5} \approx 36.9°$$

$$\frac{\sin 36.9°}{6} = \frac{\sin B}{8} \qquad \text{Find } B \text{ with the Law of Sines.}$$

$$\frac{8 \sin 36.9°}{6} = \sin B$$

$$B = \sin^{-1} 0.8 \approx 53.1° \qquad \left(\frac{8}{6} \sin 36.9° \approx 0.8 \right)$$

$$C \approx 180° - 36.9° - 53.1° \approx 90°$$

11. See Figure 13-63.

Let b represent the side of the original triangle that is opposite the angle 45°. Let w represent the side opposite $\angle W$, which is also the distance from the plane to the blue car. Two miles is $2(5280) = 10,560$ feet.

$$\sin 45° = \frac{6000}{w}$$

$$w = \frac{6000}{\sin 45°} = \frac{6000}{\frac{1}{\sqrt{2}}} = \sqrt{2}(6000) \approx 8485.3$$

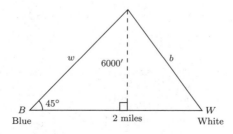

FIGURE 13-63

$$b^2 = 8485.3^2 + 10{,}560^2 - 2(8485.3)(10{,}560)\cos 45°$$

$$b^2 \approx 56{,}793{,}637.9$$

$$b \approx \sqrt{56{,}793{,}637.9} \approx 7536.2$$

The plane is about 8485 feet from the blue car and about 7536 feet from the white car.

Miscellaneous Formulas

The formulas in this section are used to find the exact value for more trigonometric ratios than the main angles—$0, \frac{\pi}{6}, \frac{\pi}{4}, \frac{\pi}{3}, \frac{\pi}{2}$. We will find angles that are half, double, or the sum or difference of these angles. We will also use the Pythagorean Identities and the Reciprocal Identities in the next section to prove identities. These formulas are also used to rewrite the functions in a form that fits a calculus formula.

1. The Pythagorean Identities

    a. $\sin^2 s + \cos^2 s = 1$

    b. $\tan^2 s + 1 = \sec^2 s$

    c. $\cot^2 s + 1 = \csc^2 s$

2. The Reciprocal Identities

    a. $\csc s = \dfrac{1}{\sin s}$ and $\sin s = \dfrac{1}{\csc s}$

    b. $\sec s = \dfrac{1}{\cos s}$ and $\cos s = \dfrac{1}{\sec s}$

    c. $\cot s = \dfrac{1}{\tan s} = \dfrac{\cos s}{\sin s}$ and $\tan s = \dfrac{1}{\cot s} = \dfrac{\sin s}{\cos s}$

3. Addition and Subtraction Formulas

    a. $\sin(s + t) = \sin s \cos t + \cos s \sin t$

    b. $\sin(s - t) = \sin s \cos t - \cos s \sin t$

    c. $\cos(s + t) = \cos s \cos t - \sin s \sin t$

    d. $\cos(s - t) = \cos s \cos t + \sin s \sin t$

e. $\tan(s+t) = \dfrac{\tan s + \tan t}{1 - \tan s \tan t}$

f. $\tan(s-t) = \dfrac{\tan s - \tan t}{1 + \tan s \tan t}$

4. **Power Reduction Formulas**

    a. $\sin^2 s = \dfrac{1 - \cos 2s}{2}$

    b. $\cos^2 s = \dfrac{1 + \cos 2s}{2}$

    c. $\tan^2 s = \dfrac{1 - \cos 2s}{1 + \cos 2s}$

5. **Half-Angle and Double-Angle Formulas**

    a. $\sin\left(\dfrac{s}{2}\right) = \pm\sqrt{\dfrac{1 - \cos s}{2}}$

    b. $\cos\left(\dfrac{s}{2}\right) = \pm\sqrt{\dfrac{1 + \cos s}{2}}$

    c. $\tan\left(\dfrac{s}{2}\right) = \dfrac{1 - \cos s}{\sin s} = \dfrac{\sin s}{1 + \cos s}$

        The sign of $+$ or $-$ depends on where the angle $\frac{s}{2}$ lies.

    d. $\sin 2s = 2 \sin s \cos s$

    e. $\cos 2s = \cos^2 s - \sin^2 s = 1 - 2\sin^2 s = 2\cos^2 s - 1$

    f. $\tan 2s = \dfrac{2 \tan s}{1 - \tan^2 s}$

6. **Product-to-Sum and Sum-to-Product Formulas**

    a. $\sin s \cos t = \dfrac{1}{2}[\sin(s+t) + \sin(s-t)]$

    b. $\cos s \sin t = \dfrac{1}{2}[\sin(s+t) - \sin(s-t)]$

    c. $\cos s \cos t = \dfrac{1}{2}[\cos(s+t) + \cos(s-t)]$

    d. $\sin s \sin t = \dfrac{1}{2}[\cos(s-t) - \cos(s+t)]$

    e. $\sin s + \sin t = 2 \sin\left(\dfrac{s+t}{2}\right)\cos\left(\dfrac{s-t}{2}\right)$

f. $\sin s - \sin t = 2\cos\left(\dfrac{s+t}{2}\right)\sin\left(\dfrac{s-t}{2}\right)$

g. $\cos s + \cos t = 2\cos\left(\dfrac{s+t}{2}\right)\cos\left(\dfrac{s-t}{2}\right)$

h. $\cos s - \cos t = -2\sin\left(\dfrac{s+t}{2}\right)\sin\left(\dfrac{s-t}{2}\right)$

EXAMPLE 13-20

Evaluate the trignometric functions.

- $\sin 75°$

  We can think of 75° as 45° + 30°. This lets us use formula 3(a).

  $$\sin(s+t) = \sin s \cos t + \cos s \sin t$$

  $$\sin 75° = \sin(45° + 30°) = \sin 30° \cos 45° + \cos 30° \sin 45°$$

  $$= \frac{1}{2}\cdot\frac{\sqrt{2}}{2} + \frac{\sqrt{3}}{2}\cdot\frac{\sqrt{2}}{2} = \frac{\sqrt{2}}{4} + \frac{\sqrt{6}}{4}$$

  $$= \frac{\sqrt{2}+\sqrt{6}}{4}$$

- $\cos 15°$

  We use formula 5(b) because $15° = \frac{30°}{2}$. We take the positive square root because 15° is in Quadrant I.

  $$\cos\frac{s}{2} = \sqrt{\frac{1+\cos s}{2}}$$

  $$\cos 15° = \cos\left(\frac{30°}{2}\right) = \sqrt{\frac{1+\cos 30°}{2}}$$

  $$= \sqrt{\frac{1+\frac{\sqrt{3}}{2}}{2}} = \sqrt{\frac{\frac{2}{2}+\frac{\sqrt{3}}{2}}{2}} = \sqrt{\frac{\frac{2+\sqrt{3}}{2}}{2}}$$

  $$= \sqrt{\frac{2+\sqrt{3}}{4}} = \frac{\sqrt{2+\sqrt{3}}}{\sqrt{4}} = \frac{\sqrt{2+\sqrt{3}}}{2}$$

- $\tan \dfrac{7\pi}{12}$

  Because $\frac{7\pi}{12} = \frac{\pi}{4} + \frac{\pi}{3}$, we can use formula 3(e).

$$\tan(s + t) = \frac{\tan s + \tan t}{1 - \tan s \tan t}$$

$$\tan \frac{7\pi}{12} = \tan\left(\frac{\pi}{4} + \frac{\pi}{3}\right) = \frac{\tan \frac{\pi}{4} + \tan \frac{\pi}{3}}{1 - \tan \frac{\pi}{4} \tan \frac{\pi}{3}} = \frac{1 + \sqrt{3}}{1 - 1(\sqrt{3})}$$

$$= \frac{1 + \sqrt{3}}{1 - \sqrt{3}} = \frac{(1 + \sqrt{3})(1 + \sqrt{3})}{(1 - \sqrt{3})(1 + \sqrt{3})}$$

$$= \frac{1 + 2\sqrt{3} + (\sqrt{3})^2}{1 - (\sqrt{3})^2}$$

$$= \frac{1 + 2\sqrt{3} + 3}{1 - 3} = \frac{4 + 2\sqrt{3}}{-2}$$

$$= -\frac{2(2 + \sqrt{3})}{2} = -(2 + \sqrt{3})$$

- If $\cos \theta = \frac{3}{5}$ and θ is in Quadrant I, find $\sin 2\theta$.

  By formula 5(d), $\sin 2\theta = 2 \sin \theta \cos \theta$. We need to find $\sin \theta$ so that we can use the formula.

$$\sin^2 \theta + \cos^2 \theta = 1$$

$$\sin^2 \theta + \left(\frac{3}{5}\right)^2 = 1$$

$$\sin \theta = \sqrt{1 - \left(\frac{3}{5}\right)^2} = \frac{4}{5}$$

$$\sin 2\theta = 2 \sin \theta \cos \theta = 2\left(\frac{4}{5}\right)\left(\frac{3}{5}\right) = \frac{24}{25}$$

- $\cos^2 \frac{\pi}{12} - \sin^2 \frac{\pi}{12}$

    The expression looks like formula 5(e), where $s = \frac{\pi}{12}$.

$$\cos^2 s - \sin^2 s = \cos 2s$$

$$\cos^2 \frac{\pi}{12} - \sin^2 \frac{\pi}{12} = \cos\left(2 \cdot \frac{\pi}{12}\right) = \cos \frac{\pi}{6} = \frac{\sqrt{3}}{2}$$

- Suppose $\cos 2\theta = \frac{1}{4}$. Find $\sin^2 \theta$.

    We will use formula 4(a).

$$\sin^2 \theta = \frac{1 - \cos 2\theta}{2} = \frac{1 - \frac{1}{4}}{2} = \frac{\frac{4}{4} - \frac{1}{4}}{2} = \frac{\frac{3}{4}}{2} = \frac{3}{4 \cdot 2} = \frac{3}{8}$$

- Write $\cos^4 x$ without squaring any trigonometric functions.

    We will use formula 4(b) twice.

$$\cos^4 x = (\cos^2 x)(\cos^2 x)$$

Pull out both $\frac{1}{2}$'s

$$= \left(\frac{1 + \cos 2x}{2}\right)\left(\frac{1 + \cos 2x}{2}\right) = \frac{1}{2}(1 + \cos 2x) \cdot \frac{1}{2}(1 + \cos 2x)$$

Multiply $\frac{1}{2} \cdot \frac{1}{2}$ Multiply

$$= \frac{1}{4}(1 + \cos 2x)(1 + \cos 2x) = \frac{1}{4}(1 + 2\cos 2x + \cos^2 2x)$$

Use the formula for $s = 2x$

$$= \frac{1}{4}\left[1 + 2\cos 2x + \left(\frac{1 + \cos 2 \cdot 2x}{2}\right)\right]$$

$$= \frac{1}{4}\left[1 + 2\cos 2x + \frac{1}{2}(1 + \cos 4x)\right]$$

- Rewrite cos 2x cos 5x as a sum or difference.

  Formula 6(c) tells us how to write the product of two cosines as a sum.

$$\cos \overset{s}{2x} \cos \overset{t}{5x} = \frac{1}{2}\left[\cos(\overset{s}{2x} + \overset{t}{5x}) + \cos(\overset{s}{2x} - \overset{t}{5x})\right]$$

$$= \frac{1}{2}[\cos(7x) + \cos(-3x)]$$

$$= \frac{1}{2}(\cos 7x + \cos 3x) \qquad \text{Because cosine is even,}$$
$$\cos 3x = \cos(-3x).$$

- Rewrite sin 3x − sin 2x as a product.
  This fits formula 6(f).

$$\sin \overset{s}{3x} - \sin \overset{t}{2x} = 2\cos \frac{\overset{s}{3x} + \overset{t}{2x}}{2} \sin \frac{\overset{s}{3x} - \overset{t}{2x}}{2} = 2\cos \frac{5x}{2} \sin \frac{x}{2}$$

 PRACTICE_____

1. Find tan 15° using the Half-Angle formula.

2. If $\sin \theta = \frac{2}{3}$ and θ is in Quadrant II, find sin 2θ.

3. Write $\sin^4 x$ using only the first powers of trigonometric functions.

4. Write cos 4x sin 6x as a sum.

 SOLUTIONS _____

1. Use formula 5(c).

$$\tan 15° = \tan\left(\frac{30°}{2}\right) = \frac{1 - \cos 30°}{\sin 30°} = \frac{1 - \frac{\sqrt{3}}{2}}{\frac{1}{2}}$$

$$= \left(1 - \frac{\sqrt{3}}{2}\right) \div \frac{1}{2}$$

$$= \left(1 - \frac{\sqrt{3}}{2}\right) \cdot 2 = 2 - \sqrt{3}$$

2. Because θ is in Quadrant II, cosine is negative.

$$\sin^2\theta + \cos^2\theta = 1$$

$$\left(\frac{2}{3}\right)^2 + \cos^2\theta = 1$$

$$\cos\theta = -\sqrt{1-\left(\frac{2}{3}\right)^2} = -\sqrt{\frac{5}{9}} = -\frac{\sqrt{5}}{3}$$

$$\sin 2\theta = 2\sin\theta\cos\theta \quad \text{Formula 5(d)}$$

$$= 2\left(\frac{2}{3}\right)\left(\frac{-\sqrt{5}}{3}\right) = -\frac{4\sqrt{5}}{9}$$

3. $\sin^4 x = (\sin^2 x)(\sin^2 x)$

$$(\sin^2 x)(\sin^2 x) = \frac{1-\cos 2x}{2}\cdot\frac{1-\cos 2x}{2} \quad \text{Formula 4(a)}$$

$$= \frac{1}{2}(1-\cos 2x)\cdot\frac{1}{2}(1-\cos 2x)$$

$$= \frac{1}{4}(1-\cos 2x)(1-\cos 2x)$$

$$= \frac{1}{4}(1-2\cos 2x+\cos^2 2x)$$

$$= \frac{1}{4}\left[1-2\cos 2x+\left(\frac{1+\cos 2\cdot 2x}{2}\right)\right] \quad \text{Formula 4(b)}$$

$$= \frac{1}{4}\left[1-2\cos 2x+\frac{1}{2}(1+\cos 4x)\right]$$

4. We use formula 6(b).

$$\cos 4x \sin 6x = \frac{1}{2}[\sin(4x + 6x) - \sin(4x - 6x)]$$

$$= \frac{1}{2}[\sin(10x) - \sin(-2x)]$$

$$= \frac{1}{2}[\sin 10x + \sin 2x] \quad \text{Sine is odd,}$$
$$\text{so } \sin(-2x) = -\sin 2x.$$

Introduction to Proving Trigonometric Identities

The previous formulas are examples of *trigonometric identities*, that is, equations that are true for every real number in the domain of the functions. Some of these are actually easy to prove. For example, we can prove the Double-Angle formula $\sin 2x = 2 \sin x \cos x$ if we assume the Addition formula $\sin(s + t) = \sin s \cos t + \cos s \sin t$. By letting $s = x$ and $t = x$, we have

$$\sin 2x = \sin(x + x) = \overbrace{\sin x \cos x + \cos x \sin x}^{\text{The Addition formula}} = 2 \sin x \cos x$$

Although you will not prove trigonometric identities in calculus, experience with these proofs will prepare you to adapt calculus formulas to fit functions that you are given. Proving trigonometric identities involves algebra skills and a knowledge of the basic trigonometric identities (especially the Pythagorean Identities and the Reciprocal Identities). Let us begin by simplifying expressions and then we will prove a few identities.

 EXAMPLE 13-21

Simplify the expression.

- $\dfrac{1 - \sin^2 \theta}{\cos \theta}$

"Simplifying a trigonometric expression" generally means to write it with as few symbols as possible, in particular, with as few trigonometric functions as possible and avoiding trigonometric functions in denominators, if feasible.

We begin by replacing $1 - \sin^2 \theta$ with $\cos^2 \theta$ (from a Pythagorean Identity). This allows us to remove $\cos \theta$ from the denominator.

$$\frac{1 - \sin^2 \theta}{\cos \theta} = \frac{\cos^2 \theta}{\cos \theta} = \frac{(\cos \theta)(\cos \theta)}{\cos \theta} = \cos \theta$$

- $\dfrac{1 - \sin^2 \theta}{1 + \sin \theta}$

The numerator of this fraction is the same as the first problem, but the denominator has a different form. Instead of using a Pythagorean Identity, we will factor $1 - \sin^2 \theta$ using the factoring formula $A^2 - B^2 = (A - B)(A + B)$. One of these factors is the denominator.

$$\frac{1 - \sin^2 \theta}{1 + \sin \theta} = \frac{(1 - \sin \theta)(1 + \sin \theta)}{1 + \sin \theta}$$

$$= \frac{1 - \sin \theta}{1} = 1 - \sin \theta$$

- $\cos \theta \tan \theta$

We write $\tan \theta$ in terms of sine and cosine, which allows us to simplify the product.

$$\cos \theta \tan \theta = \cos \theta \left(\frac{\sin \theta}{\cos \theta} \right) = \sin \theta$$

- $\dfrac{1}{1 + \cos \theta} + \dfrac{1}{1 - \cos \theta}$

We begin by adding the fractions. The LCD is $(1 + \cos \theta)(1 - \cos \theta) = 1 - \cos^2 \theta$.

$$\frac{1}{1 + \cos \theta} + \frac{1}{1 - \cos \theta} = \frac{1}{1 + \cos \theta} \cdot \frac{1 - \cos \theta}{1 - \cos \theta} + \frac{1}{1 - \cos \theta} \cdot \frac{1 + \cos \theta}{1 + \cos \theta}$$

$$= \frac{(1 - \cos \theta) + (1 + \cos \theta)}{1 - \cos^2 \theta} = \frac{2}{1 - \cos^2 \theta}$$

We can remove the trigonometric function from the denominator by using a Pythagorean Identity and a Reciprocal Identity.

$$\frac{2}{1 - \cos^2 \theta} = \frac{2}{\sin^2 \theta} = 2\left(\frac{1}{\sin^2 \theta}\right) = 2\csc^2 \theta$$

Although a trigonometric identity looks like an equation, you should not treat it like an equation. That is, do not try to move quantities across the equal sign. Begin with one side of the identity (usually the more complicated side) and use algebra and basic trigonometric identities to show that it is equal to the other side.

 EXAMPLE 13-22

Prove the identity.

- $\dfrac{\sec^2 t - 1}{\tan t} = \tan t$

  The expression $\sec^2 -1$ can be replaced by $\tan^2 t$ from a Pythagorean Identity. This substitution allows us to write the fraction in lowest terms.

  $$\frac{\sec^2 t - 1}{\tan t} = \frac{\tan^2 t}{\tan t} = \tan t \qquad \text{The identity is now proved.}$$

- $\tan x + \cot x = \sec x \csc x$

  If you do not see an obvious place to start, try writing all of the expressions on one side of the identity in terms of sine and/or cosine. This often (but not always) leads to the other side.

$$\tan x + \cot x = \frac{\sin x}{\cos x} + \frac{\cos x}{\sin x} \overset{\text{The LCD is }\cos x \sin x}{=} \frac{\sin^2 x}{\cos x \sin x} + \frac{\cos^2 x}{\sin x \cos x} \overset{\text{Add the fractions}}{=} \frac{\sin^2 x + \cos^2 x}{\cos x \sin x}$$

$$\overset{\text{Use a Pythagorean Identity}}{=} \frac{1}{\cos x \sin x} \overset{\text{Separate the fractions}}{=} \frac{1}{\cos x} \cdot \frac{1}{\sin x} \overset{\text{Reciprocal Identities}}{=} \sec x \csc x$$

- $\dfrac{\sin\theta}{\sec^2\theta - 1} = \cos\theta\cot\theta$

We begin by replacing $\sec^2\theta - 1$ with $\tan^2\theta$ (this is from a Pythagorean Identity). This reduces the number of terms in the denominator on the left side. We then rewrite the expression in terms of sine and cosine.

$$\frac{\sin\theta}{\sec^2\theta - 1} = \frac{\sin\theta}{\tan^2\theta} = \frac{\sin\theta}{\frac{\sin^2\theta}{\cos^2\theta}}$$

Simplify the fraction

$$= \sin\theta \cdot \frac{\cos^2\theta}{\sin^2\theta} = \frac{\cos^2\theta}{\sin\theta} = \frac{\cos\theta\cos\theta}{\sin\theta}$$

Separate the fractions

$$= \cos\theta \cdot \frac{\cos\theta}{\sin\theta} \quad \overset{\text{Change to } \cot\theta}{=} \cos\theta\cot\theta$$

Learning strategies for proving trigonometric identities is not easy, so you should expect some frustration.

 PRACTICE

Simplify the expression in Problems 1 to 4. Prove the identity in Problems 5 to 8.

1. $\sin x(\csc x - 1)$

2. $\dfrac{1}{1+\sin x} + \dfrac{1}{1-\sin x}$

3. $\sin t \sec t$

4. $\dfrac{\csc^2\theta - 1}{\cot\theta}$

5. $\dfrac{1-\cos t}{\sin^2 t} = \dfrac{1}{1+\cos t}$

6. $\dfrac{\cot x}{\csc x} = \cos x$

7. $(\sec t - \tan t)(\sec t + \tan t) = 1$

8. $\sin^4 x - \cos^4 x = 2\sin^2 x - 1$ [Hint: $(\sin^2 x)^2 - (\cos^2 x)^2$ and use the factor formula $A^2 - B^2 = (A - B)(A + B)$.]

SOLUTIONS

1. We begin by distributing $\sin x$ in the parentheses. We then use a Reciprocal Identity.

$$\sin x(\csc x - 1) = \sin x \csc x - \sin x = \sin x \left(\frac{1}{\sin x} \right) - \sin x$$

$$= 1 - \sin x$$

2. We add the fractions [the LCD is $(1 + \sin x)(1 - \sin x)$] and use a Pythagorean Identity and a Reciprocal Identity.

$$\frac{1}{1 + \sin x} + \frac{1}{1 - \sin x} \overset{\text{Add the fractions}}{=} \frac{(1 - \sin x) + (1 + \sin x)}{(1 + \sin x)(1 - \sin x)} \overset{\text{Simplify}}{=} \frac{2}{1 - \sin^2 x}$$

$$\overset{\text{Use a Pythagorean Identity}}{=} \frac{2}{\cos^2 x} = 2 \left(\frac{1}{\cos^2 x} \right) = 2 \sec^2 x$$

3. $\sin t \sec t = \sin t \cdot \dfrac{1}{\cos t} = \dfrac{\sin t}{\cos t} = \tan t$

4. After using a Pythagorean Identity, we can simplify the fraction.

$$\frac{\csc^2 \theta - 1}{\cot \theta} = \frac{\cot^2 \theta}{\cot \theta} = \cot \theta$$

5. We begin with a Pythagorean Identity, changing the denominator to $1 - \cos^2 t$, which factors as $(1 - \cos t)(1 + \cos t)$.

$$\frac{1 - \cos t}{\sin^2 t} \overset{\text{Use a Pythagorean Identity}}{=} \frac{1 - \cos t}{1 - \cos^2 t} \overset{\text{Factor the denominator}}{=} \frac{1 - \cos t}{(1 - \cos t)(1 + \cos t)} \overset{\text{Simplify}}{=} \frac{1}{1 + \cos t}$$

6. We begin by rewriting the expressions in terms of sine and cosine, and then we simplify the fraction.

$$\frac{\cot x}{\csc x} = \frac{\frac{\cos x}{\sin x}}{\frac{1}{\sin x}} = \frac{\cos x}{\sin x} \cdot \frac{\sin x}{1} = \cos x$$

7. After multiplying, we use a Pythagorean Identity.

$$(\sec t - \tan t)(\sec t + \tan t) = \sec^2 t - \tan^2 t$$

Use a Pythagorean Identity
$$= (\tan^2 t + 1) - \tan^2 t = 1$$

8. We begin by using the hint.

This is 1
$$\sin^4 x - \cos^4 x = (\sin^2 x - \cos^2 x)(\sin^2 x + \cos^2 x) = \sin^2 x - \cos^2 x$$

Use a Pythagorean Identity   Distribute the minus sign
$$= \sin^2 x - (1 - \sin^2 x) = \sin^2 x - 1 + \sin^2 x = 2\sin^2 x - 1$$

Summary

In this chapter, we learned how to

- *Work with the unit circle.* A point is on the unit circle if its coordinates make the equation $x^2 + y^2 = 1$ true. If we know one coordinate of a point on the unit circle but not the other, we can use the equation to help us find the missing coordinate. We would, however, need its sign.

- *Work with angles.* Radian measure is based on the circumference of the unit circle, 2π. We can use the equation $180° = \pi$ radians to convert back and before between degree measure of an angle and radian measure. Two angles are coterminal if the difference of their measures is a multiple of 2π (or $360°$). The reference angle of an angle is the smallest positive angle made between the terminal side of the angle and the x-axis.

- *Evaluate trigonometric functions from points on the unit circle.* If (x, y) is a point on the unit circle determined by angle θ, then $\cos\theta = x$, $\sin\theta = y$, $\tan\theta = \frac{y}{x}$, $\csc\theta = \frac{1}{y}$, $\sec\theta = \frac{1}{x}$, and $\cot\theta = \frac{x}{y}$. Substituting $\cos\theta$ for x and $\sin\theta$ for y changes the unit circle equation to $\sin^2\theta + \cos^2\theta = 1$, which is a Pythagorean Identity.

- *Sketch the graph of a sine function or a cosine function.* When the functions are in the form $y = a\sin[k(x - b)]$ or $y = a\cos[k(x - b)]$, the amplitude is $|a|$, the phase shift is b, and the period is $\frac{2\pi}{k}$. If we want to sketch the graph for one period of either of these functions, we plot points for $x = b$, $b + \frac{\pi}{2k}$, $b + \frac{\pi}{k}$, $b + \frac{3\pi}{2k}$, $b + \frac{2\pi}{k}$.

- *Recognize the graph of a secant, cosecant, tangent, or cotangent function.* All of these graphs have vertical asymptotes, which occur in the zeros of their denominators. The range of secant and cosecant is $(-\infty, -1] \cup [1, \infty)$ and the range of tangent and cotangent is $(-\infty, \infty)$.

- *Use trigonometry to solve right triangles.* A right triangle has three sides. The longest side is opposite the right angle and is usually denoted as c. The legs are usually denoted as a and b. The three main trigonometric ratios for an acute angle θ (an angle less than $90°$) are $\sin\theta = \frac{b}{c}$ (where b is the side opposite θ), $\cos\theta = \frac{a}{c}$ (where a is the side adjacent to θ), and $\tan\theta = \frac{b}{a}$. If we know an acute angle and one of the sides, we can "solve" the triangle, that is, find all three sides and all three angles. Using some combination of trigonometric ratios, the Pythagorean Theorem, and the fact that the sum of acute angles is $90°$, we can find the other angle and the other two sides.

- *Evaluate inverse trigonometric functions.* $\sin^{-1} x$ is the angle θ, where $\sin\theta = x$. Similarly, $\cos^{-1} x = \theta$, where $\cos\theta = x$ and $\tan^{-1} x = \theta$, where $\tan\theta = x$. If we have one of these ratios, we can construct a triangle to find the other ratios. If θ is one of the angles we know, 0, $\frac{\pi}{6}$, $\frac{\pi}{4}$, $\frac{\pi}{3}$, or $\frac{\pi}{2}$ (or similar angles in Quadrants II or IV), we can evaluate inverse trigonometric functions directly. Often we need to use a calculator, though.

- *Solve a triangle using the Law of Sines and/or the Law of Cosines.* The Law of Sines is $\frac{\sin A}{a} = \frac{\sin B}{b} = \frac{\sin C}{c}$. We can use this to solve a triangle if we know either two angles and one side or two sides and one angle opposite one of these sides. If we do not have this information, we can use the Law of Cosines, $a^2 = b^2 + c^2 - 2bc\cos A$. (In these formulas, $\angle A$ is opposite side a, and so on.)

- *Use miscellaneous trigonometric formulas to evaluate a larger family of angles.* We used the Addition/Subtraction formulas, as well as the Double-Angle and Half-Angle formulas to evaluate angles that involve the special angles (mentioned above). We also used them to rewrite expressions.

- *Prove trigonometric identities.* A trigonometric identity is an equation that is true for every real number in the domain of the expression. To prove an identity, we begin with one side of the identity, use algebra and the basic trigonometric identities (usually the Pythagorean Identities and the Reciprocal Identities) to show that it is equal to the other side.

QUIZ

When using a calculator, make sure the angle mode is correct.

1. Convert $\frac{7\pi}{8}$ radians to degree measure.

   A. $162\frac{1}{2}^{\circ}$

   B. 175°

   C. 315°

   D. $157\frac{1}{2}^{\circ}$

2. Find $\tan\theta$ if $\sin\theta = -\frac{4}{9}$ and θ is in Quadrant IV.

   A. $\frac{\sqrt{65}}{4}$

   B. $-\frac{\sqrt{65}}{4}$

   C. $-\frac{4\sqrt{65}}{65}$

   D. $\frac{4\sqrt{65}}{65}$

3. Find $\sin 2\theta$ if $\cos\theta = \frac{5}{12}$, and θ is in Quadrant I.

   A. $\frac{35}{72}$

   B. $-\frac{35}{72}$

   C. $\frac{10\sqrt{119}}{144}$

   D. $-\frac{10\sqrt{119}}{144}$

4. Find the reference angle for $-\frac{17\pi}{9}$ radians.

   A. $-\frac{\pi}{9}$

   B. $\frac{\pi}{9}$

   C. $\frac{2\pi}{9}$

   D. $-\frac{2\pi}{9}$

5. Find the phase shift for the function $f(x) = 6\cos(4x - \frac{\pi}{3})$.

   A. $\frac{\pi}{3}$

   B. $\frac{\pi}{6}$

   C. $\frac{\pi}{8}$

   D. $\frac{\pi}{12}$

6. Find the period for the function $f(x) = 6\cos(4x - \frac{\pi}{3})$.

   A. 6

   B. $\frac{\pi}{2}$

   C. 4

   D. $\frac{2}{\pi}$

7. Find $\tan(\frac{\pi}{4})$.

   A. $\frac{\sqrt{3}}{3}$

   B. $-\sqrt{3}$

   C. -1

   D. 1

8. Find $\sin[\tan^{-1}(\frac{1}{3})]$.

   A. $\frac{\sqrt{10}}{10}$

   B. $\frac{\sqrt{2}}{4}$

   C. $\frac{2\sqrt{2}}{3}$

   D. $\frac{3\sqrt{10}}{10}$

B

a

c

b

A

FIGURE 13-64

Refer to Figure 13-64 for Problems 9 and 10.

9. If $\angle A = 35°$ and $b = 8$, what is a?

   A. About 5.6   C. About 6.6

   B. About 4.6   D. About 3.6

10. If $a = 5$ and $c = 12$, what is $\angle A$?

   A. About 22.6°   C. About 65.4°

   B. About 67.4°   D. About 24.6°

11. The graph in Figure 13-65 is the graph of one period for which function?

   A. $y = 3\cos[\frac{1}{2}(x + \frac{\pi}{4})]$ C. $y = 3\cos[\frac{1}{2}(x - \frac{\pi}{4})]$

   B. $y = 2\cos[\frac{1}{3}(x + \frac{\pi}{4})]$ D. $y = 2\cos[\frac{1}{3}(x - \frac{\pi}{4})]$

12. A ladder is leaning against a wall. The base of the ladder is 2 feet from the wall. The floor and ladder form an angle of 82°. How long is the ladder?

   A. About 14.4 feet   C. About 13.2 feet

   B. About 13.6 feet   D. About 14.8 feet

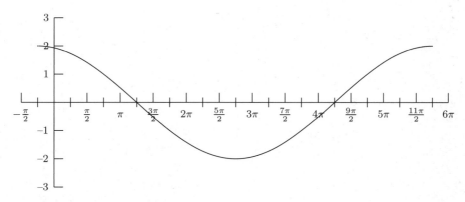

FIGURE 13-65

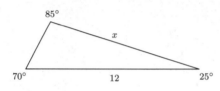

FIGURE 13-66

13. The terminal point for **t** is $\left(-\frac{8}{17}, -\frac{15}{17}\right)$. Find tan **t**.

   A. $\frac{8}{15}$

   B. $-\frac{8}{15}$

   C. $\frac{15}{8}$

   D. $-\frac{15}{8}$

14. $\cos 61° \cos 29° - \sin 61° \sin 29° = $ _____

   A. $\cos 32°$

   B. 0

   C. $\sin 32°$

   D. 1

15. Find **x** in Figure 13-66.

   A. About 11.8

   B. About 10.9

   C. About 12.7

   D. About 11.3

16. Use a Half-Angle formula to compute $\sin 22.5°$.

   A. $\frac{\sqrt{2-\sqrt{2}}}{2}$

   B. $\frac{\sqrt{2+\sqrt{2}}}{2}$

   C. $\frac{\sqrt{1+\sqrt{2}}}{2}$

   D. $\frac{\sqrt{1-\sqrt{2}}}{2}$

17. The expression $\frac{\sec^2 \theta - 1}{\sec^2 \theta}$ is NOT equal to

   A. $\frac{\tan^2 \theta}{\sec^2 \theta}$

   B. $\cos^2 \theta$

   C. $1 - \cos^2 \theta$

   D. $\sin^2 \theta$

chapter 14

Sequences

While you are not likely to see sequences in a first calculus course, you will probably work with sequences in Calculus II and in differential equations. In particular, you will work with geometric sequences and series. While the purpose of this book is to prepare you for calculus, the material at the end of the chapter will help you in your financial life. Some financial formulas are based on a combination of the formula for the sum of the first n terms of a geometric sequence as well as formulas we learned in Chapter 9. Understanding how to use the loan payment formula will help you make informed decisions when you decide to borrow money.

CHAPTER OBJECTIVES

In this chapter, you will

- Compute the nth term of a sequence
- Represent terms in a sequence with a formula
- Compute partial sums of a sequence
- Work with arithmetic sequences and geometric sequences
- See how some financial formulas are based on geometric sequences

The *n*th Term of a Sequence

A *sequence* is an ordered list of numbers. Although listing the same numbers, the sequence 1, 2, 3, 4, 5, 6 ... is different from the sequence 2, 1, 4, 3, 6, 5, ... Usually a sequence is infinite. This means that there is no last term in the sequence. A *series* is the sum of the terms in a sequence (if the sum exists). Although a sequence can be any list of numbers, we will work with sequences that can be found from a formula. Formulas describe how to compute the *n*th term, a_n. For example, the formula $a_n = 2n + 1$ gives us this sequence.

$$3, \quad 5, \quad 7, \quad 9, \quad \ldots$$
$$\underset{2(1)+1}{} \quad \underset{2(2)+1}{} \quad \underset{2(3)+1}{} \quad \underset{2(4)+1}{}$$

EXAMPLE 14-1

Find the first four terms and the 50th term of the sequence.

- $a_n = n^2 - 10$

  The first term is $a_1 = 1^2 - 10 = -9$; the second term is $a_2 = 2^2 - 10 = -6$; the third term is $a_3 = 3^2 - 10 = -1$; the fourth term is $a_4 = 4^2 - 10 = 6$; and the 50th term is $a_{50} = 50^2 - 10 = 2490$.

-  $a_n = \dfrac{n-1}{n+1}$

$$a_1 = \frac{1-1}{1+1} = 0 \qquad a_2 = \frac{2-1}{2+1} = \frac{1}{3} \qquad a_3 = \frac{3-1}{3+1} = \frac{1}{2}$$

$$a_4 = \frac{4-1}{4+1} = \frac{3}{5} \qquad a_{50} = \frac{50-1}{50+1} = \frac{49}{51}$$

- $a_n = (-1)^n$

$$a_1 = (-1)^1 = -1 \qquad a_2 = (-1)^2 = 1 \qquad a_3 = (-1)^3 = -1$$

$$a_4 = (-1)^4 = 1 \qquad a_{50} = (-1)^{50} = 1$$

You might have noticed that finding terms in a sequence is much like evaluating functions, which we learned in Chapter 2. In fact, sequences are special kinds of functions whose domain is the natural numbers (instead of intervals of real numbers).

We can write a formula for some sequences that involves one or more previous terms. For example, the next term of the sequence 3, 5, 7, 9, . . . can be found by adding 2 to the previous term. In other words, we could use the formula $a_n = a_{n-1} + 2$ to find terms for this sequence. This is an example of a *recursive* formula. A recursive formula is not of much use unless we know how to start. For this reason, the value of a_1 is usually given with recursively defined sequences. A complete recursive definition for this sequence is $a_n = a_{n-1} + 2, a_1 = 3$. Now we can compute the terms of the sequence with this formula.

$$3, \quad 5, \quad 7, \quad 9, \quad \ldots$$
$$\quad 3+2 \quad 5+2 \quad 7+2$$

 EXAMPLE 14-2

Find the first four terms of the sequence.

- $a_n = 3a_{n-1} + 5, \ a_1 = -4$

  Think of $3a_{n-1} + 5$ as "three times the previous term plus 5."

  $$a_1 = -4 \qquad\qquad a_2 = 3(-4) + 5 = -7$$
  $$a_3 = 3(-7) + 5 = -16 \qquad a_4 = 3(-16) + 5 = -43$$

- $a_n = \dfrac{a_{n-1}}{a_{n-2}}, \ a_1 = 2, \ a_2 = 4$

  Terms of this sequence are found by taking the quotient of the previous two terms.

  $$a_1 = 2 \qquad a_2 = 4 \qquad a_3 = \frac{a_{3-1}}{a_{3-2}} = \frac{a_2}{a_1} = \frac{4}{2} = 2 \qquad a_4 = \frac{a_3}{a_2} = \frac{2}{4} = \frac{1}{2}$$

A famous recursively defined sequence is the Fibonacci sequence. Entire books are written about it! The nth term of the Fibonacci sequence is $a_n = a_{n-1} + a_{n-2}$ and $a_1 = 1$ and $a_2 = 1$. From the third term on, each term is the sum of the previous two terms. The first few terms are 1, 1, 2, 3, 5, 8, 13, ...

Instead of using a formula to describe a sequence, we might be given the first few terms. From these terms we should be able to see enough of a pattern to write a formula for the nth term.

EXAMPLE 14-3

Find the next term in the sequence.

- 2, 6, 18, 54 . . .

  Because each term (after the first) is three times the previous term, the next term is $3(54) = 162$.

- $1, \dfrac{1}{2}, \dfrac{1}{3}, \dfrac{1}{4}, \ldots$

  The next term is $\dfrac{1}{5}$.

- $1, -2, 4, -8, 16, \ldots$

  The next term is $-2(16) = -32$.

  Find a formula for the nth term for the next four problems. Do not use a recursive definition.

- $3, 9, 27, 81, \ldots$

  $3 = 3^1, \ 9 = 3^2, \ 27 = 3^3, \ 81 = 3^4$

  The nth term is $a_n = 3^n$.

- $-2, \ -4, \ -6, \ -8, \ -10, \ldots$

  $-2 = -2(1), \ -4 = -2(2), \ -6 = -2(3), \ -8 = -2(4), \ -10 = -2(5)$

  The nth term is $a_n = -2n$.

- $-1, \ 4, \ -9, 16, \ -25, \ldots$

  $-1 = -1^2, \ 4 = 2^2, \ -9 = -3^2, \ 16 = 4^2, \ -25 = -5^2$

  If we want the signs to alternate, we can use the factor $(-1)^n$ (if we want the odd-numbered terms to be negative) or $(-1)^{n+1}$ (if we want the even-numbered terms to be negative). The nth term of this sequence is $a_n = (-1)^n n^2$.

- $\dfrac{1}{2}, \ \dfrac{2}{3}, \ \dfrac{3}{4}, \ \dfrac{4}{5}, \ldots$

$$\frac{1}{2} = \frac{1}{1+1}, \ \frac{2}{3} = \frac{2}{2+1}, \ \frac{3}{4} = \frac{3}{3+1}, \ \frac{4}{5} = \frac{4}{4+1}$$

The nth term is $a_n = \dfrac{n}{n+1}$.

Partial Sums for a Sequence

There are times when we want to add the first n terms of a sequence. The sum $a_1 + a_2 + a_3 + \cdots + a_n$ is called the nth partial sum of the sequence. Its notation is S_n.

$$S_1 = a_1 \qquad\qquad S_2 = a_1 + a_2$$

$$S_3 = a_1 + a_2 + a_3 \qquad S_4 = a_1 + a_2 + a_3 + a_4$$

Another common notation for the nth partial sum uses the capital Greek letter sigma, "Σ." This notation also makes use of a_n or a formula for a_n. "$\sum_{n=1}^{5} a_n$" means "add each a_n beginning with a_1 and ending with a_5.

$$\sum_{n=1}^{5} a_n = a_1 + a_2 + a_3 + a_4 + a_5$$

The subscript n is called the *index of summation*. Other common indices are i, j, and k.

 EXAMPLE 14-4

Write the sum.

• $\displaystyle\sum_{n=1}^{6} \frac{n^2}{4}$

$$\underset{\frac{1^2}{4}}{\tfrac{1}{4}} + \underset{\frac{2^2}{4}}{1} + \underset{\frac{3^2}{4}}{\tfrac{9}{4}} + \underset{\frac{4^2}{4}}{4} + \underset{\frac{5^2}{4}}{\tfrac{25}{4}} + \underset{\frac{6^2}{4}}{9}$$

• $\displaystyle\sum_{n=1}^{5} (-1)^{n+1}(3n-4)$

$$\underset{(-1)^{1+1}(3\cdot 1-4)}{-1} \;-\; \underset{(-1)^{2+1}(3\cdot 2-4)}{2} \;+\; \underset{(-1)^{3+1}(3\cdot 3-4)}{5} \;-\; \underset{(-1)^{4+1}(3\cdot 4-4)}{8} \;+\; \underset{(-1)^{5+1}(3\cdot 5-4)}{11}$$

Write the sum using summation notation.

• $1 + \dfrac{1}{2} + \dfrac{1}{3} + \dfrac{1}{4} + \cdots + \dfrac{1}{20}$

This is the sum of the first 20 terms in a sequence, so we begin by writing "$\sum_{n=1}^{20}$." The nth term of the sequence is $a_n = \frac{1}{n}$, and the summation notation for this sum is $\sum_{n=1}^{20} \frac{1}{n}$.

- $2 + 4 + 6 + 8 + 10 + 12$

This is the sum of the first six terms of the sequence whose nth term is $a_n = 2n$. The summation notation is $\sum_{n=1}^{6} 2n$.

- $\dfrac{1}{2} - \dfrac{1}{4} + \dfrac{1}{6} - \dfrac{1}{8} + \dfrac{1}{10} - \cdots + \dfrac{1}{18}$

This is the sum of the first nine terms of the sequence whose nth term is $a_n = (-1)^{n+1} \frac{1}{2n}$. The summation notation is $\sum_{n=1}^{9} (-1)^{n+1} \frac{1}{2n}$.

There are formulas for finding the nth partial sum for special sequences. Using these formulas, we can add many terms of a sequence with little work. We will learn the formulas for the sums of the first n terms for two important sequences, *arithmetic sequences* and *geometric sequences*, later.

 PRACTICE

1. Find the first four terms and the 100th term of the sequence whose nth term is $a_n = \frac{2n-1}{n+1}$.

2. Find the first four terms and the 100th term of the sequence whose nth term is $a_n = (-1)^{n+1} \frac{n^2}{2}$.

3. Find the first four terms of the sequence whose nth term is $a_n = \sqrt{a_{n-1}}$ and $a_1 = 256$.

4. Without using a recursive definition, find the nth term for the sequence
$$10, \ 5, \ \frac{5}{2}, \ \frac{5}{4}, \ \frac{5}{8}, \ \frac{5}{16}, \dots.$$

5. Without using a recursive definition, find the nth term for the sequence
$$\frac{0}{3}, \ \frac{1}{4}, \ \frac{2}{5}, \ \frac{3}{6}, \ \frac{4}{7}, \dots.$$

6. Write the sum for $\sum_{n=1}^{6} \frac{5}{2n}$.

7. Write the sum using summation notation.
$$\frac{1}{3} - \frac{1}{9} + \frac{1}{27} - \frac{1}{81} + \frac{1}{243}$$

✔ SOLUTIONS

1. $$a_1 = \frac{2(1) - 1}{1 + 1} = \frac{1}{2} \qquad a_2 = \frac{2(2) - 1}{2 + 1} = 1$$

$$a_3 = \frac{2(3) - 1}{3 + 1} = \frac{5}{4} \qquad a_4 = \frac{2(4) - 1}{4 + 1} = \frac{7}{5}$$

$$a_{100} = \frac{2(100) - 1}{100 + 1} = \frac{199}{101}$$

2. $$a_1 = (-1)^{1+1} \frac{1^2}{2} = \frac{1}{2} \qquad a_2 = (-1)^{2+1} \frac{2^2}{2} = -2$$

$$a_3 = (-1)^{3+1} \frac{3^2}{2} = \frac{9}{2} \qquad a_4 = (-1)^{4+1} \frac{4^2}{2} = -8$$

$$a_{100} = (-1)^{100+1} \frac{100^2}{2} = -5000$$

3. $$a_1 = 256 \qquad a_2 = \sqrt{256} = 16$$

$$a_3 = \sqrt{16} = 4 \qquad a_4 = \sqrt{4} = 2$$

4. $a_n = 20 \left(\dfrac{1}{2}\right)^n$ or $a_n = 10 \left(\dfrac{1}{2}\right)^{n-1}$

5. $a_n = \dfrac{n - 1}{n + 2}$

6. $\dfrac{5}{2} + \dfrac{5}{4} + \dfrac{5}{6} + \dfrac{5}{8} + \dfrac{5}{10} + \dfrac{5}{12}$

7. $\displaystyle\sum_{n=1}^{5} (-1)^{n+1} \left(\dfrac{1}{3}\right)^n$ or $\displaystyle\sum_{n=1}^{5} (-1)^{n+1} \dfrac{1}{3^n}$

Arithmetic Sequences

A term in an arithmetic sequence is computed by adding a fixed number to the previous term. This fixed number is called the *common difference*. For example, 3, 7, 11, 15, 19, ... is an arithmetic sequence because we can add 4 to any term to find the following term. We can define the *n*th term recursively as

$a_n = a_{n-1} + d$ or, in more general terms, $a_n = a_1 + (n-1)d$. In the sequence above, $a_1 = 3$ and $d = 4$.

 **EXAMPLE 14-5**

Find the first four terms and the 100th term.

- $a_n = 28 + (n-1)1.5$

  $a_1 = 28$ $a_2 = 28 + (2-1)1.5 = 29.5$ $a_3 = 28 + (3-1)1.5 = 31$

  $a_4 = 28 + (4-1)1.5 = 32.5$ $a_{100} = 28 + (100-1)1.5 = 176.5$

- $a_n = -2 + (n-1)(-6)$

  $a_1 = -2$ $a_2 = -2 + (2-1)(-6) = -8$

  $a_3 = -2 + (3-1)(-6) = -14$ $a_4 = -2 + (4-1)(-6) = -20$

  $a_{100} = -2 + (100-1)(-6) = -596$

When asked whether or not a sequence is arithmetic, we subtract each term from the term that follows it. If the difference is the same, the sequence is arithmetic.

EXAMPLE 14-6

Determine if the sequence is arithmetic. If it is, find the common difference.

- $-8,\ -1,\ 6,\ 13,\ 20, \ldots$

  $20 - 13 = 7,\ 13 - 6 = 7,\ 6 - (-1) = 7,\ -1 - (-8) = 7$

  The sequence is arithmetic. The common difference is 7.

- $29,\ 17,\ 5,\ -7,\ -19, \ldots$

  $-19 - (-7) = -12,\ -7 - 5 = -12,\ 5 - 17 = -12,\ 17 - 29 = -12$

  The sequence is arithmetic, and the common difference is -12.

- $\dfrac{5}{3},\ \dfrac{5}{6},\ \dfrac{5}{12},\ \dfrac{5}{24}, \ldots$

  $\dfrac{5}{24} - \dfrac{5}{12} = -\dfrac{5}{24},\ \dfrac{5}{12} - \dfrac{5}{6} = -\dfrac{5}{12}$

  Because the differences are not the same, the sequence is not arithmetic.

We can find any term in an arithmetic sequence if we know either one term and the common difference or two terms. We need to use the formula

$a_n = a_1 + (n-1)d$ and, if necessary, a little algebra. For example, if we are told the common difference is 6 and the 10th term is 141, then we can put $a_n = 141$, $n = 10$, and $d = 6$ in the formula to find a_1.

$$141 = a_1 + (10-1)6$$

$$87 = a_1$$

The nth term is $a_n = 87 + (n-1)6$.

 EXAMPLE 14-7

Find the nth term for the arithmetic sequence.

- The common difference is $\frac{2}{3}$ and the seventh term is -10.

  Using $d = \frac{2}{3}$, $n = 7$, and $a_n = -10$, the formula $a_n = a_1 + (n-1)d$ becomes $-10 = a_1 + (7-1)\frac{2}{3}$. We solve this for a_1.

  $$-10 = a_1 + (7-1)\frac{2}{3}$$

  $$-10 = a_1 + 4$$

  $$-14 = a_1$$

  The nth term is $a_n = -14 + (n-1)\frac{2}{3}$.

- The 12th term is 8, and the 20th term is 32.

  The information gives us a system of two equations with two variables. In this example and the rest of the problems in this section, we will add -1 times the first equation to the second. Substitution and matrices would work, too. The equations are $8 = a_1 + (12-1)d$ and $32 = a_1 + (20-1)d$.

  $$-a_1 - 11d = -8$$

  $$\underline{a_1 + 19d = 32}$$

  $$8d = 24$$

  $$d = 3$$

  $$a_1 + 11(3) = 8 \qquad \text{Let } d = 3 \text{ in } a_1 + 11d = 8$$

  $$a_1 = -25$$

  The nth term is $a_n = -25 + (n-1)3$.

- The eighth term is 4, and the 20th term is -38.

  The information in these two terms gives us the system of equations $4 = a_1 + (8 - 1)d$ and $-38 = a_1 + (20 - 1)d$.

$$-a_1 - 7d = -4$$

$$a_1 + 19d = -38$$

$$12d = -42$$

$$d = -\frac{7}{2}$$

$$a_1 + 7\left(-\frac{7}{2}\right) = 4 \qquad \text{Let } d = -\frac{7}{2} \text{ in } a_1 + 7d = 4$$

$$a_1 = \frac{57}{2}$$

The nth term is $a_1 = \frac{57}{2} + (n-1)\left(-\frac{7}{2}\right)$.

We can add the first n terms of an arithmetic sequence using one of two formulas. If $a_n = a_1 + (n-1)d$, then

$$S_n = \frac{n}{2}(a_1 + a_n) \quad \text{or} \quad S_n = \frac{n}{2}[2a_1 + (n-1)d]$$

We use the first formula if we know all of a_1, a_n, and n, and the second when we do not know a_n.

◻ EXAMPLE 14-8

- Find the sum.

$$2 + \frac{13}{5} + \frac{16}{5} + \frac{19}{5} + \frac{22}{5} + 5$$

$a_1 = 2$, $a_6 = 5$, and $n = 6$ (because there are six terms)

$$2 + \frac{13}{5} + \frac{16}{5} + \frac{19}{5} + \frac{22}{5} + 5 = \frac{6}{2}(2 + 5) = 21$$

- Find the sum of the first 20 terms of the sequence $-5,\ -1,\ 3,\ 7,\ 11,\ldots$.
  $a_1 = -5,\ d = 4$, and $n = 20$.

$$S_{20} = \frac{20}{2}[2(-5) + (20 - 1)4] = 660$$

- $6 + (-2) + (-10) + (-18) + \cdots + (-58)$

We know $a_1 = 6,\ d = -8$, and $a_n = -58$ but not n. We can find n by solving $-58 = 6 + (n - 1)(-8)$.

$$-58 = 6 + (n - 1)(-8)$$
$$-64 = -8(n - 1)$$
$$8 = n - 1$$
$$9 = n$$

$$6 + (-2) + (-10) + (-18) + \cdots + (-58) = \frac{9}{2}[6 + (-58)] = -234$$

PRACTICE

1. Find the first four terms and the 40th term of the arithmetic sequence whose nth term is $a_n = 14 + (n - 1)4$.

2. Determine if the sequence $0.03, 0.33, 0.63, 0.93, \ldots$ is arithmetic.

3. Determine if the sequence $0.4, 0.04, 0.004, 0.0004, \ldots$ is arithmetic.

4. Find the nth term of the arithmetic sequence whose first term is 16 and ninth term is 54.

5. Find the nth term of the arithmetic sequence whose sixth term is 12 and 10th term is 36.

6. Compute the sum.

$$-8 + \left(-\frac{35}{4}\right) + \left(-\frac{38}{4}\right) + \left(-\frac{41}{4}\right) + (-11) + \left(-\frac{47}{4}\right)$$

7. Compute the sum. $10 + 17 + 24 + 31 + \cdots + 108$

✔ SOLUTIONS

1. $a_1 = 14$, $a_2 = 14 + (2 - 1)4 = 18$, $a_3 = 14 + (3 - 1)4 = 22$, $a_4 = 14 + (4 - 1)4 = 26$, and $a_{40} = 14 + (40 - 1)4 = 170$.

2. $0.93 - 0.63 = 0.3$, $0.63 - 0.33 = 0.3$, $0.33 - 0.03 = 0.3$
The differences are the same, so the sequence is arithmetic.

3. $-0.0004 - 0.004 = -0.0036$, $0.004 - 0.04 = -0.036$
The differences are not the same, so the sequence is not arithmetic.

4. Because $a_1 = 16$, we have $a_n = 16 + (n - 1)d$. Using $a_9 = 54$ in this formula, we have $54 = 16 + (9 - 1)d$. Solving this equation for d gives us $d = \frac{19}{4}$. The nth term is $a_n = 16 + (n - 1)\frac{9}{4}$.

5. From the information in the problem, we have the system $12 = a_1 + (6 - 1)d$ and $36 = a_1 + (10 - 1)d$.

$$-a_1 - 5d = -12$$
$$\underline{a_1 + 9d = 36}$$
$$4d = 24$$
$$d = 6$$
$$a_1 + 5(6) = 12 \qquad \text{Let } d = 6 \text{ in } a_1 + 5d = 12$$
$$a_1 = -18$$

The nth term is $a_n = -18 + (n - 1)6$.

6. $a_1 = -8$, $a_6 = -\frac{47}{4}$, and $n = 6$. $S_n = \frac{n}{2}(a_1 + a_n)$ becomes $S_6 = \frac{6}{2}[-8 + (-\frac{47}{4})] = -\frac{237}{4}$.

7. $a_1 = 10$, $d = 7$, and $a_n = 108$. We can find n by solving $108 = 10 + (n - 1)7$. This gives us $n = 15$. $S_{15} = \frac{15}{2}(10 + 108) = 885$.

Geometric Sequences

In an arithmetic sequence, the difference between any consecutive terms is the same, and in a geometric sequence, the *quotient* of any consecutive terms is the same. A term in a geometric sequence can be found by multiplying the previous term by a fixed number. For example, the next term in the sequence 1, 2, 4, 8,

16, ... is $2(16) = 32$, and the term after that is $2(32) = 64$. This fixed number is called the *common ratio*. We can define the nth term of a geometric sequence recursively as $a_n = ra_{n-1}$. The general formula is $a_n = a_1 r^{n-1}$.

EXAMPLE 14-9

- Determine if the sequence 5, 15, 45, 135, 405, ... is geometric.

  We need to see if the ratio of each consecutive pair of numbers is the same.

  $\frac{405}{135} = 3$, $\frac{135}{45} = 3$, $\frac{45}{15} = 3$, and $\frac{15}{5} = 3$

  The ratio is the same number, so the sequence is geometric.

- Determine if the sequence -8, 4, -2, 1, $-\frac{1}{2}$, ... is geometric.

  $\frac{-1/2}{1} = -\frac{1}{2}$, $\frac{1}{-2} = -\frac{1}{2}$, $\frac{-2}{4} = -\frac{1}{2}$, and $\frac{4}{-8} = -\frac{1}{2}$

  The ratio is the same number, so the sequence is geometric.

- Determine if the sequence 2430, 729, 240.57, 80.10981, ... is geometric.

  $\frac{80.10981}{240.57} = 0.333$ and $\frac{240.57}{729} = 0.33$

  The ratios are different, so this is not a geometric sequence.

- Find the first four terms and the 10th term of the sequence $a_n = \frac{1}{100}(-5)^{n-1}$.

  $a_1 = \frac{1}{100}$

  $a_2 = \frac{1}{100}(-5)^{2-1} = -\frac{1}{20}$

  $a_3 = \frac{1}{100}(-5)^{3-1} = \frac{1}{4}$

  $a_4 = \frac{1}{100}(-5)^{4-1} = -\frac{5}{4}$

  $a_{10} = \frac{1}{100}(-5)^{10-1} = -\frac{78,125}{4}$

We can find the nth term of a geometric sequence by either knowing one term and the common ratio or by knowing two terms. This is similar to what we did to find the nth term of an arithmetic sequence.

EXAMPLE 14-10

Find the nth term of the geometric sequence.

- The common ratio is 3 and the fourth term is 54.

  $a_4 = 54$ and $r = 3$, so $a_n = a_1 r^{n-1}$ becomes $54 = a_1 3^{4-1}$. This gives us $a_1 = 2$. The nth term is $a_n = 2(3)^{n-1}$.

- The third term is 320, and the fifth term is 204.8.

$a_3 = 320$ and $a_5 = 204.8$ give us the system of equations $320 = a_1 r^{3-1}$ and $204.8 = a_1 r^{5-1}$. Elimination by addition does not work for the systems in this section, so we use substitution. Solving for a_1 in $a_1 r^2 = 320$ gives us $a_1 = \frac{320}{r^2}$. Substituting this in $a_1 r^4 = 204.8$ gives us the following.

$$a_1 r^4 = 204.8$$

$$\frac{320}{r^2} \cdot r^4 = 204.8$$

$$320 r^2 = 204.8$$

$$r^2 = 0.64$$

$$r = \pm 0.8$$

There are two geometric sequences whose third term is 320 and fifth term is 204.8; one has a common ratio of 0.8 and the other, -0.8; a_1 for both sequences is the same.

$$a_1 = \frac{320}{0.8^2} = 500 \text{ and } a_1 = \frac{320}{(-0.8)^2} = 500$$

The nth term for one sequence is $a_n = 500(0.8)^{n-1}$, and the other is $a_n = 500(-0.8)^{n-1}$.

- The third term is 20, and the sixth term is 81.92.

From $a_3 = 20$ and $a_6 = 81.92$, we have the system of equations $20 = a_1 r^{3-1}$ and $81.92 = a_1 r^{6-1}$. We solve for a_1 in $20 = a_1 r^2$. Now we substitute $a_1 = \frac{20}{r^2}$ for a_1 in $81.92 = a_1 r^5$.

$$81.92 = a_1 r^5$$

$$81.92 = \frac{20}{r^2} \cdot r^5$$

$$81.92 = 20 r^3$$

$$4.096 = r^3$$

$$\sqrt[3]{4.096} = r$$

$$1.6 = r$$

$$a_1 = \frac{20}{1.6^2} = 7.8125$$

The nth term is $a_n = 7.8125(1.6)^{n-1}$.

We can add the first n terms of a geometric sequence using the following formula (except for $r = 1$). If $a_n = a_1 r^{n-1}$, then

$$S_n = a_1 \frac{1 - r^n}{1 - r}$$

EXAMPLE 14-11

- Find the sum of the first five terms of the geometric sequence whose nth term is $a_n = 3(2)^{n-1}$.

$a_1 = 3$ and $r = 2$.

$$S_5 = 3 \cdot \frac{1 - 2^5}{1 - 2} = 3 \cdot \frac{-31}{-1} = 93$$

- Compute $16 + 8 + 4 + 2 + 1 + \frac{1}{2} + \frac{1}{4} + \frac{1}{8} + \frac{1}{16}$. $a_1 = 16$, $r = \frac{1}{2}$, and $n = 9$.

$$S_9 = 16 \frac{1 - \left(\frac{1}{2}\right)^9}{1 - \frac{1}{2}} = 16 \frac{\frac{512}{512} - \frac{1}{512}}{\frac{1}{2}}$$

$$= 16 \frac{\frac{511}{512}}{\frac{1}{2}} = 16 \left(\frac{511}{512} \div \frac{1}{2}\right) = 16 \left(\frac{511}{512} \cdot 2\right) = \frac{511}{16}$$

- $\sum_{i=1}^{6} 6.4(1.5)^{i-1}$

We are adding the first six terms of the geometric sequence whose nth term is $a_n = 6.4(1.5)^{n-1}$.

$$\sum_{i=1}^{6} 6.4(1.5)^{i-1} = S_6 = 6.4 \frac{1 - 1.5^6}{1 - 1.5} = 133$$

- $\sum_{k=0}^{7} 2(3)^{k-1}$

This problem is tricky because the sum begins with $k = 0$ instead of $k = 1$. These terms are the first *eight* terms of the geometric sequence

$\frac{2}{3}$, 2, 6, 18, 54, 162, 486, 1458, ... Now we can see that $n = 8$, $a_1 = \frac{2}{3}$, and $r = 3$.

$$\sum_{k=0}^{7} 2(3)^{k-1} = S_8 = \frac{2}{3} \cdot \frac{1-3^8}{1-3} = \frac{6560}{3}$$

• $54 + 18 + 6 + 2 + \frac{2}{3} + \cdots + \frac{2}{81}$

We have $a_1 = 54$ and $r = \frac{1}{3}$. We need n for $a_n = \frac{2}{81}$.

$$\frac{2}{81} = 54\left(\frac{1}{3}\right)^{n-1}$$

$$\frac{1}{2187} = \left(\frac{1}{3}\right)^{n-1}$$

Because $3^7 = 2187$, $n - 1 = 7$, giving us $n = 8$.

$$54 + 18 + 6 + 2 + \frac{2}{3} + \cdots + \frac{2}{81} = 54\left[\frac{1-\left(\frac{1}{3}\right)^8}{1-\frac{1}{3}}\right] = 54\left(\frac{\frac{3^8}{3^8}-\frac{1}{3^8}}{\frac{2}{3}}\right)$$

$$= 54\left(\frac{\frac{3^8-1}{3^8}}{\frac{2}{3}}\right) = 54\left(\frac{6560}{6561} \div \frac{2}{3}\right)$$

$$= 54\left(\frac{6560}{6561} \cdot \frac{3}{2}\right) = \frac{6560}{81}$$

When the common ratio is small enough ($-1 < r < 1$ and $r \neq 0$), we can add *all* of the terms in a geometric sequence. Such a sum is called a *series*. An example of a series is the sum of the terms in the geometric sequence $a_n = \left(\frac{1}{2}\right)^{n-1}$.

$$1 + \frac{1}{2} + \frac{1}{4} + \frac{1}{8} + \frac{1}{16} + \cdots$$

In the finite sum $S_n = a_1\frac{1-r^n}{1-r}$, r^n is very small when the ratio is a fraction, so $1 - r^n$ is very close to 1. Using this fact and calculus techniques, it can be shown that the sum of all the terms of this kind of geometric sequence is

$$S = \frac{a_1}{1-r} \quad \text{or} \quad S = a_1\left(\frac{1}{1-r}\right)$$

The only difference between the infinite sum formula and the partial sum formula is that $1 - r^n$ is replaced by 1. If n is large enough, there is very little difference between the partial sum and the entire sum. Let us compare the sum of the first 20 terms of the sequence whose nth term is $a_n = (\frac{1}{2})^{n-1}$ with the sum of all the terms.

$$S_{20} = \sum_{n=1}^{20} 1 \cdot \left(\frac{1}{2}\right)^{n-1} = 1 \cdot \frac{1 - \left(\frac{1}{2}\right)^{20}}{1 - \frac{1}{2}} \approx 1.999998093 \text{ and } S = 1 \cdot \frac{1}{1 - \frac{1}{2}} = 2$$

EXAMPLE 14-12

• $\displaystyle\sum_{i=1}^{\infty} 6 \left(\frac{2}{3}\right)^{i-1}$

$a_1 = 6, \ r = \frac{2}{3}$

$$\sum_{i=1}^{\infty} 6 \left(\frac{2}{3}\right)^{i-1} = S = 6 \cdot \frac{1}{1 - \frac{2}{3}} = 6 \cdot \frac{1}{\frac{1}{3}} = 6 \left(1 \div \frac{1}{3}\right) = 6 \left(1 \cdot \frac{3}{1}\right) = 18$$

• $\displaystyle\sum_{k=0}^{\infty} 15 \left(\frac{3}{4}\right)^{k-1}$

We need to be careful with this sum because the sum begins with $k = 0$ instead of $k = 1$. This means that a_1 is not 15 but

$$a_1 = 15 \left(\frac{3}{4}\right)^{0-1} = 15 \left(\frac{3}{4}\right)^{-1} = 15 \left(\frac{4}{3}\right) = 20$$

The common ratio is $\frac{3}{4}$.

$$\sum_{k=0}^{\infty} 15 \left(\frac{3}{4}\right)^{k-1} = S = 20 \cdot \frac{1}{1 - \frac{3}{4}} = 20 \cdot \frac{1}{\frac{1}{4}} = 20 \cdot 4 = 80$$

PRACTICE

1. What term comes after 18 in the sequence $\frac{2}{9}, \frac{2}{3}, 2, 6, 18, \ldots$?

2. Find the first four terms and the 10th term of the geometric sequence whose nth term is $a_n = -2(4)^{n-1}$.

3. Determine if the sequence 900, 90, 9, 0.9, 0.09, . . . is geometric.

4. Determine if the sequence 9, 99, 999, 9999, . . . is geometric.

5. Find the nth term of the geometric sequence(s) whose first term is 9 and fifth term is $\frac{729}{16}$.

6. Find the nth term of the geometric sequence whose common ratio is -3 and sixth term is -1701.

7. Find the nth term of the geometric sequence whose third term is 1 and sixth term is $\frac{27}{8}$.

8. Compute the sum.

$$\frac{3}{4} + \frac{3}{8} + \frac{3}{16} + \cdots + \frac{3}{256}$$

9. $\displaystyle\sum_{i=1}^{\infty} \frac{3}{4} \left(\frac{1}{2}\right)^{i-1}$

10. $\displaystyle\sum_{n=0}^{\infty} -4 \left(\frac{3}{5}\right)^{n-1}$

 **SOLUTIONS**

1. $3(18) = 54$

2. $a_1 = -2$, $a_2 = -8$, $a_3 = -32$, $a_4 = -128$, and $a_{10} = -524{,}288$

3. The sequence is geometric because the following ratios are the same.

$$\frac{0.09}{0.9} = 0.1, \quad \frac{0.9}{9} = 0.1, \quad \frac{9}{90} = 0.1, \quad \frac{90}{900} = 0.1$$

4. The sequence is not geometric because the ratios are not the same.

$$\frac{9999}{999} = \frac{1111}{111} \quad \text{and} \quad \frac{999}{99} = \frac{111}{11}$$

5. Because the fifth term of the sequence is $\frac{729}{16}$, we have the equation $\frac{729}{16} = 9r^{5-1}$. Once we have solved this equation for r, we are done.

$$\frac{729}{16} = 9r^4$$

$$\frac{1}{9} \cdot \frac{729}{16} = r^4$$

$$\frac{81}{16} = r^4$$

$$\pm\frac{3}{2} = r \qquad \sqrt[4]{\frac{81}{16}} = \frac{3}{2}$$

There are two sequences. The nth term for one of them is $a_n = 9(\frac{3}{2})^{n-1}$ and the other is $a_n = 9(-\frac{3}{2})^{n-1}$.

6. The sixth term is -1701 and $r = -3$, which gives us the equation $-1701 = a_1(-3)^{6-1}$.

$$-1701 = a_1(-3)^5$$

$$-1701 = -243a_1$$

$$7 = a_1$$

The nth term is $a_n = 7(-3)^{n-1}$.

7. The third term is 1 and the sixth term is $\frac{27}{8}$, which gives us the system of equations $1 = a_1 r^{3-1}$ and $\frac{27}{8} = a_1 r^{6-1}$. Solving $1 = a_1 r^2$ for a_1, we get $a_1 = \frac{1}{r^2}$. We substitute this in $\frac{27}{8} = a_1 r^5$.

$$\frac{27}{8} = \left(\frac{1}{r^2}\right)r^5$$

$$\frac{27}{8} = r^3$$

$$\sqrt[3]{\frac{27}{8}} = r$$

$$\frac{3}{2} = r$$

$$a_1 = \frac{1}{\left(\frac{3}{2}\right)^2} = \left(\frac{2}{3}\right)^2 = \frac{4}{9}$$

The nth term is $a_n = \frac{4}{9}(\frac{3}{2})^{n-1}$.

8. $a_1 = \frac{3}{4}$ and $r = \frac{1}{2}$. We know $a_n = \frac{3}{256}$ but we need n. We solve $\frac{3}{256} = \frac{3}{4}(\frac{1}{2})^{n-1}$ for n.

$$\frac{3}{256} = \frac{3}{4}\left(\frac{1}{2}\right)^{n-1}$$

$$\frac{4}{3} \cdot \frac{3}{256} = \left(\frac{1}{2}\right)^{n-1}$$

$$\frac{1}{64} = \left(\frac{1}{2}\right)^{n-1}$$

Because $2^6 = 64$, $n - 1 = 6$, so $n = 7$. Now we can find the sum.

$$S_7 = \frac{3}{4} \cdot \frac{1 - \left(\frac{1}{2}\right)^7}{1 - \frac{1}{2}} = \frac{3}{4} \cdot \frac{\frac{128-1}{128}}{\frac{1}{2}} = \frac{3}{4}\left(\frac{127}{128} \div \frac{1}{2}\right)$$

$$= \frac{3}{4}\left(\frac{127}{128} \cdot \frac{2}{1}\right) = \frac{381}{256}$$

9. $a_1 = \frac{3}{4}$ and $r = \frac{1}{2}$. This is all we need for the infinite sum formula.

$$S = \frac{3}{4} \cdot \frac{1}{1 - \frac{1}{2}} = \frac{3}{4} \cdot \frac{1}{\frac{1}{2}} = \frac{3}{4}\left(1 \div \frac{1}{2}\right) = \frac{3}{4} \cdot (1 \cdot 2) = \frac{3}{2}$$

10. a_1 is not -4 because the sum begins at $n = 0$ instead of $n = 1$.

$$a_1 = -4\left(\frac{3}{5}\right)^{0-1} = -4\left(\frac{3}{5}\right)^{-1} = -4\left(\frac{5}{3}\right) = -\frac{20}{3}$$

Now we can add all of the terms of the geometric sequence whose nth term is $a_n = -\frac{20}{3}(\frac{3}{5})^{n-1}$.

$$S = -\frac{20}{3} \cdot \frac{1}{1 - \frac{3}{5}} = -\frac{20}{3} \cdot \frac{1}{\frac{2}{5}} = -\frac{20}{3}\left(1 \div \frac{2}{5}\right) = -\frac{20}{3}\left(1 \cdot \frac{5}{2}\right) = -\frac{50}{3}$$

Payments and Geometric Sequences

When regular payments are made to a savings account, the monthly balances act like terms in a geometric sequence. The common ratio is $1 + i$, where i is the interest rate per payment period. We learned in Chapter 9 that if we leave P dollars in an account, earning annual interest r, compounded n times per year, for t years, then this grows to A dollars where $A = P(1 + \frac{r}{n})^{nt}$. (This is why i replaces $\frac{r}{n}$.)

Let us see what happens to the balance of an account if \$2000 is deposited on January 1 every year for 5 years, earning 10% interest per year, compounded annually. The first \$2000 will earn interest for the entire 5 years, so it will grow to $2000(1 + \frac{0.10}{1})^5 = 2000(1.10)^5$. The second \$2000 will earn interest for 4 years, so it will grow to $2000(1.10)^4$. The third \$2000 will earn interest for 3 years, so it will grow to $2000(1.10)^3$. The fourth \$2000 will earn interest for 2 years, so it will grow to $2000(1.10)^2$. And the fifth \$2000 will earn interest for 1 year, so it will grow to $2000(1.10)^1$. The balance a year after the last payment made is

$$2000(1.10)^5 + 2000(1.10)^4 + 2000(1.10)^3 + 2000(1.10)^2 + 2000(1.10)^1$$

This is the sum of the first five terms of the geometric sequence whose nth term is $a_n = 2000(1.10)^n$. If we want to use the partial sum formula, we need to rewrite the nth term in the form $a_n = a_1 r^{n-1}$. We use exponent properties to change $2000(1.10)^n$ to $a_1(1.10)^{n-1}$. We also use the fact that $n = 1 + n - 1$.

$$2000(1.10)^n = 2000(1.10)^{1+n-1} = 2000(1.10)^1(1.10)^{n-1}$$
$$= [2000(1.10)](1.10)^{n-1} = 2200(1.10)^{n-1}$$

Now we can use the partial sum formula.

$$S_5 = 2200 \cdot \frac{1 - 1.10^5}{1 - 1.10} = 13{,}431.22$$

The balance in the account will be \$13,431.22.

The formula for computing the payment on a loan is also based on the partial sum of a geometric sequence. Before we get to the formula, let us examine a simple loan. Ethan needs to borrow \$6000 from his parents for moving expenses to his new job. He plans to pay off the loan in 6 months. His parents have the money in an account that pays 9% interest, compounded monthly. If Ethan only makes six $1000 payments, his parents would be out of the interest that they would have made; so Ethan wants the payments to include this lost interest. If they had left the money in the account instead of loaning it, the balance after 6 months would be $A = 6000(1 + \frac{0.09}{12})^6 = 6275.11$. He wants the sum of the payments to be such that if they deposit the money in the same account right away, they would have $6275.11. Let P represent the payment. We again use the formula $A = P(1 + i)^n$, where i is the interest rate per period, $i = \frac{0.09}{12} = 0.0075$, and n is the number of payments, $n = 6$. During the 6 months of the loan, the first payment earns interest for 5 months, the second payment earns interest for 4 months, the third payment earns interest for 3 months, and so on. Here is the value of the account when these payments are directly deposited.

$$\overset{\text{Pymt \#1}}{P \cdot 1.0075^5} + \overset{\text{Pymt \#2}}{P \cdot 1.0075^4} + \overset{\text{Pymt \#3}}{P \cdot 1.0075^3} + \overset{\text{Pymt \#4}}{P \cdot 1.0075^2} + \overset{\text{Pymt \#5}}{P \cdot 1.0075^1} + \overset{\text{Pymt \#6}}{P \cdot 1.0075^0}$$

As you can see, this is the sum of the first six terms of the geometric sequence $A_n = P \cdot 1.0075^{n-1}$. We want the value of this sum to be 6275.11.

$$6275.11 = P \cdot \frac{1 - 1.0075^6}{1 - 1.0075} \qquad \text{Solve for } P.$$

$$P = 6275.11 \left(\frac{1 - 1.0075}{1 - 1.0075^6} \right) \approx 1026.41 \quad \text{The payment is \$1026.41.}$$

All of this work can be simplified with the formula

$$P = Ai \cdot \frac{(1 + i)^n}{(1 + i)^n - 1}$$

where i = interest rate per payment period, A is the loan amount, and n is the number of payments.

This formula comes from solving for P:

$$\underset{\substack{\text{Based on a formula from Chapter 9} \\ A(1 + i)^n}}{} = \underset{\substack{\text{The partial sum of a geometric sequence} \\ P \cdot \dfrac{1 - (1 + i)^n}{1 - (1 + i)}}}{}$$

 **EXAMPLE 14-13**

When Halley graduates from college, she will owe $15,000 on a student loan. She will make monthly payments for 20 years, at an interest rate of 6%, compounded monthly. What are Halley's payments?

The loan amount is $A = 15{,}000$, $i = \frac{0.06}{12} = 0.005$, and $n = 12(20) = 240$. Her payment will be

$$P = 15{,}000(0.005) \cdot \frac{1.005^{240}}{1.005^{240} - 1} \approx \$107.46.$$

Summary

In this chapter, we learned how to

- *Find terms for a sequence.* If we have the first terms of a sequence, we can use the pattern to find other terms. If we have a formula for the nth term, denoted a_n, we can use the formula to find terms. The formula for a recursive sequence involves one or more previous terms in the sequence.

- *Work with partial sums of a sequence.* The sum of the first n terms of a sequence is $S_n = a_1 + a_2 + \cdots + a_n$ and can also be represented with sigma notation. The notation $\sum_{i=1}^{n} a_i$ means to add the a_is from $i = 1$ to $i = n$.

- *Work with arithmetic sequences.* The difference between any consecutive terms of an arithmetic sequence is a fixed number, called the common difference. A formula for the nth term of an arithmetic sequence is $a_n = a_1 + (n-1)d$, where d is the common difference. The nth partial sum for an arithmetic sequence can be computed with one of two formulas: $S_n = \frac{n}{2}(a_1 + a_n)$ and $S_n = \frac{n}{2}[2a_1 + (n-1)d]$.

- *Work with geometric sequences.* The quotient of any consecutive terms of a geometric sequence is a fixed number, called the common ratio. A formula for the nth term of a geometric sequence is $a_n = a_1 r^{n-1}$. The nth partial sum for the first n terms of the sequence can be found with $S_n = a_1 \cdot \frac{1-r^n}{1-r}$. If $-1 < r < 1$ (with $r \neq 0$), the sum $a_1 + a_2 + a_3 + \cdots$ is called a series. This sum is $S = \frac{a_1}{1-r}$.

- *Use geometric sequences and a formula from Chapter 9 to develop financial formulas.* If P dollars is regularly invested into an account at an interest rate

i per payment period for n payments, the value of this account (when the last payment is made) is the sum of a geometic sequence. Each payment for a loan of A dollars to be paid by n payments with an interest rate of i per payment period is P dollars, where $P = Ai \cdot \frac{(1+i)^n}{(1+i)^n-1}$.

QUIZ

1. **Which term comes next in the sequence?**

    $$\frac{3}{4}, \frac{4}{9}, \frac{5}{16}, \frac{6}{25}, \dots$$

    A. $\frac{7}{41}$

    C. $\frac{7}{49}$

    B. $\frac{7}{36}$

    D. $\frac{7}{56}$

2. **What is the sixth term of the sequence whose nth term is $a_n = (-1)^n(3n)^2$?**

    A. -324

    C. -108

    B. 324

    D. 108

3. **Which formula generates the terms in the sequence?**

    $$5, 9, 17, 33, 65, \dots$$

    A. $a_n = 5 \cdot 2^{n-1} + 1$

    C. $a_n = 5 \cdot 2^n$

    B. $a_n = 5 \cdot 2^n + 1$

    D. $a_n = 2a_{n-1} - 1, \ a_1 = 5$

4. **Is the sequence in Problem 3 arithmetic, geometric, or neither?**

    A. Arithmetic

    C. Neither

    B. Geometric

    D. There are not enough terms to tell.

5. **Is the sequence $18, \ -12, \ 8, \ -\frac{16}{3}, \ \frac{32}{9}, \dots$ arithemtic, geometric, or neither?**

    A. Arithmetic

    C. Neither

    B. Geometric

    D. There are not enough terms to tell.

6. **What is the fourth term for the arithmetic sequence whose 10th term is 22 and 16th term is 40?**

    A. 12

    C. 4

    B. 9

    D. 46

7. **What is the sixth term of the geometric sequence whose third term is 16 and eighth term is $\frac{512}{243}$?**

    A. $\frac{128}{27}$

    C. $\frac{128}{81}$

    B. $\frac{256}{27}$

    D. $\frac{256}{81}$

8. Find the sum.

$$-8 + \left(-\frac{13}{2}\right) + (-5) + \left(-\frac{7}{2}\right) + \cdots + 7$$

A. -1

B. $-\frac{3}{2}$

C. $-\frac{11}{2}$

D. Too many terms are missing to find the sum.

9. Find the sum.

$$\frac{3}{8} + \frac{3}{4} + \frac{3}{2} + 3 + \cdots + 192$$

A. $\frac{3069}{2}$

B. $\frac{3069}{8}$

C. $\frac{3069}{4}$

D. Too many terms are missing to find the sum.

10. Find the sum.

$$\sum_{n=1}^{\infty} 36 \left(\frac{1}{3}\right)^{n-1}$$

A. 54

B. 48

C. 72

D. There are too many terms to add.

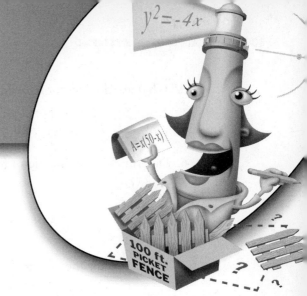

Final Exam

1. Rewrite the exponential equation in logarithmic form: $e^{x-10} = 12$.
   A. $\log_{12}(x - 10) = e$
   B. $\ln(x - 10) = 12$
   C. $x - 10 = 12^e$
   D. $x - 10 = \ln 12$

2. Find the product. $\begin{bmatrix} -4 & 0 \\ 1 & 3 \\ -2 & 2 \end{bmatrix} \cdot \begin{bmatrix} -1 & 3 \\ 0 & 1 \end{bmatrix}$

   A. $\begin{bmatrix} 8 & -23 \\ 0 & 3 \\ -2 & 5 \end{bmatrix}$

   B. $\begin{bmatrix} 4 & -12 \\ -1 & 6 \\ 2 & -4 \end{bmatrix}$

   C. $\begin{bmatrix} 4 & -12 \\ -1 & 6 \end{bmatrix}$

   D. The product does not exist.

3. Find the fourth term of a geometric sequence whose second term is $-\frac{27}{8}$ and sixth term is $-\frac{2}{3}$.
   A. $-\frac{2}{3}$
   B. $-\frac{3}{2}$
   C. $\frac{2}{3}$
   D. $\frac{3}{2}$

4. Convert $108°$ to radian measure.
   A. $\frac{4\pi}{9}$
   B. $\frac{5\pi}{9}$
   C. $\frac{4\pi}{5}$
   D. $\frac{3\pi}{5}$

5. What are the foci for the ellipse $\frac{x^2}{25} + \frac{(y-8)^2}{16} = 1$?

   A. $(0, 5)$ and $(0, 11)$ C. $(-3, 8)$ and $(3, 8)$

   B. $(0, -5)$ and $(0, 5)$ D. $(-5, 0)$ and $(5, 0)$

6. Determine if the function $f(x) = \sqrt{x^2 + 4}$ is even, odd, or neither.

   A. Even   C. Neither

   B. Odd   D. It is impossible to tell without the graph.

7. Find $x + y$ for the system $\begin{cases} \frac{3}{2}x + \frac{1}{3}y = 0 \\ x - 2y = 16 \end{cases}$.

   A. 8.8   C. -5.6

   B. 2   D. The system has no solution.

8. Find the sum.

$$400 + (-200) + 100 + (-50) + \cdots + \left(-\frac{25}{8}\right)$$

   A. $\frac{2125}{8}$ C. $\frac{2125}{4}$

   B. $\frac{6375}{4}$ D. Too many terms are missing to find the sum.

9. Find $\sin^{-1}\left(\frac{1}{2}\right)$.

   A. $\frac{\pi}{6}$ C. $\frac{2\pi}{3}$

   B. $\frac{\pi}{3}$ D. $\frac{5\pi}{6}$

10. What is the remainder for $\frac{x^4+5x^3-6x^2+2x-4}{x^2+3x+1}$?

   A. $21x + 8$ C. $33x + 7$

   B. $67x + 15$ D. $39x + 9$

11. What is the directrix for the parabola $(y + 6)^2 = 10(x - 2)$?

   A. $y = \frac{5}{2}$ C. $x = \frac{5}{2}$

   B. $y = -\frac{1}{2}$ D. $x = -\frac{1}{2}$

12. The graph of which function is given in Figure FE-1? (The dashed graph is the graph of $y = \ln x$.)

   A. $f(x) = -\ln x$ C. $f(x) = e^x$

   B. $f(x) = \ln(-x)$ D. $f(x) = -e^x$

FIGURE FE-1

13. Find the vertex for the function $f(x) = -5(x-1)^2 + 3$.
    A. $(5, 3)$ C. $(-1, 3)$
    B. $(-5, 3)$ D. $(1, 3)$

14. Find the zeros for the polynomial function $y = 3x^4 + x^3 - 71x^2 + x + 30$.
    A. $\frac{2}{3}, -5, -2 \pm \sqrt{7}$ C. $\frac{2}{3}, -5, 2 \pm \sqrt{7}$
    B. $-\frac{2}{3}, 5, -2 \pm \sqrt{7}$ D. $-\frac{2}{3}, 5, 2 \pm \sqrt{7}$

15. Find the domain for $(f - g)(x)$ if $f(x) = \sqrt{x-3}$ and $g(x) = \frac{1}{x-10}$.
    A. $(3, 10) \cup (10, \infty)$ C. $[3, 10)$
    B. $[3, 10) \cup (10, \infty)$ D. $(3, 10)$

16. Find the sum.

$$\sum_{n=1}^{10} [6 + (n-1)(-2)]$$

    A. -24 C. -28
    B. -26 D. -30

17. What is an asymptote for the hyperbola $(x-6)^2 - \frac{(y+1)^2}{9} = 1$?
    A. $y = -\frac{1}{3}x + 1$ C. $y = -\frac{1}{3}x - 3$
    B. $y = -3x + 17$ D. $y = 3x + 17$

18. Use exponent and logarithmic properties to condense the logarithm: $\frac{1}{2}\log_6 x + \log_6 y - 3\log_6 z$.

A. $\frac{\log_6 \sqrt{x}y}{3\log_6 z}$

C. $\log_6 \frac{\sqrt{x}y}{z^3}$

B. $\frac{\log_6 \sqrt{x}y}{\log_6 z^3}$

D. $\frac{\log_6 \sqrt{x}y}{\log_6 z^3}$

19. Evaluate $f(-1)$ for $f(x) = \begin{cases} 4x+7 & \text{if } x < 0 \\ x^2 & \text{if } 0 \le x \le 3. \\ 10 & \text{if } x > 3 \end{cases}$

A. $-1, 3$

C. $1, 3$

B. $-1, 3, 10$

D. 3

20. Find the 10th term of the sequence whose nth term is $a_n = \frac{n+1}{n^2+1}$.

A. $\frac{11}{101}$

C. $\frac{11}{100}$

B. $\frac{1}{10}$

D. $\frac{11}{99}$

21. What is an equation for the graph in Figure FE-2?

A. $(x-3)^2 = -3(y-6)$

C. $(x-3)^2 = 12(y-6)$

B. $(x-3)^2 = 3(y-6)$

D. $(x-3)^2 = -12(y-6)$

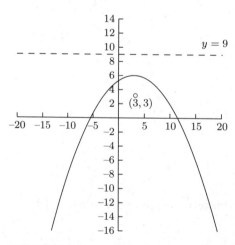

FIGURE FE-2

22. The graph of $y = -f(x - 4)$ is the graph of $y = f(x)$
   A. Shifted to the left 4 units and reflected across the y-axis.
   B. Shifted to the right 4 units and reflected across the y-axis.
   C. Shifted to the left 4 units and reflected across the x-axis.
   D. Shifted to the right 4 units and reflected across the x-axis.

23. Solve the equation: $x^2 + 6x + 12 = 0$.
   A. $3 \pm \sqrt{3}\,i$
   B. $6 \pm \sqrt{3}\,i$
   C. $-3 \pm \sqrt{3}\,i$
   D. $-6 \pm \sqrt{3}\,i$

24. Find $x - 2y$ for the system $\begin{cases} 4x - 7y = 27 \\ 2x + 3y = -19 \end{cases}$.
   A. 12
   B. 8
   C. -3
   D. 3

25. What is the center for the ellipse $x^2 - 8x + 25y^2 + 150y + 16 = 0$? (After writing the equation in standard form, you can identify h and k.)
   A. $(5, -3)$
   B. $(4, -3)$
   C. $(4, -5)$
   D. $(4, \frac{1}{5})$

26. Find the fifth term of the arithmetic sequence whose ninth term is 4 and 15th term is 13.
   A. 12
   B. -2
   C. -4
   D. There is not enough information to determine the answer.

27. Solve the equation for x: $4^{3x-1} = 50$.
   A. About 1.274
   B. About 3.631
   C. About 1.766
   D. About 2.822

28. Find the determinant for the matrix $\begin{bmatrix} -8 & 1 \\ 2 & -1 \end{bmatrix}$.
   A. 6
   B. -1
   C. 1
   D. -10

29. Find $\tan \theta$ if $\cos \theta = \frac{7}{15}$ and θ is in Quadrant IV.
   A. $-\frac{4\sqrt{11}}{15}$
   B. $\frac{15\sqrt{11}}{44}$
   C. $-\frac{4\sqrt{11}}{7}$
   D. $\frac{7\sqrt{11}}{44}$

30. A library leases its photocopier. One monthly bill was $750 for 12,000 copies. Another month, the bill was $862.50 for 16,500 copies. How much does the library pay for each copy? (Hint: Find the linear equation giving the cost in terms of the number of copies used.)

A. $0.02

C. $0.03

B. $0.025

D. $0.035

31. Find $x - y$ for the system $\begin{cases} y = -x^2 + 6x - 11 \\ x + y = 1 \end{cases}$.

A. 5 and 7

C. 4 and 9

B. −1 and 8

D. −2 and 10

32. Find the sum.

$$\sum_{n=1}^{\infty} 100 \left(\frac{2}{5}\right)^{n-1}$$

A. 250

C. $\frac{500}{3}$

B. $\frac{576}{3}$

D. There are too many terms to add.

33. A boy lies on the grass in a park, flying a kite. He has 200 feet of string out and the angle of elevation is 78°. How high is the kite? (Assume the string is anchored to the ground.)

A. About 182 feet

C. About 196 feet

B. About 189 feet

D. About 208 feet

34. Find the quadratic function having vertex $(\frac{1}{2}, 4)$ and whose graph contains the point $(-1, -14)$.

A. $y = -72(x + \frac{1}{2})^2 + 4$

C. $-\frac{40}{9}(x - \frac{1}{2})^2 - 4$

B. $y = -8(x - \frac{1}{2})^2 + 4$

D. $-40(x + \frac{1}{2})^2 - 4$

35. Solve the equation for x: $\log_3(x - 5) + \log_3(x + 5) = \log_3(8x - 5)$.

A. 10, −2

C. 10

B. $-\frac{6}{5}$

D. The equation does not have a solution.

36. Find the inverse of the matrix $\begin{bmatrix} 5 & 2 \\ -3 & 1 \end{bmatrix}$.

A. $\begin{bmatrix} \frac{1}{5} & \frac{1}{2} \\ -\frac{1}{3} & 1 \end{bmatrix}$

C. $\begin{bmatrix} \frac{1}{11} & -\frac{2}{11} \\ \frac{3}{11} & \frac{5}{11} \end{bmatrix}$

B. $\begin{bmatrix} -\frac{1}{5} & -\frac{1}{2} \\ \frac{1}{3} & -1 \end{bmatrix}$

D. $\begin{bmatrix} 19 & 12 \\ -18 & -5 \end{bmatrix}$

37. Use an Addition/Subtraction formula to compute $\cos 105°$.

A. $\frac{\sqrt{2}-\sqrt{6}}{4}$

C. $\frac{1-\sqrt{3}}{4}$

B. $\frac{\sqrt{6}-\sqrt{2}}{4}$

D. $\frac{\sqrt{2}-1}{4}$

38. Determine the average rate of change of the function $g(x) = \sqrt{x-1}$ between $x = 5$ and $x = 10$.

A. -5

C. 5

B. $-\frac{1}{5}$

D. $\frac{1}{5}$

39. Find $x + y$ for the system $\begin{cases} y = -\frac{1}{3}x + 3 \\ x + 3y = 5 \end{cases}$.

A. 3

C. -2

B. 4

D. The system has no solution.

40. What is the eccentricity for the ellipse $\frac{x^2}{29^2} + \frac{(y-3)^2}{21^2} = 1$?

A. $\frac{20}{21}$

C. $\frac{20}{29}$

B. $\frac{21}{20}$

D. $\frac{21}{29}$

41. Find the domain for $(f \circ g)(x)$ if $f(x) = \frac{1}{x}$ and $g(x) = \sqrt{x+4}$.

A. $(-4, \infty)$

C. $(-4, 0) \cup (0, \infty)$

B. $[-4, 0) \cup (0, \infty)$

D. $(-\infty, -4) \cup (-4, 0) \cup (0, \infty)$

42. Use a matrix method to solve the system. What is $x + y + z$?

$$\begin{cases} x - y - 2z = -12 \\ 3x + y + z = -7 \\ 2x - 5y + 4z = -6 \end{cases}$$

A. 1

C. 3

B. 2

D. 4

43. Find $\cos 2\theta$ if $\cos \theta = \frac{3}{4}$. It does not matter which quadrant contains θ.

   A. $\frac{1}{4}$

   B. $\frac{1}{8}$

   C. $-\frac{3}{2}$

   D. $-\frac{1}{8}$

44. Perform the division: $\frac{7+2i}{1-5i}$.

   A. $\frac{17}{26} - \frac{33}{26}i$

   B. $-\frac{9}{26} + \frac{7}{26}i$

   C. $\frac{7}{26} - \frac{33}{26}i$

   D. $-\frac{3}{26} + \frac{37}{26}i$

45. The shaded region in Figure FE-3 is the solution to which system?

   A. $\begin{cases} -7x + 4y > 13 \\ 2x - y > 8 \\ y < x^2 - 2x - 8 \end{cases}$

   C. $\begin{cases} 7x - 4y > 13 \\ 2x + y < 8 \\ y < x^2 - 2x - 8 \end{cases}$

   B. $\begin{cases} -7x + 4y > 13 \\ 2x - y > 8 \\ y > x^2 - 2x - 8 \end{cases}$

   D. $\begin{cases} 7x - 4y > 13 \\ 2x + y < 8 \\ y > x^2 - 2x - 8 \end{cases}$

46. An archeologist finds a wooden tool at a site and wants to use the tool to date the site. The tool has 90% of its carbon-14 remaining. About how old is the tool? (Recall: the half-life of carbon-14 is about 5700 years.)

   A. 422 years

   B. 866 years

   C. 1336 years

   D. 1098 years

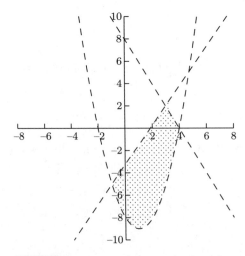

FIGURE FE-3

47. Find the determinant for the matrix $\begin{bmatrix} 2 & -1 & 0 \\ -5 & 1 & 2 \\ 0 & 2 & -1 \end{bmatrix}$.

A. 1   C. 4

B. -2 D. -5

48. Evaluate $(f \circ g)(x)$ for $f(x) = 5x + 4$ and $g(x) = 3x^2 + x - 2$.
   A. $15x^3 + 17x^2 - 6x - 8$ C. $75x^2 + 121x + 46$
   B. $75x^2 + 125x + 50$ D. $15x^2 + 5x - 6$

49. What is the period for the function $f(x) = 4\sin[\frac{1}{2}(x - \frac{\pi}{3})]$?
   A. $\frac{1}{2}$ C. $\frac{\pi}{2}$
   B. 2π D. 4π

50. Find an equation of the line that contains the point $(12, 15)$ that is perpendicular to the line $3x + 4y = 8$.
   A. $y = \frac{4}{3}x - 1$ C. $y = -\frac{4}{3}x + 31$
   B. $y = \frac{3}{4}x + 6$ D. $y = -\frac{3}{4}x + 24$

51. Find the inverse of the matrix $\begin{bmatrix} 1 & 1 & 0 \\ -3 & 2 & 0 \\ 1 & -2 & 1 \end{bmatrix}$.

   A. $\begin{bmatrix} -\frac{1}{5} & \frac{2}{5} & 0 \\ \frac{1}{5} & \frac{3}{5} & 0 \\ \frac{3}{5} & \frac{4}{5} & 1 \end{bmatrix}$ C. $\begin{bmatrix} \frac{2}{5} & 0 & -\frac{1}{5} \\ \frac{3}{5} & 0 & \frac{1}{5} \\ \frac{4}{5} & 1 & \frac{3}{5} \end{bmatrix}$

   B. $\begin{bmatrix} \frac{2}{5} & -\frac{1}{5} & 0 \\ \frac{3}{5} & \frac{1}{5} & 0 \\ \frac{4}{5} & \frac{3}{5} & 1 \end{bmatrix}$ D. $\begin{bmatrix} -\frac{1}{4} & -\frac{1}{2} & -\frac{1}{4} \\ -\frac{3}{8} & -\frac{1}{4} & -\frac{3}{8} \\ \frac{1}{2} & 0 & -\frac{1}{2} \end{bmatrix}$

52. Evaluate $(f \circ g)(4)$ for $f(x) = \frac{1}{2}x^2 + 1$ and $g(x) = x - 6$.
   A. 9   C. 3
   B. -7 D. -1

53. Find all zeros for the polynomial $x^4 + 15x^2 - 16$.
   A. $\pm 1, \pm 4i$ C. $\pm i, \pm 4$
   B. $\pm 1, \pm 4$ D. $\pm i, \pm 4i$

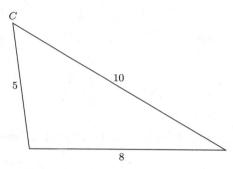

FIGURE FE-4

54. Find $\angle C$ for the triangle in Figure FE-4.

    A. 97.9°   C. 29.7°

    B. 52.4°   D. 37.6°

55. David, a salesman for a cell phone plans, earns $9 commission for selling a limited minutes plan and $16 commission for selling an unlimited minutes plan. Last month, he sold 65 plans, earning a total commision of $781. How many limited plans did he sell?

    A. 37   C. 41

    B. 39   D. 43

56. Find the domain for the function $g(x) = \sqrt{6x - 12}$.

    A. $(2, \infty)$ C. $(-\infty, 2) \cup (2, \infty)$

    B. $[2, \infty)$ D. $(-\infty, -2) \cup (2, \infty)$

57. Find the slant asymptote for the graph of $f(x) = \frac{5x^3 - 8x^2 + 2x + 3}{x^2 - x - 2}$.

    A. $y = 9x - 3$ C. $x = 2, x = -1$

    B. $y = 5x - 3$ D. The graph does not have a slant asymptote.

58. Find the maximum or minimum value for the function $f(x) = -(x - 4)^2 + 10$.

    A. The maximum value of the function is 10.   C. The maximum value of the function is 4.

    B. The minimum value of the function is 10.   D. The minimum value of the function is -4.

FIGURE FE-5

Problems 59 and 60 refer to the function whose graph is in Figure FE-5.

59. **What kind of symmetry does the graph have?**
    A. x-axis symmetry
    B. y-axis symmetry
    C. Origin symmetry
    D. The graph has no symmetry.

60. **Find the average rate of change of the function between $x = -1$ and $x = 2$.**
    A. -1
    B. 1
    C. 3
    D. -3

61. **Find an equation of the line containing the points $(-\frac{1}{2}, -3)$ and $(1, 1)$.**
    A. $8x - 3y = 4$
    B. $8x - 3y = 3$
    C. $y = -\frac{8}{3}x - \frac{4}{3}$
    D. $8x - 3y = 5$

62. **Evaluate the difference quotient for the function $f(x) = 8$.**
    A. 1
    B. 8
    C. 0
    D. It is impossible to tell.

63. **Are the lines $2x - 5y = 5$ and $5x - 2y = 1$ parallel, perpendicular, or neither?**
    A. Parallel
    B. Perpendicular
    C. Neither
    D. It is impossible to determine.

64. Find the vertex for the graph of the function $y = -0.008x^2 + 2x + 5$.
    A. $(125, 130)$ C. $(125, -15{,}620)$
    B. $(125, 380)$ D. $(-125, 380)$

65. Find the domain for the function $h(x) = \frac{1}{x^3 - 4x^2 - 5x}$.
    A. $x \neq -1,\ 0,\ 5$ C. $x \neq -5,\ 0,\ 1$
    B. $x \neq 1,\ 0,\ 5$ D. $x \neq -5,\ 0,\ -1$

66. Are the four points $(-20, 30)$, $(0, 57)$, $(40, 25)$, and $(20, 0)$ (plotted in Figure FE-6) the vertices of a parallelogram? (Hint: Compute the slope of each side and compare them.)
    A. Yes   C. It is impossible to determine.
    B. No

67. The graph of which function is sketched in Figure FE-7?
    A. $f(x) = (x - 1)^3 - 1$ C. $f(x) = (x + 1)^3 + 1$
    B. $f(x) = (x + 1)^3 - 1$ D. $f(x) = (x - 1)^3 + 1$

68. Find the vertical asymptote(s) for the graph of $y = \frac{x^2 - 4}{x^2 + 36}$.
    A. $x = -2, x = 2$ C. $x = 6$
    B. $x = -6, x = 6$ D. The graph does not have a vertical asymptote.

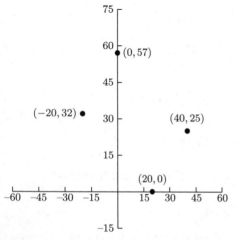

FIGURE FE-6

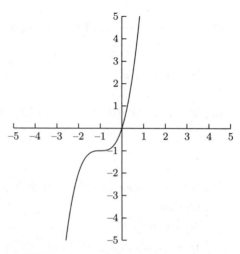

FIGURE FE-7

69. Find a fourth-degree polynomial with integer coefficients and having zeros -1, 1, and $-3 + 5i$.

A. $x^4 - 6x^3 + 35x^2 - 6x + 34$ C. $x^4 - 20x^3 + 33x^2 + 20x - 34$

B. $x^4 - 20x^3 + 35x^2 - 20x + 34$ D. $x^4 + 6x^3 + 33x^2 - 6x - 34$

70. Evaluate $g(5u)$ for $g(x) = x^2 - 2x + 4$.

A. $25u^2 - 10u + 4$ C. $5u^2 - 10u + 20$

B. $5u^2 - 10u + 4$ D. $25u^2 - 10u + 20$

71. Evaluate the difference quotient for $f(x) = 3x^2 + 4x + 6$.

A. $6a + 3$ C. $6a + 3h^2 + 4h$

B. $6ah + 3h + 4$ D. $6a + 3h + 4$

72. Find the domain for the function $f(x) = \frac{\sqrt{x-8}}{x-10}$.

A. $[8, \infty)$ C. $(8, 10) \cup (10, \infty)$

B. $[8, 10) \cup (10, \infty)$ D. $(8, 10] \cup [10, \infty)$

Problems 73 to 77 refer to the function whose graph is in Figure FE-8.

73. What is the domain of the function?

A. $[-3, 37]$ C. $[-40, 37]$

B. $[-3, 5] \cup [5, 37]$ D. $[-3, 4]$

74. What is the range of the function?

A. $[-40, 37]$ C. $[-3, 37]$

B. $[-3, 4]$ D. $[-40, 4]$

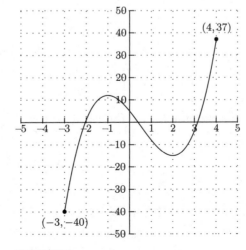

FIGURE FE-8

75. **Where is the function decreasing?**
   A. $(-3, -1) \cup (2, 4)$ C. $(-3, 2)$
   B. $(-1, 2)$ D. $(2, 4)$

76. **Is the function even, odd, or neither?**
   A. Even   B. Odd   C. Neither

77. **Evaluate $f(2)$.**
   A. $f(2) = -10$ C. $f(2) = -20$
   B. $f(2) = -15$ D. $f(2) = -25$

78. **Determine whether or not $f(x) = 4x - 9$ and $g(x) = \frac{x+9}{4}$ are inverses of each other.**

   A. Yes, the functions are inverses of each other.

   B. No, the functions are not inverses of each other.

   C. It is impossible to determine.

79. **An object is fired upward with the initial velocity of 80 feet per second from the edge of a bridge that is 20 feet above the surface of a lake. What is the object's maximum height above the surface of the water? (Hint: The position function is $h = -16t^2 + v_0 t + h_0$, where t is in seconds, h is in feet, v_0 is the initial velocity in feet per second, and h_0 is the initial height in feet.)**
   A. 110 feet   C. 125 feet
   B. 120 feet   D. 140 feet

80. **Find $f^{-1}(x)$ for $f(x) = \frac{2x+1}{x-3}$.**

   A. $\frac{3x-1}{x+2}$ C. $\frac{3x-1}{x-2}$

   B. $\frac{3x+1}{x-2}$ D. $f^{-1}(x)$ does not exist because $f(x)$ is not a one-to-one function.

81. **Find the vertical asymptote(s) for the graph of $y = \frac{x+3}{x^2+4x-12}$.**
   A. $x = 2$ C. $x = -6, x = 2$
   B. $x = -3$ D. The graph does not have a vertical asymptote.

Problems 82 to 85 refer to the graphs in Figures FE-9 to FE-12. Match the function with its graph.

82. $f(x) = |x + 1| - 3$

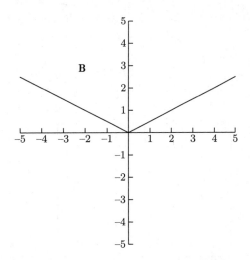

A

FIGURE FE-9

B

FIGURE FE-10

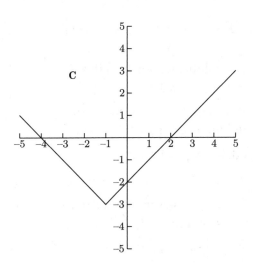

C

FIGURE FE-11

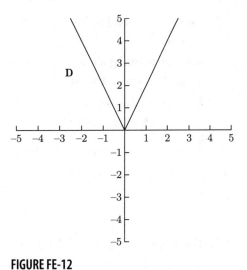

D

FIGURE FE-12

83. $f(x) = |x - 1| + 3$

84. $f(x) = 2|x|$

85. $f(x) = \frac{1}{2}|x|$

86. **A farmer wants to enclose three rectangular pens for his goat herd. (See Figure FE-13.) If he has 800 feet of fencing on hand, what is the maximum enclosed area?**

A. 18,500 square feet

B. 20,000 square feet

C. 21,500 square feet

D. 23,000 square feet

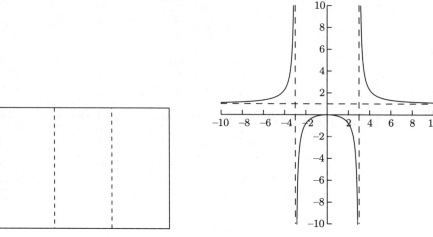

FIGURE FE-13   FIGURE FE-14

87. Describe the end behavior for the graph of $P(x) = -16x^4 + 12x^3 - 4x^3 + 3x + 8$.
   A. The graph goes up on the left and down on the right.
   B. The graph goes down on the left and up on the right.
   C. The graph goes down on the left and down on the right.
   D. The graph goes up on the left and up on the right.

88. Find the horizontal asymptote for the graph of $r(x) = \frac{4x+1}{x-3}$.
   A. $y = 4$
   B. $y = 0$, the x-axis
   C. $y = 3$
   D. The graph does not have a horizontal asymptote.

89. The graph in Figure FE-14 is the graph of which function?
   A. $y = \frac{1}{x^2-9}$
   B. $y = \frac{x}{x^2-9}$
   C. $y = \frac{x^2}{x^2-9}$
   D. $y = \frac{x^3}{x^2-9}$

90. If $2000 is invested in an account paying 4% annual interest, compounded quarterly, what is the account worth after 10 years?
   A. $2977.73
   B. $2960.49
   C. $2209.24
   D. $9602.04

Answers to Quizzes and Final Exam

Chapter 1
1. D
2. C
3. C
4. B
5. A
6. D
7. A
8. A
9. B
10. B
11. D
12. B
13. C

Chapter 2
1. D
2. B
3. A
4. B
5. A
6. C
7. D

8. B
9. D

Chapter 3
1. C
2. B
3. B
4. A
5. D
6. C
7. B
8. A
9. A
10. B
11. A
12. C

Chapter 4
1. B
2. B
3. A
4. C
5. A

6. A
7. B
8. A
9. D
10. A
11. C
12. C
13. D

Chapter 5
1. Figure 5-43
2. Figure 5-41
3. Figure 5-44
4. Figure 5-42
5. B
6. A
7. B

Chapter 6
1. A
2. B
3. A
4. C

5. A
6. D
7. B
8. C
9. B
10. D
11. C
12. D

Chapter 7
1. D
2. C
3. B
4. A
5. C
6. D
7. B
8. B
9. C
10. A
11. D
12. A

13. A
14. C
15. A

Chapter 8
1. A
2. B
3. C
4. C
5. C
6. A
7. C
8. D
9. C
10. B
11. D

Chapter 9
1. A
2. D
3. A
4. B
5. C
6. A
7. B
8. C
9. C
10. D
11. B
12. D
13. B
14. A
15. D
16. C
17. C

Chapter 10
1. B
2. A
3. A

4. D
5. A
6. D
7. D
8. B
9. B
10. C

Chapter 11
1. D
2. C
3. B
4. D
5. A
6. C
7. A
8. A
9. B
10. C

Chapter 12
1. D
2. B
3. A
4. C
5. B
6. A
7. D
8. B
9. D
10. A
11. C
12. C

Chapter 13
1. D
2. C
3. C
4. B
5. D

6. B
7. D
8. A
9. A
10. D
11. B
12. A
13. C
14. B
15. D
16. A
17. B

Chapter 14
1. B
2. B
3. D
4. C
5. B
6. C
7. A
8. C
9. B
10. A

Final Exam
1. D
2. B
3. B
4. D
5. C
6. A
7. C
8. A
9. A
10. D
11. D
12. B
13. D

14. C
15. B
16. D
17. B
18. C
19. D
20. A
21. D
22. D
23. C
24. B
25. B
26. B
27. A
28. A
29. C
30. B
31. A
32. C
33. C
34. B
35. C
36. C
37. A
38. D
39. D
40. C
41. A
42. A
43. B
44. D
45. D
46. B
47. D
48. D
49. D
50. A
51. B

52. C	62. C	72. B	82. C
53. A	63. C	73. D	83. A
54. B	64. A	74. A	84. D
55. A	65. A	75. B	85. B
56. B	66. A	76. C	86. B
57. B	67. B	77. B	87. C
58. A	68. D	78. A	88. A
59. C	69. D	79. B	89. C
60. A	70. A	80. B	90. A
61. D	71. D	81. C	

Appendix

The Distributive Property and the FOIL Method

In algebra and calculus, we often need to rewrite expressions. We might need to *expand* a product such as $(2x + 1)(x - 4)$ and use the Distributive Property to do so. According to this property, we expand this product by multiplying $x - 4$ by $2x$ and by 1, and then combining like terms. To make this process a little easier (and to make sure we get all of the correct terms), we use the letters in FOIL to expand it. **F** means to multiply **first** times **first**. **O** means to multiply **outer** times **outer**. **I** means to multiply **inner** times **inner**. **L** means to multiply **last** times **last**. After computing each of these individual products, we add them.

$$(2x + 1)(x - 4) = \overset{\text{F·F}}{2x \cdot x} + \overset{\text{O·O}}{2x \cdot (-4)} + \overset{\text{I·I}}{1 \cdot x} + \overset{\text{L·L}}{1(-4)}$$

$$= 2x^2 - 8x + x - 4 = 2x^2 - 7x - 4$$

Reversing this process is called *factoring*. To factor a quadratic expression such as $x^2 - 2x - 3$, we want to write it in such a way that the FOIL method produces $x^2 - 2x - 3$. We can always factor a quadratic expression (though not always easily). Here, we only look at expressions that can be factored easily. (In Chapter 7, we cover ways to factor other quadratic expressions.) We always begin with $(ax + b)(cx + d)$. We choose a and c so that F in FOIL gives us the first term. For $x^2 - 2x - 3$, this means we want a and c to be 1.

$$x^2 - 2x - 3 = (x + b)(x + d)$$

We now choose b and d so that $O + I + L$ in FOIL gives us $-2x - 3$. We begin by choosing b an d so that their product is -3. This leaves us with $b = 1$ and $c = -3$ or $b = -1$ and $c = 3$. If use the FOIL method on both $(x + 1)(x - 3)$ and $(x - 1)(x + 3)$, we see that the first is the correct factorization.

Solving Equations and Inequalities

Using algebra to solve equations and inequalities is important in precalculus and calculus. Usually the solution to an equation is a number or numbers. Sometimes, the solution to an equation is simply the equation written another way. To solve for x means to have x, and x only, on one side of the equation. The equation $x = \frac{y-5}{y^2+1}$ is solved for x but $x = \frac{y-5}{x^2+1}$ is not solved for x because x is on both sides of the equation. Solving for x when the equation contains more than one variable is very much like solving for x when the equation has only one variable. We move quantities from one side of the equation by adding, subtracting, multiplying, and dividing.

- Solve for x in the equation $a(x + 4) - 2a(x - 1) = 5(a + x)$.

$a(x + 4) - 2a(x - 1) = 5(a + x)$ Simplify both sides of the equation.

$ax + 4a - 2ax + 2a = 5a + 5x$

$ax - 2ax + 6a = 5a + 5x$ Collect x terms on one side of the equation.

$ax - 2ax - 5x + 6a = 5a$ Collect terms without x on the other side.

$ax - 2ax - 5x = -6a + 5a$ Simplify both sides.

$-ax - 5x = -a$ Factor x.

$x(-a - 5) = -a$ Divide both sides by $-a - 5$

$$x = \frac{-a}{-a - 5} \quad \text{or} \quad \frac{-a}{-(a + 5)} \quad \text{or} \quad \frac{a}{a + 5}$$

Quadratic Equations

Equations of the form $ax^2 + bx + c = 0$ (where $a \neq 0$) are *quadratic equations*. There are several techniques we can use to solve them—factoring, completing the square, and using the quadratic formula. The simplest quadratic equations are in the form $x^2 = $ number. This equation has solutions $x = \sqrt{\text{number}}$ and

$x = -\sqrt{\text{number}}$, or simply, $x = \pm\sqrt{\text{number}}$. For example, the solutions for $x^2 = 36$ are $x = 6$ and $x = -6$, or $x = \pm 6$.

Many quadratic equations can be solved by factoring. When there is a zero on one side of the equation, we factor the other side, set each factor equal to zero and solve both equations. This method comes from the fact that $ab = 0$ implies $a = 0$ or $b = 0$.

- $x^2 + x - 6 = 0$

  $x^2 + x - 6$ factors as $(x + 3)(x - 2)$. Set each of $x + 3$ and $x - 2$ equal to 0 and solve for x.

$$x + 3 = 0 \qquad x - 2 = 0$$

$$x = -3 \qquad x = 2$$

- $3x^2 + 24 = -18x$

  We need a zero on one side of the equation, so we move $18x$ to the other side.

$$3x^2 + 18x + 24 = 0$$

$$3(x^2 + 6x + 8) = 0$$

$$3(x + 2)(x + 4) = 0$$

$$x + 2 = 0 \qquad x + 4 = 0$$

$$x = -2 \qquad x = -4$$

Some quadratic equations are difficult to factor. The quadratic formula can solve *every* quadratic equation. If $a \neq 0$ and $ax^2 + bx + c = 0$, then

$$x = \frac{-b \pm \sqrt{b^2 - 4ac}}{2a}$$

- $3x^2 - x - 4 = 0$

  $a = 3$, $b = -1$, and $c = -4$

$$x = \frac{-(-1) \pm \sqrt{(-1)^2 - 4(3)(-4)}}{2(3)} = \frac{1 \pm \sqrt{49}}{6} = \frac{1 \pm 7}{6} = \frac{8}{6}, \frac{-6}{6} = \frac{4}{3}, -1$$

- $4x^2 + x = 1$

We need 0 on one side of the equation. Once we move 1 to the other side, we have $4x^2 + x - 1 = 0$.

$$x = \frac{-1 \pm \sqrt{1^2 - 4(4)(-1)}}{2(4)} = \frac{-1 \pm \sqrt{17}}{8}$$

A quadratic equation can have square roots of numbers as solutions that need to be simplified. The square root of a number is simplified when it does not have any perfect squares as factors. For example, $\sqrt{24}$ is not simplified because $24 = 2^2 \times 6$. We can use the exponent properties $\sqrt{ab} = \sqrt{a} \cdot \sqrt{b}$ and $\sqrt[n]{a^n} = a$ to simplify $\sqrt{24}$.

$$\sqrt{24} = \sqrt{4 \cdot 6} = \sqrt{4} \cdot \sqrt{6} = 2\sqrt{6}$$

Square roots of fractions and square roots in denominators are also not considered simplified. These numbers often come up in trigonometry. Sometimes we can multiply the fraction by the denominator over itself.

- $\sqrt{\dfrac{1}{3}} = \dfrac{\sqrt{1}}{\sqrt{3}} = \dfrac{1}{\sqrt{3}} = \dfrac{1}{\sqrt{3}} \cdot \dfrac{\sqrt{3}}{\sqrt{3}} = \dfrac{\sqrt{3}}{(\sqrt{3})^2} = \dfrac{\sqrt{3}}{3}$

- $\dfrac{10}{\sqrt{5}} = \dfrac{10}{\sqrt{5}} \cdot \dfrac{\sqrt{5}}{\sqrt{5}} = \dfrac{10\sqrt{5}}{(\sqrt{5})^2} = \dfrac{10\sqrt{5}}{5} = 2\sqrt{5}$

This trick does not work for expressions such as $\dfrac{2}{\sqrt{3}+1}$. To simplify these fractions, we use the fact that $(a - b)(a + b) = a^2 - b^2$. This allows us to square each term in the denominator individually. The denominator is in the form $a + b$ (where $a = \sqrt{3}$ and $b = 1$). We multiply the fraction by $a - b$ over itself.

$$\frac{2}{\sqrt{3}+1} = \frac{2}{\sqrt{3}+1} \cdot \frac{\sqrt{3}-1}{\sqrt{3}-1}$$

$$= \frac{2(\sqrt{3}-1)}{(\sqrt{3})^2 - 1^2} = \frac{2(\sqrt{3}-1)}{3-1}$$

$$= \frac{2(\sqrt{3}-1)}{2} = \sqrt{3}-1$$

- $\dfrac{-8}{2 - \sqrt{5}}$

  The denominator is in the form $a - b$ (with $a = 2$ and $b = \sqrt{5}$). We multiply the fraction by $a + b$ over itself.

  $$\frac{-8}{2 - \sqrt{5}} = \frac{-8}{2 - \sqrt{5}} \cdot \frac{2 + \sqrt{5}}{2 + \sqrt{5}}$$

  $$= \frac{-8(2 + \sqrt{5})}{2^2 - (\sqrt{5})^2} = \frac{-8(2 + \sqrt{5})}{4 - 5}$$

  $$= \frac{-8(2 + \sqrt{5})}{-1} = 8(2 + \sqrt{5}) = 16 + 8\sqrt{5}$$

Factoring by Grouping

Some expressions of the form $ax^3 + bx^2 + cx + d$ can be factored using a technique called *factoring by grouping*. This technique takes several steps. The first step is to factor the first two terms and the second two terms so that each pair of terms has a common factor. The second step is to factor this common factor. For example, if we factor x^2 from the first two terms of $x^3 + 2x^2 + 3x + 6$, we are left with $x^2(x + 2) + 3x + 6$. Now we look at the second two terms, $3x + 6$, and factor it so that $x + 2$ is a factor. If we factor 3 from $3x + 6$, we are left with $x + 2$ as a factor: $3x + 6 = 3(x + 2)$. This leaves us with $x^2(x + 2) + 3(x + 2)$. In the last step, we factor $x + 2$ from each term, leaving x^2 and 3.

$$x^3 + 2x^2 + 3x + 6 = x^2(x + 2) + 3(x + 2)$$

$$= (x + 2)(x^2 + 3)$$

We can use this technique to solve equations.

- $4x^3 - 5x^2 - 36x + 45 = 0$

  Once we have factored $4x^3 - 5x^2 - 36x + 45$, we set each factor equal to 0 and solve for x. If we factor x^2 from the first two terms, we have $4x^3 - 5x^2 = x^2(4x - 5)$. If we factor -9 from the second two terms, we have $-36x + 45 = -9(4x - 5)$.

  $$4x^3 - 5x^2 - 36x + 45 = 0$$

  $$x^2(4x - 5) - 9(4x - 5) = 0$$

  $$(4x - 5)(x^2 - 9) = 0$$

$$4x - 5 = 0 \qquad x^2 - 9 = 0$$

$$4x = 5 \qquad x^2 = 9$$

$$x = \frac{5}{4} \qquad x = \pm 3$$

Solving $ax^n = b$ and $a\sqrt[n]{x} = b$

Solve equations of the form $ax^n = b$ by first dividing both sides of the equation by a, and then by taking the nth root of both sides. If n is even, use a $\pm$ symbol on one side of the equation to get both solutions.

- $$4x^2 = 9$$

$$x^2 = \frac{9}{4}$$

$$x = \pm\sqrt{\frac{9}{4}} = \pm\frac{3}{2}$$

- $$8x^3 = -1$$

$$x^3 = -\frac{1}{8}$$

$$x = \sqrt[3]{-\frac{1}{8}} = -\frac{1}{2}$$

Solve equations of the form $a\sqrt[n]{x} = b$ by first dividing both sides of the equation by a, and then by raising both sides to the nth power.

- $4\sqrt{x} = 5$

$$4\sqrt{x} = 5$$

$$\sqrt{x} = \frac{5}{4}$$

$$(\sqrt{x})^2 = \left(\frac{5}{4}\right)^2$$

$$x = \frac{25}{16}$$

- $4\sqrt{x} - 3 = 0$

  This equation needs to be in the form $\sqrt{x} = \frac{b}{a}$ before we square both sides of the equation.

$$4\sqrt{x} - 3 = 0$$

$$4\sqrt{x} = 3$$

$$\sqrt{x} = \frac{3}{4}$$

$$(\sqrt{x})^2 = \left(\frac{3}{4}\right)^2$$

$$x = \frac{9}{16}$$

Inequalities

Solving linear inequalites is much like solving linear equations *except* when multiplying or dividing both sides of the inequality by a negative number, we must reverse the inequality symbol. Solutions to inequalities are usually given in interval notation. The last page of the appendix has a review of interval notation.

- $5x - 8 > 3x + 10$

$$5x - 8 > 3x + 10$$

$$2x > 18$$

$$x > 9$$

The solution is $(9, \infty)$.

- $3x + 7 \leq 5x - 9$

$$3x + 7 \leq 5x - 9$$

$$-2x \leq -16$$

$$\frac{-2x}{-2} \geq \frac{-16}{-2} \quad \text{Reverse the sign at this step.}$$

$$x \geq 8 \quad \text{The solution is } [8, \infty).$$

A double inequality is notation for two separate inequalities. They are solved the same way as single inequalities.

- $-3 \le \dfrac{4x+7}{2} \le 5$

This inequality means $-3 \le \frac{4x+7}{2}$ and $\frac{4x+7}{2} \le 5$.

$$-3 \le \dfrac{4x+7}{2} \le 5 \qquad$$ Clear the fraction by multiplying all three quantities by 2.

$$-6 \le 4x+7 \le 10 \qquad$$ Subtract 7 from all three quantities.

$$-13 \le 4x \le 3 \qquad$$ Divide all three quantities by 4.

$$\dfrac{-13}{4} \le x \le \dfrac{3}{4}$$

The solution is $[-\frac{13}{4}, \frac{3}{4}]$.

Nonlinear inequalities are solved in a different way. Below is a list of steps we will take for solving polynomial inequalities.

1. Rewrite the expression with 0 on one side.
2. Factor the nonzero side.
3. Set each factor equal to 0 and solve for x.
4. Put these solutions from Step 3 on a number line.
5. Pick a number to the left of the smallest solution (from Step 3), a number between consecutive solutions, and a number to the right of the largest solution.
6. Put these numbers in for x in the original inequality.
7. If a number makes the inequality true, mark "True" over the interval. If a number makes the inequality false, mark "False" over the interval.
8. Write the interval notation for the "True" intervals.

- $2x^2 - x \ge 3$

$$2x^2 - x - 3 \ge 0 \qquad\qquad \text{Step 1}$$

$$(2x - 3)(x + 1) \ge 0 \qquad\qquad \text{Step 2}$$

$$2x - 3 = 0 \qquad x + 1 = 0 \qquad \text{Step 3}$$

$$x = \dfrac{3}{2} \qquad\qquad x = -1$$

Step 4: Put -1 and $\frac{3}{2}$ on a number line. See Figure A-1.

FIGURE A-1

Step 5: We use $x = -2$ for the number to the left of -1, $x = 0$ for the number between -1 and $\frac{3}{2}$, and $x = 2$ for the number to the right of $\frac{3}{2}$.

Step 6: We test these numbers in $2x^2 - x \geq 3$.

Let $x = -2$	$2(-2)^2 - (-2) \geq 3?$	True
Let $x = 0$	$2(0)^2 - 0 \geq 3?$	False
Let $x = 2$	$2(2)^2 - 2 \geq 3?$	True

Step 7: We mark the interval to the left of -1 "True," the interval between -1 and $\frac{3}{2}$ "False," and the interval to the right of $\frac{3}{2}$, "True." See Figure A-2.

FIGURE A-2

Step 8: The intervals that make the inequality true are $x \leq -1$ and $x \geq \frac{3}{2}$. The interval notation is $(-\infty, -1] \cup [\frac{3}{2}, \infty)$.

If there is an x in a denominator, the steps change slightly.

1. Get 0 on one side of the inequality.
2. Write the nonzero side as one fraction.
3. Factor the numerator and denominator.
4. Set each factor equal to 0 and solve for x.
5. Put these solutions from Step 4 on a number line.
6. Pick a number to the left of the smallest solution (from Step 4), a number between consecutive solutions, and a number to the right of the largest solution.
7. Put these numbers in for x in the original inequality.
8. If a number makes the inequality true, mark "True" over the interval. If a number makes the inequality false, mark "False" over the interval.

9. Write the interval notation for the "True" intervals—make sure that the solution does not include any x-value that makes a denominator 0.

• $\dfrac{x-4}{x+5} > 2$

$$\frac{x-4}{x+5} > 2$$

$$\frac{x-4}{x+5} - 2 > 0 \qquad \text{Step 1}$$

$$\frac{x-4}{x+5} - 2\left(\frac{x+5}{x+5}\right) > 0 \qquad \text{Step 2}$$

$$\frac{x-4-2(x+5)}{x+5} > 0$$

$$\frac{-x-14}{x+5} > 0$$

$$-x-14 = 0 \qquad x+5 = 0 \qquad \text{Step 4}$$
$$x = -14 \qquad\qquad x = -5$$

Step 5: See Figure A-3.

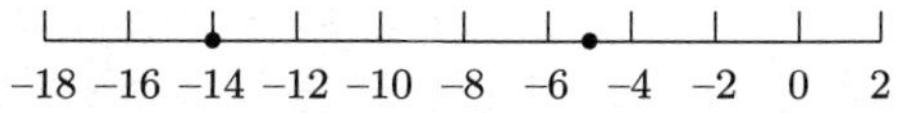

FIGURE A-3

Step 6: We use $x = -15$ for the number to the left of -14, $x = -10$ for the number between -14 and -5, and $x = 0$ for the number to the right of -5.

Step 7:

$$\frac{-15-4}{-15+5} > 2? \qquad \text{False}$$

$$\frac{-10-4}{-10+5} > 2? \qquad \text{True}$$

$$\frac{0-4}{0+5} > 2? \qquad \text{False}$$

We write "False" over the interval to the left of -14, "True" over the interval between -14 and -5, and "False" over the interval to the right of -5.

Step 8: See Figure A-4.

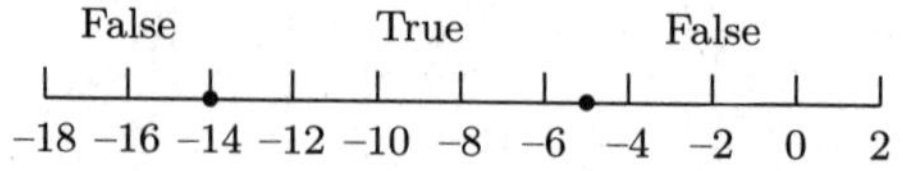

$$\begin{array}{ccc} \text{False} & \text{True} & \text{False} \end{array}$$

FIGURE A-4

The solution is the interval $(-14, -5)$.

• $\dfrac{x^2 - 3x}{x + 1} \leq -1$

$$\frac{x^2 - 3x}{x + 1} \leq -1$$

$$\frac{x^2 - 3x}{x + 1} + 1 \leq 0$$

$$\frac{x^2 - 3x}{x + 1} + 1 \cdot \frac{x + 1}{x + 1} \leq 0$$

$$\frac{x^2 - 3x + x + 1}{x + 1} \leq 0$$

$$\frac{x^2 - 2x + 1}{x + 1} \leq 0$$

$$\frac{(x - 1)(x - 1)}{x + 1} \leq 0$$

$$x - 1 = 0 \qquad x + 1 = 0$$

$$x = 1 \qquad x = -1$$

$$\frac{(-2)^2 - 3(-2)}{-2 + 1} \leq -1? \qquad \text{True}$$

$$\frac{0^2 - 3(0)}{0 + 1} \leq -1? \qquad \text{False}$$

$$\frac{2^2 - 3(2)}{2 + 1} \leq -1? \qquad \text{False}$$

See Figure A-5.

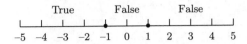

FIGURE A-5

The solution is $x = 1$ (where $\frac{x^2-3x}{x+1} = -1$) and $(-\infty, -1)$. The solution does *not* include $(-\infty, -1]$ because a bracket next to -1 indicates that -1 is part of the solution. We cannot allow $x = -1$ because we would have a zero in a denominator.

TABLE A-1

Inequality	Number Line	Interval
$x < a$	←———————○———————→ a	$(-\infty, a)$
$x \leq a$	←———————●———————→ a	$(-\infty, a]$
$x > a$	←———————○———————→ a	(a, ∞)
$x \geq a$	←———————●———————→ a	$[a, \infty)$
$a < x < b$	←———○———————○———→ a b	(a, b)
$a \leq x \leq b$	←———●———————●———→ a b	$[a, b]$
$x < a$ or $x > b$	←———○———————○———→ a b	$(-\infty, a) \cup (b, \infty)$
$x \leq a$ or $x \geq b$	←———●———————●———→ a b	$(-\infty, a] \cup [b, \infty)$
All x	←————All real numbers————→	$(-\infty, \infty)$

Index